W9-AEE-435

The design of this volume in the Handbook Series is to afford the reader a general view of the Slavonic nations from the earlier to the present time. It is made for popular use and information, and to occupy a vacant field. There are many books dealing with the subject, but most of them are in the original and inaccessible to English-speaking people. The editor has here brought together readable examples of the most important writings, and practical illustrations of the rise of learning, imagination and creative power which finally brought about the liberation of this race. There are chapters on Russia, Poland, Czechoslovakia, Yugoslavia and Bulgaria; also a selected bibliography.

SLAVONIC NATIONS

OF

YESTERDAY AND TODAY

THE HANDBOOK SERIES

THE HANDBOOK SERIES

SLAVONIC NATIONS

OF

YESTERDAY AND TODAY

SELECT READINGS AND REFERENCES ON RUSSIA,
POLAND, CZECHOSLOVAKIA, YUGOSLAVIA
AND BULGARIA

Edited by

MILIVOY S. STANOYEVICH,

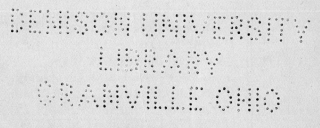

NEW YORK
THE H. W. WILSON COMPANY
1925

Published September 1925

Printed in the United States of America

PREFATORY NOTE

The design of this volume in the "Handbook Series" is to afford the reader a general view of the Slavonic nations from the earlier to the present time. It is made for popular use and information, and to occupy a vacant field. There are many books dealing with this subject, but most of them are in the original and inaccessible to the English speaking people. Well-known encyclopedias: Ottův, *Slovnik Naučný* (Czechoslovak); Efron, *Entsik-lopeditchesky Slovar* (Russian); Orgelbranda, *Encyk-lopedja Powszechna* (Polish); Stanojević, *Narodna En-ciklopedia* (Yugoslav), and Slavonic periodicals contain invaluable articles on all Slavonic nations, but who reads them? Our own object is to place before the reader select and characteristic extracts of those articles which have appeared in recent English, French and American magazines.

As this work is neither a history nor an encyclopedia, we are not forced to place all magazine writers on Slavonic affairs upon the list of those represented. Some of less note will be omitted, so that our selections from those quoted may often be of greater length than is usual in books of this kind. The editor's aim is to give distinctive and readable examples of the most important writings; to bring together practical illustrations of the rise of learning, imagination, and creative power, which finally brought the liberation of this race. The Slavonic nations are free at present from foreign oppression and viewed internationally, they are making great progress toward consolidation and stability.

It is not too much to say that already the political as well as the economic importance of the Slavonic states is making itself felt both in Europe and America. Only people possessing a real vitality could have survived so long in the struggle against assorted tyranny as these Slavonic nations. The inhabitants of these regions are industrious and the work of post-war reconstruction has gone forward despite many difficulties. The productive forces of the nations have been harnessed; raw materials utilized and manufactures re-started; the creation of commercial, financial, transport and credit apparatus is being carried forward. Preparations are made to develope to the utmost the unrivalled geographical position of these states in readiness for the time when normal trade and international relations will be in full swing. Apart from the economic progress the development of art, literature and science gives promise of an important future especially for the western Slavonic states, Czechoslovakia, Poland and Yugoslavia.

As to transliteration of the Slavonic names in this volume, it has not been thought best to follow in all cases the quaint and often inconsistent spelling to which the earlier writers were addicted. Thus for the ending of the Russian and Bulgarian proper names, whenever possible we adopt -*ov* and -*ev* instead of the antiquated -*off* and -*eff*, for old -*witsch* we use -*vitch* (in Russian) and -*vich* (for ending of Serbian proper names)—*vitch* or *vich* meaning *son of*. The Polish termination -*ski* remains unchanged, while the Russian common form is -*sky*. The older forms *Czar* (or *Tzar*) and *Tzankoff* (or *Zankof*) have been substituted with *Tsar* and *Tsankov*. For the older *sch*, we use *sh;* for the older *gh, ch* or *kh* we, use *h* (*Tchehov, Mohilev*). The French sound *j* in Russian words has been substituted with *zh* (*Zhukovsky, Voronezh*), and English *dj* in Serbian transliterations with *dzh* (*Karadzhich, Karapandzhich*). For Russian and Serbian *j* we use *y* (*Tolstoy, Yugoslavia*).

The difficulty of representing foreign names in Cyrillic characters is even greater than that which we find

in transcribing Russian names, and they may become
hardly recognizable in the process. When foreign names
so treated occur in a Cyrillic document under transcrip-
tion, they should be restored to their original form if it
can be identified with certainty. Thus where "Gertzen"
stands for a German *Herzen,* and "Mariengoff" for
Marienhof we shall write them in their native spelling
and not as "Gertzen" and "Mariengoff." Czechoslovak
and Polish employing the Latin alphabet are not subjects
for transliteration in the same way as those Slavonic
languages which employ the Cyrillic script. Some ex-
planations on orthography and pronunciation of Polish
and Czechoslovak proper names are to be found in the
beginning of the chapters on Poland and Czechoslovakia.

In compiling this collection the editor is under a
debt of gratitude to Mr. H. W. Wilson, at whose suggestion the work was undertaken. He also makes sincere acknowledgment to Miss Edith M. Phelps, who, in
addition to reading the proofsheets, has placed at the
editor's disposal her sound scholarship and wide experience, which have been most gratefully accepted.

M. S. S.

CONTENTS

CHAP. I. SLAVONIC RACE IN GENERAL

CHAP. II. RUSSIA

CHAP. III. POLAND

CHAP. IV. CZECHOSLOVAKIA

BIBLIOGRAPHY

An asterisk (*) preceding an article indicates that the article
or a part of it has been reprinted in this volume.

CHAPTER I

INTRODUCTION

THE SLAVONIC RACE IN GENERAL

American Journal of Philology. 32:431-5. O. '11.
Slavic analogy to Verner's law. E. Prokosch.

Architectural Record. 47:371-6. Ap. '20. Slav temperament in architecture. L. V. Solon.

*Canadian. 47:15-18. My. '16. The Pan-Slavonic ideal.
J. D. Prince.

Century. 88:590-8. Ag. '14. Slavs in America. E. A.
Ross.

Charities. 13:199-205. D. 3, '04. Slavs, Magyars and
some others in the new immigration. Kate H.
Claghorn.

Charities. 13:215-22. D. 3, '04. The Slavs in anthra-
cite coal communities. P. Roberts.

Charities. 13:223-6. D. 3, '04. Some industrial effects
of Slav immigration. F. J. Warne.

Charities. 13:227-9. D. 3, '04. Slavs in the bituminous
mines of Illinois. J. R. Commons.

Charities. 13:257-61. D. 3, '04. Housing and social
conditions in a Slavic neighborhood. M. B. Sayles.

Charities. 21:533-52. Ja. 2, '09. The Slavs and kindred
immigrants in Pittsburgh. P. Roberts.

Charities. 21:589-98. Ja. 2, '09. Slav's a man for a'
that. A. B. Koukol.

Charities. 14: 875-81. Jl. 1, '05. Culture which the Slav offers America. V. Svarc.

*Contemporary Review. 73: 1-13. Ja. '98. The coming of the Slav. G. Washburn.

Contemporary Review. 95: 1-14. Ja. '09. Arrival of the Slavs. W. T. Stead.

Contemporary Review. 103: 719-24. My. '13. Panslavist bubble. E. J. Dillon.

Contemporary Review. 116: 419-29. O. '16. Pan-Slavism. R. W. Seton-Watson.

Critic. 3: 305-6. Jl. 14, '83. Slavic and Latin. Dr. Abel's Ilchester lectures on literature. W. D. Whitney.

Folk-Lore. 1: 463-80. D. '90. Marriage among the early Slavs. M. Kowalewsky.

Folk-Lore Record. 4: 52-70. Je. '81. Slavonic folk-lore. W. S. Lach-Szyrma.

Fortnightly Review. 18: 325-38. S. '72. The republican movement in Europe. The Slavic peoples. Emilio Castelar.

Fortnightly Review. 20: 94-112. Jl. '73. Pan-Slavism, its rise and decline. E. L. Miyatovich.

*Fortnightly Review. 81: 371-82. Mr. '04. The Slav and his future. E. Reich.

Fortnightly Review. 92: 160-74. Jl. '09. Race questions and British policy. R. C. Long.

Forum. 52: 177-85. Ag. '14. Pan-Slavism in America. C. Townley-Fullam.

Harvard Graduate. 5: 343-6. Mr. '97. Slavic languages. L. Wiener.

Hibbert Journal. 13: 243-60. Ja. '15. The Slavophile creed. P. Vinogradov.

Independent. 79: 205-10. Ag. 10, '14. Teuton against Slav. W. M. Sloane.

International Quarterly (Monthly). 10: 32-45. O. '04. The Slavs. Peter Roberts.

*La Nation Tchèque. 1:343-9. Mr. 15, '16. Les Slaves dans le monde (The Slavs among the nations). T. G. Masaryk.

Living Age. 244:463-8. F. '25, '05. Real Slav temperament. H. M. Conacher.

Living Age. 320:156-9. Ja. 26, '24. Ingratiating Slavs. C. Treves.

Methodist Review. 74:259-66. Mr. '92. The doctrine of Pan-Slavism. S. Thomov.

Nineteenth Century. 74:283-94. Ag. '13. Pan-Germanism versus Pan-Slavism. A. S. Rappaport.

Nineteenth Century. 74:295-300. Ag. '13. The Balkan fiasco. J. W. Ozanne.

North American Review. 189:801-11. Je. '09. Achilles heel of Germany. A. R. Colquhoun.

Outlook. 67:511-20. Mr. 2, '01. Slavic characteristics. E. A. Steiner.

Outlook. 73:555-64. Mr. 7, '03. Slovak and Pole in America. E. A. Steiner.

Popular Scientific Monthly. 37:684-90. S. '90. Slavonian fairies. F. S. Kraus.

Popular Science Monthly. 63:25-32. My. '03. The Slavic immigrant. A. McLaughlin.

Popular Science Monthly. 79:498-92. N. '11. Crossing of the races. J. G. Wilson.

Proceedings of the American Philosophical Society. 59:184-93. Slav and Celt. J. D. Prince.

Smithsonian Institution. Annual Report. 1905-6. p. 399-422. The Origin of the Slavs. M. Zaborowski.

Smithsonian Institution. Annual Report. 1910. p. 599-612. Geographical and statistical view of the contemporary Slav peoples. L. Niederle.

Survey. 24:666-77. Ag. 6, '10. Peasant background of our Slavic fellow citizens. E. G. Balch.

Survey. 27:951-6. O. 7, '11. Slav farmers on the abandoned farm area of Connecticut. A. E. Cance.

CHAPTER II

RUSSIA

American Journal of Sociology. 29:493-5. Ja. '24. Sociology in Russia. P. A. Sorokin.

American Journal of Theology. 22:541-61. O. '18. The church and the religion of Russia. G. W. Richards.

American Law Review. 52:657-68. S. '18. American democracy and Russian democracy. E. P. Wheeler.

American Political Science Review. 12:181-91. My. '18. Revolutionary Russia. S. Litman.

Annals of the American Academy. 11:137-73. Mr. '98. Social theories and Russian conditions. F. Sigel.

Annals of the American Academy. 84:81-9. Jl. '19. Russia—present and future. R. M. Story.

Annals of the American Academy. 84:90-7. Jl. '19. The Russian tragedy. W. C. Huntington.

Annals of the American Academy. 84:98-101. Jl. '19. The menace of bolshevism. Baron Rosen.

Annals of the American Academy. 84:102-7. Jl. '19. Democracy and bolshevism. A. J. Sack.

Annals of the American Academy. 84:108-113. Jl. '19. The Soviet republic. S. Nuorteva.

Annals of the American Academy. 84:114-20. Jl. '19. The intelligentsia and the people in the Russian revolution. M. J. Olgin.

Annals of the American Academy. 84:121-6. Jl. '19. Economic force and the Russian problem. T. D. Thacher.

Annals of the American Academy. 84:127-45. Jl. '19. Social condition in Russia today. R. Robins.

Annals of the American Academy. 102:131-7. Jl. '22. Russia as the chief obstacle to European rehabilitation. W. E. Walling.

Annals of the American Academy. 114: 49-55. Jl. '24. Conditions in Russia. J. A. Frear.

Annals of the American Academy. 114: 56-61. Jl. '24. Underlying economic factors in the Russian situation. Leo Pasvolsky.

Annals of the American Academy. 114: 70-5. Jl. '24. Attitude of the U. S. government towards the Soviet régime. E. E. Young.

Annals of the American Academy. 114: 76-84. Jl. '24. Should America recognize Russia? J. Davis.

Annals of the American Academy. 114: 85-8. Jl. '24. Efforts of the Soviet government to block American aid to Russia. P. Mathews.

*Arts and Decoration. 13: 12-13, 52. My. 25, '20. The Russian revolution and her artists. Ivan Narodny.

Asia. 24: 372-6. My. '24. Russian soul and the Russian language. M. Eastman.

*Athenaeum. 4630: 266-8. Je. '18. Language and folk-lore of Ukraina (The literature of Ukraina). G. F. Lees.

*Atlantic Monthly. 126: 248-56. Ag. '20. Bolshevism from the inside. J. A. Gade.

Atlantic Monthly. 127: 114-18. Ja. '21. Lenin. A. Kuprin.

*Atlantic Monthly. 131: 349-409. Mr. '23. Bolshevism and religion in Russia. R. O. G. Urch.

Atlantic Monthly. 134: 393-400. S. '24. Profiteering under a communist régime. W. H. Chamberlain.

Atlantic Monthly. 134: 545-55. O. '24. Who's who in Soviet Russia. W. H. Chamberlain.

Atlantic Monthly. 135: 122-30. Ja. '25. Triumph of atheism in Russia. S. High.

Bookman. 58: 384-94. D. '23. Bolos and the arts. M. E. Harrison.

Catholic World. 119: 721-31. S. '24. Truth about Russia. C. Phillips.

Charities. 13:246-52. D. 3, '04. The Ruthenians in America. Ivan Ardan.

Charities. 13:252-6. D. 3, '04. The Duhobors. Jos. Elkinton.

Century. 97:384-90. Ja. '19. Russia, a dissolving view. L. Stoddard.

Century. 109:374-83. Ja. '25. Russia's challenge to Christianity. M. G. Hindus.

Columbia University Quarterly. 20:11-23. Ja. '18. A glimpse of Russia in the year of her revolution. H. C. Sherman.

Constructive Quarterly. 5:76-90. Mr. '17. Orthodox Russia and its orthodox priesthood. N. N. Glubo- kovsky.

Constructive Quarterly. 6:590-609. D. '18. Hopes for the Orthodox Church of Russia. L. Turkevich.

*Contemporary Review. 115:606-12. Je. '19. Pros- pects in Russia. P. Vinogradov.

Contemporary Review. 118:496-506. O. '20. The truth about Russia. A. E. Copping.

*Contemporary Review. 121:636-44. My. '22. Russian drama in XIX and XX centuries. C. Nabokov.

Contemporary Review. 122:205-11. Ag. '22. Russian literature since 1917. D. S. Mirsky.

Contemporary Review. 125:78-83. Ja. '24. What of religion in Russia? E. Bernstein.

Contemporary Review. 125:562-70. My. '24. Russia and her neighbors. H. C. Woods.

Contemporary Review. 125:657-60. My. '24. Anglo- Russian conference. G. Glasgow

Contemporary Review. 126:301-7. S. '24. The tragedy of the Russian *diaspora.* Charles Sarolea.

Contemporary Review. 126:509-18. O. '24. Russian treaty. G. Glasgow.

Contemporary Review. 126:697-702. D. '24. Case for the Russian treaties. A. Ponsonby.

Contemporary Review. 126:778-82. D. '24. Zinoviev pantomime; Anglo-Russian relations. G. Glasgow.

Contemporary Review. 127:59-65. Ja. '25. True genesis of bolshevism. E. G. Hawke.

Current History. 13:149-57. Ja. '21. The French and Russian revolutions. Charles W. Thompson.

*Current History. 18:299-304. My. '23. Religion and morals in bolshevist Russia. E. W. Hullinger.

Current History. 19:721-9. F. '24. Bolshevism and the world revolution. Charles Sarolea.

Current History. 19:776-83. F. '24. Tragic failure of Soviet policies. F. A. Golder.

Current History. 20:415-22. Je. '24. Asiatic states in the Soviet union. W. H. Chamberlain.

Current History. 20:782-6. Ag. '24. Whither goest thou, Russia? A. Margolin.

Current History. 20:943-9. S. '24. Russian communism at the crossroads. W. H. Chamberlain.

Current History. 20:960-1. S. '24. Russia's move to treat China as an equal. K. K. Kawakami.

Current History. 21:391-6. D. '24. Boris Savinkov. E. Tabenkin.

Current History. 21:534-7. Ja. '25. Soviet Russia's expansion in central Asia. J. Lewery.

Current History. 21:655-64. F. '25. Trotsky's attack on the Soviet rulers. E. Tabenkin.

*Dial. 67:14-16. Jl. 12, '19. Bolshevik Russia and Jacobin France. W. H. Chamberlain.

Drama. 9:31-61. F. '19. The Russian dramatic stage. A. Bakshy.

Dublin Review. 159:52-67. O. '16. The Russian church. R. Reynolds.

Dublin Review. 162:41-70. Ja. '18. The Latin church in Russia. A. Fortescue.

Dublin Review. 168:192-202. Ap. '21. Soviet Russia and Poland. S. Rice.

*Edinburgh Review. 232:290-306. O. '20. Bolshevism in theory and practice. G. H. Crichton.

Edinburgh Review. 234:227-43. O. '21. Russian communist experiment. P. Struve.

Edinburgh Review. 239:295-311. Ap. '24. Lenin, the man and his achievment. R. H. B. Lockhart.

English Review. 24:408-14. My. '17. Tchehov and modern Russia. H. Fyfe.

English Review. 26:523-30. Je. '18. Religion and the Russian revolution. L. Lawton.

English Review. 28:140-9. F. '19. The problem of Russia. H. Fyfe.

English Review. 28:150-9: F. '19. Indemnities and bolshevism. M. Lyon.

English Review. 39:620-5. N. '24. A plea for Tsarism. Charles Sarolea.

Foreign Affairs. 1:140-6. Mr. 15, '23. The new Russian economic policy. A. Bullard.

Forum. 65:392-7. Ap. '21. Japan, Russia, Germany. G. Brandes.

Forum. 65:497-505. My. '21. The fate of Russia. F. I. Kent.

Forum. 70:2233-42. D. '23. Russians mortal and immortal. W. L. Phelps.

Forum. 71:191-7. F. '24. Red army today. A. Lukomsky.

*Fortnightly Review. 101:606-16. Ap. '17. Russia and the Slav ideal. Z. N. Preëv.

Fortnightly Review. 111:670-7. My. '19. Western and eastern ideals in Russia. P. Vinogradov.

Fortnightly Review. 111:760-70. My. '19. Echoes from the Ukraina. K. M. Blakey.

Fortnightly Review. 119:769-76. My. '23. East and west in Russia: Peter Tchaadayev. C. H. Wright.

Fortnightly Review. 120:896-905. D. '23. Conversations with Maxim Gorky. B. H. Clark.

Fortnightly Review. 121:240-57. F. '24. My lady Bolshevik. J. Prelooker.

Fortnightly Review. 122:670-8. N. '24. The results of Leninism. L. Lawton.

Fortnightly Review. 122:830-41. D. '24. Russian dream of freedom. J. A. T. Lloyd.

Freeman. 8:202-5. N. 7, '23. Russia in reconstruction. W. H. Chamberlain.

Freeman. 8:346-8. D. 19, '23. The future of Soviet Russia. W. H. Chamberlain.

Freeman. 8:612-15. Mr. 5, '24. Russian peasant as a revolutionist. G. T. Robinson.

Harper's. 78:833-55; 79:2-24. My.-Je. '89. Social life in Russia. E. M. Vogüé.

Harper's. 138:270-7. Ja. '19. Education and self-government in Russia. M. G. Strunsky.

*Harper's. 144:611-21. Ap. '22. The Russia of tomorrow. N. D. Avksentiyev.

Hibbert Journal. 14:393-408. Ja. '16. Religion in Russia today. J. Y. Simpson.

Hibbert Journal. 14:681-90. Jl. '16. The spiritual alliance of Russia and England. W. Begbie.

Hibbert Journal. 18:209-24. Ja. '20. The Bolshevist utopia and the religious movement. E. Trubetskoy.

Independent. 114:101-3. Ja. 24, '25. Vanishing ikon. L. Fischer.

International Journal of Ethics. 30:190-5. Ja. '20. Light from Tolstoy on Russia. D. Drake.

Journal of Race Development. 11:517-28. Ap. '21. Bolshevist Russia and civilized mankind. M. I. Rostovtsev.

Journal of Race Development. 11:529-48. Ap. '21. The new Russian bourgeoisie. N. Hapgood.

Living Age. 299:733-5. D. 21, '18. The future of Ukraina. W. Czerniewski.

Living Age. 300:129-37. Ja. 18, '19. The modern Russian revolution. G. Buchanan.

Living Age. 300:723-6. Mr. 22, '19. The first step in Russian regeneration. P. Milyukov.

Living Age. 302:47-50. Jl. 5, '19. The downfall of the Russian "intellectuals." H. Brennan.

Living Age. 305:708-10. Je. 19, '20. Russia and Europe's reconstruction. L. Krasin.

*Living Age. 306:502-5. Ag. 28, '20. The great narcosis. Ivan Bunin.

*Living Age. 310:401-6. Ag. 13, '21. Russia's culture under the Soviets. A. F. Damansky.

Living Age. 310:470-5. N. 10, '23. Russia's new economy. N. Bucharin.

*Living Age. 312:270-3. F. 4, '22. Economic program of bolshevist Russia. N. U. Lenin.

Living Age. 312:274-9. F. 4, '22. Present condition of Russian industry. E. Peipers.

Living Age. 314:84-6. Jl. 8, '22. Economic organization in Soviet Russia. M. Bucharin.

Living Age. 314:585-6. S. 2, '22. Church revolution in Soviet Russia. Ivan Tregubov.

Living Age. 316:85-9. Ja. 13, '23. Petrograd and Moscow. I. Župančić.

*Living Age. 316:134-7. Ja. 20, '23. An apology for the unavoidable. N. U. Lenin.

*Living Age. 317:515-18. Je. 2, '23. The Soviets and the peasants. K. Radek.

*Living Age. 317:760-3. Je. 30, '23. An optimist on Russia. L. Krasin.

Living Age. 318:350-6. Ag. 25, '23. Soviet village life. G. Popov.

Living Age. 319:258-64. N. 10, '23. The mystery of bolshevism. G. Popov.

Living Age. 319:458-64. D. 8, '23. On the Trans-Siberian express. A. Cipolla.

Living Age. 319:514-20. D. 15, '23. Dead souls again S. R. Minzlov.

Living Age. 320: 125-30. Ja. 19, '24. Russian situation. A. Maude.

Living Age. 320: 548-51. Mr. 22, '24. Soviet diplomacy since the war. G. Tchitcherin.

Living Age. 322: 172-4. Jl. 26, '24. Haymakers, a village festival in Russia. E. Zagorskaya.

Living Age. 322: 533-40. S. 13, '24. How revolution came to Russia. A. Ransome.

Living Age. 322: 641-3. S. 27, '24. Tchastushka, Russian ballad satire. E. Nedzelsky.

Living Age. 324: 209-12. Ja. 24, '25. Peasant fires and peasant quarrels. I. Zhiga.

Living Age. 324: 366-8. F. 14, '25. Tcheka, brother to the Kremlin. G. Popov.

*La Revue de France. 1: 637-50. Ap. 15, '21. La littérature mystique au pays du bolshevisme (Mystic literature in the land of Bolshevism). H. Izvolsky.

*La Revue Mondiale. 32: 327-36. O. 1, '21. La litterature russe actuelle (Modern Russian literature). A Lévison.

London Mercury. 4: 414-18. Ag. '21. Recent development in poetry. D. S. Mirsky.

*London Mercury. 5: 276-85. Ja. '22. The literature of bolshevik Russia. D. S. Mirsky.

London Mercury. 6: 193-5. Je. '22. The literature of the emigration. D. S. Mirsky.

London Quarterly Review. 128: 1-16. Jl. '17. Thoughts on the Russian revolution. S. Graham.

London Quarterly Review. 137: 107-9. Ja. '22. Recent Russian literature. A. Clyne.

Nation. 108: 188-90. F. '19. Russia and the world. M. S. Farbman.

Nation. 108: 321-2. Mr. 1, '19. Russia at the crossroads. G. V. Lomonosov.

Nation. 119: 138-40. Ag. 6, '24. Sinclair vs. Standard oil in Russia. L. Fischer.

Nation. 119:564-5. N. 26, '24. Nepman is passing. L. Fischer.

Nation. 120:24-6. Ja. 7, '25. Lenin versus Trotsky. L. Fischer.

Nation. 120:243-7. Mr. 4, '25. Civil liberties in Russia. H. F. Ward.

Nation. 120:237-8. Mr. 4, '25. Political prisoners under bolshevism. L. Fischer.

Nation (London). 26:593-4. Ja. '20. The dismemberment of Russia. A. F. Kerensky.

*Nation (London). 27:460, 493, 520, 547, 576. Jl. 10, 17, 24, 31, Ag. 7, '20. Impressions of bolshevik Russia. Bertrand Russell.

*New Age (London). 16:219. D. 31, '14. The literature of Ukraina. V. Levitsky.

New Europe. 14:227-32. Mr. 18, '20. The church in bolshevik Russia. P. Dukes.

New Republic. 28:18-20. Ag. 31, '21. Russian intelligentsia and the revolution. M. J. Olgin.

Nineteenth Century. 85:395-408. F. '19. Behind the veil in Moscow. John Pollock.

Nineteenth Century. 86:881-8. N. '19. Democracy in Russia and the peasants' land hunger. V. Polyakov.

Nineteenth Century. 88:445-9. S. '20. The peasants under Lenin. L. Lawton.

Nineteenth Century. 89:146-61. Ja. '21. "Economists" from bolshevy. J. Pollock.

Nineteenth Century. 94:1-12. Jl. '23. Bolshevist inferno. E. C. Cox.

Nineteenth Century. 95:318-27. Mr. '24. Disgraceful act. L. F. Easterbrook.

Nineteenth Century. 96:487-93. O. '24. Soviet and our disgraceful traffic with it. W. F. Lloyd.

Nineteenth Century. 96:494-9. O. '24. Impressions of Russia today. A. Pownall.

Nineteenth Century. 96:617-25. N. '24. The friends of the Soviet. L. F. Easterbrook.

Nineteenth Century. 96:786-97. D. '24. Disgraceful Soviet. P. Hehir.

North American Review. 169:6-32. Jl. '99. A plea for a Russo-American understanding. V. Holmstrem.

North American Review. 213:539-50. Ap. '21. Proletkult, its pretensions and fallacies. Leo Pasvolsky.

Open Court. 30:335-45. Ja. '16. Russia in war and peace. M. M. Victorov.

*Open Court. 32:390-407. Jl. '18. The gloom and glory of Russian literature. M. J. Rudwin.

Outlook. 122:148-50. My. 28, '19. In the grip of the bolshevists. A. H. Carasso.

Outlook. 122:193-6. Je. 4, '19. What the bolshevists have done to Russia. A. H. Carasso.

*Outlook. 127:513-14. Mr. 30, '21. Russia in sun or shadow. Ivan Petrunkevitch.

Outlook. 130:341-4. Mr. 1, '22. Can Russia come back? J. P. Goodrich.

Outlook. 136:654-8. Ap. 16, '24. Some Russian factories. A. Ruhl.

Outlook. 138:204-6. O. '24. Russia through Russian eyes. N. de Bogory.

Outlook. 138:592-4. D. 10, '24. Business with the Bolsheviki. S. High.

Political Science Quarterly. 37:227-50. Je. '22. Sociological interpretation of the Russian revolution. Jerome Davis.

Political Science Quarterly. 38:529-51. D. '23. Soviet Russia and federated Russia. A. L. P. Dennis.

Quarterly Journal of Economics. 39:320-4. F. '25. Conjuncture institute at Moscow. N. D. Kondratiev.

*Quarterly Review. 233:272-87. Ap. '20. The contribution of Russia to learning. M. Rostovtsev.

Review of Reviews. 69: 397-400. Ap. '24. Rykov, Lenin's successor in Russia. M. D. Christophides.

Review of Reviews. 70: 523-6. N. '24. Politics versus economics in Russia. W. H. Chamberlain.

*Scribner's. 71: 515-27. My. '22. Russia of yesterday and tomorrow. J. H. Hammond.

Scribner's. 76: 272-80. S. '24. On the Soviet Trans-Siberian. K. Roosevelt.

Scribner's. 77: 156-60. F. '25. Suicide of Russia. E. Huntington.

Sewanee Review. 24: 61-8. Ja. '16. A Russian novelist's estimate of the Russian intellectual. H. S. G. Tucker.

Sewanee Review. 29: 351-9. Jl. '21. Unreality in Russian literature. C. A. Manning.

Sewanee Review. 30: 286-97. Jl. '22. Dostoyevsky and modern Russian literature. C. A. Manning.

Spectator. 129: 297. S. 2, '22. Russia abroad. B. Pares.

Survey. 53: 270-4. Public health in Soviet Russia. L. D. Wald.

Touchstone. 4: 314-21. Ja. '19. The Bolshevist and the cubist. Thomas Whittemore.

World's Work. 45: 67-80. N. '22. Contrasts between the French and Russian revolutions. R. Recouly.

Yale Review. 6: 838-55. Jl. '17. The Russian revolution. A. Petrunkevitch.

Yale Review. n.s. 13: 467-81. Ap. '24. Struggle for power in Russia. M. Farbman.

Yale Review. n.s. 14: 140-55. O. '24. In a Russian village. M. G. Hindus.

CHAPTER III

POLAND

American Catholic Quarterly Review. 42: 494-506. Jl. '17. Poland and the Poles. D. Dale.

American Economic Review. 13:593-608. D. '23. Currency inflation in eastern Europe with special reference to Poland. E. D. Durand.

Annals of the American Academy. 93:153-6. Ja. '21. The Polish group in the United States. J. K. Grove.

Annals of the American Academy. 102:32-9. Jl. '22. The finance and currency situation in Poland. E. D. Durand.

*Arts and Decorations. 12:6-7, 46-7. N. 15, '19. The art and artists of Poland. J. P. Wachowski.

*Asia. 18:1010-14. D. '18. Poland reborn. A. H. Debski.

Asiatic Review. 16:574-7. O. '20. The world importance of the Polish question. O. Novikov.

Atlantic Monthly. 124:126-31. Jl. '19. Poland, the verge of bolshevism. V. Kellog.

Bookman. 12:568-78; 13:30-42. F.-Mr. '01. The country of Sienkiewicz. L. E. Van Norman.

Bookman. 44:412-26. D. '16. Henryk Sienkiewicz's Poland. L. E. Van Norman.

British Review. 11:13-25. Jl. '15. The Polish question. J. Gabrys.

Catholic World. 110:444-55. Ja. '20. A Polish mystic on the national resurrection. M. M. Gardner.

Century. 70:451-63. Jl. '05. The future of Poland. D. B. MacGowan.

Century. 90:57-71. My. '15. Poland's story. J. C. Welliver.

Century. 93:182-92. D. '16. The Future of Poland. H. A. Gibbons.

Charities. 13:235-9. D. 3, '04. Notes on the Poles in Baltimore. L. B. Garrett.

Contemporary Review. 108:205-11. Ag. '15. Poland's ordeal and Poland's hope. L. Bariatinsky.

Contemporary Review. 108:481-90. O. '15. The resurrection of Poland. J. H. Harley.

Contemporary Review. 110:715-23. D. '16. The Polish problem. J. H. Rose.

Contemporary Review. 112:519-25. N. '17. Thaddeus Kościuszko. H. Zaleski.

Contemporary Review. 117:332-40. Mr. '20. A plea for Poland. H. N. Brailsford.

Contemporary Review. 122:174-9. Ag. '22. Great Britain and Poland. G. Adamkiewicz.

Contemporary Review. 125:299-308. Mr. '24. Revival of Poland. H. A. L. Fisher.

Dublin Review. 160:17-37. Ja. '17. Undying Poland. W. Barry.

Edinburgh Review. 221:358-84. Ap. '15. The problem of Poland. J. A. R. Marriott.

Edinburgh Review. 225:158-77. Ja. '17. Prussia, Poland and Ireland. J. A. R. Marriott.

English Review. 30:538-45. Je. '20. The Garibaldi of Poland. Thomas Barclay.

English Review. 34:183-89. F. '22. Poland and Pan-Slavism. R. Dell.

Englishwoman. 41:55-9. F. '19. The Polish question. G. Dickenson.

Fortnightly Review. 89:470-82. Mr. '08. The significance of the Polish question. R. Blennerhassett.

Fortnightly Review. 104:1046-57. D. '15. Polish memories. W. F. Bailey.

Fortnightly Review. 106:246-52. Ag. '16. The future of Poland. J. C. de Chassaigne.

Fortnightly Review. 107:373-88. Mr. '17. The Polish problem. E. J. Dillon.

*Fortnightly Review. 111:657-69. My. '19. Poland, the crime of partition. J. Conrad.

Fortnightly Review. 113:261-70. F. '20. Piłsudski and the new Poland. S. Huddleston.

Fortnightly Review. 117:39-51. Ja. '22. The Outlook in Poland. E. J. Dillon.

Fortnightly Review. 119:993-1004. Je. '23. Poland and her frontiers. R. Machray.

Fortnightly Review. 120:104-112. Jl. '23. Poland and the peace. J. H. Harley.

Freeman. 6:489-91. Ja. 31, '23. The new Poland. A. Goldenweiser.

*Geographical Review. 4:6-25. Jl. '17. Poland, the land and the state. E. Romer.

Harper's. 140:105-16. D. '19. Poland under the Poles. H. A. Franck.

Harvard Graduates. 29:199-201. D. '20. Poland to-day. W. C. Bailey.

*Hibbert Journal. 15:113-24. O. '16. Immortal Poland. G. Dennis.

Independent. 83:192. Ag. 9, '15. Helpless Poland. Ignace J. Paderewski.

Independent. 113:395-8. N. 15, '24. Danzig. R. O. F. Husband.

Living Age. 299:673-5. D. 14, '18. The attitude of the Poles. M. Seyda.

*Living Age. 301:779-82. Je. 28, '19. The future of Poland. Ignace Paderewski.

Living Age. 303:613-17. D. 6, '19. A visitor to Poland. Mrs. C. E. Chesterton.

Nation. 108:135-7. Ja. 25, '19. Poland and the Jewish problem. E. S. Bagger.

Nation. 111:65-6. Jl. 17, '20. The tragedy that is Poland. B. Ginzburg.

Nation. 112:916-17. Je. 29, '20. There is Poland. C. Fauntleroy.

Nation. 119:171-2. Ag. 13. '24. Get rich quick in Poland. A. L. Strong.

National Geographic. 27:88-106. Ja. '15. Partitioned Poland. W. J. Showalter.

National Geographic. 31:444-53. My. '17. Devasted Poland. F. Walcott.

*National Review. 75 : 278-84. Ap. '20. Inspiration of Poland. H. Hoover.

National Review. 76 : 218-27. O. '20. If Poland perish. B. J. Wilden-Hart.

New Republic. 9 : 73-6. N. 18 '16. The new Poland. R. Ussher.

New Republic. 16 : 44-6. Ag. 10, '18. America and the Polish question. Jan Kobiet.

New Republic. 20 : 78-81. Ag. 20, '19. Poland and the Jews. H. N. Brailsford.

New Europe. 16 : 203-7. S. 9, '20. Europe and Poland. P. Bernus.

Nineteenth Century. 81 : 300-5. F. '17. Danzig, Poland's outlet to the sea. L. B. Namier.

Nineteenth Century. 82 : 859-69. O. '17. Polish political parties and the war. R. A. Ussher.

Nineteenth Century. 85 : 612-25. Mr. '19. Poland and the peace. C. Battine.

Nineteenth Century. 28 : 436-44. S. '20. The council of action and Poland. R. A. Ussher.

North American Review. 211 : 751-7. Je. '20. Poland's struggle and the world's peace. S. Stojowski.

*Open Court. 31 : 372-5. Je. '17. The Polish language. L. Bloomfield.

Outlook. 88 : 541-2. Mr. 7, '08. Dispossessing the Poles. H. Sienkiewicz.

Outlook. 112 : 273-7. F. 2, '16. Poland's future. G. Mason.

Outlook. 120 : 628-31. D. 18, '18. The aspirations of Poland. W. O. Gorski.

Outlook. 122 : 147-8. My. '19. Sorely tried Poland. V. Kellog.

Outlook. 125 : 568-72. Je. 28, '20. Our debt to Poland. M. F. Egan.

Outlook. 137 : 430-1. Jl. 16, '24. Talk with the premier of Poland. E. F. Baldwin.

Outlook. 137:638-9. Ag. 27, '24. Present-day Poland.
E. F. Baldwin.

Outlook. 139:225-6. F. 18 '25. Keystone of an arch.
A. L. P. Dennis.

Overland. n.s. 83:21. Ja. '25. More excellent way.
A. Cryan.

Quarterly Review. 230:474-503. O. '18. La question
polonaise et l'Europe. W. Martin.

*Sciencia. 22:294-302. O. '17. The Polish question.
A. B. Boswell.

Scottish Geographical. 35:81-93. Mr. '19. The Polish
problem. M. I. Newbigin.

*Slavonic Review. 3:117-30. Je. '24. Literature and
national life in modern Poland. R. Dyboski.

World's Work. 37:39-44. N. '18. Prussianism in
Poland. Charles D. Hazen.

World's Work. 37:173-9. D. '18. An independent
Poland. Ignace J. Paderewski.

World's Work. 38:109-12. My. '19. Paderewski,
Piłsudski and Poland. V. Kellog.

World's Work. 43:617-30. Ap. '22. The Jews in
Poland. H. Morgenthau.

Yale Review. 9:732-43. Jl. '20. Poland in the new
Europe. C. Lubomirski.

Chapter IV

Czechoslovakia

American Catholic Quarterly Review. 46:91-103. Ja.
'21. Czechoslovakia, a modern republic. H. F.
Wright.

American Journal of Sociology. 28:76-8. Jl. '22. Czech
sociology. J. Škola.

Annals of the American Academy. 84:58-63. Jl. '19.
An experiment in progressive government. Chas.
Pergler.

Annals of the American Academy. 93:149-53. Ja. '21.
Bohemians and Slovaks. J. F. Smetanka.

Annals of the American Academy. 102:1-13. Jl. '22
Economic and financial reconstruction of Czechoslovakia. B. Štěpánek.

*Art and Archeology. 11:179-83, 213-19. My. '21. Art
in Czechoslovakia. Aleš Hrdlička.

Art and Archeology. 11:199-205. My. '21. Architecture in the Czechoslovak republic. O. Heidrich.

Asia. 18:1002-9. D. '18. The future of Czechoslovak
state. Charles Pergler.

Asia. 18:1029-35. D. '18. The singing Czechoslovaks.
L. Llewelyn.

Bankers. 108:911-26. Je. '24. Czechoslovakia's
economic resources. P. Einzig.

Bookman. 34:256-66. N. '11. The message of Bohemia.
L. Baury.

Catholic World. 107:489-95. Jl. '18. The Bohemian
situation. M. R. Ryan.

Catholic World. 112:346-53. D. '20. The Czechoslovak republic and religion. H. F. Wright.

Century. 104:261-9. Je. '22. Masaryk's fight for God.
N. M. Schoonmaker.

*Century. 104:857-64. O. '22. The Yankees of cen-
tral Europe. J. A. James.

Century. 108:517-26. Ag. '24. Around the world in
New York: Czechoslovakia. K. Bercovici.

Charities. 13:206-10. D. 3, '04. The Bohemians in
Chicago. Alice G. Masaryk.

Charities. 13:211-14. D. 3, '04. Bohemian farmers in
Wisconsin. N. Mashek.

Charities. 13:239-44. D. 3, '04. The Slovaks in
America. P. V. Rovinianek.

Contemporary Review. 108:100-4. Jl. '18. Bohemia
and the war. M. J. Landa.

*Contemporary Review. 119:310-21. Mr. '21. The
Czechoslovak republic. R. W. Seton-Watson.

Contemporary Review. 123: 598-605. My. '23. Czechoslovakia under Masaryk. S. Münz.

Current History. 10: 309-12. My. '19. Work of the Czechoslovaks in America. B. P. Matocha.

Current History. 11: 287-90. N. '19. Three founders of the Czech republic. L. Weiss.

Current History. 13: 516-18. D. '20. How the Czechs are using their liberty. E. Markell.

Current History. 14: 835-45. Ag. '21. The upbuilding of Czechoslovakia. J. H. Wallis.

Current History. 14: 942-3. S. '21. Right of Czechoslovakia to independence. Charles Pergler.

Current History. 14: 944-5. S. '21. Czechoslovakia's place in the sun. C. L. Orbach.

Current History. 15: 499. D. '21. Czechoslovakia's right to statehood. A. Poliak.

Current History. 16: 472-4. Je. '22. The Slovaks—past and present. S. J. Polickar.

Current Opinion. 66: 287-9. My. '19. The importance of the Czechoslovak state to Europe. Charles Pergler.

Edinburgh Review. 238: 209-29. O. '23. Central Europe and Czechoslovakia. R. H. B. Lockhart.

Everybody's. 40: 41-3. F. '19. Masaryk, greatest man of new Europe. W. Hard.

Fortnightly Review. 93: 541-53. Mr. '10. A visit to Bohemia. G. S. Street.

*Fortnightly Review. 100: 347-58. Ag. '13. The Bohemian Sokol. W. Jerrold.

Fortnightly Review. 120: 418-29. S. '23. Dr. Edouard Beneš. R. H. B. Lockhart.

*Geographical Review. 8: 31-6. Jl. '19. Czechoslovakia and its people. Milivoy S. Stanoyevich.

Geographical Review. 14: 561-75. O. '24. Natural regions of Czechoslovakia. J. Moscheles.

Harper's. 138: 247-55. Ja. '19. Men of Bohemia. O. Gilbreath.

Independent. 97:434-5. Mr. 29, '19. The birth of the
Czechoslovak republic. Charles Pergler.

Journal of the National Education Association. 13:207-
9. Je. '24. Czechoslovakia and education. E. V.
Lippert.

*La Revue Universelle. 6:731-5. S. 15, '21. La vie à
Prague. (Social life in Prague). P. Bouchard.

Living Age. 321:839-41. My. 3, '24. Electioneering
among illiterates. M. Brod.

Nation. 108:497-8. Ap. 5, '19. Plight in Czechoslovakia. H. G. Alsberg.

*National Geographic. 31:163-87. F. '17. Bohemia
and the Czechs. Aleš Hrdlička.

National Geographic. 39:111-56. F. '21. Czechoslovakia, key land to central Europe. M. O. Williams.

Nineteenth Century. 81:570-8. Mr. '17. The liberation of the Czechoslovaks. Joseph Forman.

Nineteenth Century. 81:579-92. Mr. '17. Czech claims
and Magyar intrigues. F. Gribble.

Nineteenth Century. 95:483-90. Ap. '24. Foreign
policy of Czechoslovakia. E. Beneš.

North American Review. 206:426-36. S. '17. Bohemia,
the submerged front. S. Bonsal.

North American Review. 208:858-66. D. '18. The
Czechoslovak nation. G. Peet and L. E. Van Norman.

Outlook. 126:547-8. N. 24, '20. The courageous
Czechs. E. Markell.

Outlook. 131:144-5. My. 24, '22. The hub of Europe.
E. F. Baldwin.

Public. 21:728-30. Je. 8, '18. Kultur and Bohemian
independence. E. F. Prantner.

Public. 22:265-6. Mr. 15, '19. Bohemia—a democracy.
E. F. Prantner.

Public. 22:540-1. My. 24, '19. President Masaryk of
Bohemia. E. F. Prantner.

Public. 22:982-4. S. 13, '19. Czechoslovakia's experiment. E. F. Prantner.

Review of Reviews. 68:80-4. Jl. '23. Breaking up of old Bohemian estates. L. E. Textor.

Saturday Evening Post. 194:16-49. D. '21. Europe in transition. The Czechoslovakian opportunity. I. F. Marcosson.

Scribner's. 69:82-98. Ja. '21. Putting a republic on the map. R. Recouly.

Scribner's. 74:596-608. N. '23. Czechoslovakia an emerging republic. V. I. Paradise and H. Campbell.

Smithsonian Institution. Annual Report. 1919. p. 471-86. Je. 30, 1919. The origin and the beginnings of the Czechoslovak people. J. Matiegka.

Studies. 11:613-20. D. '22. Impressions of Czechoslovakia. G. O'Neill.

Survey. 43:169-72. N. 29, '19. The social beginnings of the Czechoslovak republic. R. J. Kerner.

Survey. 46:327-36. Je. 11, '21. Pathfinding in Prague. R. Crawford.

Survey. 46:337-45. Je. 11, '20. Prague's window to the west. B. Lasker.

Survey. 46:346-53. Je. 11, '21. Social and economic problems; how Czechoslovakia is trying to meet them. B. Štěpánek.

Survey. 46:361-8. Je. 11, '21. Americans of Czechoslovak descent. Šarka B. Hrbková.

Theatre Arts. 7:69-73. Ja. '23. Czechoslovak pupet shows. Š. B. Hrbková.

World's Work. 35:508-11. Mr. '18. The ferment in Bohemia. R. W. Rowan.

CHAPTER V

YUGOSLAVIA

American Catholic Quarterly Review. 37:567-73. O. '12. Serbia and the Balkan crisis. R. F. O'Connor.

American Political Science Review. 9:227-51. My. '15. Southern Slav question. H. D. Harris.

Annals of the American Academy. 84:51-7. Jl. '19. An eye-witness of the Serbian apotheosis. Madame S. Grouitch.

Art and Archaeology. 17:207-8. My. '24. Earliest civilization in Yugoslavia. N. Vulich.

Art and Archaeology. 17:209-15. My. '24. Yugoslav national art. T. Gjorgjevich.

*Art and Archaeology. 17:233-40. My. '24. Modern Yugoslav art. Branko Popovich.

Art and Archaeology. 17:241-2. My. '24. Some of Montenegro's antiquities. H. R. Fairclough.

Asia. 18:1015-20. D. '18. A united Yugoslavia. V. Savich.

Atlantic Monthly. 116:119-27. Jl. '15. Serbia and southeastern Europe. G. M. Trevelyan.

Atlantic Monthly. 128:267-77. Jl. '21. The Adriatic negotiations at Paris. D. H. Miller.

Bookman. 42:335-8. N. '15. The Serbian epic. A. Yarmolinsky.

British Review. 12:179-88. N. '15. With a voluntary party in Serbia. J. W. N. Sullivan.

Canadian. 47:183-8. Jl. '16. The Cheechas of Serbia. P. F. Jones.

Catholic World. 109:229-35. My. '19. Slovenes and their leaders. E. Christich.

Catholic World. 113:599-606. Ag. '21. Reunion and fusion of the southern Slavs. E. Christich.

Catholic World. 114:667-73. F. '22. Yugoslavia, a modern kingdom. H. F. Wright.

Catholic World. 118:808-13. Mr. '24. In Yugoslavia. C. C. Martindale.

Century. 68:240-6. Je. '04. A possible American heir to the Serbian throne. A. B. Hulbert.

Century. 92:509-18. Ag. '16. Glimpses of Serbia in retreat. F. Jones.

Century. 95:687-92. Mr. '18. Yugoslavia, a new European state. Milivoy S. Stanoyevich.

Century. 98:135-9. My. '19. Adria, the troubled sea. L. Stoddard.

Century. 98:780-6. O. '19. In Montenegro today. W. Warfield.

Contemporary Review. 84:131-43. Jl. '03. Serbia and the rival dynasties. E. J. Dillon.

Contemporary Review. 101:820-30. Je. '12. Hungary and the southern Slavs. R. W. Seton-Watson.

Contemporary Review. 104:153-63. Ag. '13. A holiday among the Serbians. G. M. Trevelyan.

Contemporary Review. 107:273-83. Mr. '15. Serbia revisited. G. M. Trevelyan.

Contemporary Review. 107:515-20. Ap. '15. Zadrougas, the strength of Serbia. A. Smith.

Contemporary Review. 108:576-81. N. '15. Serbia's need and Britain's danger. R. W. Seton-Watson.

Contemporary Review. 109:437-47. Ap. '16. With the Serbian army in retreat. M. A. S. C. Stobart.

Contemporary Review. 110:510-14. O. '16. The "Slava" of a Serbian regiment. C. Askew.

Contemporary Review. 113:40-50. Ja. '18. With the Serbians in Corsica. K. Royds.

Contemporary Review. 117:531-8. Ap. '20. The Serbs as seen in their national songs. M. E. Durham.

Contemporary Review. 117:635-42. My. '20. Some Adriatic problems. H. Charles Woods.

Contemporary Review. 118:514-21. O. '20. Some sidelights of Dalmatia. L. Re-Bartlett.

Contemporary Review. 125:445-50. Ap. '24. Macedonian tangle. J. W. Collins.

Contemporary Review. 126:613-21. N. '24. A holiday in Bosnia. A. Dell.

Current History. 7:111-12. O. '17. A new phase of the Balkan question. Milivoy S. Stanoyevich.

Current History. 7:497-500. Mr. '18. The Serbian mission in America. Milivoy S. Stanoyevich.

*Current History. 13:278-86. F. '21. Yugoslavia's resources and beauty. G .W. Atwood.

Current History. 14:624-6. Jl. '21. Yugoslavia's constitutional problems. Ivan Schvegel.

Current History. 15:930-7. Mr. '22. Drifting toward a Yugoslav federation. C. Stefanov.

Current History. 16:131-2. Ap. '22. Yugoslavia's attitude toward Bulgaria. G. G. Smith.

Current History. 17:255-9. N. '22. Pacifist revolution in Croatia. L. Denny.

Edinburgh Review. 220:41-59. Jl. '14. Serbia irredenta. F. Gribble.

Englishwoman. 1917:46-55. Ja. '17. Literature of southern Slavs. P. Popovich.

Foreign Affairs. 1:82-104. Je. '23. Yugoslavia today. H. F. Armstrong.

Fortnightly Review. 53:124-35. Ja. '80. The black mountain. Hulme-Beaman.

Fortnightly Review. 85:537-45. Mr. '06. The Serbo-Bulgarian convention and its results. A. Stead.

Fortnightly Review. 91:1-18. Ja. '09. Europe and the annexation of Bosnia and Herzegovina. M. R. Ivanovich.

Fortnightly Review. 91:838-49. My. '09. The secret treaty between Serbia and Austria-Hungary. S. Protich.

Fortnightly Review. 99:125-41. Ja. '13. Masters of the southern Slav. H. Baerlein.

Fortnightly Review. 102:643-52. O. '14. Soul of the southern Slav. E. Christich.

Fortnightly Review. 111:478-91. Mr. '19. Adriatic Hungary and Serbia. G. M. Trevelyan.

Fortnightly Review. 111:385-95. Mr. '19. The Macedonian question. Charles H. Woods.

Fortnightly Review. 111:478-91. Mr. '19. Adriatic problem and the peace conference. V. Gayda.

Forum. 57:447-50. Ap. '17. Embattled Serbia. F. L. Waldo.

Harper's. 135:327-37. Ag. '17. The Serbian tragedy as I saw it. H. Corey.

Independent. 79:67-8. Jl. 13, '14. Serb and Austrian. M. I. Pupin.

Independent. 97:218-20. F. 15, '19. In justice to the Yugoslavs. V. R. Savich.

Literary Digest. 51:406-7. Ag. 28, '15. The ancient national poetry of Serbia. Charles Martin.

Literary Digest. 57:34-6. Je. 8, '18. Modern Serbian poetry. Paul Selver.

Living Age. 283:249-52. O. 24, '14. New Slav empire of the south. S. Casson.

Living Age. 307:755-9. D. 25, '20. On the Adriatic. Theo. Brekes.

Living Age. 309:193-201. Ap. 23, '21. King "Nikita" of Montenegro. Roda Roda and H. Wendel.

Living Age. 316:417-25. F. 17, '25. Land hunger. L. Kuhar.

London Quarterly Review. 130:21-33. Jl. '18. The Cinderella of the nations. W. F. Lofthouse.

Macmillan's. 1:35-44. N. '05. A sketch in old Serbia. M. E. Durham.

Nation. 105:660. D. 13, '17. New Serbia and its problems. Milivoy S. Stanoyevich.

Nation. 108:209-11. F. 8, '19. Two problems of Yugoslavia. V. R. Savich.

Nation. 110:181-2. F. 7, '20. Politics in Yugoslavia. H. F. Armstrong.

Nation. 112:510. Ap. 6, '21. Peasant rule and co-operation. I. F. Lupis-Vukich.

Nation. 120:101-2. Ja. 28, '25. Toward a Yugoslav republic. D. Mitrany.

National Geographic. 27:417-32. Ap. '15. The kingdom of Serbia. W. J. Showalter.

National Geographic. 31:383-412. My. '17. On the Monastir road. H. Corey.

National Review. 75:412-16. My. '20. A word for Serbia. F. Sandes.

New Europe. 16:196-200. S. 9, '20. The Adriatic problem and the Yugoslav merchant marine. V. Primorac.

New Republic. 4:300-2. O. 23, '15. Bulgaria's choice. H. N. Brailsford.

New Republic. 41:253-5. Ja. 28, '25. Unmaking of Yugoslavia. D. Mitrany.

Nineteenth Century. 1:359. My. '77. Montenegro. (A song). Alfred Tennyson.

Nineteenth Century. 1:360-79. My. '77. Montenegro. A sketch. W. E. Gladstone.

Nineteenth Century. 2:796-819. D. '77. South Slavonians and Rajpoots. H. S. Maine.

Nineteenth Century. 78:548-62. S. '15. Some recent experiences in Serbia. E. N. Bennett.

Nineteenth Century. 78:1021-30. N. '15. The strategical significance of Serbia. N. Županić.

Nineteenth Century. 78:1335-44. D. '15. Belgrade, the gateway to the east. W. F. Bailey.

Nineteenth Century. 78:1345-53. D. '15. The Serbian soldier in action. E. H. Young.

Nineteenth Century. 79:67-84. Ja. '16. The sacrifice of Serbia. R. Machray.

*Nineteenth Century. 86:889-98. N. '19. Italian and Yugoslav psychology. Montgomery-Campbell.

Nineteenth Century. 86:1162-9. D. '19. Serbia today and tomorrow. A. Dell.

*Nineteenth Century. 88:787-96. N. '20. The new Adriatic state. J. Leyland.

Nineteenth Century. 89:135-45. Ja. '21. The martyrdom of Montenegro. R. McNeill.

North American Review. 206:583-5. O. '17. Serbia and European peace. Milivoy S. Stanoyevich.

North American Review. 214:201-7. Ag. '21. Flivvering through Bosnia. H. F. Armstrong.

North American Review. 214:641-3. N. '21. Serbia's Westminster. H. F. Armstrong.

North American Review. 214:741-51. D. '21. Yugoslavia today. P. de Lanux.

*North American Review. 217:96-106. Ja. '23. Modern Yugoslav literature. Milivoy S. Stanoyevich.

Outlook. 37:143-4. Ja. 29, '16. Folk-poetry of the Serb. A. L. Salmon.

Outlook. 118:576-7. Ap. 10, '18. Why are the southern Slavs anti-German? Pierre de Lanux.

Outlook. 119:585-7. Ag. 14, '18. The theft of a nation. E. M. Chadwick.

Outlook. 135:586-9. D. 5, '23. Rifling the eagle's nest. B. Roselli.

Outlook. 136:434-7. Mr. 12, '24. Dalmatia, the Slav body with a Latin soul. B. Roselli.

Outlook (London). 34:267. Ag. 29, '14. What the Serbians want. Chedo Miyatovich.

Outlook (London). 34:331-2. S. 12, '14. The new Slav empire of the south. S. Casson.

Outlook (London). 38:248-9. S. 9, '16. The future of Serbia. J. E. Barker.

Overland. n.s. 48:221-8. O. '06. Overland among the Slavonians of Istria. F. J. Koch.

Quarterly Review. 226:488-507. O. '16. The mediaeval Serbian empire. W. Miller.

Quarterly Review. 236:418-33. O. '21. The Triune kingdom, political and economical. J. M. Jovanović. and P. Popović.

Review. 1:120-1. Je. 21, '19. The Italo-Yugoslav controversy. L. Pasvolsky.

Review of Reviews. 51:203-8. F. '15. Serbia's struggle. M. I. Pupin.

Review of Reviews. 58:633-5. D. '18. The glory that is Serbia. A. Stead.

Review of Reviews. 61:189-92. F. '20. Fiume, an explanation. E. Baldwin.

Review of Reviews. 61:267-72. Mr. '20. Serbia's vital problems. W. J. Doherty.

Scientific American. 112:219. Mr. 6, '15. The present geographical position of Serbia. Jovan Cvijić.

Scottish Geographical. 35:1-15. Ja. '19. The problem of the south Slavs (Yugoslavs). M. I. Newbigin.

Scribner's. 7:255-60. F. '90. The Minnesota heir of a Serbian king. E. Schuyler.

*Scribner's. 59:368-80. Mr. '16. The Serbian people in war time. S. Naylor.

Scribner's. 67:18-32. Ja. '20. The borderland of Slav and Latin. E. A. Powell.

Sewanee Review. 31:313-23. Jl. '23. The Yugoslav renaissance. Milivoy S. Stanoyevich.

Spectator. 103:547-9. O. 9, '09. Hungarian crisis and the southern Slavs. Scotus Viator. (Seton-Watson).

Spectator. 109:51-2. Jl. 13, '12. Croatia and the south Slav question. H. Hinkovich.

Survey. 29:277-86. D. 7, '12. Serbo-Croats of Manhattan. M. S. Orenstein.

Survey. 43:681-3. Mr. 6, '20. Through Yugoslavia with pen and pencil. M. Hoffman.

World's Work. 35:670-6. Mr. '18. Destroying a nation. E. M. Chadwick.

World's Work. 37:581-6. Mr. '19. The controversy between the Italians and the Yugoslavs. L. Stoddard.

Yale Review. 7:90-100. O. '17. Serbia, the buffer state. L. Markovich.

Yale Review. 8:500-12. Ap. '19. The passing of the Balkans. V. R. Savich.

Yale Review. 9:462-81. Ap. '20. The struggle for the Adriatic. Charles Seymour.

*Yugoslav Review. 2:2-7. Mr. '24. Early Yugoslav civilization. A. T. Pavitchich.

CHAPTER VI

BULGARIA

Asia. 18:918-24. N. '18. Bulgaria points the way. E. B. Haskell.

American Journal of International Law. 6:86-106, 659-78. Ja., Jl. '12. Bulgarian independence. G. Scelle.

Century. 90:251-63. Je. '15. Bulgaria's dream of empire. T. L. Stoddard.

Century. 97:237-42. D. '18. Bulgaria quits. L. Stoddard.

Contemporary Review. 104:109-10. Jl. '13. The Tsar's telegram and the smothered Balkan war. E. J. Dillon.

Contemporary Review. 104:259-80. Ag. '13. The latest phase of the Balkan crisis. E. J. Dillon.

Contemporary Review. 104:567-70. O. '13. How Bulgaria fared in the division of the spoils. E. J. Dillon.

Contemporary Review. 104:880-4. D. '13. Exit Tsar Ferdinand. E. J. Dillon.

*Contemporary Review. 114:484-8. N. '18. Bulgaria, Turkey and the war. E. Pears.

Contemporary Review. 118:784-9. D. '20. Alexander Stambolisky. J. D. Bourchier.

Contemporary Review. 121:570-8. My. '22. Bulgaria and the treaty of Neuilly. E. F. B. Grogan.

Contemporary Review. 124:321-8. S. '23. The Bulgarian coup and afterwards. J. W. Collins.

Current History. 5:70-6. O. '16. Bulgaria's part in the European war. R. A. Tsanov.

Current History. 13:217-22. N. '20. Bulgaria's novel methods of reconstruction. T. Vladimirov.

Current History. 14:272-4. My. '21. Stambolisky's reforms in Bulgaria. E. Markell.

Current History. 15:489-91. D. '21. The truth about Bulgaria. T. T. Holway.

Current History. 15:491-2. D. '21. Bulgaria's rights.
T. Vladimirov.

Current History. 17:96-8. O. '22. Bulgaria's peasant
rule and foreign foes. C. Stefanov.

*Current History. 19:636-40. Ja. '24. Bulgaria's revo-
lution of 1923. C. Stefanov.

English Historical Review. 25:276-87. Ap. '10. Bulgarian treaty of A. D. 814, and the great fence of
Thrace. J. B. Bury.

English Review. 21:405-10. N. '15. The truth about
the Bulgars. S. Graham.

Fortnightly Review. 36:284-93. S. '81. Bulgaria.
M. V. Chirol.

Fortnightly Review. 99:312-21. F. '13. After the war.
H. Vivian.

Fortnightly Review. 103:483-94. Mr. '15. Bulgaria's
attitude. F. Fox.

Fortnightly Review. 103:755-66. My. '15. Bulgaria
and entente diplomacy. E. J. Dillon.

Fortnightly Review. 104:904-15. N. '15. The Balkan
imbroglio. E. J. Dillon.

Fortnightly Review. 108:418-31. S. '17. Bulgaria and
peace. C. Price.

Fortnightly Review. 115:1034-43. Je. '21. The internal situation in Bulgaria. H. Charles Woods.

Fortnightly Review. 120:294-304. Ag. '23. The Bulgarian revolution. H. Charles Woods.

Forum. 58:25-32. Jl. '17. Bulgaria militant and misguided. F. L. Waldo.

Independent. 73:1225-9. N. 28 '12. Spirit of Bulgaria.
A. Sonnichsen.

Independent. 74:1051-2. My. 8, '13. Bulgarian election. A. Konstantinov.

Independent. 75:673-5. S. 18, '13. After the treaty
of Bucharest. H. A. Gibbons.

Independent. 84:13-15. O. 4, '15. The arbiter of Balkan destiny. S. Brooks.

Journal of Education. 68:399-400. O. 15, '08. World's nerve centres. R. Warburton.

*L'Echo de Bulgarie. 10:2634-6. Ag. 19-21, '22. Le village dans la poésie bulgare (Village life in Bulgarian poetry). N. Dontchev.

Living Age. 276:515-21. Mr. 1, '13. Secrets of the Bulgarian victories. P. Gibbs.

Living Age. 317:390-2. My. 19, '23. Rebuilding Bulgaria. G. Akbardzhev.

Living Age. 318:157-9. Jl. 28, '23. Bulgaria since the war. L. Lamouche.

Living Age. 319:500-4. D. '23. Snapshots of the Bulgarian insurrection. Dimo Siarov.

Missionary Review. 36:412-20. Je. '13. Bulgaria, the youngest kingdom. M. N. Popov.

*Nation. 109:563. N. 1, '19. Bulgaria faces the future. H. Alsberg.

Nation (London). 33:360-1. Je. 16, '23. Revolution in Bulgaria. A. J. Toynbee.

*National Education Association. Journal of Proceedings. 1915:190-3. Ag. '15. Education in Bulgaria. Stephen Panaretov.

National Geographic. 23:1104-18. N. '12. Rise of Bulgaria. J. D. Bourchier.

National Geographic. 27:377-400. Ap. '15. Bulgaria and its women. H. D. Jenkins.

New Europe. 16:63-7. Jl. 29, '20. Agrarian government of Bulgaria. G. C. Logio.

New Republic. 2:144-5. Mr. 23, '15. Bulgaria, key of the Near East. F. H. Simonds.

Nineteenth Century. 74:1342-56. D. '13. Bulgaria and her traducers. H. M. Wallis.

North American Review. 141:464-74. N. '85. United Bulgaria. E. Schuyler.

North American Review. 188:833-41. D. '08. Bulgaria and the treaty of Berlin. S. Tondzhorov.

North American Review. 198:630-9. N. '13. Bulgaria and the treaty of Bucharest. S. Tondzhorov.

North American Review. 209:763-71. Je. '19. Greece, Bulgaria and the principle of nationality. A. Andreades.

Outlook. 103:306-11. F. 8, '13. Victorious Bulgaria. A. Edwards.

*Outlook. 135:536-9. N. 28, '23. The Bulgarians, a simple folk with a heart. N. de Bogory.

Political Science Quarterly. 28:627-45. D. '13. The Balkan adjustment. S. P. Duggan.

Review of Reviews. 49:209-10. F. '14. Bulgaria after the wars. B. C. Marsh.

Review of Reviews. 52:716-19. D. '15. The Bulgarians and their country. O. Bainbridge.

Review of Reviews. 64:81-3. Jl. '21. The Bulgarian "National service" law. S. M. Feinberg and G. Georgiev.

Review of Reviews. 68:517-23. N. '23. The Bulgarian revolution. F. P. Graves.

South Atlantic Quarterly. 8:12-18. Ja. '09. Bulgaria, satisfied and dissatisfied. E. G. Elliott.

Spectator. 130:1034-5. Je. 23, '23. Bulgarian upheaval. H. Baerlein.

Survey. 29:212-14. N. 23, '12. Bulgarian in America. P. Roberts.

Westminster Review. 179:1-15. Ja. '13. Letters of a doomed sovereign. H. J. Darnton-Fraser.

CHAPTER I

INTRODUCTION

THE SLAVONIC RACE IN GENERAL

THE SLAVS AMONG THE NATIONS[1]

The five nations which will be studied here—
Russians, Czechoslovaks, Poles, Serbians and Bulgarians
—can perfectly well represent the Slavonic world. For
instance, the Serbians can represent the Croats and the
Slovenes, not only in politics but also in literature and
language. Besides, the Slavs themselves are not altogether agreed as to the number of nations into which
they must be divided. The number varies, according to
the writer, from seven to ten. It has even been
contended that it is possible to fix the number of living
Slavonic nations at fourteen, omitting those which have
become extinct. The question of the exact number of
Slavonic nations has always excited numerous discussions and roused bitter disputes between philologists,
historians of literature, and ethnographers. In my opinion, in order to complete the list of Slavonic nations of
the twentieth century, the Slovenes and Lusatian Serbs
must be added.

Do the Slavs, as a whole, constitute a true unity?
I believe that can be answered by a categoric affirmative.
We are obviously confronted by a group of distinct
nations, each with its own tongue, its national literature,
its independent history, and its peculiar civilization; but
these differences do not hide the existence among them
of a general consciousness—the feeling that they all belong to a single Slavonic organism.

This Slavonic consciousness is not developed in an
equal measure among all the Slavonic nations. It is not

[1] By T. G. Masaryk. La Nation Tchèque. 1: 343-9. March 15, 1916.

the same at all periods or among all classes of society, but it is common to all. Among the Czechs, and I speak from personal experience, it has already been very powerful for a long time. Those who do not belong to our race can easily understand the nature of this sentiment by comparison and analogy. "Latinism" gives some idea of it, though a very feeble one. The difference of language is much more accentuated among the Latin than among the Slav nations, and the racial community of the various Latin groups is as much a cause of jealousy as of unity. "Germanism"—the affinity that exists between Germanic nations, if the term is used in its widest sense as including as German not only the German but also the English and the Scandinavians—represents a less indeterminate and more precise bond, and so to a much greater extent does "Scandinavism," that is, the community of feeling which brings together the Swedish, Danish, and Norwegian peoples. But even Scandinavism does not constitute so close a relationship between the various branches of this race as that which unites the different Slavonic groups. The Slavs are much more closely united from the linguistic and intellectual point of view than the various groups of other races are with one another.

From the geographical point of view the contact of the Slavs with one another is also much closer than that of the various Germanic peoples. They are not separated by the sea. The several Slavonic nations have not wandered so far as have other peoples from the cradle of their race, where at one time they formed groups which were identical and united, or at least with very few distinguishing marks. Moreover, the slower development of their civilization, and their economic life, which is not so rich as that of other nations, have also tended to preserve the uniformity and the unity of their character.

In western Europe this common sentiment among the Slavonic nations is often translated into a political idea.

Some prefer to see in it what is called "Panslavism," that is, the design to form a colossal Slavonic monarchy under the domination of Russia, and they readily repeat the words of Napoleon on the danger of a "Cossackized" Europe.

If the numbers of the Slavonic peoples are examined, it is seen that they greatly surpass those of other nations. According to the figures of Professor Niederle, which are somewhat unfavorable to the Slavs, in 1900 there were 136,500,000 Slavs. In 1916 their number may be estimated at 156,700,000. As the Germans, who are the most numerous apart from the Russians, are only seventy million, the English forty-five million, the French forty million, and the Italians thirty-six million, it is not astonishing that a certain fear of the Panslavist peril—also called the Panrussian peril—should have arisen among the western peoples.

This danger appears to them even more threatening for the future than now. The birth-rate among the Slavs is much greater than among the Germans and the Latins, so that soon the Slavs will be twice as numerous as the other European nations. Today men are no longer content with a policy which has regard to the present alone; true statesmen also think of the distant future of their nation, and that is why the fertility of the race, or, in concrete terms, the time which a population takes to double itself, is for them a matter of supreme importance. This factor plays such a part that the youth of today will doubtless witness a complete transformation of Europe.

THE SLAV AND HIS FUTURE [1]

It has become customary of late years to look upon the Slav as something so essentially extra-European, that it comes almost as a shock when, upon examining him

[1] By E. Reich. Fortnightly Review. 81: 371-82. March 1, 1904.

more closely, we discover that he is, after all, but part and parcel of the same family to which the majority of European nations appertain. In his language there is really nothing strange to the western ear, and the student accustomed to looking at various tongues from a philological point of view is immediately struck by the close relationship evident between the numerous Slavonic languages and other branches of the Indo-European stock. Familiar sounds and words at once strike his ear, and he is delighted at recognizing, under a very thin veil of disguise, verbal terminations and inflexions already familiar to him through Latin and Greek.

If the language of the Slav is not foreign to us, even less so are his physical characteristics. We meet with the same fair hair, the same fresh complexion, the same clear, light-blue eyes which we have been wont to set down as peculiarly Teutonic, and by the time we have made out all these features of similitude, a great deal of the original feeling of strangeness was worn off, and we are prepared, as far as externals go, to accept the Slav for our kinsman. When we have learned a little more of the working of his soul perhaps we shall not have quite such a brotherly feeling toward him.

For over a thousand years the Slav, under varying styles and titles, has peopled the whole of Europe east of the Elbe River. A very great proportion of that country he may very well look upon as quite his own; over the rest he forms a very considerable percentage of the population. All about the central and lower Danubian basin he is scattered especially thick, and forms decidedly the preponderant element.

In point of language the Slav falls into three natural divisions, the southern, the central, and the northern. In character he displays very slight diversity, and the Slav from the extreme south would on most subjects find himself in complete sentimental harmony with his northern brother. His chief feature is an over-sensitive,

frequently over-sentimental, mind, easily prone to rhap-
sodic vagaries, alternating with fits of the profoundest
melancholy. Much of this is reflected in Slav music,
and nothing can equal the inexpressible depths of de-
spondency of some of their folk-songs in the minor key.
From these crises of despair they burst, without the
slightest warning, into the most extravagant hullabaloo.
For the rest of his character the Slav is stamped rather
with subtlety and cunning than with real intelligence.
He seems to prefer attaining his end by ruse and craft
rather than by open and straightforward means. The
same inequality, the same unevenness, the same extremes
which characterize the emotions of the Slav, have also
set their mark upon his education. If he is of the upper
class, be he Russian, Pole, Serbian, or Bulgarian, we
shall find him over-educated. His mind is overloaded
with instruction, and this defect is shared even by the
women, who devote themselves with enthusiasm to study,
and often take up a prominent position in the learned
professions. The number of women doctors who are
Polish and Russian is greater than that of any other
nationality.

In his intellectual pursuits the Slav enjoys the advantage of being an excellent linguist, and here we may
be pardoned a momentary digression. It has frequently
been supposed that the Slav owes his talent for languages
in no small part to the difficulties with which his own
tongue bristles. This theory is distinctly erroneous. No
Slav language can be difficult. It is only the old
languages which have for centuries been the vehicles
for every kind of thought that can finally attain that
degree of subtlety and *finesse* which render English,
German, and French especially, so exceedingly difficult.
A language which has never, or has only for some few
decades, been a literary medium, must inevitably be exceedingly simple. Extensive vocabulary Slav languages
may boast, but this is the criterion of linguistic poverty.
French and Greek, probably the most perfect instruments

of human thought, are comparatively indigent in word-forms. Whence the Slav really draws his linguistic talent is from his polyglot surroundings. In the events of everyday life, he may be called upon to employ half a dozen independent tongues. His household will certainly contain servants speaking several dialects, and in Russia he will very probably have Tatar domestics as well. French and German are essential to social intercourse, and the Slav is absolutely dependent on foreign literature to compensate for the deficiencies of his own. To the Slav, therefore, the knowledge of languages is an immense stimulus to wide reading, and the necessity of reading is an equally potent motive for the acquisition of languages. Thus it frequently happens that a Russian is quite as familiar, if not more familiar, than we are ourselves, with the works of our latter-day philosophers. It would probably be no exaggeration to say that the writings of Herbert Spencer are quite as well known in Russia as they are at home.

THE COMING OF THE SLAV [1]

The Latin and the Teutonic races have had their day, and they have failed to establish a truly Christian civilization. They have done great things in the organization of society, in the development of material wealth, in literature, art, and science, and especially in recognizing and securing in some degree the rights of the individual man; but they have exalted the material above the spiritual, and made Mammon their god. They have lost the nobler aspirations of youth, and are governed now by the sordid calculations of old age. We wait the coming of the Slav to regenerate Europe, establish the principle of universal brotherhood and the kingdom of Christ on earth.

This is the substance of an address delivered not long

[1] By G. Washburn. Contemporary Review. 73: 1-13. January, 1898.

ago by a young Slav. If it were the fancy of a single brain it would not be worth noticing: but as it is, in fact, the dream of more than a hundred million brains in Europe, it has some interest for those who are to be regenerated by the coming of the Slav. Englishmen and Americans used to have such dreams, and somehow, without much wisdom or much conscious direction on the part of their rulers, these dreams have got themselves fulfilled in a measure. If we have failed to establish a truly Christian civilization in the world, and left something for the Slav to do, it is, perhaps, our fault; but we have certainly done something toward the evolution of society. If we hear less of these dreams now, it is because we have found that the renovation of the world was a "bigger job" than we had counted upon. The Latin races had certainly failed to realize their dreams when the Teutonic races took up the work and put new life into it. If now the Slavs can complete it, so much the better for us and the world, however painful the process may be. The Latin races have lost nothing worth having by our leadership, and if the Slavs are to bring in a truly Christian civilization and universal brotherhood, then Latin, Teuton, and Slav will share alike in all the happy results which must follow. There is nothing manifestly absurd in their dream.

It must be acknowledged that there is some truth in their pessimistic view of modern civilization, and it has happened again and again in the history of the world that a new race has been called to take the lead in regenerating it. The Slavic race seems to be the only one in sight to which such a mission could be given. It is not exactly new. The Slavs have been a long time in central and south-eastern Europe. Even Russia is only relatively new. But their early development was checked by the Turkish invasion of Europe. But for this, Constantinople would, centuries ago, have been the capital of a great Slavic Empire, and central Europe might have been Slavic instead of German. As it was, all the southern Slavs fell under the Turks, and went back into barbarism. Those in central Europe were overwhelmed by the Germans, and Russia was absorbed in endless wars with her neighbors. Essentially, then, the Slavic race is a new one. It has never exerted any direct influence upon the development of European civilization until within a few years. The race is not only new, but far more numerous and powerful than any of the races that in times past have been called to overthrow or regenerate an existing civilization in Europe. It numbers more than a hundred millions under the rule or leadership of Russia.

It is interesting to know what this great race is dreaming of, but the question which interests us still more is whether the Slavic people can be depended upon to realize such an ideal civilization as they dream of. They are far enough from it now. Whatever may be said of western civilization, even enthusiastic Frenchmen have no desire to exchange it for that of Russia. This, however, proves nothing. The Slavs are just emerging from barbarism, and the Russian government is more under the influence of western than of Slavic ideals. The same thing is true of the governing class and of educated Russians generally. They may be ardent Panslavists, and believe in the mission of their race: but their faith is not in themselves—it is in the *muzhik*. When we ask for the ground of this faith, they tell us that there is something in the Slavic race which is above, or beyond, the comprehension of the western world. The very writers who give us the saddest, the most pathetic pictures of the Russian people, as they are, still profess the most unbounded faith in the *muzhik*. They believe that it is his destiny to regenerate the world. Perhaps it is: but the trouble is that they give us no sufficient reason for their faith. Even Dostoyevsky takes for his motto the lines of the poet Tutchev:

No man can comprehend Russia with his reason;
It is only necessary to believe in Russia.

In one of his novels he says: "Russia has the genius of all nations, and Russian genius in addition: we can understand all nations, but no other nation can understand us." The truth seems to lie in the first quotation. Every Russian is, to a certain extent, a mystic, who sees visions and acts upon intuitions. He believes in Russia as a Christian may believe in the book of Revelation, without understanding it. Its history, past and future, is to him a sort of Apocalyptic vision—with its mysterious seals, trumpets, and horses: its conflicts which shake heaven and earth: the final triumph of the saints of God, and, at the end, the Holy City coming down from heaven. We do not doubt the sincerity of Russian writers, but we can hardly avoid feeling that this apotheosis of the *muzhik* is largely the work of the imagination. He is the Great Unknown to educated Russians as well as to western Europe. He may be destined to overrun Europe, to revolutionize the Russian government, and to establish a better civilization in the world.

THE PAN-SLAVONIC IDEAL [1]

The Slavonic nations are in a position today very similar to that of the Italian states before the union of Italy into a compact entity in 1870, but with this important difference: the Italians have always had a commonly-recognized literary language, while all the Slavs have not as yet fixed upon any idiom which might be used as a general Slavonic medium. Outside this distinction, however, the comparison between Slavs and Italians holds good. Every Italian state before the union used its own dialect, not merely for purposes of conversation, as is still the case in most parts of Italy today, but also, to some extent, for literary purposes. In spite of this diversity of language and feeling, the House of Savoy, aided by the Garibaldian activities,

[1] By J. Dyneley Prince. Canadian Magazine. 47: 15-18. May, 1916.

seized the opportunity made by the culmination of a general discontent which had long been seething, and with a few deft strokes marvellously welded what had been a heterogeneous mass into an enduring and solid nation.

The Italian dialects differ from one another far more radically than do the Slavonic languages of our time. Thus a Piedmontese, or Bolognese, speaking in his own tongue, would be quite unintelligible to a Florentine, a Roman, a Neapolitan, or a Sicilian. The common linguistic bond between the Italian tribes is now the Tuscan idiom, which had for centuries been the higher literary medium among the educated classes of all Italy. This Tuscan language the unifiers of Italy found ready to their hand, and they made it the official language of their united country, requiring Tuscan to be taught in the army to the levies from every corner of the kingdom, so that, at the present day, it is a rare thing to find an Italian of middle age who does not speak and understand the *lingua toscana.*

Unlike the Italians, who before their union were satisfied to develop only purely local serio-comic literature in their various dialects, each Slavonic people has, most unfortunately, striven to foster a national literature in its own idiom. Of course, geographical separation is largely responsible for this tendency, which has had more effect than any other influence in keeping the Slavonic peoples apart from each other, and thus has hindered the growth of a true feeling of that Slavonic brotherhood, which has, however, arisen and grown in spite of all obstacles.

The rise of these distinctive national literatures is unfortunate also from the aesthetic point of view, in that only two Slavonic peoples have suceeded in producing truly great modern literatures. There are attempts at literature, for example, among the Bulgarians, the Slovaks of Czechoslovakia, the small Yugoslav tribe known as Slovenes, and even among the Lusatian Serbs

of Saxony who, although surrounded as they have been
for centuries by alien German hordes, have maintained
their Slavonic character and during the last fifty years
have established a *Matitsa* or literary association for the
purpose of developing a purely Wendish (Sorbian) literature. Of the peoples just mentioned, not one has
succeeded in bringing forth anything of permanent value
from a literary point of view. On the other hand, the
Serbians and Croatians, who use the same language,
have done better in fixing their idiom as a literary
vehicle. The only difference between Serbian and Croatian is the fact that the Serbs, who are Orthodox in religion, write their language in the modern modification
of the Cyrillic alphabet, while the Croats, who are chiefly
Roman Catholic, use the Latin letters.

Among the Yugoslavs there have existed from very
early times certain popular epics and lyrics of considerable literary value which were collected in the eighteenth
century by Mioshich and in the nineteenth century by
Karadzhich. These songs attracted the attention of
Goethe himself, owing to their simplicity and beauty
of form. The little mediaeval republic of Dubrovnik
(Ragusa) was for centuries the center of a very charming lyric literature, the productions of which, although
greatly influenced by the Italian style, are none the less
characteristically Slavonic. The Czechs in Bohemia also
have produced a well-marked national literature which
has considerable merit, although in this branch of
Slavonic expression, more than in any other, it is possible to feel the Germanic spirit; a not unnatural result
of the historic position of Bohemia during the middle
ages.

It was reserved for Russian and Poland to develop
a really great line of literary men who have brought
forth two European literatures second to none in pro-
fundity of thought and beauty of expression. West-
erners may find fault with the analytical sadness of much
of the Russian literature, the introspective character of

which has been attributed by some critics to Scandinavian influence.

The prevailing tone of sadness in some of the Russian expression is undoubtedly due to the joy in gloom inherent in the northern Slavonic nature, not unlike the marked delight in sorrow perceptible among the Irish and Highland Scottish Celts. No one can deny, however, that Russian literature is the exponent of a genuinely great effort. Moreover, the Poles have been excelled by no modern people in poetry, for which their imaginative national character has peculiarly fitted them. It is a pity that Mickiewicz wrote practically for the Poles alone: that much of this poetical effort is masked from the world by the intricacies of the most difficult Slavonic language. It is true, we know something of Polish prose literature from the excellent translations of the late Jeremiah Curtin who rendered Sienkiewicz's stirring style into vigorous and idiomatic English, but of the great mass of Polish literary effort we know as yet but little. Tolstoy, Dostoyevsky, Turgenev and other great Russian names are also well known through English and French translations, but it must be regretted that unhealthy productions such as *Sanin* and the *Millionnair* of Artsibashev should have such vogue among the English speaking peoples as to give an unpleasant color—one might almost say "unpleasant odor"—to modern Russian literature.

With such a diversity of interest and so much feeling of separatism as exists among the Slavonic nations, it is not difficult to see that these people are still far from a common Slavonic ideal, although the underlying impulse to incline toward each other is undoubtedly there. The various Slavonic idioms are really mutually comprehensible. It is possible for an orator to deliver an address in any Slavonic language to a mixed audience of Slavs and make himself generally understood. The present writer has often spoken in Russian to hearers of every Slavonic tribe and been followed well enough to be questioned as to the points of his address by non-Russian Slavs speaking their respective idioms. Here, then, there exists a possible connecting link for a common Slavonic fellowship, and, at the same time a cause of disunion, as all these nations are still very jealous regarding their own vernaculars. For example, Poles are apt to feel offended if they are addressed in Russian: they ridicule Bohemian and despise Slovak. In fact, the Poles at the present moment are the *enfants terribles* of possible united Slavia. Their horizon is, as a rule, bounded by the limits of their own language and they are opposed to all efforts to promote a common Slavonic feeling, not being far-sighted enough to perceive that only in this way can the smaller Slavonic nations hope to preserve their individuality in the readjustment of national values after the great war.

CHAPTER II

RUSSIA

RUSSIA AND THE SLAV IDEAL [1]

It may surprise most readers to learn that the Slav movement as a force in Russian political life was formulated in the first quarter of the nineteenth century. Slavism has been preached in the 'twenties by such brilliant apostles as Kireyevsky, Koshelev, Venevitinov, Homyakov, later by Samarin and Aksakov, and in a modified, broader, and more progressive form by Dostoyevsky and Solovyëv; but until the World War it has never entered the sphere of practical politics in Russia. As a matter of fact, it did play a part in Russian political life, and a very important part indeed, but it was a "part" in the play-acting sense, a part in the great game of political make-believe.

The Slavophils have always taken the greatest interest in the fate of smaller Slav nations, such as Bohemia, Serbia, Bulgaria, and wholeheartedly supported every action of the Russian government calculated to alleviate their fate. Their concern for the small Slav nations has always been genuinely altruistic, prompted by religious and racial sympathies. They dreamt their dreams of a great Slav brotherhood of nations, but neither any Slavophil nor any responsible Russian statesman has formulated yet a practical policy of bringing the smaller Slav nations into the orbit of a Slav federation with Russia as the leading and controlling member. Nor has the Slavist movement ever shown any tendency toward world domination. On the

[1] By Z. N. Preëv. Fortnightly Review. 101: 606-16. April, 1917.

contrary the Slavophils were strongly opposed to territorial aggrandizement, and saw in the innate Russian
love of peace and good-neighborliness a sign of the
superiority of Russian civilization over that of western
Europe. They even believed that this peaceful Russian
civilization would supplant the aggressive western civilization, but not by force.

The great Russian Slavophil Ivan Kireyevsky
expressed a belief of all Slavophils when he wrote that
Russia's contribution to the world's progress will consist
of a new policy of internal and external development
conditioned by the difference between the Russian and
western culture. The basis of western European
progress, wrote Kireyevsky, is Roman civilization with
its cold mentality (*razsudotchnost*). This cold, calculating attitude of mind has permeated the western church
and state, the latter built mostly by aggression and conquest. As the evolution of a state is merely a development of its foundations, of the principles on which it has
been built, so all European progress is but a chain of
aggressive actions, *viz.*, revolutions. Under the influence
of cold mentality a corporate, national spirit has given
place to a selfish party spirit. Russia, on the other hand,
developed without any Roman influence. The pure
Russian mind has developed on the lines of Christian
love and wisdom. "Russian culture originated from the
primary source of all Christian culture, from Constantinople, Syria, and the Holy Mount; and this pure
Christian source strongly influenced all classes of the
Russian nation, all their moral, legal, and social ideas."

The Great War has thrown all Russian pre-war ideas
and national aspirations into the melting pot. For the
first time the problem of Russia's relation to the other
Slav nations has passed from the sphere of academic
discussions and day-dreams into the sphere of stern
reality. For many nations the last war was a crisis the
like of which they have never had to go through in
the whole course of their history. Many nations were

groaning under the heavy heel of war, but no race was feeling it so heavily, no race was suffering so much, as the Slavonic races.

Of Anglo-Saxon races, the British have been spared the worst suffering of war. British women and children, the civil population, have been at least spared the shame and tortures of enemy invasion. The Dutch and the Scandinavians were enjoying, if only half-heartedly, the blessings of peace. Of Latin races, the Italians were waging war in the enemy's territory; the Spaniards and the Portuguese were safe within their national boundaries. But the Slavs, all and every one of them, were called upon by the merciless god of war to sacrifice freely not only the flower of their manhood, but their homes, their womenfolk and children. Wherever one looked on the vast horizon of Slavdom he could see the terrible ravages of war. Russia was invaded, Serbia and Montenegro have been devastated, the Poles, the Ukrainians, and numerous other Slav races whose territories have been divided between Russia, Germany and Austria. These Slavonic races were subjected to the most cruel form of torture, and were forced to fight against their own brothers; Poles against Ukrainians, Czechoslovaks against Russians, and Bulgarians against Serbians.

This common martyrdom has awakened in Russia a new Slavophilism, a new consciousness of race. It is no longer confined to Russian conservatives, but is shared by liberals and radicals. It is no longer a purely orthodox, religious sentiment, but is based on a broader, human and racial sympathy. The well-known Russian publicist, Nikolay Berdyayev, who is one of the ablest exponents of the progressive Russian nationalism, thus describes the difference between this new Slavism and the old Slavism:

The Western (Cosmopolitan) movement in Russia did not recognize the intrinsic value of nationality. Russian liberals and Russian revolutionaries were strangers to the Slav idea.

The advanced political thinkers recognized only the claims of oppressed nationalities. Such nationalities had their sympathy and protection. They had to be freed. But this sympathy was purely cosmopolitan, free from any racial element, devoid of any instinct of racial solidarity. Our progressive parties recognized the Polish and Georgian nationalism, because these nationalities were suffering under Russian rule, but they had no room for Russian nationalism, because the Russians were the ruling nationality. But only those can truly understand and sympathize with other nationalities who are conscious of their own nationality. We must realize, however, that Slav solidarity is impossible on the old basis of traditional Westernism. A Slav unity will never be achieved if we persist in looking on the Orthodox religion as the only source of Slav culture, for we would thus finally alienate from us the Poles and all Slav Catholics. The spiritual basis of the Slav movement must be broader, must be capable of embracing more than one religion. We must overcome our religious nationalism.

Such a basis is offered by the universal idealism of the Russian soul, by the Russian yearning for the City of God. It is enough to get to know intimately the Russian soul to see what a wealth of universal idealism and unselfish love it possesses, a wealth unknown to other nations. Our old Slavophils never rose above narrow nationalism. It will be the task of new Slavism to make the world believe in the purity of our national ideals, to make it forgive the historical sins of our statesmanship. The world has never known our real national aspirations, but it knew only too well the heavy hand of Russian statesmanship. This heavy hand frightens the world. Now the hour has struck for the Slav races to enter the arena of the world's progress. The idea of Slav unity means not merely an external, political unity, but a deep spiritual unity, a unity of ideals and culture. The future of the Slav movement cannot depend on the changing political passions, on the fortunes of war, or on the bargains of astute diplomatists. Its aims are too great, too high, for that.

What are these aims? The old Slavism was too much concerned with the religious and internal aspects of the Slav idea to evolve a definite policy to guide the Russian statesmanship in its international relations. The new Slavism is still too young to do so. It is more an awakening of the national consciousness than an organized movement. We can foresee its future course only by understanding the general trend of thought of the Russian people.

Great as the difference between the various sections of the Russian public opinion are, they all share one fundamental belief, a belief in a distinct Russian mission in the world, in Russia's "Messianism," as the Russians call it. This belief is common both to the most pious of Orthodox Greek churchmen of the type of Homyakov and liberal thinkers of the type of Professor Milyukov, to such primitive Christians as Tolstoy and such confirmed atheists as Herzen. Ask a pious Slavophil of the old school what Russia's mission is, and he will tell you that it is to lead mankind to the City of God, to the true religion from which men could learn how to live *po-bozheski* (according to God's desire). Ask the most advanced social-revolutionary, and he will tell you that it is the mission of the Russian agricultural proletariat to evolve an equitable social system which would supplant the unjust capitalist system of western Europe.

Both these extremists, no matter how divergent are their starting premises (spiritual with one, and materialistic with the other), are equal believers in Russia's Messianism. Between these two extremities there is the great mass of Russian moderate opinion equally confident that Russia is destined to give to the world a great gift, to contribute to the world's progress a culture and civilization of its own, a nobler, a more comprehensive and universal civilization than that evolved by western Europe, a civilization which will be as much an advance on the latter as Christian civilization was an advance on the materialistic Roman civilization.

Not only in the domain of religion and sociology; but in the domain of art, science, literature, in all the spheres of human activities, Russia, enriched by a close communion with her Slav sisters, is destined to reach the heights unseen yet to the vision of the present generation. Such is the belief of all Russians, and in this they are all Slavophils, whether they are conscious of their Slavism or not.

The Russians believe that they are destined to reconcile west and east, to bring into harmony the over-materialized individualistic civilization of western

Europe with the over-spiritualized contemplative civilization of the east, by inoculating their western neighbors
with some of the idealism of the east, while enriching
herself and her eastern neighbors by the political, social,
and economic benefits of western civilization and the
rich spiritual fruits of western culture. Russia's central
position between east and west, geographically, ethno-
graphically, and mentally, seems to predestine her for
such a mission. That the Russian people are spiritually
fitted for such a mission few of those acquainted with
Russian literature and Russian learning can doubt.

THE CONTRIBUTION OF RUSSIA TO LEARNING[1]

Russian learning grew up and developed in close con-
junction with one of the most important but least known
institutions of Peter the Great—the Russian Academy
of Science. This academy laid the foundation of systematic learned inquiry and created higher Russian
education. It still remains the central point of the vast
and complicated network of institutions having a purely
scientific object. I will not write of the history of the
Academy of Science, for such a digression would take
up too much time. I will confine myself to remarking
that, after a number of years when the members were
exclusively foreigners, chiefly Germans, the academy
became purely Russian as regards its membership as well
as its methods of learned work. Let me describe the
constitution of the academy. There were in it three
departments: first, the Department of Mathematics and
Physics; secondly, the Department of Russian Language
and Literature; and thirdly, the Department of History
and Philology. Each of these departments was divided
into a series of "chairs," which were sometimes held
jointly by several specialists. These "chairs" formed

[1] By M. Rostovtsev. Quarterly Review. 233: 272-87. April, 1920

groups called divisions, *e.g.* that of Oriental Language and Literature, that of Classical Philology and Archaeology, that of History, etc.

All the members of the academy were employed by the state, received salaries, and devoted themselves to learned work. Several of them were at the head of some learned institution or other, itself concerned with similar learned work. Many of these institutions had a world-wide reputation; for instance, the famous Observatory of Petrograd in Pulkovo; the Meteorological Institute, combined with a Seismological Institute having had many branches in the country; a splendid Zoological and Palaeontological Museum, one of the best in the world; a Museum of Ethnography and Anthropology; an Asiatic Museum containing a unique collection of Oriental MSS., etc. You may judge of the productiveness of the academy by the number of its publications. The academy had the exclusive use of a large printing-house which employed some hundreds of workmen; but even this establishment was unable to deal with the whole of the material supplied by the members. All the contributions and books printed by the academy were subjected to a vigorous censorship by the academy itself, which determined their scientific value; and they were only printed after they had been accepted at the general meeting of the department.

Nor was the work of the eleven universities of Russia [Moscow, Petrograd, Kazan, Kiev, Odessa, Harkov, Perm, Saratov, Tomsk, Voronezh, Yuryev (Dorpat)] less productive. As regards their constitution these universities most closely resembled the German model, but they had their own peculiarities which were chiefly due to their local position and their history. The general boards of professors which governed the universities did their best not only to transmit knowledge to the students, but also to make the universities so many laboratories in which learned inquiry could be pursued. The academic qualifications demanded of a professor were of a more stringent nature than was customary in western Europe or in America. On leaving the university, every candidate for a professorship was obliged to pass a severe and complicated examination in his special subject. He was further obliged to write, print and defend two original learned theses at a public meeting of his faculty. He thus became possessed, one after the other, of the degrees of Master and Doctor. The standard demanded in these theses became higher every year. Only Doctors of the corresponding branches were entitled to chairs in the university. It was the aim of the university to create as many learned workers as possible. The most capable students remained attached to the university in some permanent way. They received bursaries and were sent abroad so that they might embark upon original work of their own. Every attempt was made to secure the best possible libraries, laboratories and clinics in every university. Excellent work was done in the medical faculties. The Institute of Experimental Medicine in Petrograd, the Military Medical Academy in the same city, the clinics of Moscow and Odessa, have always been true seminaries of scientific knowledge. Good work was done in the fostering of scholarship among the students by the so-called "Seminaria," which possessed special libraries. In each seminary the students formed a group round the professor, and were engaged on advanced studies. These universities have been no less active in the solving of learned problems than has been the academy itself, and we are indebted to them not only for a series of wonderful discoveries, but also for the deepening and broadening of our knowledge of Russia. We also owe to them the fact that the highly qualified scholars of Russia may now be numbered, not by tens, but by hundreds and perhaps by thousands.

A very prominent part in the development of Russian learning has been taken by private learned societies and by certain official state organizations having some learned purpose in view. The great work done for the study of the geography and ethnography of Russia was done almost entirely by the Russian Geographical Society. Most of our knowledge of the Archaeology of Russia was due to the great Archaeological Societies in Petrograd, Moscow and Odessa, to the State Archaeological Commission, and to the periodical archaeological congresses. The study of the geology of Russia has been concentrated in the hands of the State Geological Committee. The work of collecting, classifying and studying the extensive records of Russian history was chiefly done by the State Archaeographic Commission and by many private societies, both in Moscow and Petrograd. The private societies of Kiev, Odessa and other towns and many provincial Record Commissions, as well as the archives of certain state institutions, have taken an important part in this work.

Let me now explain a little more in detail about those aspects of the study of Russia with which I am most familiar; I refer to the study of the prehistoric, protohistoric and historic past of Russia. The historical evolution of that country is exceedingly complicated and difficult to analyze. The study of Russian history is closely connected with that of the development of the national psychology. It presents problems more difficult and more complicated than any to be found in the history of the western European peoples. First of all you must take into consideration that the Slavs, as a nation, have well-defined peculiarities and .are quite different from the other branches of the Indo-European family. Besides this, one must always remember that the evolution of the Russian part of the Slavonic people is closely connected with the cultural development of the lands in which the Slavs settled and remained, both in the pre-Slavonic and in the Slavonic period of their history. Russia was always a bridge between the great Oriental or eastern and the great western civilizations. She was imbued with both influences, absorbed them both, and, thanks to the creative genius of her inhabitants, transformed these elements into a new, original and quite independent form of culture. At the same time the eastern and western centers of culture bordering on Russia were the cradles of powerful and warlike states for which Russia was ever an attractive prey, owing to the fact that she was not separated from them by any natural barriers. The defence of her own independence, on this account a very difficult task, was further complicated by the mixture of races in a land which was geographically and economically predestined to form one state.

The economic life of Russia is also very complicated. Russia tends on the one side toward the Baltic, on another toward the White Sea, and on a third toward the Black Sea. Great commercial highways, whether by land or water, radiate through the country in all directions. At the same time it is important to point out that Russia forms one whole with the very peculiar world of northern and central Asia. These facts add to the complexity of the tasks before the historian and archaeologist of Russia. The archaeological materials are enormous and remarkably divergent in character. Their ordering can only be achieved by scholars who are entirely familiar with the archaeology of the west as well as with that of the east, and especially with the archaeology of central and farther Asia, a country still very little explored. Not less rich and various are the literary documents. Through Lithuania and Poland, Russia has always been in touch with western Europe, chiefly with Germany, and through the Black Sea with Byzantium and afterward with Turkey. Moreover, the southern steppes of Russia cannot be separated from Iranian and Turco-Mongolian portions of central Asia, which in their turn are closely connected with India and China.

Thus it is that the task of studying Russia historically is an enormous one. Nevertheless Russian scholars,

though aware of the complexity of the task, boldly and
patiently set themselves to solve it. The archaeological
study of Russia is not more than a hundred years old,
but a huge mass of material has already been collected,
and many difficult problems have been solved. Year by
year, excavations are made in Russia, and step by step
her prehistoric and protohistoric destinies are being
elucidated. The very rich barrows of south Russia
have shown how closely the northern slopes of the
Caucasus and the northern shore of the Black Sea were
connected with the great Oriental civilization—with
Mesopotamia, Elam and Iran. We clearly see now how
old and how rich this civilization was. From the third
millennium B.C. onward the south of Russia was one of
the most interesting centers of civilization. During the
neolithic period, there dwelt on the banks of the
Dnieper and the Bug an agricultural population which
produced uncommonly artistic painted pottery of the
same type as the oldest painted pottery of Elam. In the
copper age the river Kuban in north Caucasus was one
of the chief centers of the civilization which afterward
impregnated Europe. During the early and late iron
age, that is to say, at the time when the great Assyrian
Kingdom and later that of Persia arose in the east, and
the great city states flourished in the west, the steppes
of south Russia formed the center of a mighty state
closely connected on the one side with Iran and on the
other with Greece. This state imbibed simultaneously
the cultural elements of west and east, and, thus
nourished, created an independent civilization.

During the Roman period these cultural ties became
stronger; and, beginning with the third century A.D.,
the civilization of south Russia became fused with the
German civilization from the north and thus renewed
and enriched the civilization of western Europe. The
rich cultural life of the south influenced northern and
central Russia, and created there, chiefly in the east, on
the river Kama, very important and opulent centers of

civilization which were closely connected with the shores
of the Baltic and the steppes of Siberia. This prehistoric civilization became, as it grew, the basis of the
culture of the Slavonic peoples, and formed the background against which the historical life of the Russian
state developed.

I am of course far from having exhausted, in these
short remarks, the material I could and ought to use in
an attempt to describe the state of scientific inquiry in
Russia. But I think that I have said enough to show
the direction which humane learning has taken in
Russia, and the results which it has achieved.

Not being a specialist, I have no right to speak of
what has been done by Russian scholars in the domain
of mathematics and of natural science. But, like every
educated man, I know the great names of renowned
Russian mathematicians, Lobatchevsky and Tchebyshev;
of the physicists and chemists, Lomonosov, Mendeleyev,
and Lebedev; and of the physiologists and physicians,
Pirogov, Metchnikov, Pavlov, and others. I cannot
undertake to describe what they have done, but I will
venture to bring before you the testimony of some of
the most eminent English specialists regarding them.
The number of such tributes could be multiplied at will.
This is what one of the most distinguished scholars of
the age, Sir Joseph Thomson, writes to Professor Sir
P. Vinogradov about the late Professor Lebedev of
Moscow:

I think Lebedev's investigations on the pressure of light, in-
volving as they did the measurement of extraordinarily minute
effects, are among the most striking triumphs of Experimental
Physics. The results he arrived at are of first-rate importance in
the general theory of radiation.

I think these remarks will suffice to show how high
is the standard of Russian work in the domain of scholarship. I hope that, although my sketch is neither ex-
haustive nor comprehensive, it will be successful in con-
vincing you that Russian learning has done and is doing
its share in building up our common treasury of culture.

It remains for me to express a hope that, in these sad times, Russian scholars will, in spite of their dreadful sufferings, retain faith in themselves, in learning, and in the future of civilization.

RUSSIA IN SUN OR SHADOW?[1]

H. G. Wells speaks of "Russia in the Shadows," and thinks that not a beam of light, not a ray of hope, will penetrate it. Indeed, the powder smoke of war has enveloped Russia since the moment when Germany, feeling too crowded, decided that her neighbors should draw closer together to give her room and began to exert force against them. France and Belgium have greatly suffered from their powerful enemy. Yet, being richer, more civilized, and better armed than Russia, they have finally overcome their enemy with the aid of England and America and with the approval of almost the entire world. They taught Germany a wholesome lesson. But Russia, weak, badly armed, and still worse governed, got into the clutches of the Bolsheviks and lies prostrate, battered, exhausted, and disarmed, yet still alive, still struggling. Those whom Wells calls adventurers and brigands are in reality true representatives of the unconquerable spirit of the people, the champions of freedom and of the Revolution of March, 1917, not of Tsarism or of the old régime.

States do not collapse as suddenly as do badly built houses. Similarly, a people with a history stretching over a thousand years, having just overthrown autocracy, certainly have not done this merely to accept a new tyranny and then to die. We Russians do not doubt that the struggle will go on, whatever reverses we may suffer, since no defeats can change our belief that sooner or later victory will be on the side of the people and not on the side of the usurpers.

If Bolshevism crushes Russia, it will be a *memento*

[1] By Ivan Petrunkevitch. Outlook. 127: 513-14. March 30, 1921.

mori to Great Britain and America. The spiritual bareness of Bolshevism is best expressed in the words of one of its prophets: "If three-quarters of the population of Russia should perish of hunger and cold, then one-quarter will remain which will achieve the glory of the world revolution." Only such glory, only such new happiness, can Bolshevism promise humanity hoping for the regeneration of the world.

The existence of Russia, the Russian problem in its full scope, is at present the foremost problem of international policy for all countries. No country can settle it from the point of view of its own interests alone without taking into account the interest of other countries as well.

The Russian problem in its world significance has found a lucid interpreter in the person of John Spargo, who follows untiringly the evolution of Bolshevism in Russia and who is a profound student of Russia. In his address before the Cleveland Chamber of Commerce some time ago Spargo denounced Bolshevism as the chief cause of Russia's ruin. He holds that every country into which Bolshevism penetrates will suffer the same fate as Russia. The same opinion is held by the best minds of Europe.

The vacillating attitude of England since the proposal of the Prinkipo conference leaves little hope that she will agree with Spargo. Unquestionably the internal difficulties of England are great. The Irish question and the triple union of workers cause heavy disturbance in her life. Yet every thinking Englishman knows that the Irish question, being more a problem of geography than of politics, is beyond the power of either Englishmen or Irishmen to solve. As for the labor problem, the advanced political development of the English people serves as guaranty for the inviolability of parliamentary rule and Constitution as long as the madness of Bolshevism will be kept powerless to fetter the will of Englishmen as it has fettered H. G. Wells. Lloyd George's

government has seemed ready to sacrifice England's
traditional pride, ready to forget all the epithets by
which it has characterized the political and moral features of the Moscow usurpers, ready to forgive all the
crimes against Englishmen in Russia. It has been ready
to do all this in order to rejuvenate English trade, dispose of English goods, and give work to the unemployed.
The English government knows that the trade agreement
with Soviet Russia will not bring England either raw
products or other advantages, but hopes that it will
thus deprive the Opposition of one of the weapons used
against the government. The act of signing a trade
agreement by England will have served as a signal for
similar action by many other countries. It is a new
and heavy blow to the Russian people.

The Moscow Soviet government has placed both itself and the country in a hopeless situation; it finds itself
without means of transportation, without bread or clothing. All complaints against and references to the blockade lack foundation because Russia has never existed
on imported grain, nor can she buy clothing if she has
no bread for export. Bolshevism has recklessly squandered the national wealth, and in complaining of the
blockade is only attempting to shift the guilt from its
own shoulders to those of foreigners. Bolshevism more
than any blockade has destroyed Russian industry.

As a losing gambler, Bolshevism has sought material
support in western Europe and in America because any
help would prolong its existence; it would, in the words
of Lenin, give a temporary respite, which has been
already more than once its salvation. A splendid example
of this policy is the Riga peace with Poland. Bolshevism
does not doubt that the world revolution will wipe out
all assumed responsibilities and destroy the existing
order.

We would not consider ourselves entitled to protest
against the ending of the political isolation of the Soviet
government by foreign countries if that government had

the sanction of the Russian people. We protest because
the idea of the sovereignty of the people forms the
foundation of modern constitutional law and is recognized by all countries. The Soviet government has denied
the people the very right to sovereignty. It seems that
outside of Russia many are thinking that the revolutionary origin of the Soviet government does not differ
materially from the origin of the first provisional government, which came into existence after the March
revolution, just as the Soviet government did in November. Yet their respective positions differ greatly. The
provisional government, having deposed the Tsar and
proclaimed the republic, issued an electoral law never
surpassed in democratic spirit. It considered its mission
to be fulfilled when the Constituent Assembly elected by
the people should have taken over the reins of government. The temporary character of the government was
accepted by every one. The Soviet government, having
overthrown the provisional government, dispersed by
armed force the Constituent Assembly on the first day
of its opening, when it became clear that the government did not possess a majority. The Soviet government declared that the dictatorship of the proletariat
does not require recognition by the people. Therefore,
whereas the provisional government, having deposed autocracy, transferred the sovereignty to the people, the
Soviet government denied the people their sovereignty,
denied to them the right to arrange their own affairs,
and established the autocracy of Lenin and Company.
The Bolshevik government has been conscious of the
illegality and uncertainty of its own existence. It has
held out only through its barbarity, its cruelty, its
shameless dishonesty. The cruelty and stupidity of the
Tsar's régime called forth the just indignation and condemnation of the European and American democracies.
But the sympathy of the same democracies for a régime
the wickedness and absurdity of which cannot be ex-
cused by any reasons of a political or commercial nature

is beyond comprehension. What shall the same democracies feel and say when they find that in demanding of their government recognition of the Soviet government they have lent support to adventurers, and thus helped to kill, torture, plunder, and ruin, not only capitalists alone, but the most genuine democracy—the Russian peasants—as well?

Wells does not know Russia. He knows Russia no more than he does the Martians. He has visited Russia only twice, the first time before the war and the second time in the autumn of 1920, when he spent in Russia only fifteen days. Both times he has seen only Petrograd, possibly its surroundings, and Moscow. Could he behold Russia from there? Could he see the Russian village, the peasants, and country priests of whom he speaks? I think that Spargo is right when he says that Wells could see them only from the window of the train, and, I may add, only over a comparatively short stretch of country.

Yet Wells asserts that Russia possesses no elements for the creation of a government except those very Bolsheviks who ruined Russia. "The peasants are absolutely illiterate," writes Wells, "and collectively stupid, capable of resisting interference, but incapable of comprehensive foresight and organization. They will become a sort of human swamp in a state of division, petty civil war, and political squalor, with a famine whenever the harvests are bad; and they will be breeding epidemics for the rest of Europe. They will lapse toward Asia."

The collapse of the civilized system in Russia into peasant barbarism means that Europe will be cut off for many years from all the mineral wealth of Russia and from any supply of raw products from this area, from its corn, flax, and the like. . . .
Their cessation certainly means a general impoverishment of western Europe.

Wells the democrat who feels contempt for the masses, Wells the socialist who clears the way for adventurers, Wells the champion of civilization for

Europe and of Bolshevist communism for Russia, so
characterizes the peasantry, which represents 85 per
cent of the population of Russia. I cannot accept his
judgment of the Russian peasantry. It is true that
Wells is equally merciless toward the other classes of
the Russian people—the clergy and the intellectuals; but
these classes are insured against the scorn of the celebrated English writer by the fact that they have produced representatives of Russian literature, science, art,
etc., no less celebrated than their severe critic. But
the peasantry remains unprotected, and I think that I
am better acquainted with my derided fellow-citizens
than Wells is, because more than half of my long life
has been spent in the country in close touch with the
peasantry, and I can say a few words in their defense.

Undoubtedly the Russian peasants, like peasants in
all other European countries, represent the least educated class. But, like every other class, it contains men
differing from one another in mind, character, and
moral principles. To judge them wholesale, as Wells
does, deprives that judgment of all value. If Wells
were also better acquainted with Russian literature,
which to all appearance interests him but little, he
would know that the mass of Russian peasants possess
intelligence, talent, religious feeling, and kindness. Their
shortcomings are caused by their former serfdom and
their lack of education. The former was abolished only
in 1861, and literacy has been increasing among the
peasants very rapidly ever since. Only old people remain illiterate. Men of middle age and younger people
have mostly passed through the *Zemstvo* or town
schools. Wells has seen only two schools in Petrograd,
one of which apparently is being specially used to ac-
quaint distinguished foreigners with the progress of
education under the Bolshevik régime. If he desired to
learn the standard of literacy among peasants, he should
have gone to villages far from the capitals, as in the

wilds of the government of Perm or Viatka. There
was no nobility there; it was the country of the peasantry, yet school education was very well developed.
The Russian peasant created long ago, in his serfdom,
the village commune (*obshtchina*), with redistribution
of land in accordance with the increase in the number
of the family and consequent working capacity. He
created the *mir*, or peasant assembly, for the settlement
of the peasants' own communal affairs. *Obshtchina* and
mir saved the peasants from complete tyranny under
serfdom. One of the greatest Russian writers, A. I.
Herzen, saw in these institutions the nucleus of Socialism. Premier Stolypin fought them, but could not van-
quish them. One cannot doubt that the peasant *mir* is
much more stable and sagacious than the Bolshevist
communism rejected by the peasants.

Probably Mr. Wells does not know either that,
following upon the reactionary reforms of 1890 involv-
ing local self-government and limiting peasant representation, the peasants began gradually to form cooperative
associations. Up to the Bolshevik overthrow there were
about thirty-five thousand cooperative associations in
existence, numbering some twelve million members, or
some sixty million participants if the families of the
members are taken into account. The majority were
peasants. Unquestionably the peasants need the help
of intellectuals, but they understand also how to value
this help better and more wisely than the communistic
government which sends professors and engineers to
clean cesspools and streets, while ignoramuses run universities and factories. The cooperative associations
flourished before their destruction by the Bolsheviki,
while the Bolshevist communistic system of the preference of ignorance to knowledge has killed the universities, factories, and industry. The peasantry constantly
produced from its midst men who entered the ranks of
the intellectuals. When Russia became for the first

time a constitutional country of the European type, the
peasants sent so many representatives to the First
Duma that their party was the next strongest after the
Constitutional Democratic party, which consisted of
educated people who directed the policy of the first
Russian parliament.

What would Wells say if he had heard on the floor
of the First Duma a country peasant arguing in defense
of freedom, right, and European civilization with full
understanding of these matters? Would he then have
said that the Russian people can furnish no backbone to
support the state and that they need such experienced
political builders as Lenin, Trotsky, and Company? The
overwrought imagination of Wells bowed before the
audacity of Lenin's thought and the boldness of Trotsky's action. He was interested to learn, not Russia—
this would require too much time—but the plans of
Lenin, which appealed to Wells by their immensity and
far surpassed in originality his travels to the various
planets of the solar system. A fortnight's sojourn in
Petrograd was needed as a stage for the encounter of
the two reformers of a world awaiting its fate. One of
the two rebuilt the world only in imagination, the other
put his dreams into reality, having subjugated one hundred and fifty million men to his will. The conversation did not last long but ended in full agreement. Wells
remembered his own dreams about Mars and decided to
help Lenin in his plans by recommending European
powers to recognize the Soviet government and to in-
trust them with the salvation of Russia, as otherwise
Russia would perish not later than in a year and Europe
would forever lose her source of raw products and become, therefore, impoverished.

It seems to me that by his trip to Russia Mr. Wells
has given himself the pleasure of meeting and talking
with Lenin, but has added nothing to what he could
have written without leaving England.

RUSSIA OF YESTERDAY AND TOMORROW[1]

Russia embraces one-sixth of the surface of the earth. Its extreme dimension from east to west is six thousand miles—almost twice the distance from Maine to California, with a stretch of twenty-three hundred miles from north to south. European Russia alone is larger than all the rest of Europe. The total population is one hundred and seventy million, of which one hundred and thirty million are in European Russia. The largest city is Petrograd which, until recently, had a population of two million—almost as large as Berlin or Vienna. There are in Russia thirty-five cities with an average population of over one hundred thousand, and three thousand towns having from three to ten thousand. Upward of 80 per cent of the population of Russia, being agriculturists, dwell in villages.

With the exception of America, there is no other country under one flag with so great a variety of climate, of soil, and of mineral wealth. It is often stated by enthusiasts, in describing Russia, that her potential resources are greater than those of any other country. This is true if we make the single exception of our own great land, for I believe that America has been blessed in respect of its natural resources in a far greater degree than any part of the globe comprising a like area.

Within the boundaries of Russia are the most extensive timber tracts in the world. In European Russia alone they cover a territory ten times the aggregate area of our New England states. The timber industry of Russia is capable of enormous development and expansion.

Before the World War Russia produced more wheat, rye, and oats than any other nation. There are in Russia extensive deposits of iron, coal, lead, copper, gold, platinum, petroleum, and other valuable minerals.

[1] By J. H. Hammond. Scribner's. 71: 515-27. May, 1922.

The country too will be able to provide an abundance
of labor. While the labor is as yet crude and lacking
in technical skill, it is the opinion of Americans who
have conducted mining and other industrial operations
in that country that there is the possibility of developing a most efficient class of artisans from the great
Russian proletariat. All agree that while the Russian
peasant is illiterate and ignorant—densely ignorant indeed—he possesses in an exceptional degree resourceful-
ness and "native wit." Physically he is equal to, if he
does not excel, the peasant of any other European country. Given native intelligence and industry, which the
Russian has, and educational advantage, which he will
have, one is justified in having an optimistic view of
the future man-power of Russia. The Russian peasant,
contrary to the popular impression, has a peaceful and
kindly disposition, but as his knowledge of the world is
extremely limited, he has become an easy prey to the
false political and economic doctrines foisted on him by
unprincipled political agitators.

The opinion often expressed is that Russian political
thought is so thoroughly indoctrinated with socialistic
theories that it will take a long time to eradicate Bolshevism from the body politic; and that it will require
not years but generations to restore economic and social
order from the chaos incident to the aftermath of the
Soviet régime. I do not share this view, for even now
the Bolshevik dictators themselves acknowledge the
ignominious failure of that fatuous and tragic experiment in Marxian economics, and from sources unbiased
and authoritative we learn that Bolshevism virtually has
spent its force, not only outside of its own boundaries,
but within the confines of Russia itself. There may be,
most likely there will be, a recrudescence of Bolshevism
in certain European states and elsewhere, where the
political conditions are unstabilized, as the result of the
débacle following the World War. But future attempts
to establish Sovietism as a principle of government will

be sporadic only, and foredoomed to failure, incompatible as it is with the genius of modern civilization.

Many persons unfamiliar with their history question the capacity of the Russian people for self-government. This unwarranted pessimism arises from the misconception that the *de facto* government is the exponent of Russian political belief. Nothing is further from the truth. History has repeatedly shown that in the political evolution of autocratic governments (especially where the administration was in the hands of a narrow bureaucracy, as was the case in Russia), men who were leaders for political reforms, whether by peaceful or by revolutionary measures, have almost always been theorists and visionaries.

These men had not the advantage of actual administrative experience, and for this reason they often advocated utopian reforms which, however, they were quick to repudiate when later they themselves were confronted with the responsibility of the conduct of government. Russia has been cursed as well as blessed by a class of *intelligentsia*, which in other countries as well often renders a great disservice to the cause of real reform and progress, through advocacy of unrealizable ideals. Many of the leaders of reform could be justly stigmatized as unintelligent intellectuals. This will explain the attitude of mind of many upright and patriotic Russians who are affiliated with the proletariat dictatorship, under the less reputable leadership of Lenin and Trotsky. There is another class of statesmen, who served under the former Russian bureaucracy; these have been proscribed by the Soviet dictators, and now reside outside of Russia. They will fortunately be available for future administrative service.

It is the deliberate judgment of those who are familiar with the history of the Mirs, the Zemstvos, the Cooperatives, and the more recent Dumas, that the Russian people possess no mean capacity for self-government. These institutions, which contributed such

signal service in the amelioration of the conditions of the
peasants, following their emancipation in 1861, (and
who subsequently aided the proletarians of the vast industries established under the fostering administration
of Witte), have been almost entirely suppressed by the
political vandals of Soviet Russia. While the function
of these institutions legally was economic and sociologic,
the people were nevertheless afforded considerable
opportunity to learn something of the political phase of
government. But these institutions will be revivified, and
will become important factors politically in the regeneration of Russia, which country under a constitutional
form of government is destined to be one of the greatest
of the great world-powers.

BOLSHEVISM IN THEORY AND PRACTICE [1]

It is seldom that a government exercises a severe
and repressive censorship on the writings of its opponents, and at the same time with vast patience and industry collects statistics and issues propaganda which inad-
vertently provide a thorough condemnation of its own
policy. This however is exactly the position of the
Soviet government in Russia. The Soviet leaders combine, like all revolutionaries, a great ingenuity in agitation
and argument with an incapacity to understand ordinary
men and everyday things.

It is not necessary to go further than the pamphlets
of the Bolsheviks, and Russian newspapers which have
escaped the censorship, to find a most reliable exposure
of the latest development of communism. Pro-Bolshevik
observers like Mr. Goode, the late correspondent of the
Manchester Guardian, also give valuable information so
far as it goes. Although this last class of documents are
of course entirely one-sided they are first-hand, or practically first-hand, records of the Bolshevik policy; omis-

[1] By G. H. Crichton. Edinburgh Review. 232: 290-306. October, 1920.

sions or deficiencies in accounts of this kind have as great a significance as the criticism of hostile observers.

The Bolshevik republic now extends over the greater part of the former Russian Empire. It has been subjected to formidable attacks, which, whatever may be their ultimate result, appear to have impressed on the Bolsheviks the urgent need of some accommodation with western Europe, so as to secure peace and capital and give their infant state the power of continuing and maintaining its threatened existence. The Bolsheviks can undoubtedly claim no small measure of military success. What they lose at one point they regain at another, and more than once they have made a marvellous recovery after a heavy series of reverses. In estimating the achievements of the Bolsheviks it is necessary to remember two facts—that they inherited an empire three-quarters ruined by war, and that they inherited the results of their own propaganda; the latter has proved the worse inheritance of the two. In a country of such vast physical resources as Russia material losses may easily be made good, but discipline and order once lost are hard to restore.

Moral anarchy is the only expression fit to describe the primary results of the revolutionary propaganda. Russian writers, and foreign observers competent to form an opinion, alike agree in representing the Russian *muzhik*, even in ordinary times, as being intensely ignorant and capable of fierce outburts of brutality. In moments of excitement or drunkenness he behaves like a ferocious animal, and when he comes to himself displays an equally violent and unrestrained remorse. Marie Botchkareva, the commander of the Women's Battalion of Death, in her memoirs recounts an episode which illustrates this. At the time when the committee system was being introduced into the army and discipline was as a result non-existent, an officer, beloved by his men, while attempting to restrain his own regiment from an act of violence, was literally stamped to death; within an hour the same troops formed a funeral procession and, weeping, accompanied his remains to the grave. This is but one instance of many such described in that work, and it shows with some degree of probability what the average Russian peasant is like when the restraints of civilization are removed. The Bolsheviks have had to reconstruct a society whose foundations they had knocked away. This is the difficulty which the absurd logic of revolutionaries always ignores, that you cannot make a man into an angel by first making him into a beast.

In his pamphlet written in April 1918 "The Soviets at Work," Lenin himself admits the moral ruin that accompanies revolution. He says: "A great revolution and especially a socialist revolution, even if there were no external war, is inconceivable without an internal war, with hundreds and millions of cases of wavering and desertion from one side to the other, and with a state of the greatest uncertainty, instability and chaos." It is characteristic of Lenin that he abhors and repudiates sentiment and makes no attempt whatever to cast a romantic glamor over revolutionary propaganda or its immediate effect on mankind. The idealism of Kropotkin and the humane element of the Russian revolutionary movement awake no sympathy nor respect in his heart. To him their due meed is not praise but condemnation, and there seems but little doubt that to the old-fashioned type of Russian idealist and liberal reformer, if any such still remain within the limits of the Bolshevik dominion, there is no choice between death or exile, or acceptance and approval of the Bolshevik policy. Maxim Gorky, formerly an opponent of the Bolsheviks, is now their adherent, perhaps from sincere conviction, perhaps from prudence. The way of the Russian idealist has always been hard and demanded high courage. The repression and cruelty of the old empire have been greatly exaggerated, but beyond all doubt its hand was heavy on the too zealous reformer. The same courage and more is required today, when an offence against the government is punished with far greater severity.

The interest of Lenin's writing is two-fold. He explains logically how society is to be destroyed and how it is to be rebuilt on the lines laid down by Marx; while in the pamphlet "The Soviets at Work," he gives an equally clear picture of the inevitable results of destroying social sentiment. His writings are also interesting as revealing the workings of the bleak and bitter mind of a political fanatic. He perverts history, has a superstitious reverence for formulae and, even in the twentieth century, sees no absurdity in declaring, or rather assuming, that the fundamental facts on which every social system has always hitherto been based can be altered in a generation.

These characteristics appear in a marked degree in his pamphlet, "The State and Revolution," written in August 1917, before the Bolshevik revolution. This pamphlet has for its sub-title, "Marxist Teaching on the State and the Work of the Proletariat in the Revolution." It was not completed because the Bolshevik revolution took place in November of that year, and the author explains that his plans for completing the work were interrupted. "It is more pleasant," he remarks in the postscript, "and more useful to live through the experience of a revolution than to write about it." The work is, as its subtitle shows, an exposition of the Bolshevik view of Marxian teaching on revolution of the state. It contains likewise a bitter attack on various other Socialist groups, condemning their attitude to the war, their patriotic bias, their subservience to the bourgeoisie, their opportunism and their vulgarization and misinterpretation of Marx. The Fabians and the I.L.P. in England, Kautsky and his followers in Germany, among other socialist sects, whether disciples of Marx or not, are the objects of Lenin's unmeasured contempt. He denounces such renegades from the true revolutionary faith, as "Lackeys of the Bourgeoisie, Social-Democrat Traitors and Putrid Philistines." All this abuse is of no interest in itself, except as another instance of the egotism, vanity, and mutual hatred which, as is well known, always exist among the leaders of revolutionary movements, and which may be taken as a truer indication of their feeling toward their brother men, than their bombastic pretensions of sympathy for the working classes.

It is strange with what academic precision Lenin analyses his master's work. He examines every passage to bring out what he considers to be the true meaning, and he adds to each work of Marx an appropriate historical comment to show the gradual development of Marxian revolutionary philosophy.

By the middle of the nineteenth century, Marx had spent a considerable time in the study of the philosophy of Hegel, history and political economy, as a result of which he became convinced of the necessity for the complete destruction of the existing form of society. In every country there existed a large number of persons who were oppressed and exploited by a few tyrants. The form which this oppression took was the state, which existed, not to reconcile the different classes of the people, but to enable the few to wage a ceaseless economic war on the many. The army, the police, the judges, the civil service, parliamentary institutions, religion, formed the state; that is, they were the instruments created by the capitalist class to oppress and deceive the workers. The whole system had to be shattered and shattered by violence.

What however was to take its place? At first Marx did not know, but the experience of the Commune of 1871 in Paris enabled him to complete his theory. The proletariat rose in Paris and swept away the government, the police force, in short everything, and replaced the old system by a simple expedient. The people took over the business of administration, and formed a new kind of society on the principle of communism. The workers in the different districts of Paris elected certain of their number to perform public functions. These representatives had to answer to their electors for what they did. They had to make regulations and carry them out, and could be dismissed at any moment. This system was in reality of short duration, but it gave Marx the ideal of a new society of self-governing communes in which state machinery would be unnecessary.

It is on this point that the Bolsheviks differ from other socialists in their interpretation of Marx. There is amongst advanced revolutionaries apparently complete agreement that the capitalistic state must be destroyed, but the anarchists on the one hand are content to destroy the state without troubling about what is to come after. They trust to the natural perfection of the proletariat to solve all difficulties. The Bolsheviks on the other hand maintain that while the new society of communes is in process of formation, a new temporary state must be created, with exactly the same purpose as the old, namely, oppression; only the roles of oppressor and oppressed are now reversed. Masters are slaves; slaves, masters. Naturally the bourgeoisie will not submit quietly to such a process. They will resist, at first with arms, later by sabotage, by strikes, by all sorts of counter-revolutionary intrigues and agitations to render unworkable the new civilization. It will take a long time to destroy and suppress these agitators, hence the need of the state. As the agitators grow fewer the state grows weaker, and gradually disappears. The more violent of the bourgeoisie will be killed, some will die, some will make terms with the workers. Lenin, here using Marx's terminology, describes this process as "the withering away of the state."

Lenin also suggests another reason for "the withering away of the state," and that is that the functions formerly discharged by an infinite number of parliamentary representatives, police, judges and other government officials, are really very simple and can be done by anybody. Any difficulty they may present in the capitalistic order is due to profiteering, which renders an elaborate system of book-keeping necessary. When profits are abolished an immense organization is simply unnecessary. In the ideal state the work of government will consist of a few easy operations, giving receipts, keeping registers, and simple accounting. Anyone can do these things, and when communism is fully developed, everybody will take his turn at administration. Again, parliamentary institutions in capitalistic society only exist to gull the workers; they contain however two principles necessary for the development of communism, namely, representation and universal suffrage. Representatives of the workers will manage communal affairs and will act as boards of directors of industrial undertakings.

The name of the temporary oppressive Bolshevik state which leads up to this ideal regime is the "Dictatorship of the Proletariat." The Bolsheviks do not profess to know how long the process of "withering away" will take. Some time must elapse before bourgeois ideas can be eradicated from the minds of the workers who have been corrupted by them. Gradually however the conception of different classes inevitably coexisting and receiving unequal rewards for their labor will vanish. After the revolution everybody must at once receive an equal wage, the wage of an ordinary working man. Later however this bare equality will give place to a new principle by which each citizen will give what he can and receive what he needs. The period which ensues when this new conception has been fully realized is called the period of higher communism. Communism, Marx thought, would grow out of capitalism naturally by an evolutionary and revolutionary process, after a series of abortive revolutions, taking over when it was first established all the technical development of capitalistic society. These are the lines upon which the Bol-

sheviks propose to carry out the transition from capitalism to the higher communism.

THE SOVIETS AND THE PEASANTS[1]

For the first time since the revolution, the representatives of the Russian workers and peasants assemble
to discuss the questions of their struggle without the
participation of their sorely stricken comrade Lenin,
who has showed them the way to battle and to victory.
This fact lies like a cloud over the spirits of the party's
members; yet never has the situation of the Soviet
republic and the task of the Russian Communist Party
been so clear as at the present moment. And never
before have the responsible representatives of the Russian Communist Party found it so easy to reach an agreement with regard to the course which the ship of the
Communist Party must hold over the waves of revolution.   Realities speak an unmistakable idiom.

The Congress meets in an international situation
which tells the Russian workers clearly that the way of
the Soviet power and of the Russian Communist Party
was the only right one.   When the former meeting of
the communists gathered, the congress of the representatives of the bourgeois governments, which was devoted
to the subject of the revival of the world's economic
system, was just beginning in Genoa.   With the far-
sightedness that is characteristic of him, Comrade Lenin
declared to the Eleventh Congress that the Genoa Conference, which had been loudly heralded by the press
of the international bourgeoisie, sought to impose a
new burden under the guise of world economic restoration; that they would demand that Soviet Russia should
impose this burden upon the shoulders of the workmen
and the peasants, which would make it possible for the

[1] By K. Radek.   A speech before the Red Congress at Frankfort in
1923.   Living Age.   317: 515-18.   June 2, 1923.

international bourgeoisie to fix their mastery upon the whole world. Comrade Lenin showed that the international bourgeoisie was divided against itself into struggling parts capable of common exploitation of the workers but incapable of restoring the shattered economic system of the world. A year has passed since the Genoa Conference. Its hero, Lloyd George, now has leisure to write long articles about the harmfulness of the Versailles Treaty—which, be it said by the way, was the work of his own hands—and moreover to contend that the war may lead to the downfall of Europe.

Not only was there no agreement between international capital and Soviet Russia in Genoa and The Hague, but the greatest capitalist states in the world, as the events of the Ruhr make perfectly clear, were in no position to come to agreement among themselves, in order to restore the world's trade and to build it up on a capitalistic basis. When they called the Genoa Conference the capitalist lords cherished the hope that hunger would compel Soviet Russia to capitulate and to impose a heavy burden on the Russian laboring classes, in order to secure the necessary credit. The harvest of the year 1922 and the measures taken by the Soviet régime against the famine make it possible for them to refuse all demands of the Allies.

Soviet Russia declared herself ready for great sacrifices in order to secure from foreign capital the means for the speediest possible restoration of the Russian national economic system and the alleviation of the situation of the workers and peasants. It declined, however, to sell its birthright for a mess of pottage consisting of vague promises and to accept conditions that would burden the workers of Russia heavily for generations to come. Soviet Russia will wait until international capital convinces itself that the Soviets are not frightened by the financial blockade and will not sacrifice the fundamental strength of the October revolution.

Soviet Russia was not inclined to hand back the factories and industrial plants into the private ownership of foreign capitalists and to burden the working masses with the Tsarist debts until international capital provided the means to hasten the reconstruction of Russia. But there is no doubt whatever that, if Soviet Russia begins economic revival with her capacities, international capital in its own interests, because of the search for new sources of raw material and new markets for export, will have to make an agreement that is advantageous for the Soviets also.

In spite of its gigantic military superiority, which is assured by its wealth and the tremendous preponderance of its military technique, which is related thereto, international capital has no strength for beginning international meddling anew. A fresh breathing space is assured Soviet Russia through the quarrels of the international robbers who are making ready for war one against another, and who can come to no agreement and cannot form a single military front against Russia. The war in the Ruhr, the ill-feeling between France and England in Europe, Japanese and American conflict of interests in eastern Asia, the chaos in China and India— all these are weights of lead upon the feet of international capital.

When, in March of 1921, the Congress of the party decided to abandon the system of requisition and to levy taxes in kind,—that is, to give the peasants economic freedom and the right to carry on trade with what they produced in excess of their own needs,—this was, to use Comrade Kamenev's striking expression, a renewal on a new basis of the October league between the proletariat and the peasants. In October 1917, the peasants rose with the working class against the Russian and international bourgeoisie and the large landowners, for the working class helped the peasants to get rid of the iron shackles of the World War and to drive the great landowners from the soil. For three years in succession the peasants adhered to this league, helping the working class to defend the Soviet republic against attacks of the international and the Russian bourgeoisie. When the peasants shed their blood for the leadership of the proletariat, they knew that this blood was the price of keeping the great landowners away from the soil. Vexatious though the policy of requisitions and compulsory contributions was for them, the peasants never refused them, although the proletariat took their crops without complete reimbursement. This furnishing of bread was also part of the price of seizing the land of the gentry.

The wreck of intervention and the victory won in the peasants' war against the counter-revolution of the great landowners produced a new situation for the peasants. It was a question whether they would be in a position to work on their own soil or whether the proletariat would attempt to extend by force to the villages the socializing policy which the small peasant-proprietors opposed in spite of all the assurances of the Soviet republic.

At its Tenth Congress the Communist Party replied to the peasants: "We do not intend to extend socialism by force to the villages. That is an impossibility, and we have no such intention whatever. We regard the system of small peasant-proprietors as a backward institution which is not advantageous even for the peasants themselves. But we shall put the question of socializing the villages on the program for the first time when we are in a position to prove to the peasants with facts that we can help them to a more expedient and advantageous economic system, when we are in a position to give them farm machinery and to relieve them of the heaviest part of farm work by the aid of electricity. Until we reach this stage we pledge ourselves that we will exact from the peasants as taxes only what is necessary for the support of the red army which is protecting their soil, and what is absolutely indispensable for the state administration." The peasant had to make this sacrifice if he did not want to see the return of the power of the great landowners.

The year following the Tenth Congress was one of incredible hardship for the masses of the peasants. They struggled not only against the consequences of the imperialist war and the war of the bourgeoisie, but also against the famine that afflicted Soviet Russia.

But even this famine could not conceal from the peasants the gigantic reality that the new economic policy gave them a chance to escape from misery. The famine never led to a peasants' rising. In 1922 the peasants paid their taxes in kind without necessity for coercive measures. In their attitude toward the taxes in kind they generally showed that they understood the necessity and hoped that the new economic policy would eventually deliver them from their suffering.

The present Party Congress, the twelfth, must pay closest heed to the question of the peasants if we are not to come into a state of selfish dependence upon international capitalists and accept loans from them at usurious rates of interest. For the present the peasants are the most important source for the rehabilitation of heavy industry and they are the chief means for the further development of Soviet Russia.

If anyone fails to understand that the proletariat has no special guilt in treating the question of the land with the greatest heed, and that it must do this in its own interest and to protect its own power in the country, he fails to comprehend the fundamental realities of Russian economic life and the policy of the Russian working class. Those who gossip about a peasant tendency in the Party, and a degeneration of the Russian Communist Party into a Peasants' Party, those who say that the interests of the proletariat are being sacrificed to the

interests of the peasants, have already been answered
by Comrade Lenin, who said clearly that the poor Russian peasant nag had to be brought out on to a level
road.

The attitude toward this unfortunate creature will
be determined by the Twelfth Communist Congress in
discussing the question of our tax policy toward the
village. Our whole system of taxes, manifold in number,
bears heavily and abnormally upon the peasants. The
party is looking for a way to alleviate this tax burden
through a practical study of the question, and they will
prove to the peasants that they regard the improvement
of the situation of the peasantry as their next task.

This improvement, however, cannot come through
reforms of our financial policy alone. It demands still
other measures. Most important of these is support
of the peasants so far as the increase of the area under
cultivation and the strengthening of farming interests
is concerned. If the present year gives us a good harvest,
another step will be an organization for the export of
Russian crops into foreign countries. Otherwise we shall
again be faced by a danger of a decrease in our crop
area because of the falling of the price of wheat. The
export of wheat abroad will lend the peasants the means
for the purchase of industrial products, and in this way
the improvement of the peasants' situation will be at
the same time a means for the further development of
industry.

As the Soviet administration moves along the way
to the new economic policy, many are saying that this
policy is leading to a break between the Soviet government of the Russian Communist Party and the working
class. Today, however, it is no longer necessary to
prove the baselessness of this opinion. The last celebration of the first of May, the demonstration at the time
of the Soviet trials, the fifth anniversary of the October
revolution, and the twenty-fifth anniversary jubilee of

the party—all these clearly show the spontaneous growth of sympathy on the part of the workers outside the party for the Russian Communist Party. This growth progresses with the improvement of the situation of the peasantry, without which the obvious developments in our light industry would not have been possible.

BOLSHEVIK RUSSIA AND JACOBIN FRANCE [1]

So far there has been little adequate appreciation of the spiritual kinship between the French and Russian revolutions. Those who form their impressions of Soviet Russia from the testimony before the Overman Committee and similar sources naturally see nothing in the Bolshevik upheaval except a gigantic and altogether unparalleled outburst of criminal lunacy. Apologists and sympathizers with revolutionary Russia sometimes cite the French Reign of Terror as a precedent for the excesses of the Bolsheviki; but here their sense of historical resemblance seems to stop.

Now the use of terror is one of the least significant of the many features which are common to the two great revolutions. Both in general form and in minute detail there is a striking likeness between the completed structure of revolutionary France and the incomplete edifice which is still being built up in Russia. This likeness is especially marked in the closing stages of the two movements, in the period dominated in France by the Jacobins, in Russia by the Bolsheviki. Both revolutions were directed against peculiarly abominable systems of tyranny and injustice. Both, at their inception, won the admiration and sympathy of the whole world by their moderation and bloodlessness. In each case sympathy and admiration were gradually transformed into disgust and horror as the upheaval assumed more and more violent aspects, sweeping away one cherished

[1] By W. H. Chamberlain. Dial. 67: 14-16. July 12, 1919.

tradition after another in a hurricane of blood and fire.

Alike in Russia and in France there was a time when it seemed that the abuses of the old régime might be gradually removed without recourse to violence, civil war, and the definite alignment of class against class. The end of this period in France was marked by the expulsion of the Girondist deputies from the Convention in June 1793; in Russia it was signalized by the overthrow of the Kerensky government and the subsequent dissolution of the Constituent Assembly. In France this transition period occupied nearly four years; in Russia only eight months elapsed between the downfall of the Tsar and the Bolshevist coup. This acceleration of the last stage of the revolution in Russia can be accounted for by the pressure of the war and the weakness of the Kerensky government.

Judged by any abstract theoretical standard the sailors who dispersed the Constituent Assembly and the armed Parisian mob which forced the convention to expel its Girondist deputies committed an outrageous violation of all democratic principles. And yet it is difficult not to feel that both these acts, violent and arbitrary as they were, marked an inevitable forward step in the advance of the two revolutions. It was only after the exclusion of the Girondists that the feudal dues were definitely and completely abolished, that adequate steps were taken to confiscate the huge estates of the emigres and divide them up among the poverty-stricken peasants. In the same way it was only after the transfer of power to the Soviets that the Land Law, with its companion pieces of social legislation, came into being. There is still another fact, usually ignored or glossed over by conservative observers, which must be taken into consideration. France in 1793, like Russia in 1917, was living under the perpetual shadow of a possible counter-revolution. Had the plots of Kornilov and the French royalists succeeded, the most moderate social and political reforms would certainly have been swept away in a torrent of reaction. That they did not succeed was chiefly due to the stern and inflexible revolutionists who snatched the power away from the vacillating Kerensky and the unreliable Girondist.

Bolshevik Russia and Jacobin France were both compelled to face large armies of foreign enemies. In each case there was the same underlying motive for intervention—the instinctive jealous hostility of the established order toward a new movement which seemed to threaten the very foundations of society with destruction. The effects of intervention were also quite similar. Foreign invasion produced an extraordinary, almost a miraculous, recrudescence of fighting spirit in the French and Russian peoples. There is a dramatic contrast indeed between the royalist French army which fled in disgraceful panic before a handful of Prussians at Rossbach and the revolutionary levies that hurled back the superior forces of the coalition at Valmy and Jemmapes. And there is an equally striking contrast between the helpless, disorderly mob that threw down its arms and refused to fight before Brest-Litovsk and the resolute, effective red army that drove the Czechoslovaks from the Volga and the French from the Ukraine. It is quite true that, in Russia and France alike, the revolutionary governments employed conscription in raising their armies. But it is equally true that conscription would have proved altogether ineffective in practice if it had not been supported by a spirit of ardent and unquenchable popular enthusiasm.

Another effect of intervention, regrettable but inevitable, was an appalling increase in the use of terror on the part of the revolutionists. The most abominable cruelties of the French Revolution, the September Massacres, the drownings at Nantes, the wholesale shootings at Lyons and Toulon, can be directly ascribed to the presence or proximity of foreign invaders. It was certainly no mere coincidence that the worst acts of the much exaggerated red terror in Russia were committed during the late summer of 1918, when it seemed that any day might witness the fall of the Soviet republic before the Allied and Czechoslovak armies. It is impossible to justify deeds of ruthless violence and terrorism under any conditions. But, when we recall the hysterical eagerness with which certain elements in England and America seized upon every opportunity to persecute real and imaginary cases of "pro-Germanism," it is surely easy to understand the frenzy that possessed the ignorant, oppressed French and Russian masses when they saw their revolution, their only hope of a better future, assailed and threatened with extinction by hosts of foreign bayonets.

The characters of the Bolshevik and Jacobin leaders are generally cast in a common mold. With few exceptions they are men fanatically devoted to their ideals, reckless of their own lives, and of the lives of others, supremely disinterested, and through this very disinterestedness devoid of pity for those whom they consider enemies of the revolution. Among them, as among the English Puritans of the seventeenth century, the most burning enthusiasm for a doctrinaire ideal is often combined with great shrewdness and practical sagacity. Coming down to specific examples, the resemblance between Lenin and Robespierre is unmistakable. The Russian is a devotee of Karl Marx; the Frenchman an ardent worshiper of Rousseau. Both men are characterized by inflexible will-power, and by a personal integrity that extorts the reluctant admiration of their bitterest enemies. Lenin has a more enlightened mind, a wider international background. Perhaps the best proof of his mental superiority lies in the fact that he has never fallen a victim to Robespierre's fatal delusion that terror is an effective means of securing the fruits of revolution. Yet in essential outlines the two types of

character are quite similar. In the same way a fore-
runner of Trotsky appears in St. Just, the fiery young
enthusiast whose boundless energy and passionate eloquence contributed so much to the organization and victories of the revolutionary armies.

Russia, like France, has had her emigres; and here
again the parallel is obvious. The Russian grand dukes.
like the French nobles, are naively convinced that their
régime of cruelty and rapacity, extravagance and oppression, has somehow endeared them to the masses of
the common people. The whole revolution, in their eyes,
is the work of a few bad men, anarchists, criminals;
all that is needed to destroy it is a little modest outside
help in men and money. In Russian and French aristocrats alike is found the same inability to appreciate
realities, the same ferocious hatred of their own people,
the same disgraceful willingness to make any sacrifice of
their country's peace and happiness that may help to
give them back their old privileges and possessions.
Prince Lvov and his associates in Paris protesting
against every suggestion to relieve starvation in Bolshevist Russia are worthy successors of the French
emigres who applauded the savage and bloodthirsty
manifestoes of the Duke of Brunswick from their safe
retreat at Coblenz. In exile as in power the Russian
and French ruling classes consistently uphold their
previous record of cruelty and selfishness.

Jacobins and Bolsheviki alike were called upon to
face the most difficult and exacting problems of administration. They were obliged simultaneously to repress
domestic plots, to repulse foreign invasion, to save their
people from absolute starvation as a result of the
abnormal conditions created by war, revolution, and
previous maladministration. That they succeeded in
maintaining their hold upon the government in the face
of all these obstacles was not due solely, or even primarily, to the remarkable organizing capacity of some of

their leaders. It was due rather to the intensely active cooperation of the revolutionary elements among the masses. In Russia these masses organized themselves in local soviets. In France they created the patriotic societies which radiated all over the country from the Jacobin stronghold of Paris. These active popular bodies formed the very backbone of the French and Russian revolutions. Out of them came the best soldiers for the armies, the best workmen for the factories. It was due to their vigorous exertions that the supply of food and clothing and munitions was somehow kept up, that both revolutions did not perish in a welter of sheer chaos and anarchy.

Both movements temporarily inaugurated a new style of diplomacy. The fundamental spirit of Tchitcherin's recklessly unconventional state papers is summed up in the famous announcement of the convention that it was "the friend of all peoples and the enemy of all governments." In consistently making desperate and more or less successful efforts to supplement arms with propaganda, to break the iron ring of their enemies by fomenting domestic uprisings, the Bolsheviki are only following in the footsteps of the Jacobins. Other points of resemblance between the two movements are a pronounced anticlerical tendency, a passionate fondness for fetes and celebrations, an ardent and almost pathetic zeal for the speedy diffusion of enlightenment among the illiterate masses.

The French and Russian revolutions both have their dark and bloody aspects. Through both there runs a strain of fiery fanaticism, the natural product of cruel and prolonged repression. This fanaticism often finds expression in acts of shocking and senseless brutality. Revolution like war, makes men dangerously susceptible to the passions of suspicion, intolerance, and mob violence. The fruits of the French Revolution were partially lost through its excesses. Russia may have a similar experience. But, whatever the crimes and mistakes of the Jacobins and the Bolsheviki, the reactionary legends that represent them as monsters of unmitigated iniquity are certainly very far from the truth. To their account must be laid not only the terror, but also nearly all the glorious positive achievements that are associated with the two great modern efforts to realize a freer and better world. If, in the course of the struggle, they often had recourse to stern and bloody methods, it should be remembered that, in this respect, their opponents were equally guilty. The Vendean counter-revolutionists of 1792, like Koltchak's Cossacks were notorious for their remorseless and diabolical savagery. French and Russian revolutionists alike were animated by the loftiest ideals, ideals that are admirably expressed in the great blazing watchword: Liberty, Equality, Fraternity. And, though these ideals might be often forgotten or trampled under foot in the heat and fury of a desperate civil and foreign war, yet somehow they impress upon both movements an unmistakable character of beauty and nobility. Jacobin France did not develop into Rousseau's ideal state; yet there are few intelligent Frenchmen who would wish to see the years of the revolution blotted from their country's history. Bolshevik Russia will probably not evolve into the perfect Marxian commonwealth; but future history will scarcely deny that the Russian Revolution played a part, and a very important part, in the advance of the human race toward spiritual and material freedom.

ECONOMIC PROGRAM OF BOLSHEVIST RUSSIA [1]

The best way to celebrate the anniversary of a great revolution is to center all attention on its unsolved problems. Such a celebration of a revolution is especially

[1] By Nikolay Lenin. Living Age. 312: 270-3. February 4, 1922.

necessary and proper when there are in existence basic problems that require solution; and when it is necessary to do things that are quite novel, from the point of view of the course that the revolution has run hitherto, in order to solve those problems.

What is new and novel at the present moment, so far as our revolution is concerned, is the necessity which compels us to adopt a "reformist," gradual, cautious policy toward fundamental economic questions. This "novelty" raises many doubts of both a theoretical and a practical nature.

The first theoretical question is: How can we justify our change from revolutionary to "reformist" policies, when the revolution as a whole marches on triumphantly? Is this not "giving up positions," "acknowledging failure," or something of that sort? All our enemies say that it is. And even our friends are puzzled.

For three years, up to the spring of 1921, our plan was to revive our large-scale industries and to organize a system of exchanging their products with the peasants, while endeavoring to socialize agriculture. In order to revive our large-scale industries, we proposed to take from the peasants a certain amount of foodstuffs and raw materials as a sort of loan, by means of requisitions. This was the revolutionary approach to the problem of breaking up the old social and political order and of substituting for it a new order.

Since the spring of 1921, we have been trying— though we have not as yet really introduced it—another plan, which is reformist in its character. We are no longer trying to *break up* the old social and economic order, with its trade, its small-scale economy and private initiative, its capitalism, but we are now trying to *revive* trade, private enterprise, and capitalism, at the same time gradually and cautiously subjecting them to state regulation just so far as they revive.

This is an entirely different way of attacking the

problem. By comparison with the preceding revolutionary method, it is reformist; since a revolution shatters
the old to its very foundations, instead of reforming it
slowly, gradually, and cautiously, with as little disturbance as possible.

Now, if after testing revolutionary methods, we declare them a failure and substitute reformist methods,
does that mean that we pronounce revolution itself a
blunder? Does not this prove that we should not have
begun with the revolution in the first place, but with
reforms?

Such a deduction is either sophistry or plain dishonesty, when advanced by men who have gone through
the actual experience of a great political overturn. A
real revolutionist's greatest danger lies in exaggerating
revolution, in forgetting the limitations to a successful
and proper application of revolutionary methods. Most
real revolutionists have brain storm when they begin to
write the word, "Revolution," with a capital R, when
they begin to exalt revolution to a divinity. They lose
their heads and become incapable of coolly and sanely
deciding at what moment it is necessary to apply revolutionary methods, and when it becomes essential to use
reform methods. Real revolutionists perish—not through
defeat from without, but through failure from within—
just as soon as they lose their sanity and begin to fancy
that the "great, triumphant, world revolution" is a final
end in itself, and that all problems, under all conditions,
in all fields of action, can and should be solved solely
by revolution. Such thoughts are stupid, and in the
heat of fighting, since the revolution is the most intense
of wars, the price paid for stupidity is defeat.

Engels was wont to stress the fact that stupid and
foolish things are done in the course of a revolution, as
well as in other times. It should be our endeavor to
commit as few stupid and foolish actions as possible, to
repair those already made, to determine as carefully as

possible what can be accomplished by revolution, and what cannot. Our own experience shows us that the Brest-Litovsk peace was not a revolutionary, but a reformist act, or even worse than reformist; since, as a general thing, reformist activities usually move forward carefully, slowly, cautiously, but still forward, while our act at Brest was a step backward. Yet the correctness of our tactics in concluding the Brest-Litovsk treaty has now been so thoroughly proved, that there is no use wasting words arguing about it.

First, we thereby withdrew from the imperialistic World War and effectually interfered with the mutual slaughter of two groups of international capitalistic vultures. As far as we Russians are concerned, our job here is finished. The entire completion of the work can come only as a result of a revolution in the important countries of the world.

We created the Soviet state, which incorporates the dictatorship of the proletariat. A world change has taken place. The epoch of bourgeois-democratic parliamentarism is over. A new chapter of the world's history has begun: the epoch of proletarian dictatorship. Much of the work here has not yet been carried to completion. It would be unpardonable to overlook that. More than once shall we have to make over, to start again at the beginning, to change things around. Every step forward and upward in developing the productive forces of the country, and in advancing its culture, will have to be accompanied by changes in our Soviet system; and we are still on a very low stage of development with regard to our productive forces and our culture. Many changes are still in store for us, and it would be absurd or worse than absurd to let that fact trouble us.

We have begun to lay the foundation of the new Socialist order. In this field, the most fundamental things still remain undone. And we here face the most important of our tasks, from the viewpoint of theory, of the practical needs of the Russian Soviet republic, and of the international proletariat.

In April 1918, in *The Current Tasks of the Soviet Authority,* I wrote:—

It is not sufficient to be a revolutionary or a follower of Socialism and Communism generally. It is necessary to be able at each given moment to find that special link of the chain which should be grasped with all our strength in order to keep the whole chain in its place and to prepare the transition to the next link; and it should be also remembered that the order of these links, their form, their joints, their difference from each other in the historic chain of events, are by no means as simple as in an ordinary chain, forged by a blacksmith.

At the present moment the link we have to deal with is reviving internal *trade* under proper government regulation. Trade is the link in the historic chain of events, which we must forge in the period of 1921-22. If we forge this link sufficiently strong now, we shall surely make good our title to the whole of the chain. Otherwise we shall not obtain possession of this chain and shall not be able to lay the foundation of socialism in other fields of production.

No doubt, this appears strange. Communism and private trading! There seems to be such a distance between the two, such an incongruity in the bracketing of the two together. But if we think economically for a moment, we shall see that the two are no more incongruous than the existence side by side of communism and of patriarchal, small-peasant agriculture.

When we shall have conquered the whole world, I think we shall use all the gold in the world for making public lavatories in the streets of some of its largest cities. That would be the most appropriate and instructive use to which gold could be put; for those generations will still remember how for the sake of gold, ten million men were killed and thirty million were crippled in the "great and liberating" war of 1914-18,

in that war which was fought for the purpose of deciding which peace treaty was worse, the Brest or the Versailles. That generation also will remember how, for
the sake of that same gold, twenty million men were
killed and sixty million crippled in a war fought in 1925,
or possibly in 1928, between Japan and America or between England and America.

But no matter how "appropriate," how useful and
humanitarian, it would be thus to employ our gold, we
must admit that it will take a decade or two of labor
as intensive as that of 1917-21, and on a much larger
scale, before we shall be in a position to do this. In the
meantime, we must take good care of our gold in Soviet
Russia, sell it for as high a price as possible, buy goods
for it as cheaply as possible. When you live with the
wolves, you must howl as they do. And as for extermin-
ating the wolves as would be proper in sensible human
society, we must remember the good Russian proverb:
"Don't boast when you go into battle; boast when you
return from battle."

Private trading is the only possible economic connection between tens of millions of peasants and our
large-scale industries, so long as we do not have dispersed among these peasants an excellently developed
industrial system, with a net-work of electrical connections and with a local organization that can supply these
small-scale farmers with better goods, in larger quantities, more cheaply and more quickly than heretofore. On
a world scale this "if" is already a reality, this condition
is already a possibility; but it happens that Russia, economically one of the most backward capitalistic countries, in attempting to change its system at once, and to
establish new connections between industry and agriculture, has not succeeded in its "storm attack," and finds
itself forced to resort to slow and gradual "siege" operations.

A proletarian state authority can take control of

trade, direct it into the necessary channels, and give it the proper guidance. Here is a very simple illustration. In the Donetz coal basin there is a noticeable revival of activity, which is the result of increasing the output of the larger state-owned mines, and also of introducing a system of leasing small mines to the peasantry. The state thus obtains a certain amount of coal at a certain price and sells it to other state institutions at, say, 20 per cent profit and to private individuals at, say, 40 per cent profit. These are not the exact figures, for I do not know what the exact calculations are and would not make them public at this time if I knew them. But I give them as an illustration of how we are beginning, little by little, to acquire control of the exchange of commodities between industry and agriculture, of wholesale trade, of small-scale industry which is still at work or large-scale industry which is badly disorganized. By stimulating trade in any of these fields, we impress the peasant, who is the true representative of the masses; and we systematically and persistently pursue our larger goal of reviving large-scale industries.

Let us not fall into the abyss of emotional socialism, that old Russian, semi-aristocratic, semi-peasant patriarchal contempt for trade. It is permissable and imperative to employ any transitional form which may prove expedient to bring the peasantry and the proletariat together and to stimulate agriculture in our disorganized and suffering country, as a first step toward reorganizing industry and hastening more important and far-reaching measures, such as electrification.

After the victory of the proletariat, at least in one country, we have a new relation between revolution and reform. Why could we survive the Brest retreat? Because we had gone so far forward, that we had room for a retreat. In the course of a few weeks, between November, 1917 and the Brest peace, we made a bewildering advance, constructed the Soviet state, withdrew from the war in a revolutionary fashion, finished the

work of the bourgeois-democratic revolution.   Consequently, even the great backward movement which the
Brest peace forced upon us still left us enough positions
to reform our battalions and then to move triumphantly
forward, against Koltchak, Denikin, Yudenitch, Piłsudski, and Wrangel.

Before the victory of the proletariat, reforms are
subsidiary agencies in the revolutionary class struggle.
After the victory, while still subsidiary on an international scale, they become for the country in which the
victory has been won a necessary and proper device for
relieving a maximum strain on those forces of the revolution that may have become temporarily insufficient
for the accomplishment of this or that specific task. The
victory does, however, so add to our power, that it is
possible for us to survive a retreat with ample material
and moral resources.   Material resources mean such a
reserve of strength that the foe cannot crush us completely.   Moral resources mean immunity against internal demoralization and disorganization, cool nerves,
courage, capacity to retreat no matter how far, but never
too far, and then to turn at the right moment and re-
sume our advance.

We retreated to state capitalism. But we retreated
just far enough. We are now retreating to state regulation of trade. We shall retreat only far enough. There
are already indications that the end of our retirement
is in sight, that in a future not very distant, it will be
possible to stop the retreat. The more sensibly, the more
ably we conduct our retirement, the sooner it will be
possible to stop, and the swifter and farther will be our
subsequent triumphant advance.

BOLSHEVISM FROM THE INSIDE [1]

The greatest problem facing the Soviet government
at present is that of transportation. This is almost para-

[1] By J. A. Gade. Atlantic Monthly. 126: 248-56. August, 1920.

lyzed. The inefficiency and corruption of the Tsarist government, the wear and tear of the war, when everything was sacrificed to meet temporarily the demands of the western front, and finally the incompetency and negligence of the Soviet government, are now all bearing fruit. Rolling-stock cannot be renewed, as there are not domestic workshops and no foreign deliveries. Such skilled workmen as Russian railroads possessed were either called to the red colors or, as is the case to a great extent, have become commissars and refuse to turn back into mechanics and engineers. Stecklov recently stated that foreign engineers, skilled workmen, and master-mechanics were just as badly needed by Russia as foreign locomotives and cars. It is now hoped that Scandinavian mechanics, and especially Swedish, of socialistic and communistic tendencies, may be lured to Russia by liberal pay and assurance that their families will be taken care of during their absence. The very best mechanics, especially from the metal and textile industries, were early sent to the front with the first detachment of soldiers from Petrograd and Moscow; most of these perished along the Don and in the Ukraina. The red armies swallowed up what skilled mechanics were left, as well as the best workmen from Petrograd, Moscow, Ivanovo-Voznessensk, and the Ural.

Lomonosov, who is considered an expert in everything pertaining to railway matters, has declared that traffic could be kept up, even to its present miserable condition, only if the Bolsheviki repair five times the number of locomotives they are now repairing, namely, 10 per cent instead of 2 per cent of those now broken down. Russia has only about twenty-seven hundred "sound" locomotives. Firewood being the only fuel naturally decreases capacity. Before the war the average through train made about one hundred versts a day, but the present speed of the few trains that are despatched and not stopped or robbed *en route* is about sixty versts. Sixty per cent of the scanty and wholly insufficient pre-war engines are now out of commission, and almost all are badly worn. About two hundred are discarded every month.

Lomonosov looked facts in the face when he concluded a recent speech in Petrograd by saying:

> The facts are very simple: as we have no engines, we cannot carry goods. Superhuman efforts are needed. If we continue as heretofore, spring will find us with 8o per cent of the engines out of commission, and this means that our trains will stop. Even if our negotiations with the western powers and the United States are successful, we shall get nothing for some time. The fate of the republic depends today upon its railways, and these upon the engines. Three months ago Brother Trotsky cried: "Proletarians—to horse!" The Russian proletarian mounted, and the victory was won. Let the cry now be: "Proletarians—to your lathes! We have succeeded in defeating Koltchak and Denikin; now we must defeat engines."

In southeast Russia, in the Ural and Ufa districts, enormous grain stocks, enough to feed starving Russia and western Europe, are rotting in storehouses and granaries. Those who could repair locomotives and freighters are permitted to use the small available rolling stock for the transport of a load of produce to their own factory or village. Such precious freight must, however, be well guarded on the way, and the percentage of foodtrains which have been started and have got through to Petrograd and Moscow has been exceedingly low.

While cabinets and labor unions are squabbling in western Europe and America about ten- and eight- and six-hour working-days, despite the crying necessity of "speeding up" production, the Soviet government, anticipating a similar danger, passes resolutions for a double and triple shift on its railroads and in its boiler-works. The working-day is prolonged beyond eight hours, and the Saturday half-holiday goes by the board. Even the First of May, the great fête-day of the proletariat, is to be celebrated as a day of unusual toil, and all between the ages of eighteen and fifty, who have, during the last two years, done any railway work whatever, have been mobilized for this purpose.

The few trains running are practically at the service only of the military or government officials. Much "pull" and many permits are requisite to procure a ticket, while the general public is forbidden access to the stations.

The case of the Moscow textile district, which requires a monthly delivery of over half a million poods of Turkestan cotton, illustrates sufficiently how industry is affected by the lack of rolling-stock. At present only two trains a month are running, and at this rate it would take more than a score of years to deliver the eight million poods of cotton now awaiting transportation to the factories. An equal period would be required for the delivery in central Russia by the one monthly train of the ten million poods of metals stacked in the Ural district.

When the Soviet government "took over," it found nothing but worn-out machinery from which the more valuable parts, such as copper, brass, and bronze, had been removed. Belting had all been cut up for shoe-soles. The existing machinery is principally "scrap"; factories must be reequipped if industrial life is to be started on the most modest basis. Indeed, so far as industrial undertakings go, the Soviet government has to a certain extent been forced to acknowledge its erroneous course. It has recognized that it is impossible to run elaborate machinery and intricate manufacturing without technical experts and men of trained organizing and managing capacity, who could now be found only among the detested bourgeoisie.

The All-Russian Council has thus recently been obliged to acknowledge the necessity of seeking technical experts among the bourgeois class, and has even urged the communist workmen to receive them in a spirit of comradeship. "The Council believes that a blinding self-conceit led the working class to believe it could solve the vital questions now facing Russia without employing bourgeois specialists in responsible positions." The pill is sugared by all manner of further recommendations as to a rapid technical education of the proletariat, which would fit its members in the immediate future to assume positions of responsibility in the management of industry. Commissars of trade are to be appointed, standing in the same relationship to the general managers of all plants in which the military commissar stands to the regimental commander. No doubt the industrial chiefs' life will thereby be made as thoroughly miserable as that of many an officer whom I have heard bless the fate which delivered him from the claws of his tormentor.

But apart from human sacrifice, Russia needs the wherewithal to start work—tools and agricultural machinery and medicines and, most of all, rolling-stock and the food this can distribute. The smaller Russian industries have been consolidated into larger institutions under government control, or absorbed directly by the government. About four thousand larger plants have been nationalized, or, to use Rykov's recent words, "The entire Russian industry has been transferred to the hands of the government and Soviet institutions, and private industry is destroyed. Of Soviet Russia's entire industry, 41 per cent, employing 76 per cent of the laborers and representing three fourths of the national production, is now carried on by nationalized factories." Power-plants are being erected for their supply, and new branches of industry are being developed, since Russia was forced by the blockade to depend upon herself. The procuring of all raw stuffs, as well as their distribution, is controlled by the Supreme Soviet of National Economy, assisted by the numberless affiliated local economic soviets.

Russia's principal industries are textile and metal. Of the eleven hundred and ninety-one metal industries, six hundred and fourteen have been nationalized and one hundred and sixteen united into trusts. Russia now produces about one-third of the machinery she made before the war, when most of her stock was reasonably new and whole. Only 7 per cent of her seven million spindles are at work and only 11 per cent of her one hundred and sixty-four thousand looms are weaving. The textile industry, which, in pre-war days, was surpassed by England and Germany only, is completely broken down. These are appalling figures and facts, but they are quoted from the best authorities.

The section of the Donez Basin was naturally of enormous importance to the Bolsheviki; but there again they are helpless, from lack of cars and the destruction of the bridges.

The desperate economic conditions are being met by conscription of labor and the conversion of various armies into so-called "labor armies."

With the defeat of the white armies and the resulting reduction of the red forces, the Soviet government has been faced with the same problem as all other participants in the great war—namely, how to assimilate its soldiers. They were of particular danger to the Soviet republic. Trotsky and Lenin conceived the idea of labor armies, thus putting off the evil hour. They have assisted the government on an enormous scale, in chopping trees, sawing wood needed for fuel, clearing streets and railroads, repairing roads and bridges, mending broken agricultural implements, accumulating and concentrating food-stuffs, and meeting in every way the transportation difficulties, and in fact rehabilitating industry, as well as agriculture, by ploughing and seeding the fields.

The trade unions have vigorously opposed the complete enslavement of labor, with the result that they have been loudly berated by the Soviet government.

Discipline in the red armies improved greatly as time went on. Punishments were frequent and merciless. It is naturally far more difficult to maintain discipline in regiments roaming over several square miles of forest, or over the horizon-wide *polya*. The soldiers cannot see why they should not be filling their own wood-sheds or ploughing behind their home barns. As a result, desertions have occurred on a large scale, and "starvation punishments" have been imposed.

Many of the skilled laborers have left the factories, tempted by the larger prospects of speculation. The *Ekonomitcheskaya Zhizn* quotes a recent congress as follows: "Inasmuch as enormous masses of laborers have run away from cities into villages, labor-mobilization had best take place in the matter." Premiums are paid in the form of increased rations or pay for exemplary "labor behavior," while special prison camps have been established for the deserters, as also punitive deserter-labor-companies, whose duties are far from pleasant.

It is doubtful whether the labor-armies will, as Trotsky believes, acquire the military qualities which are of vital importance—namely, promptness and the same obedience that would be given to military orders. According to Zinovyev, the future outlook of the labor armies is not very cheerful. "They will have to remain mobilized for several years."

All labor soldiers are provided with labor books, which must always be found in order when inspected if the holder is to receive his alloted rations.

It speaks volumes for the extraordinary power exercised by the government that the weak and unhomogeneous Russia of today is capable of putting forth, if only temporarily, so mighty an effort toward economic reconstruction as that of the labor-armies.

The Soviet government, knowing very well how little is to be expected from the great powers, really believes that a pound of flesh will be exacted in return for everything that is given. Convinced that it must rely upon itself and its own energy, it follows that any regeneration must very largely come from within—from Russia herself. Every other nation, if sane, is busy setting its own house in order. America alone might enter Russia with altruistic motives. Her Red Cross or child-feeding organizations might be willing to labor in the name of charity. All others will come for concessions and selfish gain. The Bolsheviki have no illusions. Radek, the world's first propagandist, also knows that a world-revolution is for the time being out of the question, and that any *rapprochement* to the western world is possible only if the Bolsheviki first promise to stop their propaganda. As a result, the Soviet government is now ready to promise this or anything else demanded in order to reestablish relations. The future will take care of itself, and, the doors once open, it will undoubtedly prove very easy to start the old underground propaganda machinery going all over the world.

THE GLOOM AND GLORY OF RUSSIAN LITERATURE [1]

THE TRAGEDY OF RUSSIAN LITERATURE

Russian literature is a faithful record of the history of Russia. In her literature, hapless and helpless, Russia has recorded her grief and sorrow. In her song and story she has uttered her heaven-rending cry of anguish. Russia's fiction is the direct outcome of the sufferings of her people. The misfortunes of Russia are darker and deeper, her shrieks of agony are louder and longer than those of any other country. Her literature is sadder and gloomier than that of any land. It is the literature of a country which is always "complaining and sighing and wailing." If the joys of Russia are bitterly ignored in her literature, it is because in truth they cannot be said to exist. The humorous details in Russian literature often hide a most tragical background, which all of a sudden breaks through. Russian literature is indeed a faithful reflex of the life and character of the land and the people. When Gogol read to Pushkin the manuscript of his novel "Dead Souls," Pushkin exclaimed: "My God, how sad our Russia is!" In speaking later of this novel to others,

[1] By M. J. Rudwin. Open Court. 32: 390-407. July, 1918.

Pushkin added: "Gogol invents nothing; it is the simple truth." Nor did any of the later novelists, following in the footsteps of their master, invent anything. They told the simple truth, the terrible truth about the fate of their country, and about their own fates.

The same adverse fate which has brooded over Russia has in a like manner inexorably pursued her writers. In the writers of Russia are mirrored the life and character of their country. They on their part reflect in their works their own sad lives. In the creations of their imagination they reproduce their own sufferings, griefs and fears. With many a Russian author it is as though he had dipped his pen in his own blood. *Le malheur d'être poète* is not wholly a Russian trait. Sappho and Tasso are classical examples of the tragic fate of a poet. In all lands have the writers drunk of life's cup of bitterness, have they been bruised by life's sharp corners and torn by life's pointed thorns. Chill penury, public neglect, and ill health have been the lot of many an author in countries other than Russia. But in the land of the Tsars men of letters had to face problems and perils which were peculiarly their own, and which have not been duplicated in any other country on the globe. It was a great misfortune in Russia to possess a talent. "The devil," cried Pushkin in despair, "has caused me to be born in this country with a talent and a heart." The literary career was especially filled with danger in Russia. Every man of letters was under suspicion. The government of Russia treated every author as its natural enemy, and made him frequently feel the weight of its heavy hand. The wreath of laurels on the brow of almost every poet was turned by the tyrants of his country into a crown of thorns.

The hatred of the rulers of Russia against writers had its good reason. They saw in them their literary chastisers. Russian authors were enthusiastic supporters of the dream of social justice. They were, indeed, fighters for liberty on a battlefield where the pen was a sword. Russian literature in the last century was actuated more than any other by a powerful social instinct. It reflects more than any other the main tendencies of the social and political movements of the day. In Russia more than in any other country, literature was a vehicle for social ideas. A country without free speech and free press must needs turn to literature for the discussion of its social and political problems. In its literature at first did it try to solve in an ideal way the problems which it hoped would some day be solved in reality. A novel, a story, a poem, an essay on literature, when reading between the lines was not neglected, was a political *manifesto*. The Russian expected to see in the work of every writer of note a new program of social and political reform. He was accustomed to regard a good writer as a prophet. The best of the Russian authors became indeed the guides of their people. They were not only writers, but apostles and martyrs, who in the cause of Holy Russia faced imprisonment, exile and death.

Oppression and persecution bred demigods. "The madness and pride to starve and to die will never be wanting me," writes Belinsky not merely of himself, for it was true of any of the best Russian men of letters. Their history is, indeed, a catalog of tragedies. It is hard to mention a single great writer in Russia, who was not condemned to death, or sent as a convict prisoner to the mines of Siberia, or put as a conscript into a disciplinary battalion, or was not exiled to remote provinces, or interned on his estate, or silenced by the censor. Of all the men of letters of the world, those of Russia can surely boast of the greatest number of martyrs. Alexander Herzen calculated that during the reign of Nicholas I, the most typical and the most determined adversary of the freedom of the press that Europe has ever seen, within a period of thirty years, the three most illustrious Russian poets were either assassinated, or killed in duel, three lesser ones died in

exile, two became insane, two died of want, and one by
the hand of the executioner. The writers who saved
their lives by flight to foreign countries pined away with
homesickness and loneliness in their voluntary exile.
Turgenev, for instance, declared that in a strange land
a man lived isolated, without any real props or profound
relation to anything whatsoever. These Russian exiles
used to say, in bitter irony, that they could see their
country, the object of their study and love, better from
a distance. In foreign lands such an unfortunate did
not feel at least the torments of being a burning dreamer
in a land of eternal snow. Herzen, the creater of a
public sentiment in Russia from his refuge in London,
could well say to his countrymen: "Here in a foreign
land I am your uncensored speech, your free voice."
But it was the voice of a preacher in the wilderness.
Herzen lived in London a stranger. In the British
metropolis he felt, before he was joined by Bakunin
and other countrymen, as isolated as he had been in
exile in Russia. Russian fugitives felt their exile more
keenly than their German or French comrades. Those
who had to flee from Germany or France for their
political views found a congenial atmosphere in Switzerland or Belgium. But there was no free Slavonic
country which could offer the Russian exiles a pleasant
asylum, one in which they would not feel totally strange
ground under their feet.

Many a Russian writer, who did not seek safety
in flight, smothered his inspiration, or broke his pen in
despair before his time, or sought to forget his disappointment in drink, or lost his mind, or took his own
life! Attempts at suicide were very common among the
younger generation of Russian writers. If they did not
end their lives themselves, consumption as a result of
privations and overwork, or *delirium tremens* as a consequence of the drink habit, or insanity, which developed
from melancholia, a disease so common among Russian
authors, lay in wait for them. Many Russian writers

died just when or even before they had reached the
full development of their talents. The knell of every
ambition sounded for them just when the first rays of
glory touched the long despised brow. "Whom the gods
love die young." They preserved by this means many a
Russian writer from a worse fate. Death saved Pushkin, Gogol, Nadson, and Tchehov from insanity, and
death saved Belinsky from prison. The cause of early
death of such a great number of Russian authors lay
not wholly in the stark misery of their youth, although
many authors of plebeian descent had to acquire an education under the most terrible privations. The brief
span of life allotted to these Russians is chiefly due to
the sudden transition from an uncultured state to strenuous mental activity. It is but natural, says Brückner,
that a generation so suddenly brought into contact with
an ocean of new ideas should turn giddy on the edge of
the abyss and lose its balance.[1]

PESSIMISM IN RUSSIAN LITERATURE

"Sadness, scepticism, irony," said Alexander Herzen,
"are the three strings of Russian literature." Pessimism
and scepticism are Russian national traits of character.
The Russian is the spirit of negation become flesh. He
is the spirit of doubt and denial. His heart is the abode
of *der Geist der stets verneint*. "Truly," said Dostoyevsky, "the Russian soul is a dark place." The Russian
soul, alas! has always been fed on the milk from what
Nietzsche calls "the udders of sorrow." Profound pessimism is as distinctive a feature of Russian literature
as it is of Russian temperament. As far as we can trace
back the history of Russian literature, we find these
traits of the national character permeating it. The
plaintive note of their national music, the soul-gripping
melancholy of their folk-songs, the dreary sadness of
their folk-tales, the overwhelming pessimism of their

[1] By A. Brückner. A Literary History of Russia. Chap. 19, p. 528.
New York, 1908.

literature, all are the manifestations of these national
characteristics of the Russians. All the chords of the
Russian lyre are strung to the same tunes of mental sadness, moral scepticism, and spiritual despair. The only
muse which the Russian poets seem ever to have invoked
is the muse of Hypochondria. "I owe my early inspiration to the muse of sobs, of mourning and of pain—the
muse of the starving and the beggar." What the poet
Nekrasov says of himself is true of nearly all Russian
writers.

All men of letters in Russia express this national
trait, but it differs with each individual in accordance
with his own temperament. The pietistic melancholy of
Zhukovsky, for example, differs from the indignant melancholy of Gogol; Lermontov's militant melancholy
stands in contrast to the sceptical, almost ironical melancholy of Pushkin; the idealistic melancholy of Turgenev is different from the fatalistic melancholy of Tolstoy; the meek melancholy of Garshin forms a sharp
contrast to the bitter melancholy of Gorky; Korolenko's
melancholy is not the heartrending, cheerless kind of
melancholy of a Baratinsky or Nadson; Tchehov's pessimism is not as cynical as that of Pisemsky. But dark
despair has taken possession of the souls of all Russian
writers. There are pessimists among the great men in
all literature, but the Russians are especially sad.

"No novelist in western Europe," says Brandes, "is
so sad as Turgenev." [1] Professor Phelps says he heard
Professor Boyesen remark that he had never personally
known any man who suffered like Turgenev from sheer
despair. [2] It is so characteristic of Turgenev that the
last page written by him bore the very title "Despair."
His pessimism is fundamental. Melancholy was with
him a matter of conviction as well as of temperament.
It was due to his losing all faith in God and man.
Seated one day in a garden, he became the solitary

[1] By Georg Brandes. Impressions of Russia. New York. 1899. p. 273.
[2] By William Lyon Phelps. Essays on Russian Novelists. New York.
1911. p. 70.

witness of a struggle between a snake and a toad. This made him first doubt the providence of God. Whatever he saw later in life confirmed him in the conviction that nature is totally unconcerned about insect or man, that nature treats the man of the noblest aspirations and the man of the most brutish disposition with equal indifference. And so all ideals of the human race are in his opinion a matter of total indifference to it. He loved the good and the true, but he had no faith in the triumph of the good and the true. Turgenev anticipated by half a century the naturalist's point of view of our own day.

Turgenev's views of nature are most admirably set forth in his sketch "Nature," which appeared in his Poems in Prose:

I dreamt that I entered an enormous subterranean hall with high vaults. It was all filled with an even, subterranean light.

In the very center of the hall sat a majestic woman in a flowing garment of green color. Bending her head on her hand, she seemed to be buried in deep meditation.

I saw at once that this woman was Nature herself, and, with a sudden chill, a reverential awe entered my soul.

I approached the woman who was sitting there, and making a respectful bow: "Oh, our common mother!" I exclaimed. "What are you meditating on? Are you, perchance, pondering on the future destiny of the human race? Or, how it may reach the highest possible perfection and happiness?"

The woman slowly turned to me her dark, piercing eyes. Her lips moved, and there issued from them a ringing voice, like the clanking of iron.

"I am thinking how to add greater strength to the muscles of a flea's leg, that it may more easily save itself from its enemies. The equilibrium between attack and defense has been impaired—it must be reestablished."

"What?" I lisped in answer. "Is it that what you are thinking about? But are we men not your favorite children?"

The woman barely frowned: "All creatures are my children," she spoke, "and I take equal care of them, and equally exterminate them."

"But goodness—reason—justice—" I muttered again.

"These are human words," was heard the woman's voice. "I know neither good nor evil—reason is not my law, and what is justice? I have given you life, and I shall take it from you and shall give it to others, worms or men—it makes no difference to me—you defend yourself in the meantime, and do not bother me!"

I wanted to retort—but the earth around me gave a dull groan and trembled, and I awoke.

The uselessness of the struggle for existence, and the necessity for resignation is the prevailing theme of Russian literature. Through the mouths of the children of their sorrows the Russian authors express their renunciation of hope, their weariness of the world. Many a Russian writer reminds the reader of a monk who would fain drag down all men to the level of his own renunciation. As life had never given anything to him, he could not realize that it might have something to give to others. Some of the characters in Russian literature in their sad weakness resemble the aged saints in Russian sacred pictures. The call to physical joy and physical revolt, which is the predominant note in most recent Russian literature, is alien to the Russian temperament. This self-asserting individualism, which has found its strongest and fullest expression in Artsibashev's novel *Sanin,* has its origin in the philosophies of Max Stirner and Friedrich Nietzsche. How it will blend with the Russian temperament is hard to foresee. It is a part of the great Russian enigma.

Russian writers do not consider life the supreme possession of man. Lermontov calls life "a stupid jest." Tchehov speaks of the nothingness of life, the absurdity of life. Nadson believes that the only goal of man is non-existence. Andreyev shows us the weakness, vanity and vacuity of life, nay, the nonsense of life. Turgenev, although he loves life, sadly realizes its fleeting nature.

But in spite of this *taedium vitae,* these Russians fear death. This fear of death, which in an intensely intellectual people like the Russians is an obsession of terror, is found in almost all the works of the best-known Russian writers. It runs all through Tolstoy's diaries and novels. It is eloquently expressed in certain pages of Turgenev's "Poems in Prose."

Suffering is the foundation of Russian literature, as it is the essence of Russian life. The poetry of the sorrow of man is the *Leitmotiv* of many and many a Russian song or story or drama. The Russian capacity for suffering is the text of the great works of Russian literature. The patience and passivity *smirênié i dolgotêrpenié* (the humility and long-suffering) of their nation are stressed in the writings of all of Russia's representative men. Dostoyevsky, who fully understood the hearts of his countrymen, in perfect accord with the national temperament, regards suffering as a blessing, shows the transports of dejection and despair, describes the purification of character through grief and sorrow.

The great and glorious result of this suffering as set forth in the lives and works of Russian men of letters is universal compassion and commiseration for suffering humanity. Pity, as all the world knows, is a fundamental trait of the Russian character. Pity is also the keynote of Russian national literature. Gogol was the first writer to point out this trait in the Russian temperament—the tolerance and forbearance, the kindness and tenderness for the poor, the ignorant, the weak —nay, even for those who have sunk to the very bottom of the Inferno of Life. Russian pity extends even to the dumb beasts. "The death of a horse described by one great Russian novelist," says Bazan, "is more touching than that of any emperor." [1]

This trait of the Russian national character has found its most perfect expression in the novels of Dostoyevsky. In them we learn "the charity that passeth all understanding, and the pity that is a folly to the worldly wise." [2] Dostoyevsky loves more than any other Russian writer, for he has suffered more than any other. There is nothing on which he would not take pity. With him, suffering puts a halo even around sin, it sanctifies the wretchedness of the most wretched and the ugliness of the ugliest. In his novel "Crime and Punishment"

[1] Emilia Pardo-Bazan. Russia, Its People and Its Literature. Chicago. 1890. p. 204.

[2] Ibid. p. 246.

the assassin kisses the feet of the harlot and exclaims:
"I do not bow down to you personally, but to suffering
humanity in your person." This evangelical charity for
sinful humanity was raised by Dostoyevsky to the highest degree of piety, to "pious despair," a phrase coined
by the French critic Vicomte Melchior de Vogüé. Dostoyevsky loved erring humanity, and did better than
judge it—he pitied it. "If there ever was a person," a
writer has said, "who would forgive any human being
anything seventy times seven, the individual was Dostoyevsky." To him Christianity is reduced to the three
parables of the repentent thief, the prodigal son, and the
woman taken in adultery. His whole religion is summed
up in the one verse: "Judge not, and ye shall not be
judged; condemn not, and ye shall not be condemned;
forgive, and ye shall be forgiven" (Luke iv. 37). In
the novels of Dostoyevsky as in the writings of other
great Russians we find the essence of Christianity. It
is, indeed, remarkable what analogies the Russian writers offer to the early Christians. Turgenev was an
atheist, but his life may have been more pleasing to God
than that of many a self-styled believer. Professor
Phelps claims that Turgenev was a true Christian in the
definition of Edwin Booth, who said that a Christian
was a man who rejoiced in the superiority of a rival. [1]
Turgenev was always happy over the success of a rival.
Tolstoy may have been anathematized by the church, but
with his principles he indeed had a better claim to Christian fellowship than the members of the church of his
country, and of many another country.

MODERN RUSSIAN LITERATURE [2]

I

Nothing is more difficult than to sum up the present
state of Russian literature, or to give a satisfactory

[1] William Lyon Phelps. Op cit. p. 73.
[2] By A. Lévinson. La Revue Mondial. 32: 327-36. October 1, 1921.

estimate of it as a whole. It has undergone a double crisis of incalculable importance during the few years since the declaration of war. From that moment there appeared a departure, which grew more and more obvious, from the traditions that had previously seemed fundamental. Later the Bolshevist domination—either by wiping out the intellectuals or by sending them into voluntary exile—set up a new and highly complex movement which was definitely to change the direction of the current. The attitude that gave the Russian literature of the days before the war its "heroic character"— according to the famous formulas enunciated by Professor Vengerov—was that of a continuous and formidable protest against the existing state of things.

This mental attitude took, on the one side, the form of direct criticism of the old régime; a criticism which directed itself as much against the methods of repression practised by Tsarism as against its thirst for conquest— as for example in Leonid Andreyev's "The Seven Who Were Hanged," and "The Red Laugh." In its other respect it suffered "the torment of the beyond," a romantic refusal to accept creation as it is, an attitude exemplified in Dostoyevsky. The last act of Tolstoy, his flight from his home and family, was such a protest; the picturesque insolence of Gorky's "lost ones" was such a defiance. The saddened lyricism of a Tchehov found its consolation in the fact that "life will be beautiful in two or three hundred years." And what do the deliriums of an Artsybashev or the mystic frenzy of Merezhkovsky's group represent, if not the need to escape from the brutal realities of the reactionary powers triumphant over the revolutionists of 1905.

The very idea of the fatherland—identified with an official Russia and overwhelmed by the bureaucracy— scarcely figures among the familiar conceptions of the Russian writers. Their inspiration was the "muse of vengeance and of sorrow" invoked by Nekrasov, and their characteristic attitude was indignant denial and fervent hope for utopia. Literature was either an unparalleled weapon, or else a powerful narcotic, a source of forgetfulness, and "artificial paradise."

Ten years later the duel with Japan called forth no literature except a flood of pamphlets and revelations. It was a general *j'accuse*. The writers constituted themselves the idealists of literating defeat. Such works as Kuprin's "The Encounter," which made his name illustrious, exemplify the intellectual party's condemnation of the military state.

But, before the great conflict which brought the great empire to blows with Germany, a subtle and almost complete change was produced. The best literature ranged itself by the side of the government, which proclaimed that the cause of liberty was its own—just as, a century before, the future Decembrists had attacked the Napoleonic tyranny. It was the lyric poets who put themselves at the head of this spontaneous movement, and others followed with enthusiasm. To find a precedent for this patriotic fever one must go back to the days of the burning of Moscow, or seek for the demonstrations of the Slavophiles Homyakov and Tutchev, celebrating the defeat of the Polish insurrection. If the "sacred union" was nothing but a generous illusion for Russia, which could not last, it at least seized the imagination of the great symbolist poets, Sologub and Alexander Blok. One of the chiefs of the younger generation, Serge Gorodetsky, the interpreter of the primitive mythology of the Slavs, had proclaimed the "communion of the Tsar with the people," though it is true that today we see him celebrating in dithyrambic verse the sickle and the hammer, emblems of the Soviet and the energy of the Bolshevik.

The martyrdom of Belgium was an inexhaustible source of inspiration. In the theater, productions of the day multiplied. But only Leonid Andreyev's drama, "King, Law, and Liberty" kept its place on the boards.

The action of this piece is built around the noble figure of the poet, modeled upon Maurice Maeterlinck, who inspires the king to the supreme sacrifice—the opening of the dikes. Since that time a fragment of a dialogue between William II and a Russian scientist, a volunteer in the Belgium army, has been found among the papers of Andreyev, who died in Finland. This imaginary dialogue proves the constant preoccupation of the moralist haunted by the problem of his responsibility.

The story-tellers followed the poets closely. We see remarkable writings gathered up in *Lukomorié,* a collection edited by one of the members of the Suvorin family, the son of the great reactionary journalist. Kuzmin, Sologub, even the socialist Oliger, contributed mediocre and inferior productions to these collections.

Those works dealing with the war are characterized by almost the same stereotyped ideas. There is always a German, the hypocritical fiancé of the heroine who, once war is declared, reveals himself as the worst sort of a brute, and a spy besides. Battle-scenes are described with equal artificiality—reproductions of the sound of the detonations, or the enthusiastic shouts of the assault. The writers far behind the line are less concerned with the bloody reality of war than with its glorious trappings. One can imagine Merezhkovsky's indignation as he protested against "these nightingales singing in blood." Having broken with the great pacifist traditions set up by Tolstoy, and being deprived of immediate impressions, these writers experimented with —or else, less conscientious, actually produced—"pretty writings"; and so today not a line survives of their hasty sketches.

Another literary *genus* established itself, however, that of the war-correspondent. Many eminent authors attached to the auxiliary service of the army sent their stories of the war to the great periodicals. The novelist, Alexis Tolstoy, the poet Valery Bryusov, and many others were in the number of the correspondents. A

philosopher, Fedor Stepun, published, under a pseudonym, "The Letters of a Second Lieutenant of Artillery,"
a work which will live. Gumilev, a young schoolmaster,
twice decorated and then wounded, wrote verses "On
the Holiest of Wars," as he advanced through east
Prussia at the head of his hussars. It is to him also that
we owe the chronicles of the campaign. But these
anguished, or merely picturesque, descriptions of the
war, seen at first-hand, do not by any means constitute
works of art. We possess in them only the scattered
elements of a great epic that is yet to be written.

The war was accepted by all the literary groups as
a necessity imposed by the German menace, or as a
renewal of the national life. Only one man stood out
against the current—Maxim Gorky. He had left Italy
in order to establish at Petrograd the review *Letopis*
(Annals), an organ of internationalist propaganda.
Except for this he abstained from any political activity.
In a leading article which was violently discussed, he
set side by side the two souls of Russia—the soul of
Europe, bent on action, contrasted with the soul of Asia,
dreamy and inactive. There followed two works that
reestablished Gorky's artistic prestige, which had been
weakened by his novels, highly artificial in conception,
on socialist themes. In "Childhood" and "Among Men"
he described the early years of his life. There is nothing more moving than to follow the formation of this
soul, developing amid the most poignant scenes,
picturesque or burlesque, of popular life on the Volga.
This animated biography takes its place among the
classics, the memories of childhood of an Aksakov or a
Tolstoy.

However great the temptation to go on with a general picture of Russian literature today, I must give
some attention to individual work. During the years of
the war, although no new literary form was developed,
the art of the novel was enriched by three remarkable
productions. "Alexander I," by Merezhkovsky, is a

chronicle of the reign which fixed the destiny of Russia
for a century. Merezhkovsky proceeds by antithesis. In
the "Trilogy," to which he owes his distinction, he
opposed Christianity to paganism. In his mystic philosophical works he tried to establish a synthesis, the religion of the Holy Spirit.

In "Alexander I" we see the forces of reaction in
conflict with the youthful nobility stirred by revolutionary fervor. The soul of the Emperor is sadly divided,
and he fails to meet the dilemma. The throng of historical personages who play a part in this drama of a
whole country present themselves to us in two aspects:
real so far as precise documentation and the painting
of historical settings are concerned: fictitious so far as
these characters are intended to be twisted to the pre-
conceived ideas of the author, although the book itself
was conceived in the years which preceded the war.

"That Which Was Not," a novel by Boris Savinkov,
the famous political adventurer, is equally representative
of a page of more recent history. It is a picture of the
revolution of 1905 and its defeat—a work based on the
sensations and personal memories of the author, who
was a very active terrorist organizer. The literary
qualities of this novel were not solid enough to allow
of its survival after a sensational but ephemeral success.

I may also mention another work of distinction:
"Petersburg," by André Bely, one of the most remarkable men of the symbolist generation: poet, novelist,
critic, and anthroposophist. As a thinker Bely leans
upon German philosophy and ultimately on that of
Steiner; and in his quest after a new form of expression, he presents himself as a rival of the great French
imitators, as a Mallarmé or a Rhimbaud. For the overwhelming task of making over the novel, he prepared
himself by a series of "symphonies in prose." "Petersburg," based on a fantastic conception of the capital—
"the most artificial in the world" as Dostoyevsky would
say—has special value because of the word-study of the

author. This clever rhythmic prose, surcharged with
assonances and other phonetic tricks, enriched with
grotesque or pathetic metaphors and suggestive epithets,
forms a whole that is as complicated as a labyrinth, yet
lightened by gleams of genius. To read "Petersburg"
is a labor; and yet this book, so full of suggestions,
seems to mark an important change in the evolution of
the Russian language.

II

The moment was approaching when all literary
aspirations were to grow somber in the torment of the
revolution. When, after a year of convulsions, the communist dictatorship was established, it had an important
effect upon literary production. In view of the situation
that was forced upon the intellectuals by triumphant
Bolshevism, literature could adopt only one attitude
without perishing: silence. Authors resolutely refrained
from writing, for had they dared to speak, measures
would have been taken to deal with them. Once all
publications outside the official press had been
eliminated, printing material declared state property,
distribution of paper subject to control, nothing remained for men of letters who refused to rally to the
support of the new régime. Misery was their lot so
far as material things were concerned.

One man alone accepted the task of maintaining if
not literature, at least the existence of literary men. This
was Maxim Gorky. Some hundreds of literary men owe
to him liberty, the food that saved them from famishing,
very often life itself. I do not regard myself as qualified to discuss the political conduct of this man, who is
so generally attacked. Some day a resurrected fatherland will judge him. To combat the bad faith of a
hypocritical and brutal government, he had to struggle
without truce in the cause of the intellectuals. I can-

not speak here of his purely humanitarian undertakings, but his enterprise of "World Literature" ought to be mentioned. It is a series of translations of all the distinguished literary work that appeared on the two continents from the dawn of the French Revolution to our day. The plan of these publications was worked out independently by a chosen body of literary men and scientists; and all the competent men were gathered together in this design of unification and civilization.

By the making of translations, the writing of notes and prefaces, they endured the worst times somehow, although the situation of all these authors condemned to translating the works of others and forbidden to produce anything themselves, was somewhat paradoxical. There is no need to say that "World Literature" was nothing but a generous illusion. By a clever manoeuvre, the men at the head let the writers go on with their work, but did not give them the paper necessary for publication. In this way "World Literature" won resounding acclaim, even dazzled credulous people in other countries; but, as a matter of fact, it was reduced to nothing.

Gorky, wearied by the burden of irreconcilable responsibilities, and a struggle without glory and without effect, himself produced very little. A play for the popular theater, "The Workman Who Talks Well," designed to cure the victorious proletarian of his distaste for work and his love of talk, was hissed, and then forbidden, on the ground that it was an attack on the majesty of the people. Some "Memories of Leo Tolstoy" were much admired but in playing the rôle of the devil's advocate in a panegyric of Lenin, he had definitely alienated the people's minds.

In view, however, of the silent but obstinate protest of the literary men, the need for an official art was brought home to the despots. There were the futurist poets, who had just come to the front with their new master, Mayakovsky, at their head. They saw in the

distress of the national soul "the means to arrive." Their
leader, a man of talent but wholly devoid of scruples and
athirst for notoriety, put at the service of the most
debased demagogues his poetry, with its powerful rhythm
and its marked sonority, abundant in images of deliberate and unexampled brutality. His "Mystery Play," a
kind of comedy in the manner of Aristophanes, in which
he makes a chorus of workmen pass through hell and
heaven so that they may come out at last in the promised land of communism, crowned with the greatest
pomp, fell flat. People were stupefied to see the shade
of Tolstoy scoffed at in the open theater by a Russian
poet. A new poem, "The One Hundred and Fifty
Millions" proclaimed the so-called Bolshevist faith of
the Russian masses.

Mayakovsky was supported by other adepts no less
observant of the official ideals—Klyuev, a peasant of
the government of Olonets, drawing his inspiration from
the primitive direct speech, chief of a mystic sect in his
own country, the panegyrist of Bolshevism, in his poem,
"A Copper Whale;" Esenin; Valery Bryusov, "the
faultless master" of the symbolist group, and the
imaginist, who, with Shershenevitch and Marienhof,
"the syndicate of poets," know how to win the good-will
of Lunatcharsky, and to secure many a subsidy from
him.

At the same time, efforts were made to replace what
was called bourgeois poetry by proletarian art. Everywhere the "Proletcults" were found—associations destined to support this movement, hothouses in which these
artificial flowers were cultivated. The workman poets,
or those who so styled themselves, a Gerasimov, a Gas-
tev, are the relentless imitators of Verhaeren, of Walt
Whitman, the great American, and of their bourgeois
colleagues. Their works are nothing but *pastiches,* of
merely relative importance.

But the great Bolshevist cataclysm, the frenzied outbreak of the masses, the moral overthrow, the destructive

madness of a few crazy people destroying themselves,
would still have had to wait for literary expression
if one inspired and remarkable poem had not appeared. This is "The Twelve," by Alexander Blok, the
poet of "The Fair Lady," the well-beloved mystic, whose
previous work had been the last flowering of an exhausted but still captivating romance. This poem, the
song of songs of the October Revolution, describes the
lugubrious night march of the red guards with a phantom Petrograd for a setting. At the end of the poem you
see a blasphemous conclusion—Christ appearing through
the whirling snow and pointing out the way to the
ghastly squad. By a kind of Messianic mysticism, the
poet attributes to these sinister figures an unconscious
mission, which is almost divine.

No work has stirred up such vehement discussion,
for the Bolsheviki themselves feared a trick hidden in
this apotheosis of their own ideas; but the skill and
intuition of the artist are marvelous. He employs a
composite style, in which the *argot* of the pavement and
the prison mingles with the jargon of public meetings,
popular refrains, orthodox prayers, and the seraphic,
winged sweetness of the words describing the appearance of the Christ.

Were we to confine ourselves to printed works, we
should now have given a fair summary of the state of
literature during the Soviet régime. But the authors,
forbidden other ways of securing a public, bethought
themselves of communicating their writings orally to
readers equally exasperated by the requirements of the
official press. Little by little lectures, then the
"almanacs," and then the "spoken reviews" increased in
number. We may see Remisov reciting his learned and
delightful paraphrases of the old popular dramas; we
may see Zamyatin reciting striking short stories, vivid in
style and grotesque as silhouettes; and we may see the
critics analyzing these unpublished authors by word of
mouth. No repression could wipe out completely the

whole force of a literary generation. Though her hands were bound, the muse sang during her time of torture.

In his celebrated work on the literary movement of the nineteenth century, the Danish critic, Georg Brandes, entitled one of the two volumes devoted to France: "The Literature of the Exiles." Some day, perhaps, the literature of the Russian exiles will form a collection no less imposing; but today there is little to presage such an event. Russian literature abroad, though it is rich in names already illustrious, is lacking in new writers, and struggles in vain to raise itself; for it is an uprooted literature, the work of men fascinated by the spectacle of their agonized fatherland, overwhelmed with an irremediable nostalgia, left alone in a world which is making itself anew, and separated from their land and from their dead.

Paris is the sheltering place of precious *débris*. There is Bunin, who is the natural chief of this group, an undoubted master. His pessimism, his objective method, the austere character of his style, make one think of a Flaubert, but a terrorist Flaubert. His work cannot be reduced to brief formulas. He swears an implacable and uncompromising hatred of Bolshevism, making himself, as it were, a counterpoise to Gorky, whom he attacks with fierce invectives and ferocious irony. There are also the novelist Kuprin; the poet Balmont, the idol of the young men of 1905, who writes a good deal with the fieriness of youth; Grebenshtchikov, who paints the life of the Siberian desert in a powerful yet simple way; Madame Teffi,[1] who, though she cultivates writing of the amusing sort, is by no means lacking in agreeable lyric qualities; Aldanov, the historian of Lenin, who recently published a novel on Napoleon "in the manner of Anatole France."

Sometimes it happens that it is the books and not the authors who are exiled. Merezhkovsky published in Paris his novel, "December Fourteenth" (the date of the

[1] Pseudonym of Nadezhda Butchinskaya.

military insurrection against Nicholas I in 1825), although he wrote it in Soviet Russia. This was the subject that haunted Leo Tolstoy, and it will be remembered
that the last part of "War and Peace" might have served
as a transition to a volume on the Decembrists. Fedor
Sologub, who is now living in Russia was able to publish his novel, "The Snake-Charmer," abroad—a rather
insignificant episode and somewhat tainted by a certain
opportunism. The charmer is a young girl of the working class, good, beautiful, and intelligent, who succeeds
in completely transforming the character of her bourgeois patrons. One cannot be very much astonished to
see the style, even of a celebrated writer, going to pieces
under the influence of this factitious piece of work,
which is optimistic without conviction. This enfeebling
of a powerful talent is a symptom of the incurable disease that is affecting all Russian creative endeavor.

But Russia's terrific misfortune has not destroyed all
sources of inspiration. Count Alexis Tolstoy has recently finished a book of the greatest scope, "The Road
of Torture," a novel published in the Russian review,
Contemporary Notebooks. The action takes us from the
beginning of the war to the beginning of the revolution.
Numerous persons, drawn from the most diverse social
classes of Russia, move through the action, of which
the declaration of war, the offensive in Galicia, the flight
of the hero from an Austrian prison-camp, the murder
of Rasputin, and the upheaval of 1917, are the principal
incidents. The book is a monument erected to the
martyred people, an effort to untangle the causes of the
catastrophe; and it is also a novel of adventure, full of
surprises and striking episodes. "The Road of Torture," is not a first book, for the third Tolstoy has
already published many a novel, captivating alike for
the interest of a story well told and for the beauty of
its style. His heroes of everyday life, grotesque and
ludicrous as they are, the last wearers of gentlemen's
cast-off clothing, eccentrics indulging their manias, win

for him a place apart among Russian novelists. It is
even possible that "The Road of Torture," may carry
Tolstoy to the head of the literary movement of exiled
Russia.

I trust that, in this very summary study, though
striving to avoid fastidious classifications, I have
asserted the essential facts, whose more extended
analysis would serve to give a complete picture of the
Russian literature of our day. I have abstained from
all prophecy; but who can doubt the inexhaustible resources of the Russian genius? The day, no doubt, is
near at hand when the soul of Russia will again burst
into flower amid the rubbish; when Lazarus will break
from the grave and rise to light and liberty.

RUSSIAN DRAMA IN THE NINETEENTH AND TWENTIETH CENTURIES [1]

In the nineteenth century the Pantheon of Russian
art and literature was a temple which was visited by only
a few isolated foreigners. In the course of the decades
which followed the advent of the two greatest Russian
geniuses—Pushkin and Glinka—a whole pleiades of servants of Euterpe, Erato, Thalia, and Melpomene surrounded the pedestals upon which these two *dii majores*
dwelt. So vast and resplendent did the Pantheon become
that its fame reached the west. Guided by a handful
of enlightened and enthusiastic pioneers, western Europe
found access, in the first decade of the nineteenth century,
to the Russian Pantheon, and some of the immortal
writers and composers were recognized as world geniuses. Suffice it to mention a few names familiar to
every British reader; Glinka, Borodin, Rimski-Korsakov,
Musorgsky, Pushkin, Gogol, Turgenev, Leo Tolstoy,
Dostoyevsky, Tchehov.

One of the wings of the Pantheon remained, however,
almost unexplored—that which belonged to the worship-

[1] By C. Nabokov. Contemporary Review. 121: 636-44. May, 1922.

pers of Thalia and Melpomene. Yet anyone who over-looked this portion would gain but an imperfect knowledge of the creative genius of Russia in the domain of art which reflects, perhaps more faithfully than any other, the true spirit of the people.

Difficult indeed is the position of a guide who knows every aspect of a picturesque panorama or every canvas of a vast picture gallery through which he is leading an impatient tourist whose time is strictly limited. The guide would halt at every turn of the path, or linger in front of each picture in order that the visitor might enjoy its beauty. But time is short, and they must hurry along. One is confronted with the same difficulty in endeavoring to introduce the reader to the Pantheon of Russian drama of the past and present centuries. From Pushkin to our contemporaries—Gorky and Andreyev, we see a vast gallery of playwrights who have been proclaimed immortal throughout Russia. Griboyedov, Gogol, Ostrovsky, Count Alexis Tolstoy, Count Leo Tolstoy, Turgenev, Tchehov, have written plays which will be played in Russian theaters as long as these theaters exist. Their tragedies, dramas, and comedies embody types as immortal as the heroes of "Anna Karenin, "War and Peace," or as may be found in the novels of Dostoyevsky and Turgenev. Apart from the above-named "classics" of the Russian drama, there have been, in the course of the last fifty or sixty years, many authors whose works have remained on the repertory, as well as innumerable falling stars whose passage through the stage firmament has been as rapid as that of a still vaster number of their *confreres* of the British dramatic world.

Of the inferior category of Russian writers we need say but little. Our visit to the Pantheon is of short duration, and we must not linger in front of perishable figures, when there is so much eternal marble to explore. Sins of omission in so brief a survey are inevitable, and for these, allowance must be made by the student.

Many are the factors that have contributed to the rapid growth and luxuriant blossom of the tree of Russian dramatic art and literature. There are, however, a few fundamental factors which are the more notable in that they obtained in Russia owing to historical and social conditions differing from those of western Europe.

The period of Russian history toward the close of the sixteenth century—the old age and death of Ivan the Terrible—till the election of the first Romanov in 1613, offers, however, ample material for historical drama, and of this material two of the Russian immortals—Pushkin and Count Alexis Tolstoy—as well as several other prominent writers, have taken full advantage.

Pushkin's drama "Boris Godunov" has been admirably rendered into English verse by Mr. Alfred Hayes. The student of Russian drama has thus been given the opportunity of judging for himself the merits of this work. He will doubtless recognize the influence of Shakespeare, whose tragedies Pushkin accepted as a model. The scenic production of "Boris" is an extremely difficult task, as twenty-four changes of scenery are required if the play is to be produced as it is written. "Cuts," on the other hand, such as are universally applied to Shakespearean plays, would appear to the Russian public an inadmissable sacrilege. Some of the scenes are very short indeed. But the amount of dramatic movement and significance which Pushkin succeeds in putting into a few lines is, perhaps, unequalled even in Shakespeare's plays. Thus in the last scene there are but twenty-five lines. And yet it is a drama in itself, with a strong touch of truly Maeterlinckian suggestiveness, offering boundless possibilities to a talented stage-manager.

Count Alexis Tolstoy, one of Russia's foremost poets, belonging to a later generation than Pushkin, is the author of a trilogy in verse, "The Death of Ivan the Terrible," "Tsar Feodor," and "Tsar Boris." Having made a care-

ful study of the history of Russia of the period preceding the so-called "Troubled Times," and gained complete mastery of the language of that period, Tolstoy
gave, in the trilogy, an extraordinarily vivid picture of
the events and psychological atmosphere of Moscow at
the end of the sixteenth and the beginning of the seventeenth centuries, and some of the main characters of his
dramas are portrayed with striking vividness. Tolstoy
thus describes the basic idea of the central drama "Tsar
Feodor:" "Two parties in the state are struggling for
power—the representative of the old times, Prince
Shuiski, and the representative of reform, Boris Godunov. Both parties are trying to capture the weak-willed
Tsar Feodor as a weapon for the attainment of their
wishes. Feodor hesitates between the two, instead of
yielding to one or mastering both. . . . The tragic guilt
of Ivan the Terrible lay in his trampling upon all human
rights for the benefit of the power of the state. The
tragic guilt of Feodor lay in his exercise of absolute
power in spite of complete moral impotence."

This tragedy was "passed" by the censor at the end
of the nineteenth century. When the basic idea of the
drama was disclosed to the public with perfect clearness
owing to an extraordinarily gifted impersonation on the
part of the principal characters, the censor became aware
of his error of judgment, but it was too late. The public
realized that "history was repeating itself." The struggle
of the progressive and reactionary parties around a weak
Tsar was then being waged in Russia with peculiar intensity, and the weak Tsar Feodor who says, "What
a Tsar am I? It is so easy to mislead and deceive me,"
was recognized as the prototype and double of Nicholas
II. To withdraw the play would be to emphasize the
analogy. Apart, therefore, from the intrinsic merits of
the play and the very high level of the performance, the
success of "Tsar Feodor"—which was without parallel
in the history of the Russian stage—was due to a great

extent to the element of political satire which the play contained at the particular moment when it first saw the footlights.

Of the Russian Tsars who reigned in the nineteenth century, the most enigmatic and captivating personality was that of Alexander I. The legend of his escape from Taganrog, where a dying guardsman was believed to have been substituted when the Emperor was on his deathbed, and of his prolonged survival in a hard labor prison in Siberia under the name of Feodor Kusmitch, was but recently refuted upon careful investigation. History admits, however, the Tsar's secret connivance in the plot which culminated in the murder of his father, the crazy Paul I. Merezhkovsky, the contemporary Russian writer whose works are familiar to the British reader, has endeavoured to dramatize the subject. His drama "Paul I," produced in Russia after the revolution, is based upon unimpeachable historical evidence. In spite of its high literary merits, however, the play cannot be described as a masterpiece of dramatic art, and it is not likely to achieve the same success in Russia as the works of Alexis Tolstoy, Leo Tolstoy, Gogol, and Turgenev, the great masters who possessed a dramatic technique equal to their descriptive genius. As we have already said, the works of these masters form the basis and mainstay of the modern dramatic repertoire in Russia. Their novels and stories have been translated into English, some of their plays (Gogol's, Tolstoy's, and Tchehov's) have been produced in England. We should, therefore, risk entering up a path already explored by more competent critics were we to endeavor to present a detailed analysis of the plays of these authors.

One cannot but feel that the recent elemental upheaval which has shaken Russia to her very foundations throws a new light upon two works of dramatic art which may, therefore, be specially mentioned. We refer to Count Leo Tolstoy's comedy, "The Fruits of Culture," and to his drama, "The Power of Darkness."

The first of the above-named plays, as is well known, was written by the aged recluse of Yasnaya Polyana at the instance of his family *ad hoc*. There was a large gathering for a family holiday, and the young people were planning amateur theatricals. So the old Count was asked to write a farce. Never had he tried his hand at playwriting before. This, his first effort, made in jest, is as vivid a picture of the life of the Russian landowner and peasant classes as were the satirical plays of Griboyedov and Gogol. In a few strokes Tolstoy drew a good-natured caricature of the Russian "upper classes," separated from the peasants by an impassable gulf. Through the light veil of comedy, the spectator discerns the tragic substance—the birth in the "lower" strata of society, of an angry consciousness of the abnormality of existing conditions, a social order which sanctions the idleness, greed, and haughtiness of one class, and the submissiveness, need, and hard toil of the other. Common sense, in the "Fruits of Culture," is always on the side of the simple folk. "Useless"—that is the unspoken verdict of the peasant on the landlord. From the awakening of that consciousness to the consummation—the destruction of the "useless"—the distance has proved shorter than the latter ever dreamed.

In the "Power of Darkness," on the other hand, Tolstoy draws a tragic picture of the cruelty, ignorance, and callousness of the Russian peasant, born of the wretched existence which was his lot. At the same time, unlike some of the present-day Russian writers, whose professed creed has always been "love of the people," but who now declare that they "hate the peasant who is cruel and averse from progress," Tolstoy convinces us that in the soul of the most dastardly criminal there still lives the consciousness of the highest law of truth and goodness. The gradual fall of the hero of the play, Nikita, and his final moral ressurection and confession appear to us a striking prophetic symbol of the spiritual turmoil through which the Russian people is now passing.

The playwright Alexander Ostrovsky (1848-88) occupies a unique position among Russian dramatists. Unlike the Russian writers already mentioned, he was a playwright only. Of the forty odd plays he has written, tragedies as well as comedies, more than a score represent as it were the permanent element of the repertoire of every dramatic stage in Russia. In his plays Ostrovsky depicted chiefly the life of the merchant class, the petty landowners and *bourgeois* and the lower bureaucracy. In Tchehov's plays, which picture more or less the same social strata of a later period—that of the nineties of the nineteenth century—there is rarely a plot in the accepted sense of the word. Ostrovsky, on the other hand, always presents a plot which he weaves and unravels with the utmost skill; the dramatic interest is sustained until the last minute. So strange to western Europe, however, is the life described by Ostrovsky, so different the outlook and psychology of his heroes (resulting from their surroundings, customs, and class traditions) from the life which prevails in most European countries, that his plays will hardly ever gain admittance to the European stage. Ostrovsky's language, moreover, presents almost insuperable difficulties for the translator. Nevertheless, his dramas and comedies, as a whole, represent the truest and most comprehensive mirror of Russian middle-class life of the sixties and seventies of the last century. In that respect we doubt whether a parallel could be found in English dramatic literature. Had Charles Dickens written for the stage and his novels and stories been given dramatic form, his work, in importance and scope, might have been the nearest approach to Ostrovsky's.

There are several names which we should be tempted to add to the gallery of classical writers for the Russian stage whose works will never cease to form the basis of the Russian dramatic repertoire. Pisemsky, Suhovo-Kobylin, Shpazhinski, Prince Sumbatov, and others have each enriched the inheritance with works of enduring value and beauty. As for the minor writers who have come and gone, their name is legion.

For the last twenty years there has developed a tendency to dramatize classical novels, which grew with great rapidity after the prodigious success of the dramatized version of Dostoyevsky's "Crime and Punishment," produced in 1899. Since then, "The Idiot" and "The Brothers Karamazov" have also been adapted for the stage. "Dostoyevsky should have been a playwright," said a famous Russian critic after the first performance of "Crime and Punishment." "Almost every chapter of his great novels contains situations of dramatic intensity unrivalled in the works of any other Russian writer." So true is this appreciation that the skilful adaptation of Dostoyevsky's novels, and in particular of "Crime and Punishment" and "The Idiot," may truly be described as belonging to the most successful dramatic productions of the later period of the Russian theater.

Of contemporary foreign playwrights, Maeterlinck, Hauptmann, d'Annunzio, Knut Hamsun, and Bernard Shaw are those whose plays have "become naturalized" in Russia, if such an expression may be applied to works of art. Rostand, Brieux, Sardou, Bernstein, Maurice Donnay, Alfred Capus, and other French dramatists have also enjoyed a certain popularity, as well as Roberto Bracco and Marco Praga. Their success, however, has been somewhat transitory. That the cargo of modern French dramatic literature, and of the two above-named brilliant Italians, is of the nature of "perishable goods" seems incontestable. The emotional appeal is often artificial and superficial, the characters and plot are commonplace, and the superstructure of social or national conventions is so high as to dwarf the intended human fundamentals of these works.

We have thus made a rapid survey of the Russian dramatic Pantheon, from immortals to the "naturalized aliens." We have endeavored to show that in spite of the fetters of a narrow-minded censorship, and of gen-

eral political and social conditions prejudicial to the free
development of culture, the Russian genius has manifested itself, in the domain of dramatic art, in a manner
in which the Russian people may indeed take just pride,
and which offers every ground for the faith that when
normal conditions of civilized intercourse prevail once
more in that unhappy country, when the only censorship
that is consistent with the requirements of a civilized
community, namely, the judgment of an intelligent audience, remains in force instead of the arbitrary ruling of
individuals, Russian drama will continue to enrich the
treasure of world culture.   However backward Russia
may have been in statesmanship, in social and economic
development—in artistic achievement she has been precocious.   In the course of a century of semi-cultured
existence she has acquired the right to rank as an equal
among the older nations of Europe.   That this applies
to Russian music and literature the British reader recognized as soon as he became acquainted with the works
of Russia's composers and writers.   Commenting upon
Taine's "History of English Literature," Goncourt said
that Taine spoke of English literature as a man would
speak of fresh fruit who had tasted nothing but jam.
The student of Russian drama will always remain, to
a certain degree, under this disability.   A foreign language, a foreign school of acting, and a stage setting
necessarily similar to, but not identical with, that of the
native stage, are unavoidable elements which tend to
transform fresh fruit into jam—to borrow Goncourt's
expression.   The same might be surmised, of course, in
regard to the production in Russia of the masterpieces
of foreign dramatic literature.   But the educated Russian, as a rule, possesses the power of assimilation to a
greater degree than most of his fellow men in foreign
countries, and has a more extensive knowledge of the
cultural inheritance of the west.   The "jam" he produces
is therefore nearer in taste to fresh fruit than that with

which the west has hitherto been served in the guise of productions of Russian plays.

THE LITERATURE OF BOLSHEVIK RUSSIA [1]

Official Bolshevism has failed to create a literature, but near and around Bolshevism a literature has sprung up, which permits us to speak of these years as of a time of exceptional flourishing. The most interesting and characteristic group of writers, and at the same time the nearest to Bolshevism, are the Scythians or Left Social Revolutionaries. They are very characteristically Russian in the most accepted sense of the term. I would even say they were very Slav, if such general racial appellations were not deservedly suspicious. But here the word would be less obnoxious than in any other place, because of the very striking resemblance of their revolutionary mysticism to the Polish revolutionary mysticism of 1830, the Messianism of Towianski. The resemblance is manifold; as Towianski, a man of secondary literary importance, profoundly influenced the overtopping geniuses of Mickiewicz and Słowacki—so Ivanov-Razumnik becomes the teacher of men of far greater talent, Blok and Bely. Bely is as profoundly mystical as Słowacki and as romantic and dynamic in his art; though, of course, Słowacki is an incomparably greater genius. The doctrines themselves, though one is acutely national and the other is professedly international, are intimately akin. A vague and practically irreligious mysticism; the thirst for martyrdom; the belief in the cosmical character of their country's mission; the powerful attraction exercised by the Images of the Passion, and a tendency to identify the nation's agony with the agony of the Lord, a tendency often verging on blasphemy rather than on piety, are characteristics both of the Russian and of the Polish

[1] By D. S. Mirsky. London Mercury. 5: 276-85. January, 1922.

movement. But Towianski was a son of the Church of Rome, and believed in the Immaculate Conception as firmly as in the mission of the Poles. Whereas for Ivanov-Razumnik Christ is only the greatest of Lenin's forerunners and the historical church the incarnation of the forces of darkness. The thirst for martyrdom has degenerated with the Scythians into a yearning after defeat and dishonor. When Trotsky concluded the peace of Brest—that masterpiece of modern diplomacy and political foresight—the Left Social Revolutionaries clamored for what one might call parodying the French formula, *la défaite intégrale*. Russia was to be delivered armless and defenceless to the Germans, and the utter and final defeat of Russia as a nation was to be the triumph of Russia's spiritual force as a cosmic idea. And Ivanov-Razumnik, commenting on Bely's "Christ Is Risen," draws a parallel between Russia under the foot of the Germans and Christ on the Cross. But not only defeat and political degradation appeal to them, they love the moral degradation of Russia. All that which has been called by Vyatcheslav Ivanov Ahriman's Russia is to them as the manure from which must flower the immaculate lily of mystical socialism.

Some time before the revolution Blok wrote a short poem, which is worth many volumes; in short and drastic phrases he draws the Karamazov-like Russian character, exalting it to a symbol of all Russia—this mixture of drunken filth and drunken devotion—and finishes up:

> Yes, and even such, my Russia
> I love thee more than any other country.

This *amo quia odiosum,* if I may be allowed thus to paraphrase Tertullian, is extremely characteristic of the hysterical mysticism of the Scythians. But it is most certainly also in the tradition of Dostoyevsky. It is not only the old filth that they thus exalt; they have no illusions as to the high moral character of their friends the Bolsheviks. "Twelve" is much more obviously a hideous portrait of the red guards than a glorification of their unconscious mission. And in "Christ Is Risen" Bely explicitly says: "We are robbers and bullies." And he thus describes the victory of the Bolsheviks:

A Browning explodes in the air with red laughter. The body of a blood-besmeared railwayman falls under the rolling thunder. He is carried by two miscreants. Somebody is being killed. But the engines answer to the cries and tears and sing in chorus about the fraternity of peoples.

It is more like a Jewish prophet glorifying the Assyrian than a European exalting the victory of his party. There is something extremely unhealthy in this love for things professedly hideous and wicked, unchristian and unmanly. But there can be no doubt of their profound, sincere, hysterical love of revolution and of Russia. It may be possible even that they love Russia more than revolution, and no Russian heart is unmoved when we hear Bely exclaiming:

Russia, Russia, Russia,
Messiah of the days to be;

or Blok threatening our western neighbors:

You are millions; we are clouds, and clouds, and clouds—
try and fight us;

and then with something of the savage lust of the gorilla:

Will it be our fault if your skeleton cracks in our heavy, caressing paws?

The national and Christian current of Russian thought, as opposed to the main international and humanitarian stream, was rapidly gaining in importance for several years before the war. The elect were becoming orthodox and patriotic and leaving the agnosticism and socialism of the nineteenth century to the half-educated classes. The enthusiasm that followed the outbreak of the war seemed to prove that the idea of country had won the nation. But this enthusiasm was short-lived, and the half-educated class remained the bulwark of internationalism. Still in one way or another all the more cultured part of the nation was gained by these new forms of thought. We have seen the forms taken by nationalism in the poetry of the Scythians, and a very similar doctrine is that of Merezhkovsky, though he himself is as violently anti-Bolshevik as he was fiercely anti-monarchist. He regards Bolshevism as a wrong turn in Russia's way to the revolutionary Damascus, but he is as convinced as Ivanov-Razumnik that Russia's mission is the revelation of a mystical socialism. But a more important group of writers, both from a literary and from a philosophical point of view, are those who were united round the *Landmarks* and the *Russkaya Mysl* and whose spiritual genealogy goes back to Vladimir Solovyëv.

They are all very different—Struve, a journalist, an economist, and a practical politician; Berdyayev, a metaphysician comparable with Bergson; Bulgakov, an economist and a divine; Vyatcheslav Ivanov, a great poet, an exquisite stylist in prose and one of our most learned classical scholars; but their common feature is their love for historical Russia and their identification of the destinies of Russia with the destinies of the Russian Church. Except Struve, who is a positive politician and a very remarkable historian of economics, all these writers would be strange and difficult reading to a foreign reader. One must be at home with the ideas of the Slavophiles, of Dostoyevsky and Solovyëv to understand their mode of thought, their symbolism and their historical philosophy. Bulgakov's book of dialogues, "At the Feast of the Gods," which was written between the peace of Brest and the downfall of Germany, and which is, I think, being translated into English, is a fair specimen of their work. In these dialogues he tries to understand the phenomenon of Bolshevism from various standpoints of Christian thought. Struve's "Reflections on the Russian Revolution" is a much more secular book; but Struve also analyses Bolshevism *sub specie æternitatis*. This metaphysical attitude toward Bolshevism enables these writers to take it very seriously, and not dismiss it in a few easy formulas. As a matter of fact, Russian mystic philosophy had always foreseen the advent of Bolshevism, and this is especially certain in the case of Dostoyevsky. I have already mentioned the symbolism of these writers. This symbolism as regards Russian history was perhaps most lucidly and simply developed by Vyatcheslav Ivanov in an article published just before the revolution. He distinguishes three leading spirits in the history of Russia, or rather three aspects of Russia; Lucifer's Russia, which is the spirit of revolt, reason, and earthly perfection—from Peter the Great to the best of the revolutionaries; Ahriman's Russia, the spirit of sloth, lust, and cruelty; and Holy Russia. Historically, Holy Russia was always entangled in the meshes of Ahriman; but Bolshevism is the alliance of Ahriman and Lucifer. These conceptions are at the base of the most remarkable poetical work produced during these years beyond the Scythian group—the poetry of Maximilian Voloshin. From this poet we could hardly have expected such an achievement. A man of wide but essentially cabinet culture, he has suddenly caught hold of the very nerve of Russian history and of Russian mystery. Quite unexpectedly he has become a great poet. The great figures of Russian history have become in his hands eternal and undying symbols of the elemental forces which rule Russia. The Pseudo-Demetrius, Razin and Peter the Great acquire the stature of nature-myths. His verse has become perfectly adequate, simple, full-weighted, and terse. And he has found piercingly beautiful words to speak of Russia, the bride who threw away all the wealth accumulated by generations of kings and

delivered herself to the robber and the thief, put fire to her houses and crops, destroyed her ancient home, and went forth humiliated and a beggar, and a slave of the vilest slave.—*Holy Russia.*

This is not the rejoicing in disgrace of Blok and Bely. It is a firm faith in the purifying and sanctifying power of the fires of purgatory, and also a deep conviction that all the kingdoms of this world are not worth the Kingdom of Heaven.

In 1917 and 1918 an attitude of disgust toward the Russian people was prevalent among the non-Bolshevik part of the nation. Then Voloshin wrote his terrible prayer that Russia should be punished for her treasons and crimes. "Send us the German from the west, the Mongol from the east." But "Holy Russia" ends very differently:

Shall I dare throw a stone at thee, shall I not understand thy passionate and delirious fire? Shall I not go on my knees before thee, my face in the mire, blessing the print of thy bare foot— thou—homeless, and drunken Russia, thou fool in Christ?

That previous attitude of disgust and shame is gone for good. It may be sweepingly said that an exasperated and exclusive nationalism is the unexpected product of the revolution, and this in all parts. In Soviet Russia this hostility to the foreigner is bred by the isolation in which the country is kept by the powers on one side and by the prevalent part of the aliens in government on the other; among the emigration it is fostered by the continuous intercourse with foreigners, whose hatred and fear of Russia is displayed at every moment. With hardly any exception all Russians today believe in their intrinsic superiority over the rest of mankind. In Soviet literature this conviction is nowhere more strikingly displayed than in Blok's Scythians. In emigration literature two books are especially characteristic, the more so that they come from widely different parts: "The Destinies of Russia," by Bunakov, one of the leaders of the Social-Revolutionary Party, and "Europe and Humanity," by Prince Nicholas Trubetskoy, son of the philosopher Prince S. Trubetskoy, and now Professor at the University of Sofia. Trubetskoy (who, by the way, has written an excellent preface to Wells' "Russia in the Darkness," a masterpiece of scathing sarcasm) attacks the whole of western civilization, affirming that judged only by standards military or mercantile can "Romano-German" culture be considered superior to the civilizations of the east. As to moral standards the Europe of Versailles is in no way superior to the Hottentots or the Australian aborigines.

Bunakov in a much more serious and less paradoxical manner tells us how all the great spirits of Russia had the sense of Russia's superiority over the west, and proves that Russia is the only nation capable of creating a really universal civilization, a civilization that would weld east and west in the way first accomplished by the Empire of Alexander the Great.

This nationalism may be dangerous in many ways; it will be salutary at least in the sense of the German saying—*Mut verloren Alles verloren.* We have not lost our spirits, nor do we appear likely to lose them.

In the whole course of this survey I have not mentioned one single work of prose fiction. The fact is due neither to chance nor to neglect. Prose fiction, which had always been the pride of Russian literature, has sunk into comparative insignificance. Of our few outstanding novelists, Gorky and Sologub write little fiction, and what they do write is decidedly bad. Andreyev is dead. Ivan Bunin is by far the greatest of our living and active novelists. Every new work of his is an achievement higher than the preceding one. But though he has mixed in political polemics and written angry articles, his artistic work is always *au dessus de la mêlée.* His genius is extra-temporal, his attitude toward life that of a Brahmin or a Parnassian. The younger generations are somewhat more prolific. But the best of them, Michael Prishvin, has not published a line

for many years. Zamyatin, who roused such hopes by
his admirably terse and racy stories of provincial life,
just before the revolution, is said to have written many
remarkable stories, but they remain unpublished.

The most interesting novel depicting contemporary
Russia is thus Alexis Tolstoy's *Hozhdenié po mukam*
(Journey Through Hell), which appeared in monthly
instalments in the Parisian *Sovremmeniya Zapiski*. It
has all the qualities and all the defects of his work; an
absolute inability to tell a story and a great power of
painting character; an intimate knowledge of the Russian *intelligentsia* and a total ignorance of all that tran-
scends everyday life—war, for instance, and revolutions,
in trying to present which he pitifully fails. He has also
a peculiar liking for caricatures of living men, so in this
novel the poet Bezsonov is a scarcely dissembled caricature of Blok. His girls are sweet and healthy, but de-
pressingly the same in all his books. All said and done,
the novel is good reading, especially before you get to
the war, which is the pitfall of so many novelists.

The poorness of fiction as compared to poetry is
natural in a time when stories are spun by life and history is being made, not studied. The poet's attitude
may be only lyrical, and the novelist must either be
above the evil of the day or succumb to the whirlwind
of events. The time for narrative may come later.

What the Russian novel of tomorrow will be we can
only guess, but it is probable that it will not be like the
novel of today. It will make a fresh start.

MYSTIC LITERATURE IN THE LAND OF
BOLSHEVISM [1]

For the last few years, the most profound mystery
has veiled Russia, a mystery that should be explained,
were it only to aid in comprehending the Bolshevist men-

[1] By H. Izvolsky. La Revue de France. 1: 637-50. April 15, 1921.

ace, which weighs so heavily upon the civilized world. One must seek first to understand the soul of a people violently shaken by revolution, for Bolshevism is not merely a social and economic phenomenon, but is also— and perhaps especially—a psychological phenomenon of extreme complexity.

The mysterious soul of the real Russia is not at all incomprehensible. It is taking form, little by little, giving outward manifestations of itself, notably through the written word. There is a Bolshevist literature and (what especially concerns us here) a Bolshevist poetry. "Moscow," the Russian publishing house, is issuing in Berlin a literary review, "The New Russian Book," edited by A. S. Yashtchenko, the former professor of international law. This periodical offers a curious approach to Russian literary life under the communist régime, from which we may gain some precious information.

Russian men of letters are divided into two groups, one of which has settled itself abroad, Merezhkovsky, Bunin, Kuprin, Count Alexis Tolstoy, and others, all distinguished writers; whilst the other larger group has remained in Russia and has attached itself, more or less, to the Bolsheviki. We say "more or less," for it would be a blunder to think that all of those who live and work in Russia are of necessity active Bolsheviki. Without doubt there are Bolshevik writers, pure and simple, who serve the cause of the Soviets; but there are also literary men who live and write under the new régime, which is quite another matter; and who are often kept in Russia by force. Finally, there are those to whom Bolshevism is a bad dream, a passing cloud, but who live within themselves, afar from all political agitation. We might accuse them of indifference; Dante would have placed them between Heaven and Hell.

In spite of the appalling economic conditions of Russia, the lot of literary men is relatively pleasanter than that of the other subjects of the republic of Soviets. No doubt because they have no desire whatever to imitate Plato's example, the Bolsheviki have not driven the poets from the communist paradise and have, quite the contrary, offered them refuge and protection. But, on the other hand, they keep a vigilant watch upon all their literary work, and the liberty of the press is dead in Russia, along with all the other liberal "prejudices" of the old order of things. A play of Gorky's was withdrawn from the repertory because of its anti-revolutionary character, and it is the group of so-called "Proletarian poets" who enjoy all the favors of the government. "Proletarian poets," "imaginists," "Scythians"—thus are the cenacles of the Bolshevik Parnassus entitled. This has aided an extraordinary poetical flowering during the last few years. Professor Yashtchenko writes:

In an epoch when the complete absence of indispensable books, of paper, of scientific, historical and political works, is making itself felt, the most useless "articles of luxury" in literature are thrown upon the market in the form of lyric poetry. Is it because the popular mind, unable to give itself to quiet reflection, overflows into sentiments which seek expression in songs at once so melancholy and so dreamy? Or else, have we come back to the earliest springs of our historic life, and, after everything has been lost, does nothing remain to us but fairy stories and lyric poetry, the initial manifestations of a people's consciousness?

It is important to observe that a great number of the poets celebrated even before the revolution have remained in Russia—such men as Gumilev, Alexander Blok, Vyatcheslav Ivanov, Serge Gorodetsky, Valery Bryusov, Anna Ahmatova, Andrew Bely, whose names have survived through Bolshevism as they have survived through the old régime in Russia, because they belong to literature and not to politics. Unfortunately, we have very little information as to their present activity. The greater part are at work for the literary section of the Commissariat of Public Instruction, or for the anthology called "Universal Literature," which Gorky is editing and which publishes translations of foreign masterpieces.

Novaya Ruskaya Knyiga (The New Russian Book) gives a list of the principal translations, as well as the titles of new works which have appeared or which are to appear in Russia.

Some Russian publishers installed at Berlin, have recently issued several little collections of prose and verse, signed by five Bolshevik writers, of whom four are poets. These are Alexander Blok, Andrew Bely, Serge Esenin, and N. Kluyev, whom Yashtchenko calls the "Revolutionary Slavophiles," and who have formed a revolutionary group of "Scythians," wishing to imply by their name that they defy the classic civilization of the Occident. Add to these names that of Ivanov-Razumnik, fanatic communist theorist, commentator on the work of the Scythians and their eloquent defender. Ivanov-Razumnik is earnest and genuine, and gives evidence in his writings of a fairness and a candor which are not discoverable among the Scythians. However, he is not an adept in official Bolshevism, and is even perceptibly at some distance from it. Thus he writes:

> The dictatorship of a party, the grasp of iron, already begin to make themselves felt and cannot continue. I know that terror within and without is not my pathway, but what road am I to follow? The only road: not to wash my hands of it, not to consecrate to destruction the evolution of the true revolutionary socialism. The press is destroyed—let us fight for the resurrection of the press! Political foes are hurled into prison—let us demand proceedings and judgment for them! We must make straight again the line of revolutionary action, which Bolshevism, drunk with victory, runs the risk of distorting. Did I not understand Lenin to say that as soon as the social revolution has triumphed in Russia, a world war ought to commence, since it is only at the point of the bayonet that the Idea can be carried throughout the world? I believe in that Idea, but I do not believe in bayonets' points. I am against all war, and so against revolutionary war.

It is with complex and troubled feelings that we have leafed through these little volumes of Russian poetry, which open strange vistas into the Bolshevist world. In the first place, there is "Twelve" by Alexander Blok, a poem written in 1917, that is to say, at the dawn of

Bolshevism, which is certainly the strongest of work and the most faithful reflection of the Russian revolutionary period. No tinsel fripperies adorn this red epic, sober-hued and realistic, ironic and bitter. The twelve are red guards who, with bayonets fixed, are making a revolutionary march. A snowstorm whirls about their steps, balls whistle in the deserted streets, and death is all about them. They push on, feverish, uneasy, going from love to slaughter, from ecstasy to blasphemy. On the snow the corpse of a woman—slaughtered by one of the twelve.

A little farther on, the twelve meet a bourgeois, "*the* bourgeois*,*" attended by a mangy dog with thick fur and a short tail. The poet explains to us that this famishing dog, the dog without a kennel, who rubs himself against the bourgeois, is the "old world," at the dawn of the new Russia. Rifle-fire is always crackling.

> Trakh-takh-takh! The echo after
> Rolls through houses, rattling how,
> And the storm with rumbling laughter
> Rings and jingles in the snow. . .
> With that sovereign step they're walking
> At their heels the hungry hound;
> While in front, the red flag bearing,
> In the snow storm undetected,
> From the bullets free, protected,
> Walks with soft and gentle measure,
> Through the snow's clear pearly treasure,
> In a wreath of roses white,
> Jesus Christ—the guiding light.

What is the meaning of this mystic end to a realistic poem—the appearance of Christ's face beneath the hail of rifle balls, amid the raucous cries of the soldiery? What did Alexander Blok want to say when he placed the Christ at the head of the twelve? By what supreme irony, or by what morbid exaltation of a faith reversed, has he placed between His hands the bloody standards?

Yet it is strange that this face of Christ seems to haunt not only the author of the "Twelve," but the other Bolshevist poets as well. They wish the Christ

to be with them, although at bottom they hate Him.
They wish to enlist Him, too, and to push Him before
them on the "revolutionary march."

So the communist thinkers have not escaped from the
mysticism of their race. In their very denial of all the
ancient dogma, they still have need of a dogma of some
sort, and they find in socialism less the reversal of economic and social values, than the reversal of moral values.
Bolshevism, for them, is not a political system, but a
religion, the necessary evolution of Christianity, something which is to acquire in the eyes of humanity the
same mystic value as the teachings of the Gospel.

It seems to us, however, that these thinkers have
not known how to create a new God, and that their ges-
tation of their philosophic idea has not been long enough
nor serious enough. In fact, they are content to transform God into their own image, and to stick a red flag
into His hand. It is not a new Christ, whom they
adore, but rather Anti-Christ, whom they had need to
invent. Serge Esenin, who is the chosen prophet of this
new revelation, cries, "Lord, I shall make Thee different!" or again "May my voice devour Thee, O my Lord!"
It is always by means of violence that he proceeds, and
this is what he tells us:

> I do not seek Redemption
> Through his Passion and his Death;
> Mine is another teaching
> That shall outlast the stars.
>
> I stretch hands toward the moon,
> I shall crush it like a nut.
> I seek no reachless heaven;
> I want no falling snow.
>
> .   .   .   .
>
> A new Faith, without Cross or Passion.
>
> .   .   .   .
>
> Rejoice, Zion,
> Scatter thy light.
> A new Nazareth
> Flowers in heaven.

> A new Savior, riding on an ass,
> Comes from the Universe.
> Our Faith is Force,
> Our truth ourselves.

We seem to have heard that before!

Esenin promises to the faithful a new city where dwells "The God of the living," a terrestrial paradise—that is to say, a communist paradise. And this is how Ivanov-Razumnik sums up the new religion:

The poet has perceived a new universal Word, and it is in its name that he battles against the ancient God, as once Jacob wrestled in the desert. There is no blasphemy here, but a fight with God, and every fight with God is a divine confirmation of a new Word. In Christianity, the sufferings of one man are to save the whole Universe. In the Socialism which is coming, by the suffering of the Universe, every man is to be saved.

Ivanov-Razumnik is a genuine fanatic; he wants to save the face of Bolshevism at any price, and to explain to perplexed outsiders the prophecies of Esenin, but the essence of these prophecies seems to escape his candor. He does not recognize that Esenin is a false mystic, and that, if he struggles with God, it is by a destructive rather than a creative instinct.

"Lord, I will make Thee otherwise," and "I want no reachless Heaven"—these are the dominant ideas of this strange philosophy. To found a paradise on earth, to set the ideal close to the soil, to bind Heaven to earth by a ladder which our poet may scale without effort or fatigue—such is the dream of Esenin.

The prophet, however, is better endowed for poetry than for mystic revelations. His work is extremely original, sometimes strong, always bold. There are unexpected glittering passages, which strike and delight the imagination. The insolent defiance which he throws out to God, is invested with an almost Biblical solemnity. These are the strange images of a very Bolshevist Cosmos through which Esenin passes, walking "head down, on the clouds, as on a field of wheat":

With the scream of the tempests' dread,
I'll break in two the Earth, our Mother,
The way one crumbles bread.
The thin Equator I'll erase,
Beneath my knees' fierce rubs,
And four Suns shall go rolling
Down hill like golden tubs,
Their golden hoops a-shaking,
Whilst a Universe is breaking.

I crush the earth beneath my feet,
As great Tsar Peter did.
In a maudlin trance
I make death dance
To drunk accordion music.

In spite of such an unchained Scythian gait, Esenin undeniably has much talent. But he has no grace, tenderness, nor true emotion. This is, perhaps, too much to ask of a barbarian—for Esenin is a barbarian—and a violent individual who proposes to take Heaven by assault.

The thought of Andrew Bely is less dull, his mystic symbolism less disturbed than that of Esenin. In his view, Russia has been crucified, buried, left for dead. But she must revive, she is reviving, and soon she is to save the world.

This idea of Russia as a national and religious Messiah is not new. It has already been expressed by the Slavophiles of the old régime, and, in magisterial fashion, by Dostoyevsky. He, too, was proclaiming the mystic calling of Russia when he wrote: "He who believes in Russia, knows that she will endure absolutely all things, and will remain in essence the same Holy Russia that she has always been." "Holy Russia," "land of miracles," "the Russian people," "the bearer of God," that is the idea which incessantly reappears in Russian literature of the nineteenth century. Bely merely takes it up again to transform it according to the Bolshevist dogma, for to him Bolshevism is the dazzling confirmation of this conception of Russia as the redeemer of humanity.

> Russia, my country,
> Spouse clad in sunlight,
> Toward whom rise
> All men's eyes—
> Clearly I see thee,
> Bearing God,
> O'er the serpent triumphant.
>
> .   .   .   .   .
>
> In my breast something stirs
> With keenest emotion.
>
> .   .   .   .   .
>
> Sons well-beloved,
> 'Christ is arisen!'

"The Christ is Risen," by Andrew Bely, is a powerful poem, infinitely more powerful and profound than the incantations of an Esenin. Some of these lines cause the soul of a veritable mystic to stand out in sharp relief:

> A sadness, divine and intense,
> Falls like the violent blows
> Of Heaven upon the immense
> Globe, heavy and old.

But this sounds the hour of resurrection:

> Russia, today a bride,
> Receive the news of Spring!
> Salvation!   Resurrection!
> All things, all, all
> Proclaim what could not be.
>
> The screaming locomotive
> That flies along the rails
> Repeats, 'Long may it live—
> 'The Internationale!'
>
> The misty drops of rain,
> The telegraphic wires
> Cry, and repeat again,
> 'The Internationale!'

Thus does the sacred joy of Bely break out. This holy joy, one must admit, is inexplicable in view of the present spectacle of ravaged and bloody Russia. Is it not rather a burial than a resurrection? It is precisely this optimism, pushed to the extremes of exaltation which is most striking among the Bolshevist poets.

What! Not a cry of anguish? Not a note of doubt? And is the Bolshevist world, after years of terror and famine, really the best world, in the eyes of the Esenins and Belys?

It is with a feeling of deep relief that we have run through the last of these little miscellanies, signed by the poet Klyuyev. Klyuyev is of humble peasant origin, and his work breathes the odors of the earth, of the fields, and of labor. His "Songs of the Izba" and "Earth and Iron" reveal a poet at once profound and tender, who makes one think of Robert Burns. Un-luckily, it is almost impossible to translate his work, essentially Slavic and rustic, which holds all the riches of the popular language of Russia, which remain un-known to the writers of the city. In these poems, still so close to primitive inspiration, reappear the sweet and humble landscapes of peasant Russia, the wood village, the *izba* (hut), and all its familiar surroundings. It is the shut-in, dreamy life of the long winter evenings about the big stove, it is the glebe moistened by the rains, gilded by the sun-light. It is all the mystery of the Russian country-side, which pursues its existence, scarce-ly troubled by the distant revolutionary turmoil of the great cities. Klyuyev surely has the stuff of a true poet, perhaps of a great poet.

Here, under the roof of the *izba,* there are neither shrieks of pride nor delirious prophecies. The Russia of the farms, plunged in its dream, prays, meditates, works and sows. In the midst of the Russian chaos, the peasant, perhaps alone, retains his sober judgment and recognizes the true value of simple things. Is not here the place to look for salvation? For the poems of Klyuyev give an impression of freshness and blessed harmony—infinitely blessed after the phantasmagoria of the "Scythians."

Klyuyev has a delicate and lively imagination, like a child's. The world of the *izba* is for him a marvellous world, warmly colored, where everything, even to the familiar animals, even to the utensils of the humblest home, is filled with a mysterious life and seems to speak with him or to make him magic signs. As in "The Blue Bird" of Maeterlinck, things have names of their own, and play a helpful rôle in the life of man. At the death of his mother, like himself a peasant, Klyuyev felt a profound nostalgia descend upon the *izba*:

The stove is an orphan. The saucepan, all in tears
Keeps murmuring to the andirons, that its mistress is dead.
The pail sighs to the mop-cloth,
For the porch is washed no more.
Oh, how joyously the water used to ripple when she cleaned!
The lad, squatting behind the stove, prattles,
He says that the cemetery is pleasant to the newcomer.
And that the crosses of the tombs murmur amongst themselves,
Telling of the Eternal, which has no name.

The *izba* frowns, and a window
Transfixes the moist obscurity
With its eye of lead.

The death of this peasant mother reappears in another poem of Klyuyev's. In his eyes, as in those of all the Russian people, death is no menacing phantom, but a kindly visitor; for death is the natural and necessary passing of a gray and humble life to a marvellous life, a happy migration to the land of fairy tales. This is again the *izba*, which

Breathes like a fir-tree, bent beneath the snow.
In every corner, clustered shadows whisper,
And from its stall the lean calf lows.
Blown by the wind, past garden flower beds,
A handkerchief goes tossing, like a veil.
The silence groans.

The cranes afar are crying:
We bear the mother soul beyond the seas,
Where by the Dawn the surging Sun is cradled.
There dwell the saints, Dmitry, Nikolay, Vlas,
The holy ones, clad in their glorious robes.
And in a cope of living colors, there Saint John
Lays Jordan's water on their holy heads.

The paradise of Klyuyev is hardly an abstract heaven, and his saints clad in glorious colors, are real flesh and bone. For him, as for every soul at once mystic and naive, heaven is a transcendent image of the earth, or rather (and this is perhaps the essence of the true Russian mysticism) the earth is a confused image of heaven, a formal image of a real and better world, which already appears. The earth is holy, the *izba* is holy, the work of the laborer is holy, for these are all symbols. And nature herself is a holy temple, full of the Divine mystery, a

> Forest, where each branch is like a taper,
> Where from the pine the Cherubin
> Sets altar lights a-gleam, and gives
> Communion to all those that hear the voice
> Of the all-mother, guardian of the tombs.
> There, as I laid my kiss on Youth,
> I heard Dawn answer Dawn,
> I heard the storm-cock sing,
> Whilst like a swarm of Stars,
> The Face rose with a thousand eyes.
>
> Time drops a veil, obscures the image
> But since that time flute music rings about me.
> I have seen the face of Sound and have known music,
> Setting my lips to flowers,
> Far from your mildewed lips.

In these lines the poet of the *izba* and the soil rises to a very high pitch of inspiration, and seems to live, like a true seer, in a luminous world of his own of an intense spirituality. This subtle spiritualizing of the earthly life appears equally in a little poem of Klyuyev's dedicated to the peasant's horse:

> The sledge is wise, the cart has wit,
>   For all its wooden dress,
> The little horse has many a thought
>   He never dares express.
>
> At the vespers of the cattle,
>   Within the stable's shade,
> The murmur of the ewes is sad
>   As that the wind has made.

> Like the repentant publican's
>   Is the little horse's sigh,
> "My Father and my Lord, my God,
>   Now near to Thee am I?"
>
> "The dreams I dreamed beneath the yoke
>   Shall they be all in vain?
> Shall I drink waves celestial
>   To ease me of my pain?"
>
> Poor jade, companion of my life,
>   Toiler in lowly things,
> You are the symbol of all God's
>   Horses with flaming wings.
>
> Labor is joyous, harvest rich,
>   Your toil, from dawn to dark,
> Has made our common stable grow
>   A likeness of the Ark.

A beam from heaven seems to brighten the wooden village of Klyuyev, a ray of consolation and of hope. Is it not from this very humble Ark that the Russia of tomorrow may come forth?

Such is the present state of literature in the land of the Soviets. In writing these lines, we have made a great effort for impartiality in measuring (so far as a contemporary can) the true rank of these writers. In spite of the goodwill of the Maecenases of Moscow, it seems hard to believe that the age of Bolshevism can ever be regarded as a golden age in Russian art or literature. For the creation of a perfect art, there must be a people who have attained a perfect equilibrium, whether spiritual or intellectual, an equilibrium which is the culminating point of a powerful and definite evolution.

Fortunate peoples have no history; but have unfortunate peoples an art? In any event, how can this equilibrium essential to the development of art and creative thought be had in a country which is in an epoch of violent transition? Bolshevist poetry is a strange flower, sometimes captivating, but it is a flower soon withering, precocious and diaphanous, overwhelmed with bitterness,

burnt by the torrid breath of a gigantic brasier. Flower
of madness, flower of pride, too, for the Bolsheviki have
colored it with all their hopes.

Yet it happens, sometimes, that a fire passing through
a forest spares by a miracle some solitary tree, which
in the midst of disaster, goes on with its normal growth,
happy and necessary. So it is that in this troublous literature, in which resound "the drunk cries of the accordion," a word, a thought, a harmonious and powerful
rime surging suddenly out, brings to the reader a precious
and subtle joy. The accordion of the red prophets has
not been able to deaden the mysterious tones of that
flute which haunts the memory of Klyuyev. Russian
literature is not dead and will not know death, for it
is the emanation of a national genius, infinitely more
profound than Bolshevism. One need not partake of
the somewhat superficial optimism of Bely, or wish
to prophesy after the fashion of Esenin, in order to
pronounce here with confidence the word, "resurrection."

LANGUAGE AND FOLKLORE OF UKRAINA [1]

An Englishman who wanted to give his fellow countrymen an idea of the beauties of the Ukrainian tongue
once advised his readers to combine, mentally, classical
Greek with modern Italian. But probably neither Greek
nor modern Italian, with their softer tones, possess the
force of Ukrainian, a force derived, says Vladimir
Stepankovsky, a well-known authority, from its strange
consonantal combinations and an abundance of the deep
sounds of y (ui) and u. It is this peculiarity which has
made a modern English authoress speak of its "haunting
musicality." One of its distinguishing features is its
unparalleled aptitude for forming diminutives. They
are made not only from substantives, as in other
languages, but also from adjectives, adverbs, and even

[1] By G. F. Lees. Athenaeum. 4630: 266-8. June, 1918.

verbs. This gives that singular charm referred to by
P. Chevalier in 1781: "The language of Ukraina is very
beautiful, abundance of diminutives and pretty fashions
of elegant speech making it very delicate."

Among its other peculiarities, the fleeting accent of
its words, as well as an aptitude for its deliberate extension or cutting down of the number of syllables in the
majority of its grammatical forms, together with the
retention of some very archaic features, as the dual
number, must be mentioned. These qualities make the
language wonderfully adapted to verse, and the possibilities of its expressiveness and harmony when handled by
a native are almost unbounded.

Another very important feature of the Ukrainian
tongue is its curious homogeneity. Spoken by forty
million souls, in an area larger than Germany, it exhibits
no traces of dialect or differences in pronunciation worth
mentioning. Even the fact that the nation has been dis-
membered for centuries has not affected this remarkable
unity of its language. A Cossack of Kubagne, the most
eastern member of the race, when talking to a Galician
will hardly notice any difference in the other's speech.

A natural question that may occur to students of
language is how far Ukrainian is removed from Polish
and Russian, its two neighboring languages. But to
those who do not know at least one of these languages
it is very difficult to define exactly the extent of its re-
moteness, unless one employs a comparison. The position of Italian with regard to French and Spanish may
illustrate very nearly the relationship between Ukrainian, Polish and Russian.

These remarks refer to the spoken Ukrainian
language, the literary use of which began to be considerable from no later date than the end of the
eighteenth century, when a rich and varied vernacular
literature sprang up. Until then, in Ukraina as in other
Slavonic countries, the literary means was supplied by
the so-called Church-Slavonic, the rôle of which in east-

ern Europe may be compared to the part played in the west by Latin. As is well known, Church-Slavonic was a scholastic product, artificially evolved under the influence of Greek, from the Slav dialects of Macedonia.

The use of the spoken tongue as the literary language of Ukraina is gaining fresh ground every day and triumphantly marching toward complete victory. Just before the outbreak of the World War there were no fewer than several hundred daily, monthly, and weekly periodicals published in it. Thousands of books in Ukrainian were published yearly. In the local parliament, or Diet, of Galicia the debates were carried on in Ukrainian and Polish. Ukrainian became the language of the state railways, the post office, the courts, and the administrative offices of the province. Public instruction in the elementary, secondary, and high schools was, and is still, carried on in Ukrainian. But before the revolution the Ukrainian language was in Slavonic Russia banned from every official or public use, and was barely suffered to appear in the press and literature of the day. Even such employment of it is of recent date, since Ukrainian was strictly prohibited until 1905, the year that saw the decreeing of the Russian Constitution. Up to that time its use was confined by a Ukase to poetry and tales, and even then it had to be spelled in accordance with the Russian mode of spelling. It is a curious fact that the Bible in vernacular Ukrainian, published, after its prohibition, by the British and Foreign Bible Society, was regarded as a revolutionary publication, and anyone found in possession of a copy was punished accordingly.

It was the appearance of a great poet in the middle of the last century—a man who dared to write in the spoken language of his country—that solved at a stroke the problem of the future literary language of Ukraina. This writer was Taras Shevtchenko, the centenary of whose birth was celebrated in 1914 in all the towns and cities of Ukraina, and especially at Kiev and Lwów.

> Dig my grave and raise my barrow
> By the Dnieper-side
> In Ukraina, my own land,
> A fair land and wide.
> I will lie and watch the cornfields,
> Listen through the years
> To the river voices roaring,
> Roaring in my ears.

So sang the exquisite poet who, as has been well said by Mrs. E. L. Voynitch, whose admirable translation I quote, "has done for the Dnieper country what Burns did for Scotland." [1] His wish, written in the disciplinary brigade, in the first or second year of his martyrdom at the hands of those who accused him of "composing in the Little Russian tongue verses of a most abominable character," was carried out. There on the banks of the mighty and beautiful river, in view of Kiev and the Steppes, he lies. [2]

There is no need to relate once more all the incidents in Taras Shevtchenko's dolorous life. They have been given in sufficient detail in Mrs. Voynitch's little volume. Suffice it to say that these six masterpieces sum up a whole life of misery and shattered hopes, while at the same time they express the writer's undying love for his "dear lost Ukraina."

A Ukrainian never forgets his native land. However far away he may travel to the north of Russia, however long he may live away from his homestead, his thought always returns to Ukraina, the banks of the Dnieper, and the Steppes. The songs of his native land are ever singing in his heart.

These folk songs, many of which have now been

[1] "Six Lyrics from the Ruthenian of Shevtchenko." Rendered into English verse with a biographical sketch by E. L. Voynitch. Elkin Mathews. 1911.

[2] The poet, in 1847, was arrested on a charge of belonging to a seditious body called the Brotherhood of SS. Cyril and Methodius, and "in consideration of his robust constitution," he was sentenced to military service in the Orenburg "special" (disciplinary) brigade. He suffered many years of torture at the hands of military tyrants, until at last his heart, as he himself said, was "beggared."

translated into English by Miss Florence Randall Livesay, form a valuable section of Ukrainian literature.[1]

"Italian songs are glorious, but the singing of the Ukrainian is also a precious pearl in the common treasury of mankind," writes Paul Crath in the introduction to this collection of old ballads and songs, taken down from the lips of Ruthenian or Ukrainian immigrants in Winnipeg:

It was born out of the beauty of the Ukraina, and it is beautiful; it was born on the Steppes, and as the Steppes it is wide; it was born in battles, and it is free; it was born of the tear of a lonesome girl, and it rends the heart; it was born of the thought of the Kobzars, and its harmonies are pregnant with thoughts—this is Ukrainian song.

Rudansky, Vorobkyevitch and Fedkovitch are also singers of Ukraina. Though of lesser importance than the great poet of the Ukrainian movement for autonomy, they have written many poems which are treasured throughout their country. Fedkovitch, whose work is marked by great lyrical beauty, first wrote in German, but on returning to his native Bukovina, to find that he had become famous, he followed the advice of some well-known patriots to write in Ukrainian. His first sixteen poems in that language were published in 1861.

Turning to Russian writers, we see what a debt they owe to Ukraina. Ukrainian folk songs have been largely drawn upon by both authors and composers, Russian as well as Polish. The chief person to stamp his individuality on the Russian literary language and literature was Nikolay Gogol, whose style of writing—best seen in "Taras Bulba," "The Cloak," and that inimitable tale, "How the Two Ivans Quarreled"—is typically Ukrainian. It should be noted that Gogol's great ambition throughout his literary life was to write a ponderous history of Ukraina. He studied much toward that end, he made innumerable notes, but never got beyond his

[1] "Songs of Ukraina: with Ruthenian Poems." Translated by Florence Randall Livesay. Dent & Sons. 1916.

Introduction. However, his investigations had the result
of focusing his attention on an inexhaustible source of
material, some of which he used to very telling effect in
"Evenings on the Farm Near the Dikanka."

In "Taras Bulba" we find that Gogol had noted all
the characteristics of the Ukrainian, whether of the past
or of the present; his warlike spirit, his hatred of the
Poles, his love of drinking and smoking. It was through
Taras Bulba's inordinate love of his pipe that he was
captured by the foe. At the same time this great novel
contains some of the finest descriptions of the Steppes
of Ukraina ever penned. [1]

Finally, it should be pointed out that Tchehov,
Korolenko, and Dostoyevsky were also Ukrainian by
origin.

THE LITERATURE OF UKRAINA [2]

The modern literature of the Ukraina is scarcely a
hundred and fifteen years old; it has passed through
a speedy and successful development, and is today
worthy of general attention.

It was in the eighteenth century that the Ukraina
ceased to be politically independent. In 1764 the office
of "Hetman" was abolished, and the republic of the
Ukraina on the right bank of the Dnieper was incor-
porated into the Russian Empire as "Little Russia."
Austria received a portion of the former Empire of
Halitch in 1772 and called the country Galicia. Then
in 1775 the Sitch and the Zaporog Republic on the left
bank of the Dnieper, after being destroyed, became
known as "New Russia."

The nation that had come to grief politically was
to be restored intellectually. In the year 1798 appeared

[1] "Taras Bulba: and Other Tales." By Nikolay V. Gogol. Dent &
Sons. "Everyman's Library."
[2] By Vasyl Levitsky. New Age. (London). 16: 219. December 31,
1914.

the first cantos of the "Aeneis" by Ivan Kotlarevsky.
This epic travesty ushered in the revival of Ukrainian
literature. In this work the poet set up a memorial to
his politically moribund nation by transferring the unhappy state of things in the Ukraina to the city of Troy,
and applying to the Trojans, hounded from their home,
the sympathetic features of the scattered Cossacks.
Euphonious language and a regular metrical form endowed the work with that stimulating power which was
necessary in order to arouse and renew intellectual
activity. In Poltava, where Kotlarevsky lived and
labored, there is today a monument in his honor. There
also exists a special Kotlarevsky Society, which was
founded at Lwów, and which is concerned with the cultivation of dramatic art and literature.

It was not until some decades later that Galicia,
separated politically, was awakened. In 1837 there appeared at Budim (Hungary) the *Rusalka Dnistrovaya*
(Fairy of the Dniester), a collection of Ukrainian folk-
songs, interspersed with songs by several young poets,
under the editorship of Markian Shashkevytch. It was
in 1911 that the centenary of this poet was celebrated.
Together with three young associates, N. Ustianovytch,
J. Holovatsky and J. Vahilevytch, he founded in Galicia
the first scientific and literary society that set itself the
task of furthering the development and elaboration of
the Ukrainian language and literature, in order to raise
and enlighten the Ukrainian nation.

It was even later still that the Bukovina was aroused
to fresh vitality. Here, in the year 1859, J. G. Fedkovitch began his valuable literary activity. This Austrian lieutenant, who had served with his Ukrainian
regiment in the campaign against Italy, and who at first
wrote German poems, turned his attention to his
deserted race. The poet's stories and tales, in which
he deals with idyllic lives led by his fellow-countrymen,
his love of personal freedom and the freedom of his

mountains, are worthy of comparison with the best short stories of other literatures. He also wrote a number of dramas; but, unfortunately, the greater part of his work was still in manuscript when the poet withdrew into solitude and made no further attempt to achieve literary fame. It was only a few years ago that arrangements were made to issue all his works in printed form. Four volumes, published by the Shevtchenko Society at Lwów, have already appeared, and the remaining volumes are in preparation. This poet died in 1888.

Hungary was the only country where the Ukrainian nation was in a very backward stage of its development, and took scarcely any share in the intellectual life of its members in Galicia, Bukovina and the Russian Ukraina. It may be said that the people of the Ukraina, which had been divided into four parts politically, first began to unite again intellectually about the middle of the last of expansion. This significant intellectual union was brought about by Taras Shevtchenko, the greatest Ukrainian poet. Besides his verses he also wrote "The Artist," an autobiographical novel. In this work, the curious vicissitudes of Shevtchenko, who was free only for twelve years of his life (he was first a serf for twenty-four years and later banished for a full decade into the Kirghiz steppes because of his spirited chants), are related partly in diary form, partly in the more elaborate manner of fiction. Much can be learned about Shevtchenko, the great poet, painter and martyr, by reading his lyrical verses. But his epic poems, breathing as they do the youthful fragrance of Ukrainian poetry, also deserve to be studied. In his "Bandits," he left a splendid and a true memorial to those heroes who in 1768 prepared a St. Bartholomew's Eve at Uman for their Polish oppressors, and made a final attempt to shake off the foreign yoke and to gain freedom and independence for their native country. In his ballads the Ukrainian steppe, with the magic of its landscape, and its romantic traditions, is infused with fresh life.

Thousands of Ukrainian pilgrims, like Mohammedans seeking the grave of their prophet, visit Shevtchenko's resting-place and mound at Kanev on the Dnieper, and sing and recite the stern words in their poet's bequest, which in its second clause ("Ye shall bury me, then arise, shake off the foreign yoke and purchase liberty with the blood of foes") is still striving toward fulfilment.

Since the year 1873 there has been in existence a Shevtchenko Literary Society with its centers at Lwów and Kiev. It is soon to be raised to the status of an academy, and in addition to the literary monthly *Vistnyk* (Bulletin) it also issues "Communications of the Shevtchenko Society" and arranges systematic reprints of literary monuments.

Soon after the death of Shevtchenko (February 21, 1861) Galicia became the focus of intellectual life, and assumed the intellectual leadership for a lengthy period. The guiding spirit here was Ivan Franko, who is still living. The latest instalment of the *Vistnyk* (Vol. IX. 1913) is entirely devoted to the poet Franko, as a mark of respect for a literary activity extending over forty years. Franko has issued numerous volumes of poems; in his lyrics he imitates Heine and his pessimism. In his satires he makes unmerciful attacks on all empty patriotic show and middle-class prejudices. The tendency of his works is, on the political side, liberal; from the ethical aspect, individualistic. He aims at freeing himself and his friends from all shackles. Hence he infused the patriarchal, uncorrupted literature of a primitive people with many new elements, which were very rarely constructive, and frequently only destructive. He did not always succeed in moulding his style so as to attain ease in form; often enough he was over-ruled by a predilection for the base and ugly. He brought about a period of storm and stress in the intellectual life of his nation. Nearly all the works of Franko and his great school, which eked out an existence till the end of the nineteenth century, foster radicalism and free-thought. The same is true of his tales and novels. Perhaps Franko's greatest merit lies in the fact that by his translations he made the great works of literature known to his people, and thus trained a whole generation. He translated the "Faust" and other works of Goethe, the "Don Quixote" of Cervantes, and introduced the literature of western Europe to his fellow-countrymen. To-day the inhabitants of the Ukraina hold Franko's versatile activity in high esteem, and his fiftieth year was marked by festive gatherings in his honor.

Franko's school, the so-called "Young Ukraina," remained faithful to its master by treating political and social questions in his manner. Occasionally, however, a quieter key-note was struck, as, for instance, in the peasant tales of Vasyl Stefanyk. The youngest generation has emancipated itself completely from Franko's influence, and treads its own independent paths.

THE RUSSIAN REVOLUTION AND HER ARTISTS [1]

The Russian revolution was made and led by artists and authors. Siberia was the great Golgotha of Russian æsthetic evolution. Stage, printing-shop, bookstore, picture gallery and studio were usually the feared hot-beds of the rebellious spirit. The Russian artists and writers, critics and students mirrored the sentiments, joys and sorrows of the country, and in this they differed greatly from those of Europe or America. They were all men of active life, men and women of the people, who became artists only on the urgency of their inspiration. In fact, many of the Russian artists, musicians, composers, authors, earned their living in some field of activity other than art or literature. And when they be-

[1] By Ivan Narodny. Arts and Decoration. 13: 12-13, 52. May 25, 1920.

came professionals in art, they never made out of this a trade, but kept it an ideal, a religious part of their life.

When we consider the great Russian writers, musicians and artists of the past generations, and in fact of the present, we find them all living a double life: one for their art and the other for earning their living. Glinka, the founder of the Russian school of music, was a functionary of the old régime; Musorgsky, the foremost composer of the country, was an army officer and statistician of an official bureau; Rimsky-Korsakov, the greatest musical genius of the twentieth century, was a naval officer; Vereshtchagin, the celebrated painter of battle-scenes, was an army officer and surgeon; Tolstoy considered himself a farmer and educator; Tchehov was a celebrated surgeon; Andreyev was a journalist and lawyer. Thus we can enumerate most of the great Russian artists and authors and find them all leading many-sided lives.

It gradually became a tradition in Russia that an artist or an author who did not take an active part in the question of liberty was considered a lickspit of bureaucracy. It was considered a degree of honor for an art-critic or story-writer to spend some time in jail for his radical views or revolutionary propaganda. Every one who made up his mind to become an artist or writer knew that Siberia and jail stood before him, and that eventually he would land there as a convict. But it did not scare or intimidate any one of the determined mission. Dostoyevsky, the great master of fiction, was sentenced to be executed in Petrograd, and he was already on the scaffold when the order came from the Tsar to transmute his death sentence to compulsory labor for life in Siberia, where he spent eight years. There civilization was nothing; its tragedies were played behind closed curtains. People outside of Russia heard little of them.

How sure the Russian critics and artists were of the eventual advent of revolution has been illustrated

by the startling statement made by Dimitry Merezhkovsky, one of the foremost art critics of Russia, four
years before the storm took place. This is what he
wrote in 1910:

Russia differs from the West as the eye differs from the
ear. While one organ can only see the world, the other can
only hear it. America is the absolute eye; Russia is the absolute ear; the one is purely objective, the other purely subjective.
America's sphere is utilitarian, Russia's transcendental. In
America lives Apollo; in Russia, Dionysius. America can
reason and compromise, for that reason she came out from her
revolutions with a watchword for law and constitution. America
became the absolute positive pole of action. But Russia hates
law and hates reasoning; she wants to feel everything and lives
only by intuition. For America, politics is a science; for Russia,
a religion. For that reason the coming Russian revolution will
differ greatly from the American and the French, as it will be
brought about not by economic, but by æsthetico-fanatical motives. This is most difficult for the West to understand, where
art, religion, literature and life have long become politics. Politics in Russia means religion, a belief in some superior power,
be it bureaucratic, ecclesiastic, socialistic or atheistic. The Russian municipal politics, the so-called *Zemstvo, Volost* and
Obshtchina have remained always sacred public institutions, with
a religious or æsthetic halo around them. They were just as clean
and noble as the others were corrupt. For that reason art was
cultivated and supported by all the local governments, but persecuted and watched by the national administration. In fact,
an artist with Russian *muzhiks* became a modern saint, a wizard
of beauty.

From time immemorial the Russians have considered the
æsthetic issues as the basis of all the physical systems and governments, therefore autocracy with us was an assertion of an
absolute holiness in a mystical sense. The racial traditions do
not permit us to leave that order. The rejection of an absolute cannot help being the assertion of the opposite: holiness
against holiness. Autocracy with us has been a religion, as is
our revolution. Least of all do the revolutionists themselves
realize this peculiar state of affairs. In their conception a socialist or bolshevik is a godless being. To a Russian, liberty
in its highest metaphysical sense is not a political but a religious
feeling. All the most brutal crimes of Russia's revolutionists
will be committed as fanatical acts of Inquisition.

When ultimately all historic forms of Russian government
and church will be overthrown, then in the political and religious consciousness of the people will appear such a chasm of
emptiness that to fill up the gap with the already existing forms
of Western governments, such as the constitutional *bourgeois*

republics of America or France, will be impossible. To overthrow a structure thousands of years old a shakeup like an earthquake will be needed. None of these will the Russian revolution accept. Then, what will it accept? Further lies a jump into the transcendental, a flight into the sky, the eye always looking beyond any boundaries. Russian revolution will be absolute, brutal and corrupt, as absolute as the autocracy it rejected. Its conscious empiric limit will be perhaps a kind of socialistic ecclesiasm, an unconscious mystical religious community. The dream of an average Russian, be he a *muzhik* or nobleman, is the æsthetic ideal, art and literature. The final assertion of a new religious governmentless community is a new religious consciousness and activity—a new religious uniform of personality and society, one and all—boundless freedom and boundless love. True absence of power is power of God. Russian revolution will be brought about by art and literature; art and literature only can finish and even it out. These words are enigmatical, let them remain so.

It is remarkable how this prophesy of Merezhkovsky has come true so far, and how well it explains much that is unclear to the mind of the west. Irrespective of all his aristocratic conditions and peculiar attitude of mind, Tolstoy was to Russia what Jean J. Rousseau was to France: advocator of spiritual revolution among the intellectuals. Like all the individualists of Russian revolution, Tolstoy condemned the use of force by governments. He was a great friend of the late Ernest Grosby of New York, with whom I visited the old author, and this is what he told Mr. Grosby:

Despising the political power which is founded on violence and explosives, the people have misunderstood me. The government in which I believe is that which exercises a moral authority only. Great writers and artists are to me the great high-priests and leaders of evolution, the real sovereigns, who rule, not by force of guns and armies, but by moral authority. Just as I hate a hereditary potentate, so do I hate a cheap Parliament. Government cannot improve the moral nature of man by its political laws, and brute force always defeats its object. Every law must have the sanction of the free will, for there can be no coercion of the soul.

The younger Russian writers like Gorky, Korolenko and Sologub did not like Tolstoy's preaching of revolution so explicitly, and often maintained that it would have been better for his reputation if he had died fifteen years earlier, after publishing his "Anna Karenina." Gorky said publicly: "I admire Tolstoy, but at the same time I pity him, for as a preacher he is an amateur and cannot compare with Tolstoy the artist of fifteen years ago."

Tolstoy's revolution was directed against the Greek Church and the Holy Synod, as in his case art was the coming religion of humanity. He quoted Christ just as much as he quoted Buddha and Lao Tse. Though somewhat similar to Rousseau in many traits, he differed from the great French writer in this: while the former was a destructive giant of the rationalistic school, Tolstoy remained one of the emotional æsthetic type. Rousseau's works stimulated the French people to rebellion by stirring up their reason and ambition for action, while Tolstoy's intention was to conquer every social evil by passive resistance; one was a great leader and reformer in his Latin character of influencing the will power; the other's greatness is shown in his Slavic character of influencing the feelings and emotions. However, Gorky became himself a revolutionist and is now with the Soviet government.

Russia, previous to the revolution, was a shaky social-political machine, run by a handful of politicians and bureaucrats as far as the economic side of life was concerned, but from the æsthetic point of view she was perhaps more free even than France, not to speak of England and this country. The country was in the last years so free that vaudevilles and the dramatic stage became indirectly open forums for revolutionary propaganda. Cabinet ministers, political leaders, high fuctionaries and court favorites were made into ridiculous burlesque-heroes or allegorical villains. One of the most daring operas of the pre-revolutionary era was Mme. Stassova's *Vstrepenulis* (Waked-Up), music by R. Gliere, in which the theme is a pure and simple uprising of the *muzhiks* in the village. Seventy-five per cent of the Russian revolutionary spirit was spread by the country's artists and writers. Labor played a very insignificant rôle in it until the Bolshevik forces took the leadership. For that reason the American politicians and bureaucrats cannot judge Russia after their national patterns and accept it as a fact that Russia is going through the stage of economic sickness through which they went long ago. The American colonies went through their political turmoil with a very definite political ideal in view, which the Russians do not possess. That is the trouble with the chaos which prevails in the people's minds, as they have rather hazy views of political nature; therefore the foreigners who wish to cure the Russian ills with their past pills are greatly mistaken. It would have been all right had the Russians not been a nation of the very opposite racial character, and had their dramatic-mystic dreams not driven them against the bloody wall of Bolshevism. Russia does not want to imitate the commercial west, nor the fanatic east. She is engaged in searching for some solution from her own æsthetic past, her art and literature. That is the reason for all the absurdity of her present experiments and agony. Now let us get a comprehensive picture of the kind of men who were the real founders of the Russian revolutionary movement, besides the above-mentioned few semi-revolutionary big celebrities of art and literature.

The first two pioneers of the Russian revolutionary movement in 1845 or thereabouts were Alexander Herzen and Nicholas Tchernishevsky, both the foremost literary critics and authors of their day. Graduates of the universities, men of tremendous literary talent and noble character, they were both arrested, kept in solitary confinement and then exiled. While Herzen died an exile in Switzerland, where he escaped from Siberia, Tchernishevsky died in Siberia. Their crime was revolutionary agitation, which they kept up all the time during their

banishment and imprisonment. It was their electrifying
criticism and inspiration which produced for Russia
such novelists as Turgenev, Dostoyevsky, Tolstoy,
Tchehov and the rest. Those two men are considered
as the fathers and founders of the great Russian literature and art of the nineteenth century, and at the same
time spiritual fathers of the revolution.

But perhaps more picturesque and prominent figures
than those two in the Russian movement for liberty were
Mihail Bakunin and Prince Peter Kropotkin. There
has hardly been a more dramatic figure in any other nation's history than was Bakunin. By profession an army
officer, son of a diplomat, and a graduate of the philosophic faculties of Russia and Germany, Bakunin acquired a brilliant style of writing even as a young man.
Much as he was interested in literary work, the political
situation of Europe in 1849 thrilled him more. As a
student in Germany he became interested in the German
revolution and took an active part in the Dresden uprising, where with Richard Wagner he helped to build
the barricades. It was said that he advised that the
celebrated paintings of the Dresden Gallery be placed on
the barricades, to prevent the Prussians from shooting
at them. Yielding to the superior forces, the insurgents
surrendered and Bakunin was arrested, tried and sentenced to death in 1850 at the fortress Königstein, in
Saxony. Six months later the death sentence was commuted to life-long imprisonment in the fortress. But
having been previously one of the leaders of the Austrian
uprisings, he was turned over to the Austrian government. He was tried in the fortress of Prague in 1851
and was again sentenced to death, but the sentence was
again commuted to life-long imprisonment, as Count
Orlov, the Prime Minister of Russia, requested that
Bakunin be sent over to Russia, to be tried for political
crimes he had committed there. Tsar Nicholas the
First sent him to the fortress of Schluesselburg, to be

kept prisoner there all his life. After having been for six years in solitary confinement in this fortress he was exiled to Tomsk, whence, four years later, he escaped to Japan, America and finally to London. But a year thereafter he joined the Italian revolutionists and almost started a revolution in France, from which country he was compelled to flee to Switzerland. In 1864 he met Marx in London and discussed his theories of socialism. Though Bakunin considered himself a socialist, and organized the "International Union of Social Democracy" in Switzerland, he was never an orthodox socialist of Marx's type. Bakunin in his revolutionary essays declared that he considered himself an atheist and desired the absolute abolition of classes, and stood for the political, economic and social equality of all individuals of both sexes. He advocated that the land, factories, mills, railways and public utilities should become the collective property of the community. In the eyes of Wagner, Bakunin was the most wonderful spirit of the century, and he dedicated to him his opera "Rienzi."

Prince Peter Kropotkin was the next most interesting figure among the Russian bohemians to devote himself to the cause of the people. A son of the most aristocratic family of Russia, educated with the grand dukes, and a functionary of the court, he was more interested in literature and art than he was in his brilliant political or diplomatic career. At the age of thirty, in 1872, he resigned from all official functions and went to Switzerland to study the activity of Bakunin and observe the European social conditions. Upon his return to Petrograd he joined the *Narodniki,* organized by Tchaykovsky for the purpose of educating the peasants, and was deeply absorbed in the work for a year when in 1874 he was arrested and sent to a solitary cell of the fortress St. Peter and Paul. He escaped from the military hospital by the help of a group of artists and writers, and particularly of a celebrated violinist who gave him code-signals with his music, as he played at the open window of a house opposite the hospital. When the proper moment was indicated by the violinist, Kropotkin made a dash for the gates, outside of which his friends were waiting for him in a closed carriage and fled to London. Here he began to write literary essays and revolutionary pamphlets smuggling them into Russia with the help of sailors and business men. Like Bakunin, he participated in the European revolutionary movements on a larger scale. In 1882 he was asked to help the strike of the French weavers in Lyons, and he came to France to lecture for their cause. The French government arrested him and sentenced him to five years' imprisonment. An appeal signed by Victor Hugo, Zola, Herbert Spencer, Swinburne and other prominent artists of France and England had no influence. Ultimately he was released in 1886, and since then he has made London his headquarters. Prince Kropotkin has written a number of brilliant books, essays and the memoirs of his life, most of which are published in English.

Next to these two celebrated leaders of Russian revolution, we could name at least a hundred or more heroic figures, all of whom have been either journalists, artists, novelists, dramatists or scholars. Not one of them is a professional politician or leader of a labor organization. Take, for instance, Nicholas Morozov, whose books on chemistry, physics and mathematics class him with the foremost scholars of Europe, and we find that he was kept for twenty-five years a prisoner in solitary confinement in the fortress of Schluesselburg, for his active part in the revolutionary propaganda with Nicholas Tchaykovsky. Morozov was still alive in 1917.

The participants in the Russian revolution were not only men but also women-authors, women-writers and women-artists. Miss Vera Figner and Mme. Vera Zasulitch were the most popular figures. While Mme. Zasulitch published a remarkable book on the life of the

exiles in Siberia, for which she was persecuted and
arrested, Vera Figner was the sister of the most celebrated opera singer of Russia, and an artist herself of
great talents. Young girls when they began their crusade, they were arrested and kept in solitary confinement,
the former fifteen, the latter seventeen years—and then
they were sent to Siberia, where they were kept until they
were aged, gray-haired and broken in health. Mme.
Catherine Breshkovskaya, the so-called Grandmother
of Revolution, and Maria Spiridonova are the two next
more or less conspicuous women figures of similar type.

Taken as a whole, Russia has been thrown into the
prevailing agony and chaos by her artists and authors,
students and dreamers, but not by any precalculated plans
of politicians; thus she can be saved from further sufferings by the same kind of minds and efforts, as perhaps
the immediate future may prove. Out of the ruins of
the past traditions may yet rise new life and new art, as
art has been always such a vital force of Russia's national culture for so many generations.

BOLSHEVISM AND RELIGION IN RUSSIA [1]

In the world and in man [says Merezhkovsky], *there are two
poles or contrasts: the passive and the active, the submissive
and the heroic, the eternally feminine and the eternally masculine; in the perfect man, the Man-God, these two contrasts
are combined. When the Son appeals to the Father, He is
passive, submissive, feminine: "Not my will, but Thine be
done!" When He addresses the world, He is active, heroic,
masculine: "I have overcome the world!" In the Russian
people there is only one of these two poles—the religious-
feminine. In contrast to the Western Catholic masculine
Christianity, the Eastern Byzantine Christianity is feminine.
Thus, in the Orthodox religion and the Russian people, we
have the doubly feminine, a combination of the feminine and
the feminine.*

Attractive as this crisp definition may be, there are
undoubtedly elements in the Russian nature which are

[1] By R. O. G. Urch. Atlantic Monthly. 131: 394-406. March, 1923.

not so easily explained—elements from the east, which have not fully blended with those from the west. Thus, we are often confronted with unexpected outbursts on the part of individuals, and sometimes of the whole nation, which speak of lack of balance, an absence of harmony among the ingredients that compose the Russian character. Facts may be quoted proving almost any of the theories that have been put forward to explain the attitude of the Russian people toward the process which has overthrown the autocracy of the Tsar, and is now attacking the foundations of the orthodox church; but, nevertheless, all theories are satisfactory. The average Russian may with truth be described as in a high degree either brave or cowardly, patient or impatient, honest or dishonest, tolerant or intolerant, humane or cruel. He is all this and more; he is, as has often been said before, a mixture of unblended extremes, from which the only thing that one may definitely and constantly expect is the unexpected.

The Russian writer Leskov gives a picture of a typical Russian, who sits, day in, day out, behind the counter of his little shop, spending most of his time in quietly sliding backward and forward the balls of his abacus (a counting-frame used in all Russian shops and offices), alternating this occupation by sipping his tea from a saucer which he skillfully balances on three fingers. Here he is the most harmless, the most patient creature in the world. But once or twice in a year, an uncanny feeling steals over him; he becomes restless, just as if a thousand devils were tormenting him. At last his condition becomes unbearable, and he decides to exercise his tormentors. His one and only sovereign remedy is vodka. This he takes at first with caution; but his dose increases, and he is soon engaged in a real orgy, during which he smashes up furniture, hews down trees, tortures gypsies, and destroys whatever comes in his way. When the spell passes, he goes to the public baths, and thence to the church. Here he penitently throws himself before a Holy Picture, and with his forehead pressed to the mosaic floor, confesses his sin. He rises freed from all his devils, and the next day finds him behind his counter again, with his saucer of tea balanced on his three fingers as usual.

There is little hypocrisy about the average Russian; he is one of the sincerest of men. He is childlike in his faith; and when he has confessed and been forgiven, his sin troubles him no more. He has literally laid the burden of it all on his God.

Quoting Constantine Aksakov and B. Rozanov, Merezhkovsky continues: —

The essence of Russian history is abnegation, renunciation of authority, religious anarchy within a political monarchy. Sovereignty never tempted the Russian people; the people never strove to dress itself in state authority; but by giving up this authority to its chosen sovereign, itself wished to remain in its own vital, feminine, submissive element. It is just as if the Russian people separated from itself all that it had of the masculine, and gave it up to the ruling autocrat. All that was masculine in Russia was concentrated in the Tsar. The Tsar fell, and this fell, too, leaving only the absolute feminine. Instead of conscience, remained instinct. The religious instinct of the Russian people had been deceived by orthodoxy and autocracy. The Tsar was from God; while there was a Tsar, there was a God; the Tsar ceased to exist, God also ceased to exist. This is why the transition to complete atheism was as easy as going into a bath and bathing in new waters: unchristening was accomplished in a moment.

There may be much truth in what Merezhkovsky says, but all his absolutisms hardly seem to be borne out by historical facts.

The Tsar was nominal head of the orthodox church. He fell in March, 1917; and there is no evidence to show that the church fell too, or that any considerable anti-religious movement became general among the people. On the whole, the churches continued to attract worshipers; the people performed their devotions before Russia's many shrines; in Moscow, foot-passengers, cabmen, the fares in street-cars, continued to bare their heads and cross themselves on passing a church.

These were the ordinary outward signs of religious feeling, and, as such, may have been mere habit, which could not be thrown off in a moment; they are not conclusive proof that the heart of the people had remained unchanged. But, surely, if there had been a general change in the people's faith, these symbols of religion would gradually disappear, and there would arise some hostility toward the church, which had proved such a deceiver. There were no great outbursts against the church. Atheism was widely expressed, it is true, among the so-called *intelligentsia,* but this had been openly preached by them for two-score years, and was not a product of the revolution; and the *intelligentsia* was certainly not the "people."

The March Revolution was rather unreligious than anti-religious; the people acquiesced in it for economic reasons, but showed no hostility to the church. Indeed, the church itself was, in the main, with the people in this revolution; neither the one nor the other played any serious part in it, but just accepted it. The active anti-religious elements came from abroad, later. Look even now at the leaders of Bolshevist Russia: Lenin, Trotsky, Zinovyev, Kamenev, Radek, Litvinov, Tchitcherin, and the rest. Few of the men who grasped the reins of government were in Russia in the spring of 1917. Few of them are of Russian nationality. They are the men who made the October Revolution; the Russian people as a whole had little active part in it then, except as instruments; just as they have had little more than a passive part since. Russia's great millions are being herded and persecuted by a few men, mostly aliens, suffering untold privations, slaughtered in their thousands, yet still clinging to their religion. Their strange passivity may perhaps be explained by the peculiarly strong "feminine" characteristic which Merezhkovsky ascribes to them.

Many Russian writers emphasize the Russian's deep consciousness of his own sinfulness. He goes to the church for relief, rather than for strength to help him resist temptation in the future. He is convinced that he cannot resist; but he is just as convinced that the church will cleanse him again. How can a man bear a lasting grudge against such an indulgent church? He may scoff at religion for a time; but all the while he *knows* that he will eventually come back and be forgiven. It is just to this extremely indulgent attitude that the church owes its power over the Russian people. The church was, in the past, a bridge which spanned the gulf between the aristocracy and the peasantry: it was the one thing they had in common.

The Tsar was the nominal head of the church. Under him the church was governed by the Holy Synod, at the head of which was the Procurator, a layman, who was in fact the minister of religion, being a member of the government. After the March Revolution, the Provisional government appointed V. N. Lvov as Procurator of the Holy Synod; and a convocation of bishops met in Moscow on August 15, 1917. This convocation was one of the greatest things in the history of the Russian church; it decided to revive the patriarchate, which had been abrogated by Peter the Great two hundred years before; and steps were taken to elect a patriarch.

Three candidates were chosen by the members of the convocation—the metropolitans of Harkov, Novgorod, and Moscow. The names were written on slips of paper, and placed in an urn before the Vladimir Ikon of St. Mary, which had been brought to St. Saviour's Cathedral. The choice among the three was left to "the Will of God"; and while the whole convocation was bowed in prayer, a bishop drew out one of the slips; it bore the name of Tihon, Metropolitan of Moscow, who was now proclaimed duly elected Patriarch of Moscow and All Russia. (Tihon had spent some years in America as a missionary.)

The election took place while the eight-day street

battle for supremacy was in progress at Moscow, between the Bolsheviki and the Provisional government.
It was fortunate that the election had not been delayed,
for the Bolsheviki now had to deal, not with a church
without a head, but with an organized body, which had
the universal support of the people. The patriarchate
was not an innovation, but simply a return to the old
constitution of the orthodox church; and there was no
question that the restoration was popular. In the fall
of the Tsar, the church had lost its lay head, but it had
regained its ancient spiritual head.

RELIGION AND MORALS IN BOLSHEVIST RUSSIA [1]

I

SEPARATION OF CHURCH AND STATE

The bells of Moscow still ring. Revolution, famine
and civil war have been unable to mar what for centuries has been one of Moscow's most distinctive and
charming features, the evening concerts of church bells
at sundown calling the faithful to worship in Moscow's
sixteen hundred churches and chapels. Moscow has
more churches than any city of her size in the world.
What Mecca is to Islam, Moscow is to Russia.

Every Saturday evening as the great clock in the
Kremlin tolls six up there above the white towers which
have been quiet for five years, sixteen hundred men of
God draw their robes tighter about them and climb
winding stairs into sixteen hundred belfries, there to
convert the entire city into a strange bedlam of harmony
and discord which drowns the ordinary noises of the
street and sets the listener to dreaming. From the street
below I have often watched the black-robed, monkish

[1] By E. W. Hullinger. Current History. 18: 299-304. May, 1923.

figure swaying with the rhythm of the bell, a medieval miniature framed in the whiteness of the lower tower.

Peasant women, passing in the street, face the belfry, and silently drop to their knees on the cold pavement. Droshky drivers, pitching through the deep ruts in rickety carriages, slow down to a walk, and place their caps against their breasts; then they whip up their horses and become the same garrulous, jolly copeck seekers of a moment before. Pious country folk passing on the Sophiskaya Naberezhnaya pause and face the Kremlin across the river. There is something pathetic in those bent figures and bared heads, bowing to the mute turrets of that ancient religious citadel, where all Russia's Tsars were crowned, and from which the Bolsheviki drove its inmates, to fill its monasteries and palaces with "atheist" officials and red soldiers. During this holy moment of the day, while the bells peal out anew their centuries-old admonition, the real heart of Russia lies exposed in all its tenderness, mysticism, childlikeness and simple beauty.

Revolution has not taken an iota from the religious ardor of the Russian masses, nor has government opposition diminished the tremendous rôle the church has always played in the lives of the Russian people. Although the first signs of a new orientation in religious thought are commencing to show themselves among higher ecclesiastical circles, the masses of the Russian congregation still adhere to the precepts of their ancestors, much as they received them. Like children, hurt and troubled, they have sought the comfort of their mother, the church, and here, midst drifting incense, flickering candles, in sanctuaries whose golden vases, silver urns, mosaic pillars and rich altars satisfy every childish dream of Oriental splendor and beauty, they have found forgetfulness, kneeling to the accompaniment of chants of invisible choirs and the intonations of richly robed priests.

It is doubtful if there exists in the world a more beautiful ritual than that of the Orthodox Russian Church. It was this, in fact, that in the tenth century largely influenced St. Vladimir's small staff of religious advisers, specially appointed to investigate all the religions of the world, to cast their deciding ballot in favor of Greek orthodoxy. It was the service at St. Sophia's, now a Moslem mosque, in Constantinople, that so impressed the wise men from the steppes. Through the centuries, the Russian church has preserved most of its original Byzantine splendor and traditions. In most remote provinces and tiniest villages I found veritable temples, imposing edifices of white stone, topped by multicolored or golden cupolas and containing veritable Aladdin's caves of gold, treasures and art.

In the silent fatalism of their religion the peasants find a comfort that all else denies them, and in unshaken faith in the "will of God" they have died by the thousands and hundreds of thousands. For days I drove through a plain of cold, lingering death—death in stuffy, foodless huts; death on frozen, snow-banked roads that led not to food but oblivion; death on the lonely steppes, without a living, moving thing in sight to cheer one; death under the eaves of railway stations, while trains rolled away filled to the limit. It was an ordeal to try the stoutest, to break faith in heroes and the self-restraint of martyrs. Yet not once in all that time did I hear one word of hate, a curse, a blasphemy. I cannot remember a single harsh voice in the many homes I entered and slept in. Russia knows how to suffer and die.

In the cities, churches are crowded as never before. In fact, many could not have been so jammed before— the Tsar's gendarmes, who maintained order in the temples on feast days, would not have permitted such mobs. The congregations are shabby; they always were. The poor always went in rags and stood humbly by as the great swept by in fine raiment. There is now

no fine raiment; there are no "great," and the rags are
more tattered than ever. Pilgrims still flock every hour
of the day to the tiny Iberian shrine (hardly twelve feet
square inside) in Moscow, to benefit from the alleged
healing powers of the icon within. Formerly the priests
used to come out every day at noon and march around
the Red Square in solemn procession, carrying the icon,
so that all might profit from its miraculous properties.

During the confiscation of church treasures "for
the famine," the government plastered the walls of the
city with gaudy yellow posters, showing the Patriarch
seated upon his piles of treasures amid a ring of famine
victims. The posters produced only smiles and shrugs,
despite the fact that the attack was justified by facts.
More than a year the church had sat idly by with
its cellars literally teeming with jewels, whose value
was estimated at a minimum of $500,000,000, while
thousands were dying of starvation on every hand.
Surely, it was a golden opportunity for the communists, if ever, to turn the people from the church.
Their attempt collapsed, owing to the general lack of
confidence in the honesty of the Kremlin. "They won't
use the jewels for the famine victims. They'll put them
into their pockets; the famine is only a pretext," was
the comment I heard from peasants and droshky drivers
to college professors and aristocrats. The Patriarch and
his advisers cleverly countermoved in the form of a
policy of "passive resistance," which enabled the church
to assume the pose of a martyr, and actually resulted in
a number of open fights between enraged parishioners
and red guards, sent to take the treasures right from
under the eyes of the churchgoers. Several times the
soldiers fired, wounding and killing. The eventual
arrest of fifty or sixty of the most conspicuous priests
and the sentence to death of some of them intensified
popular sympathy for the church and increased the
masses suspicion of the government. The act was interesting, however, as an illustration of the sense of

security of the powers that be, without which they never would have dared it. As witness to the hearings at court, I often saw those gentle, martyr-like fathers, with their long hair and beards, in their black robes, in the middle of a ring of bayonets, and I know now how Christ and His followers looked in the hands of the Roman warriors.

Dramatic, indeed, has been the change in the relationship between state and church in this, theocracy's last stronghold in Europe. Inseparably united under the Tsar, head of both civil and ecclesiastical governments, the church and state are now more completely divorced in Russia than ever in America. As in France, the church has no legal standing other than that of a religious society. As in France, the church marriage ceremony has no legal value.

The communists tolerate religious services—I saw no attempt to interfere with them—but they make no secret of their hostility to organized religion. And in Russia, it must be admitted that there is a certain historical foundation for their charge that the church was used as an "instrument" by the monarchy to retain its political hold on the people. Throughout the centuries, church and state marched hand in hand, or rather, the church obediently placed its hand in the state's guiding hand. How complete was its subservience was pathetically illustrated by its attitude in the middle of the nineteenth century on as great a moral issue as serfdom.

II

Marriage, Divorce and Morals

The separation of church and state has exercised a strong influence on marriage, as well as on its corrollary, divorce. It has been pointed out that marriage by the church has no legal value. To be married and divorced in a half hour is an actual legal possibility in Soviet Russia, unless, of course, the queues in front of the respective registrar's tables happen to be too long. Or, if the couple are of a sentimental turn of mind, they may revert to wedlock in the specified time, if the officials are not too busy.

Ease of marriage and even greater ease of divorce, is one of the communist government's answers to three of the world's greatest social problems: matrimony, morality and illegitimate children.

The simple act of both persons appearing before a magistrate and signing a marriage contract constitutes the only marriage ceremony recognized by present law in Russia. There is not even the formality of the spoken vows. Both applicants, however, must present themselves.

Divorce is still easier, in that the desire of only one of the two parties affected is sufficient. Either husband or wife may obtain abrogation of their marriage by appearing at the registrar's office and indicating that continuance of conjugal relations is no longer craved. There is no trial, no appeal. The dissatisfied husband simply signs a paper and walks out a free man. If there are children, however, he does not escape responsibility for support. This latter point, as well as several other correlated legal phases of the divorce question, are still a bit vague, owing to the fact that Russia has no written code of statutes. The only law that exists consists of a few decrees promulgated by the Kremlin and the common sense and conscience of the official. Stripping it of all the sentiment and religious background surrounding marriage in the legal systems of the west, the communist approaches the institution of wedlock as a purely civil procedure, just like any other contract between two persons. The church ceremony has no legal value in Russia, although most people still go through the gesture, as in France, where a similar situation prevails.

On Kuznetski Most, Moscow's Wall Street, is a bare room containing four tables. These four tables represent the complete possible cycle of human life. To the first, in one corner, come happy young fathers to register the birth of their babies. To the second, in another corner, come young couples for their marriage contracts. The third line is a curious mixture of pathos and blasphemy; here divorce papers may be obtained. The fourth is the death certificate table. Often there are lines in front of all four tables, their lengths varying in accordance with the severity of the times and the relative movements of the curve of life in these four departments of human existence. The wedding queue always has the headstart, of course, because two persons must appear for every document given out.

There are many similar rooms in Moscow. They are scattered in cities and towns throughout Russia. They take the place of the elaborate social machinery that performs similar functions in the capitalistic countries of the west.

Make it easy for every one to marry, and you remove one of the great causes of illicit cohabitation and illegitimate children. Make it easy for any one to obtain a divorce and why should any one live with another man's wife, or another woman's husband? In the majority of cases, people would prefer regular unions. So runs the reasoning of the communists, so outlined to me by one of the veteran members of the party. This reasoning furnished the basis for the communist government's approach to several great social problems. That the above formulae do not, however, completely cover the human dilemma, that mere possibility of obtaining marriage papers does not dispose of that dreaded economic factor, one of the worst deterrents to marriage, is admitted in another section of provisional by-laws covering the legal status of children born outside of wedlock. In these instances, the mother has the right to go to the birth registrar and have her child put down regularly, in which case the baby acquires the same legal position as any infant born in regular wedlock. She also may name the father and hold him responsible for part of the child's maintenance.

Having thus "furnished every person with the legal possibility to marry," the Soviet government approaches the question of commercial vice from an angle decidedly in contrast with the customary continental attitude of "toleration." In espousing the American theory of "suppression" of vice, modern Russia has the distinction of making an interesting departure from the traditional policies which have governed Old World treatment of the problem thus far. "You can't stamp out vice," the Old World has said for centuries, "so it is better to admit the inevitable and regulate it." With characteristic opportunism, France goes one step further, and says, "Since you must regulate it, why not make the 'profession' pay for the process?" So the French government grants prostitutes permits for specified terms, as in the case of any other professional. In Russia, the Tsar's government also followed the policy of toleration, and the "yellow tickets" carried by legalized streetwalkers are famous in literature.

It remained for America, a new nation, unburdened with long experience and the consequent despair and pessimism of the Old World, to launch the novel idea of war upon vice, on the ground that vice was an offense against society and should be stamped out like any other social crime. The pros and cons of this thesis are debated, I know, even yet in America. The fact remains, however, that the moral level in America is infinitely higher than that of Europe. Other factors enter this preeminently, in my opinion, our system of co-educational schools which throws young people of both sexes together from infancy up on a basis of healthy comradeship, furnishing them with a wealth of mutual interests in addition to that of sex. (Russia, by the way, is now also trying an experiment in co-educational schools.)

Russia's experiment with the American policy began under anything but encouraging auspices. Russia had always been known as a country of, perhaps, not immoral, but certainly unmoral proclivities. The Tsar's government legalized commercial vice in the cities, and in the country the peasants were never too strict. Even in many upper circles of society considerable laxness prevailed. Evidence of this is seen in the conventional barriers by which society strove to defend itself. Young men and women of better families were never permitted to go to a theater unaccompanied, or to remain alone long without a policeman in the person of a chaperon. They could not be trusted. The rottenness of the court was notorious.

The revolution and general disruption of life which it brought did not improve matters. Many of both sexes were often obliged to occupy the same sleeping compartment, owing to the shortage of rooms. Men, women, boys and girls were crowded promiscuously into the same prison cell. Freed from the reins that had held them in leash, many others hastened to exploit the unparalleled opportunity for licentiousness. At the same time an unfortunate blunder of the government gave rise to a sudden wave of juvenile immorality.

Without warning, Russia's two sets of schools—one for boys, the other for girls—were abruptly combined into one great co-educational system, and boys and girls of all ages were thrust together in the same school for the first time in their lives. Completely lacking the community of interests instilled into the youth of America by constant companionship from childhood, their minds naturally turned to the one theme they had in common. The consequence was a terrible tide of immorality which swelled so rapidly during the first years that parents trembled to see their children depart for school. "I was against this abrupt move," Lunatcharsky, Soviet Commissar of education, said to me. "I advised gradual extension of co-education, beginning with the infants, then adding the second class the next year, and so on, as the different ages grew accustomed to each other. The more revolutionary plan carried the day, however." Having gone in for it, Lunatcharsky had the faith in the American idea to persevere despite all setbacks, until finally conditions are beginning to improve. Four new classes have now entered, who know no other system, and Lunatcharsky, reported steady improvement of conditions. The Kremlin will continue co-education, he said, believing its beneficial effects will eventually have an influence on society as a whole.

It was upon this disheartening field that the Commissariat of Health undertook to "suppress" vice in Russia. What was the result? It is too soon to form a permanent judgment. Any great social experiment requires a longer span of time than four or five years to justify or condemn itself. Social forces move too deeply in the human heart to be deviated in a moment. But it is possible to record a few of the surface phenomena.

Certain it is that there are not the same surface evidences of vice in Moscow that there are in other continental cities. Moscow is the only large European capital I have seen whose streets are not open markets for women of easy virtue. Moscow has no "segregated" district. The Soviet government closed houses of prostitution and annulled the famous "yellow tickets" of the old days.

Certain it is that vice has been driven to cover fairly effectively, as in the United States. It is also certain, however, that a terrible wave of immorality swept Russia in the wake of the revolution, due to causes enumerated above. Communist circles themselves cannot claim absolution on this score, as many prominent party people have failed to live up to the precepts of their credo.

Nicholas Semashko, Commissar of Public Health, insisted to me that this wave is now on the decline. He went so far as to maintain that "conditions now cannot be compared with conditions under the empire, when no government attempt was made to curb vice." He cited the success of the campaign against vice in the army, which, he said, had reduced the percentage of soldiers infected with venereal diseases from 14—the record under the Tsar—to 1 per cent, a new record for the continent. Even in "moral England" the percentage runs as high as seven in every hundred soldiers, he said. Semashko admitted, however, that the new economic policy, reviving the unemployment problem, had been accompanied by a certain increase in street walkers. Hundreds of thousands of women who had been working in government offices for four years were suddenly thrown out upon the street, often with no means of support.

From all I saw of conditions, and from all I heard, I am inclined to agree with Semashko that immorality is on the decline, as compared with the last four years, but I fear he is a trifle optimistic in his comparison with pre-war days. From all I learned, there is not a great deal of difference. The government has succeeded in checking the revolutionary wave of immorality, and it has driven vice pretty well under cover. How soon conditions are positively improved over the old will depend upon the success of the two sociological experiments now in progress—the policy of suppression and the plan of co-educational schools.

RUSSIA'S CULTURE AND THE SOVIETS [1]

"The Unified Labor School"—that is what the Bolsheviki proudly call the system of education they have established in Russia.

[1] By A. F. Damansky. Living Age. 310: 401-6. August 13, 1921.

This new type of school is a sort of amalgamation, a welding together of all the types of schools that existed before. All the gymnasiums, the *realschule*, the institutes, all the private, municipal, and elementary schools, have been abolished, and their place has been taken by "unified labor schools," which are divided into the elementary classes, known as the first stage, and the more advanced classes, known as the second stage.

The former teaching personnel has thinned out very considerably. Many have died, many have been executed, many have fled to the villages and abroad. Of course, the number of pupils has also decreased. The population of Petrograd (Leningrad) for example, is now officially put at eight hundred thousand, and according to unofficial, and probably more correct, information, it is only about half a million. Nevertheless, there is an appreciable shortage of teachers, which has to be made up in every possible way. Usually those who have nothing else to do go into teaching. Women preponderate in the profession.

The main idea of the new schools is to bring up children in the spirit of proletarian class-consciousness, and to inculcate in them a proletarian ideology. The immediate object of education is to rid the younger generation of the bourgeois spirit. For this purpose great care is taken to mingle children from various social strata. Those who used to attend the gymnasiums, mostly from well-to-do educated families, have been moved to what were formerly municipal schools, attended by children from the lower classes. The parents are not given a right to choose the schools which their children are to attend. Nevertheless, it has been found most difficult to inculcate a really proletarian spirit in the higher grades. In order to promote this, special permission has been given to workmen to attend advanced classes as "extra" students, even if they have not had any previous education.

The new schools are co-educational, following the

American system, which is the outgrowth of long years of cultured life. In some places they copy American boarding-schools, with living quarters for the pupils. In this way, children from the streets, who have not received any moral training, thoroughly undisciplined, in many cases already corrupted, are suddenly brought into intimate social contact with children of refinement. By the end of the very first year of "unified labor schools" many girls of fourteen and fifteen in these boarding institutions were found to be pregnant.

At Petrograd, during the winter, the children came to school at nine-thirty. Since there were no janitors, or these neglected their duty, the first task devolving on the children was to bring in wood, start fires, and shovel away the snow. Sometimes the whole school would be taken to another part of the city, where there was a load of wood intended for this particular school. The children would haul this wood on sleds. The teachers either helped the children, or else gathered aimlessly in the "teacher's room," trying to get warm.

The first class-period usually began about noon. Returning from their work, excited and already physically tired, the children would throw themselves down on the benches just as they were, in overcoats and caps, and struggle through the studies of the "academic hour," that is, forty minutes. After that they all marched to the ill-kept dining-hall, where they received their lunch, consisting of a half-pound of bread and some millet gruel. After lunch there was another forty-minute period. The teachers, exhausted by undernourishment or cold, and by constant worry about their families, which can do little more than starve on the salary allowed them, also sat in their overcoats and caps, struggling through their class-work by main force. The second period ended the school-day, and the children were dismissed.

There was enough for them to do at home. They had to help their mothers chop and carry wood, if there was any left, or hunt for some if there was none. They had to carry water up the tenement stairs.

No home work is assigned the pupils. If such work had been given, none of the children could have done it. Homes which have electric light get current for about an hour or an hour and a half a day; and most of the time get no current at all. Kerosene and candles are not to be had. The people of Petrograd wander through their dark rooms in the evenings, like cattle in their pens. When an emergency arises, they burn kindling-wood for light. Mostly they go to bed at sundown; for after dark it is scarcely possible to take a dozen steps in an average Petrograd home without knocking against something.

Teachers are required to cultivate the interest of their pupils in the political life of the country. This means merely taking part in the numerous communist festivals. Pupils welcome this kind of instruction, especially when the festival happens to be on a school day. Of course, they actually learn little when they come to school; but in any case it is much pleasanter to march through the streets with flags and music, than to sit in cold and dirty classrooms.

In the spring of 1920, when the British labor delegation visited Petrograd, all the children were ordered to march to the Uritsky Square. The pupils of the higher classes, where the bourgeois elements are still strong, were warned that, if they did not come, they would be deprived of their lunches for the following week. The Englishmen, no doubt, were impressed by the revolutionary enthusiasm of the Russian youth, who gathered to greet them as representatives of the British proletariat. In a similar manner the children were forced to parade the streets in honor of the Third Internationale.

It is not difficult to predict the results of unified-labor-school instruction. Last year the number of graduates of all the secondary schools of Petrograd was three hundred and fifty, of whom three hundred asked to be registered at the Army Medical Academy and only fifty at all other higher institutions. The reason for the popularity of the Army Medical Academy is very obvious. The course of studies has been reduced to three years. It is a great advantage to qualify as a physician in so short a period of time. According to the latest ruling, even this short course has been greatly simplified. The student immediately upon his entrance is asked to choose a specialty, and after that he is not asked to encumber his head with the study of the pathological conditions of any other organs of the human body. In the reformed, democratized medical school, a student specializing in the diseases of the eye will know nothing about lungs or kidneys, while a student specializing in therapeutics will not need to explore such out-of-the-way corners of science as the structure of the brain and of the nervous system. Only three years of study, and the specialist is an adept of proletarian science!

Conditions in the rural schools are still worse. They lack even the most elementary equipment. The teaching personnel is also very small. The privations of these teachers are indescribable. They live and teach in cold, dirty huts, for beggarly pay.

In making my escape from Soviet Russia, it was necessary for me to get from Petrograd to Pskov. I succeeded in obtaining an assignment from the Herzen Institute to deliver a course of lectures on foreign literature at the summer courses for rural teachers in the latter city. This gave me an opportunity to see daily for a whole month a rather large group of teachers from different parts of 'the government of Pskov. Their stories of the way they lived pictured an utterly inconceivable, bestial existence. Some of them, for example, told me that during the whole preceding winter they did not go out of their huts once, because they had nothing to wear except indescribable rags. Some had nothing to eat during the whole winter, save frozen potatoes and bread, without a particle of sugar or fat.

It is easy enough to see how much energy, enthusiasm, and joy these prematurely aged men and women bring to their teaching labors. And the summer courses at which I lectured were just as much a house of cards as the other "constructive work" of the Soviet régime. Both the lecturers and the students received starvation rations. The minds of all were on the one problem of food. The lecturers' thoughts were far from their lecturing, the listeners' thoughts still further from the topic under discussion.

A strange picture was presented last winter by any university lecture-room. At the place where the rostrum was supposed to be, there would be a person wrapped in nondescript clothes and rags, as if he had prepared for a far-off polar expedition. This would be professor. In front of him, on the benches, there would be five or six, rarely ten or twelve, students, in tightly buttoned coats, hats, and galoshes.

Not only the professors, but the students also, receive a salary. That is a special inducement for them to come and study. But neither the seven thousand rubles they receive every month, nor the food-ration, consisting of a pound of bread of mysterious ingredients and a handful of millet seed, is enough to feed them. They are young, they must eat. So they go to work—teach wherever they can. And, of course, they all go into "speculation."

The salary given students and their special food-ration are proudly termed by the Bolsheviki "social insurance." But in reality they are just as much a house of cards as the whole institution of "social insurance" itself. A half pound, or three-quarters of a pound, or, in the best of cases, a whole pound of inedible bread, a handful of millet seed, at rare intervals, a piece of herring, and a cold, filthy, dark, lice-ridden corner for a home—these can save no one.

Nowhere else on the earth today are entertainments and concerts so plentiful as in Petrograd and Moscow. The theater, the ballet, all forms of music, are like opium or hashish, which the Soviet régime uses to conceal its own spiritual sterility—with which it anæsthetizes the masses to endure its crude Communist surgery.

Actors, singers and musicians have been mobilized. At the state theaters performances are given only for soldiers, sailors, and members of the trade-unions. The Alexandrinsky Theatre is open to the general public for an admission price only on Sunday evenings. The Marinsky Theatre is open in the same manner twice a week. Other theaters are obliged, at the first demand of the government, to discontinue the sale of tickets and shut their doors to the general public. Places of amusement are always full, and soldiers' and sailors' blouses predominate at every performance.

It is impossible to describe the way plays are produced nowadays. There is no canvas or paint for the scenery—no way to replace the costumes and furnishings that have worn out or have been stolen. Not many actors and singers remain on the heights of their old artistic standards. Many have succumbed to the demoralizing influences under which they work; for the theaters are now run by men with very little appreciation of art or even education. So actors show a distinct tendency to descend to the artistic level of the "street," which now fills the theater, rather than to lift the masses to their own cultural level.

There is no spiritual sympathy between actor and audience. Still less is there the inspiring enthusiasm that lends wings to the work of stage performers. The crowds that pack the theaters consist of hungry, wearied men, women, and children. Their cry for bread is stifled by threats. Entertainments are provided for them to still their craving for food. This condition of the audience cannot but affect the work of the artists. It is now impossible for them to improve their voices, to perfect their acting, to deepen their talent. They work as they can, to give the least and get the most.

Singers and actors known to all Europe are compelled to appear at several entertainments the same evening. There are no cabs or automobiles, and trolley-cars stop running at six o'clock, or even earlier. So special trucks are provided to carry the artists from one smoke-filled theater to another. In the summer, when it is still light during early theater hours, it is possible to see almost any evening a truck crawling slowly down the street; it cannot run faster because its engine is partly disabled. It is filled with the former idols of the Russian capital, the pride of Russian art. Among them you note Ershov, Akimova, Bosse, Tcherkassky, Makletsova, Smirnova, Vill, Luckom. Their faces betray their fatigue and irritation. No doubt, it is not the first time that evening that they have been thus transferred from one theater to another. Here is another truck. In it you discover Vedrinsky, Domasheva, Brian, Leshkov. Where are they being dragged now? It was in just this way, in the time of serfdom, that peasant-musicians were shipped from one landlord's estate to that of his neighbor.

Actors permit themselves to be dragged thus from one theater to another because it brings them extra piles of colored paper—so necessary if they and those dear to them are not to starve.

Equally tragic is the lot of painters. They have nothing to paint on, nothing to paint with; no canvas no colors. Those who get these have no place to work, for their own living quarters are too cold and cramped. And to this is added the constant, soul-extinguishing thought of food; and the eternally corrupting question: "How much will we get?"

This question may be read always in the eyes, and heard from the lips, of scientists, professors, famous singers. "What will they give us?" That is the opening phrase of every conversation—and its closing chord.

Worst of all, most tragic of all, is the fate of writers. By the first anniversary of their régime, the Bolsheviki could already boast their cultural work in this field was done. There was not a newspaper, a magazine, a publishing house left, except those which the Soviet government owned and controlled. Not a periodical to write for! No opportunity to print! Only an author can understand the tragedy of these words, only a person who lives for his writing, for whom it is just as essential to write as to eat or breathe. In Soviet Russia, the writer, the poet, the man of letters is like a prisoner chained in his cell. He is robbed of his most elementary need, the freedom of travel. In order to go ten versts out of Petrograd, you have to spend weeks in different Soviet institutions, begging for permits. Recently even a fingerprint system has been introduced. The writer has no opportunity to get new impressions. A realization that he is cut off from the rest of the world encloses and stifles him like prison-walls.

Every time a theme is born in the writer's mind, every time an artistic image rises before him, every time words begin to string themselves into periods, this sentence of doom sounds in his ears: "That cannot be written. What if there should be a sudden search? They might hale you before the Extraordinary Commission for that!" For the government's motto is: "All who think differently are anathema." Therefore, the inspired words die away, the image disappears, the theme fades into nothingness. Literary talent is like a spirit in a cage, like thought bound with fetters. It loses faith in itself, languishes, and finally expires.

IMPRESSIONS OF BOLSHEVIST RUSSIA [1]

I entered Soviet Russia on May 11 and recrossed the frontier on June 16. The Russian authorities only

[1] By B. Russell. Nation (London). 27: 460-2. July 10, 1920.

admitted me on the express condition that I should travel with the British Labor Delegation, a condition with which I was naturally very willing to comply, and which that delegation kindly allowed me to fulfil. We were conveyed from the frontier to Petrograd, as well as on subsequent journeys, in a special train *de luxe*, covered with mottoes about the Social Revolution and the Proletariat of all countries; we were received everywhere by regiments of soldiers, with the Internationale being played on the regimental band while civilians stood bareheaded and soldiers at the salute; congratulatory orations were made by local leaders and answered by prominent Communists who accompanied us; the entrances to the carriages were guarded by magnificent Bashkir cavalrymen in resplendent uniforms; in short, everything was done to make us feel like the Prince of Wales. Innumerable functions were arranged for us: banquets, public meetings, military reviews, etc.

The assumption was that we had come to testify to the solidarity of British Labor with Russian Communism, and on that assumption the utmost possible use was made of us for Bolshevist propaganda. We, on the other hand, desired to ascertain what we could of Russian conditions and Russian methods of government, which was impossible in the atmosphere of a royal progress. Hence arose an amicable contest, degenerating at times into a game of hide and seek: while they assured us how splendid the banquet or parade was going to be, we tried to explain how much we should prefer a quiet walk in the streets. I, not being a member of the delegation, felt less obligation than my companions did to attend at propaganda meetings where one knew the speeches by heart beforehand. In this way, I was able, by the help of neutral interpreters, mostly English or American, to have many conversations with casual people whom I met in the streets or on village greens, and to find out how the whole system appears to the ordinary non-political man and woman. The first five days we spent in Petrograd, the next eleven in Moscow. During this time we were living in daily contact with important men in the government, so that we learned the official point of view without difficulty. I saw also what I could of the intellectuals in both places. We were all allowed complete freedom to see politicians of opposition parties, and we naturally made full use of this freedom. We saw Mensheviki, social revolutionaries of different groups, and anarchists; we saw them without the presence of any Bolsheviki, and they spoke freely after they had overcome their initial fears. I had an hour's talk with Lenin, virtually *tête-à-tête;* I met Trotsky, though only in company; I spent a night in the country with Kamenev; and I saw a great deal of other men, who, though less known outside Russia, are of considerable importance in the government.

At the end of our time in Moscow, we all felt a desire to see something of the country, and to get in touch with the peasants, since they form about 85 per cent of the population. The government showed the greatest kindness in meeting our wishes, and it was decided that we should travel down the Volga from Nizhni Novgorod to Saratov, stopping at many places, large and small, and talking freely with the inhabitants. I found this part of the time extraordinarily instructive. I learned to know more than I should have thought possible of the life and outlook of peasants, village schoolmasters, small Jew traders, and all kinds of people. Unfortunately, my friend, Clifford Allen, fell ill, and my time was much taken up with him. This had, however, one good result, namely, that I was able to go on with the boat to Astrahan, as he was too ill to be moved off it. This not only gave me further knowledge of the country, but made me acquainted with Sverdlov, Acting Minister of Transport, who was traveling on the boat to organize the movement of oil from Baku up the

Volga, and who was one of the ablest as well as kindest people whom I met in Russia. . . .

One of the first things that I discovered after passing the red flag which marks the frontier of Soviet Russia, amid a desolate region of marsh, pine wood, and barbed wire entanglements, was the profound difference between the theories of actual Bolsheviki and the version of those theories current among advance socialists in this country. Friends of Russia here think of the dictatorship of the proletariat as merely a new form of representative government, in which only working men and women have votes, and the constituencies are partly occupational, not geographical. They think that "proletariat" means "proletariat," but "dictatorship" does not quite mean "dictatorship." This is the opposite of the truth. When a Russian Communist speaks of dictatorship, he means the word literally, but when he speaks of the proletariat, he means the word in a Pickwickian sense. He means the "class-conscious" part of the proletariat, that is, the Communist Party. He includes people by no means proletarian (such as Lenin and Tchitcherin) who have the right opinions, and he excludes such wage-earners as have not the right opinions, whom he classifies as lackeys of the *bourgeoisie*. The Communist who sincerely believes the party creed is convinced that private property is the root of all evil; he is so certain of this that he shrinks from no measures, however harsh, which seem necessary for constructing and preserving the communist state. He spares himself as little as he spares others. He works sixteen hours a day, and foregoes his Saturday half-holiday. He volunteers for any difficult or dangerous work which needs to be done, such as clearing away piles of infected corpses left by Koltchak or Denikin. In spite of his position of power and his control of supplies, he lives an austere life. He is not pursuing personal ends, but aiming at the creation of a new social order. The same motives, however, which make him austere make him also ruthless. Marx has taught that communism is fatally predestined to come about; this fits in with the Oriental traits in the Russian character, and produces a state of mind not unlike that of the early successors of Mahomet. Opposition is crushed without mercy, and without shrinking from the methods of the Tsarist police, many of whom are still employed at their old work. Since all evils are due to private property, the evils of the Bolshevist régime while it has to fight private property will automatically cease as soon as it has succeeded.

These views are the familiar consequences of fanatical belief. To an English mind, they reinforce the conviction upon which English life has been based ever since 1688, that kindliness and tolerance are worth all the creeds in the world—a view which, it is true, we do not apply to other nations or to subject races.

In a very novel society, it is natural to seek for historical parallels. The baser side of the present Russian government is most nearly paralleled by the Directoire in France, but on its better side it is closely analogous to the rule of Cromwell. The sincere Communists (and all the older members of the party have proved their sincerity by years of persecution) are not unlike the Puritan soldiers in their stern politico-moral purpose. Cromwell's dealings with Parliament are not unlike Lenin's with the Constituent Assembly. Both, starting from a combination of democracy and religious faith, were driven to sacrifice democracy to religion enforced by military dictatorship. Both tried to compel their countries to live at a higher level of morality and effort than the population found tolerable. Life in modern Russia, as in Puritan England, is in many ways contrary to instinct. And if the Bolsheviki ultimately fall, it will be for the reason for which the Puritans fell: because there comes a point at which men feel that amusement and ease are worth more than all other goods put together.

Far closer than any actual historical parallel is the parallel of Plato's Republic. The Communist Party corresponds to the guardians; the soldiers have about the same status in both; there is in Russia an attempt to deal with family life more or less as Plato suggested. I suppose it may be assumed that every teacher of Plato throughout the world abhors Bolshevism, and that every Bolshevist regards Plato as an antiquated *bourgeois*. Nevertheless, the parallel is extraordinarily exact between Plato's Republic and the régime which the better Bolsheviki are endeavoring to create.

Bolshevism is internally aristocratic and externally militant. The Communists have all the good and bad traits of an aristocracy which is young and vital. They are courageous, energetic, capable of command, always ready to serve the state; on the other hand, they are dictatorial, lacking in ordinary consideration for the plebs, such as their servants, whom they overwork, or the people in the streets, whose lives they endanger by extraordinarily reckless motoring. They are practically the sole possessors of power, and they enjoy innumerable advantages in consequence. Most of them, though far from luxurious, have better food than other people. Only people of some political importance can obtain motor cars or telephones. Permits for railway journeys, for making purchases at the Soviet stores (where prices are about one-fiftieth of what they are in the market), for going to the theater, and so on, are, of course, easier to obtain for the friends of those in power than for ordinary mortals. In a thousand ways, the Communists have a life which is happier than that of the rest of the community. Above all, they are less exposed to the unwelcome attentions of the police and the extraordinary commission.

The communist theory of international affairs is exceedingly simple. The revolution foretold by Marx, which is to abolish capitalism throughout the world, happened to begin in Russia, though Marxian theory would seem to demand that it should begin in America. In countries where the revolution has not yet broken out, the sole duty of a Communist is to hasten its advent. Agreements with capitalist states can only be makeshifts, and can never amount on either side to a sincere peace. No real good can come to any country without a bloody revolution: English labor men may fancy that a peaceful evolution is possible, but they will find their mistake. Lenin told me that he hopes to see a labor government in England, and would wish his supporters to work for it, but solely in order that the futility of Parliamentarism may be conclusively demonstrated to the British working man. Nothing will do any real good except the arming of the proletariat and the disarming of the *bourgeoisie*. Those who preach anything else are social traitors or deluded fools.

For my part, after weighing this theory carefully, and after admitting the whole of its indictment of *bourgeois* capitalism, I find myself definitely and strongly opposed to it. The Third Internationale is an organization which exists to promote the class-war and to hasten the advent of revolution everywhere. My objection is not that capitalism is less bad than the Bolsheviki believe, but that socialism is less good, at any rate in the form which can be brought about by war. The evils of war, especially of civil war, are certain and very great; the gains to be achieved by victory are problematical. In the course of a desperate struggle, the heritage of civilization is likely to be lost, while hatred, suspicion, and cruelty become normal in the relations of human beings. In order to succeed in war, a concentration of power is necessary, and from concentration of power the very same evils flow as from the capitalist concentration of wealth. For these reasons chiefly, I cannot support any movement which aims at world revolution. The damage to civilization done by revolution in one country may be repaired by the influence of another in which there has been no revolution; but in a universal cataclysm civilization might go under for a thousand years. But while I cannot advocate world revolution, I cannot escape from the conclusion that the governments of the leading capitalist countries are doing everything to bring it about. Abuse of our power against Germany, Russia, and India (to say nothing of any other countries) may well bring about our downfall, and produce those very evils which the enemies of Bolshevism most dread.

The true Communist is thoroughly international. Lenin, for example, so far as I could judge, was not more concerned with the interests of Russia than with those of other countries; Russia is, at the moment, the protagonist of the social revolution, and, as such, valuable to the world, but Lenin would sacrifice Russia rather than the revolution, if the alternative should ever arise. This is the orthodox attitude, and is no doubt genuine in many of the leaders. But nationalism is natural and instinctive; through pride in the revolution, it grows again even in the breasts of Communists. Through the Polish war, the Bolsheviki have acquired the support of national feeling and their position in the country has been immensely strengthened.

The only time I saw Trotsky was at the Opera in Moscow. The British Labor Delegation were occupying what had been the Tsar's box. After speaking with us in the ante-chamber, he stepped to the front of the box and stood with folded arms while the house cheered itself hoarse. Then he spoke a few sentences, short and sharp, with military precision, winding up by calling for "three cheers for our brave fellows at the front," to which the audience responded as a London audience would have responded in the autumn of 1914. Trotsky and the red army undoubtedly now have behind them a great body of nationalist sentiment. The re-conquest of Asiatic Russia has even revived what is essentially an imperialist way of feeling, though this would be indignantly repudiated by many of those in whom I seemed to detect it. Experience of power is inevitably altering communist theories, and men who control a vast governmental machine can hardly have quite the same outlook on life as they had when they were hunted fugitives. If the Bolsheviki remain in power, it may be assumed that their communism will fade, and that they will increasingly resemble any other Asiatic government—for example, our own government in India.

AN APOLOGY FOR THE UNAVOIDABLE [1]

I am going to speak of the results of our new economic policy. In 1921 this policy was still nothing but a vague idea. After we came victoriously through the most important phase of the civil war, there arose the great—the greatest, in my opinion—domestic political crisis that we have faced in Soviet Russia: namely, the discontent of great masses not only of the peasants but of the workers as well. What was the cause of it?—it was the fact that our demands were too far-fetched, that we did not make sure of our foundations. The masses already felt what we still failed to realize. But even we were soon convinced that an immediate transition to a socialist redistribution of wealth was beyond our power. We saw that we were sure to perish if we did not make concessions that would give us a breathing space to devote to minor problems.

Therefore, in the spring of 1921, we decided by practically a unanimous vote, to embark upon the new economic policy. Has the result of this step been beneficial, and have we saved ourselves? I believe these are questions of the utmost importance for all Communists. Because, if the answer is no, we shall all go under together.

I think, however, that we can, with a clear conscience,

[1] By Nickolay Ulyanov-Lenin. A speech before the Third Internationale. Living Age. 316: 134-7 January 20, 1923.

answer this question in the affirmative; that the last year and a half have justified us.

I shall now prove my assertion. For this purpose, I must summarize the factors in Russia's economic situation.

First, public finance and the famous Russian ruble. I believe that we can rightly call the ruble famous, if for no other reason than that it now numbers something like one quadrillion. (General levity.) A quadrillion is no trifle. An astronomical figure! I am sure that many of you do not know just how much that is. But from the economic standpoint the number of rubles is unimportant: we could even cross out the zeros. (General levity.) In this field we have already accomplished much and shall accomplish more. The important thing is the stabilization of ruble exchange.

If we succeed in stabilizing the ruble for a considerable period, and later permanently—we shall have won. After that, these astronomical figures will do no harm. Then we shall be able to put our finance and industry on a firm foundation, and to keep them on a firm foundation. Concerning this question, I believe I can present to you some important and decisive facts. In 1921 the ruble only continued stable for three months. In 1922 this stability has lasted five months. I think this is sufficient. These figures show that since 1921, when we first inaugurated our new economic policy, we have learned how to move ahead. Unless we now do something very foolish, we are sure to make further progress. Although we are only beginning to follow our new economic policy systematically and deliberately, yet we have already held the ruble at the same value for five months instead of for three months as last year. I believe we should feel satisfied, because we stand alone, and we have done this without foreign aid. We have received no loan—no help from any one of those capitalist states that manage their own affairs with such amazing competency that even

today they still do not know how their own finances
stand!

Their Versailles Treaty set up a financial system that
they do not understand themselves. If that has happened
in those great capitalist states, how much more satisfied
should we feel, in our backward, uncivilized country, at
having accomplished the most important thing: stabilize
our money!

I shall now describe conditions among our different
social classes. The most important, of course, is the
peasantry. In 1921 dissatisfaction reigned supreme
among them. Afterward we had the famine that afflicted the peasants worst of all. Naturally, the whole
outside world shouted: "Look—this is the result of Bolshevist economics!" Naturally, they did not shout it
was the result of the civil war. All the landowners and
the bourgeoisie who fought us in 1918 now represented
the famine as a result of applying socialist theories.

Now, what is the situation after this unexpected
calamity? I say, the answer is clear to every observer.
Within a year, the peasantry have conquered the famine,
and have managed to bring in their taxes in kind to such
an extent that we now possess hundreds of millions of
poods of grain, and this almost without having recourse
to compulsion. Up to 1921, peasant uprisings were common—now they have almost entirely ceased. We can
say with assurance that the peasants are satisfied with
their present situation. We believe that this fact speaks
clearer than all the statistics and official reports we could
publish. The present condition of the peasantry is such
as to make future uprisings against us highly improbable. To be sure, they may still have some grievances;
but serious discontent has been banished.

As regards handicraft and factory industries, I can
say with full assurance that a general improvement is
to be noted. And in close connection with this, the living conditions of workingmen have improved both in

Petrograd and in Moscow. This is not so apparent else-where, since what we call heavy industry is of relatively more importance outside the capitals. And the condition of heavy industry is quite a different story.

There we still meet serious difficulties. A slight im-provement took place in 1921 and up to 1922. Conse-quently, we may hope that our mines, furnaces, and works will show still better results in the future. In a capitalist state, any betterment of these industries would unavoidably require hundreds of millions of new capital in the form of loans. We do not have such loans. All we hear about concessions and the like, is nothing but empty talk. In spite of this, we already witness a good modest revival.

Besides, our commerce has brought us in a little capi-tal—something like 20,000,000 gold rubles. At any rate, we have made a start. Our trade is bringing in money with which to restore our heavy industries. This is still "music of the future," however. Our heavy industries are in a very precarious state. Nevertheless, it is ap-parent that we are able now to put something aside—and we shall do so. We know that unless we restore our mines, furnaces, and other primary industries, we shall have no industry at all. Without heavy industries we shall be altogether lost as an independent country. Good crops and prosperous secondary industries alone will not save Russia. Without primary industries we cannot sur-vive as a civilized nation—much less as a socialist state. The amount we have been able to appropriate for their restoration up to the present is still less than 20,000,000 gold rubles.

On the whole, however, I think myself justified in concluding that the new economic policy has brought us positive gains. We have shown that we can engage in commerce as a state, and at least maintain manufactur-ing and agriculture at their present level and make slow progress.

For five years we have been defending the power of the working class; and this in war time. It was natural that the peasantry, on the whole, should be for us. They understood that behind the white stood the landowners, whom they hate above everything else in the world. This, however, does not mean a great deal: it only means an issue as to whether peasants or landlords were to run things. That is much too little for us. You understand that we seized the government for the workers; and that our aim is to erect a socialist society with the help of the workers. Consequently, the all-important question for us was to lay the economic foundations of a socialist society. We could not do it outright, and so we have tried to do it indirectly.

We are in possession of all strategic points; we keep our title to the land, which is the property of our state. This is very important, no matter what our opponents say. It has the greatest practical meaning, even for agriculture. We have made the peasants contented, we have begun to revive industry and trade.

As far as trade is concerned, I want to emphasize that we propose to found mixed companies, that is, concerns where part of the capital will be foreign private capital and the other part will come from us. First of all, we shall in this way learn how to trade—and we need such training. In the second place, we shall be able, if it proves desirable, to dissolve such companies. So we really run no risk. Undoubtedly, we have committed many follies and we are going to commit more. No one is in a better position to judge of this and to see it objectively, than I am.

Why have we made those foolish mistakes? This is clear. First: because we are a backward country. Second: we have but a minimum of education. Third: we receive no help; no civilized state comes to our assistance; they all work against us. Fourth: there is the outstanding question of government-machinery. We took the old state-machinery over from those whom we succeeded.

In 1917, when we came to power, the old function-aries sabotaged. We shouted to them: "Please come back!" And they came back, all of them. This necessity was our misfortune. Oftentimes, while all is running smoothly at the top of the government, because there we are in power, our underlings run things arbitrarily at cross-purposes, and manage to defeat our objects. We cannot remedy this in a moment. We shall have to work for years to perfect our government-machinery. As it is, we are going ahead at great speed—at too great a speed, perhaps. If we do not act too hastily, we shall have a force of young officials in a few years, who will be able radically to reform our government-machinery.

When our opponents reproach us by saying that Lenin himself confesses to an enormous amount of foolish mistakes, I want to tell them this: "You know, just the same, that our foolishness is altogether different from yours."

We have just begun to learn, and we are learning in such a systematic way that we are sure to obtain results. However, in answer to our opponents, the capitalists, who reproach us for our foolish missteps, I shall cite an example from a famous Russian writer. I shall change this example somewhat so that it reads as follows: when a Bolshevik makes a mistake, he says: two times two makes five; but when a capitalist makes a mistake, he says: two times two makes a stearin-candle. This is not difficult to prove. Take, for instance, the agreement between Koltchak and America, France, England, and Japan. Are there stronger and more civilized states in the world? They promised to help Koltchak, and made a fiasco of it that I find it humanly impossible to understand. Now for the second example—the Treaty of Versailles. What did those highly enlightened powers concoct at Versailles? How are they now to find their way out of that mixup, that nonsense? I do not think it is an exaggeration if I assert that our follies are as nothing compared to those of which the capitalist world is guilty.

I believe the most important thing for us all, Russians

as well as outsiders, is the fact that now we are finally in a position to learn. I do not know how long the capitalist powers will leave us in peace, so that we may learn. But we must use every minute that we have free from war, for the purpose of learning. And we Russians do learn.

THE RUSSIA OF TOMORROW [1]

In Russia, which is pre-eminently an agricultural country, the peasantry has always played a prominent part in the economic life of the state. And now this rôle has come to be the dominating and paramount feature in the whole situation. In present-day Russia the peasantry is the only productive element. It is the only class that has retained, and even strengthened, its social position in the state. It stands today unchallenged. The feudal system of large estates has been overthrown forever. Industry and the class dependent upon it—labor and the bourgeoisie—are, at least for the time being, crushed, weakened, and unproductive. In the future they will, of course, play an important part. For the moment, however, they are helpless.

This condition is reflected in psychological changes also. The peasants now clearly see that all the strands of life are gathered in their hands. If the peasant will furnish bread, the city, the army, and the government officials will live; if he refuses they will perish. The former psychology of semi-serfdom is now making room for a new consciousness in the peasant—that of being the real master and ruler of the country, the real "boss" of his own Russia. The peasant is now undergoing a process of self-discovery as a *citizen*. To dispose freely of this destiny, of his heritage, of his own self, and to build the edifice of his existence as a free and sovereign citizen—these are the practical lessons derived by the Russian peasant from the school of revolution.

[1] By N. D. Avksentiyev. Harper's Magazine. 144: 611-21. April, 1922.

The revolution has brought about still other favorable changes in the psychology of the peasantry. Driven by hunger, the more cultured city population was forced to seek bread in the villages, creating there new interests and demands. Having no money to give for its bread, the city has had to barter, bringing to the village new articles unknown there before. This has inevitably created entirely new wants among the peasantry.

Century-old relationships, traditional forms and molds, have been destroyed by the revolution. That which had previously seemed to be simple and pre-established, to be accepted without question, is now subjected to analysis and explanation; hence a tremendous increase in the demand for knowledge on subjects political, scientific, and technical. "The thirst for learning is overwhelming!" says a report of the Commissariat of Education. "In southern Russia peasant children have now made their appearance in the intermediary schools, making up in some cases as much as 40 to 60 per cent of all pupils. Formerly there were none. . . . In a large number of provinces private schools have been opened which are being maintained by the peasants at their own expense, all contributing to the upkeep." People who have the opportunity to observe this process on the spot say that "the face of new dawning Russia may be perceived in this movement of the peasantry toward light and knowledge."

Another great gain has been made as a result of four years of sore trial. These difficult years have not only awakened a keen and vital sense of citizenship, but they have also forced the people to live through and feel intensely, and to realize clearly, the need for *statehood, for the unity of the state*.

The Russian people—builders of one of the greatest empires of the world—have often been accused of failure to appreciate sufficiently the importance of the state, of lack of patriotism. But the Bolshevist anarchy has forced the people to realize and understand that the violation of the functions of the state spells the ruin of all social life in all its forms and manifestations. The thirst for social and political order has been aroused by life itself and will not rest until it is satisfied.

The civil war, which split Russia into isolated sections and domestic battle fronts, was equally responsible for awakening an active desire for unity. People began to realize clearly what had not been felt before—that Russia is not a mere mechanical conglomeration of individual parts, but a single political and economic organism, held together by a network of railways, ports, and other common bonds. The same stern lessons of life have intensified also the meaning of "country," have made that term a tangible reality. The disintegration of the state, its losses and calamities, the national dishonor which had to be endured more than once—all this could not fail to cause a keen realization of the vital importance and significance of a native country, of a motherland.

Finally, the destruction of economic and cultural values, the senseless experimentation of the Bolsheviki, the impossibility of creative work—all this has tended to arouse an irresistible desire for creative, productive work, for the healing of the wounds dealt to the country and its economic life by the mad and destructive policy of the Bolsheviki. The thirst for vital and fruitful activity is on the increase.

I have spoken of the peasantry, for it is this class that is ultimately bound to shape Russia's destiny. A sound, mature peasantry is the economic and social foundation of the whole edifice of the Russian state. Upon this solid foundation, after the passing of the present evil days, will be reared a sound and free industrial system, with sound and prosperous classes of labor and bourgeoisie. The spiritual and intellectual formulation of this fact will be supplied by the "brains" of the nation, the *intelligentsia*. And no matter how much these classes of the population have been crushed down, they are already in many respects undergoing the same evolution as the peasantry—a process of spiritual and political growth.

Today Russia is prepared for democratic, creative effort more than ever before. In her sufferings Russia is developing a new fortitude. And of her—this truly national Russia—it may be said in the words of Russia's greatest poet, Pushkin:

> A heavy sledge
> May shatter glass,
> But also forge the sword.

Under the sledge-hammer blows of seemingly unendurable affliction Russia has not been shattered like fragile glass. Russia has merely learned to forge a new, indomitable will, her liberty and her glorious future.

Notwithstanding all her vicissitudes, Russia will recover economically faster than may appear possible at first sight. In this respect we may apply to Russia that old Russian proverb, "There would have been no good luck if ill luck had not helped."

Russia's misfortune prior to the revolution consisted in the poor development of her productive resources, of her industry. But it is due to this very fact that Russia's chief resources are not on the surface, but still in the bowels of the earth. Destruction, therefore, has failed to reach the most important economic resources of the country—her mineral wealth, boundless forests, and most fertile sections of land. The exploitation of all this wealth is left to the future. And therein—combined with the energy of the people and a rational system of work—lies the possibility of the rapid recovery of that richest of countries. Under conditions of free labor and individual initiative, and with the vigorous cooperation of the whole nation, Russia will be able to march forward on the road of economic evolution in seven-league boots.

Of course, an indispensible condition of such quick progress and rapid healing of wounds must be close co-operation with foreign capital. Foreign capital should prove beneficial to Russian labor as well as to a proper utilization of natural resources. Given these conditions, it is possible that Russia may see a development comparable to that of the United States after the Civil War. Foreign capital played a most important part in American reconstruction.

Such cooperation on the part of American capital would be particularly welcomed by democratic Russia. In the first place, American capital is at the present moment the most powerful. In the second place, America has been throughout Russia's period of revolutionary trials exceptionally well-meaning and unselfish. The United States has always been, just as she is today, the champion of Russian democracy and of the integrity of Russia's territorial and sovereign rights. It is America that has come to the relief of Russia's dying, famine-stricken population. This will never be forgotten by future Russia. It establishes a solid basis for peaceful cooperation of both countries in the domain of world politics as well as economics.

AN OPTIMIST ON RUSSIA [1]

On my way from Moscow to London I had to cover in an aeroplane several hundred miles of Russian territory. It is the fourth time that I have made this trip from Moscow to Königsberg and back, and the landscape from an aeroplane is well known to me. This year I and my colleagues noticed a new streak of color on the gray background of the Russian peasant cottages—the roofs and thatch of new buildings shining brightly. This is a

[1] By Leonid Krasin. Living Age. 317: 760-3. June 30, 1923.

fact of the utmost importance; it shows that the Russian peasant not only is recovering from the consequences of the war and blockade; but is able to sink a certain amount of capital in building up his village again.

There can be no doubt concerning the economic reconstruction of the village. Not only is the arable land increasing, but agricultural methods are becoming improved. The peasantry has undergone during these last years the greatest psychological change. The Russian peasant is today no more a forgotten slave or serf, as he was under the Tsarist régime. The peasant is today the citizen and lord of all the Russian realm. All the land belongs to him, and he is not afraid of the restoration of the landlord or the Tsarist régime. Together with the old régime has disappeared, too, the traditional shortsightedness of the Russian peasant. Millions of peasants have been to the front during the Great War; millions of peasants have been imprisoned abroad; they have learned to know the motor car, tractors, tanks, electrical power in the trenches, as well as European methods of tilling the soil. Many of them during their imprisonment were working on the biggest estates in Germany, Hungary, and Austria, where they had a chance to run tractors and to work the soil with the most perfected implements.

Again, during the civil war the peasants left their own villages and fought for the freedom of their land on the north, south, east, and west. Hundreds of thousands and millions of peasants were thrown from the Volga to the Urals and from the Urals to the south of Russia; then once again to the Finnish border, and from there to the frontier of the Baltic states and Poland, or to liquidate the white guard bands in Transcaucasia. The peasant during these five years of Soviet rule has played, and is playing, an active part in the direct administration of the state, from the village council to the most important state institutions.

It is difficult to grasp the magnitude of the change

that has taken place during this time. This change could not but have its effect on the productive capacity of the Russian peasants, and the reforms that, under the old régime, would have taken tens of years to introduce—and that by crushing down the conservative obstinacy of the peasant, who had been intentionally left ignorant by the régime of the Tsar—are today introduced in a period of a few months by a simple decree of the Soviet government, that is, the government of the workers and peasants.

Paradoxical as it may seem, the reconstruction of agriculture is going all the quicker owing to the low cultural and productive level of the economic system inherited by the peasants as a legacy from the old Tsarist régime. In practically no European country is it possible to increase agricultural productivity by 30 per cent, or even by 15 or 10 per cent, for in all civilized countries the productive maximum of arable land has already been attained. Things are different in Russia. Without considering the area of untouched land, there exists the fullest possibility of an extraordinary increase in production, even without very large investments in artificial manures or agricultural implements, by simply bringing methods of production up-to-date.

The Russian peasant used to produce under the Tsar not more than one-third, and sometimes one-fourth, of what could have been produced on the given area by using even a slightly more modern system of agriculture. Such simple measures as earlier ploughing, the use of better-selected seeds, the introduction of the system of rotation of crops, the sowing of edible roots, a little more accurate tilling of the soil, and the use of the most elementary agricultural implements; all these simplest measures could alone increase the crop of the peasant farms by 150 or 200 per cent. The Russian peasantry is working feverishly in this sense, and the Soviet government is doing its best to speed up and strengthen this development.

The most decisive element in this is the increased requirements of the peasant's family during the war and revolution. In Russia, as everywhere else, the war created exceptionally favorable conditions for the production of agricultural crops. During the war the Russian peasant used to sell or exchange his agricultural products in the towns at a very high price, receiving not only money, but also furniture, clothes, shoes, hardware, articles of comfort, and even jewelry. In the Russian peasant home (*izba*) you can frequently see very expensive furniture and wares obtained in the towns. Neither the wife nor the daughter of the peasant is any more satisfied with the standard of living usual before the war; and the peasantry has received an unprecedented stimulus to increase agricultural production and to offer the maximum amount of products on the foreign market.

This is the reason why, notwithstanding the extremely difficult conditions, the area of arable land is becoming larger, and the crop every year is increasing. This is why everyone who comes back to Russia after a few months' absence is bound to notice the exceedingly rapid and striking increase in the general well-being of the rural population. Parallel to the reconstruction of agriculture there is a revival of the light and handicraft industries directly connected with the working up of the rural raw-material, as well as with the city industries working for the inland market. At the same time, the Soviet government is making heroic efforts to rebuild transport and heavy industry. Here the task is somewhat more difficult, as the destruction and exhaustion of big factories and works, as well as the expenses involved, are in this case far more considerable than in the middle and light industries. Nevertheless, the great majority of branches have succeeded in maintaining their basic equipment in a more or less satisfactory state.

Notwithstanding all difficult conditions, and the havoc of the civil war, the railways are slowly but ceaselessly increasing their efficiency and the number of cars furnished every day for loading and unloading at a given place surpasses the maximum figures of the last five years. The textile and chemical industries are producing one-third of their pre-war figures. The position is somewhat worse in the coal-mining industry, where the equipment was exhausted before the revolution—especially the boilers—and where it was difficult to secure the power required. The oil industry at Baku is yielding already 50 per cent, and in Grosny even 80 per cent of the pre-war figures. Poland and Rumania, who experienced neither blockade nor intervention, and who, on the contrary, have received, and are receiving, foreign help in the form of loans, can hardly boast of the better state of their oil industries.

On the whole we see, therefore, a slow but progressive reconstruction of Russian economic life, the quickest and most successful development being visible in agriculture and the small handicraft industries. Little by little, in keeping with the general internal recovery of the country, is proceeding the development of our foreign trade. The first year after the blockade, in 1920, Soviet Russia could not export any kind of goods, and was obliged to restrict its purchases to the most indispensable machines and materials, paying for the same in gold. The chief purchases were railway materials, locomotives, agricultural implements, machines and tools for the forest and other producing industries. About ten million pounds sterling were spent in the buying of eight hundred locomotives, rails, and other railway requisites. As the British government at that time hesitated to reopen solid economic relations with Russia, the biggest part of these orders had to be placed in Germany and Sweden. Only from the end of 1920 and the beginning of 1921 we began more regular purchases in England.

The bad harvest of 1921 forced Russia to spend large sums upon imports of foodstuffs and seeds, in order to save the lives and livelihood of the peasants in the famine-stricken areas. The total imports for 1920 were about £5,000,000. In 1921 they amounted to about £20,000,-000; while in 1922 they ran to £27,000,000. Of course, the government is taking all possible steps to reduce imports, in order to spend the least possible amount of gold abroad.

It was only in 1921 that Soviet Russia made timid attempts to export her first cargoes of flax, timber, skins, hides, and furs. The rapid growth of our exports is shown by the figures of timber exports. In 1920 they were quite insignificant: about two hundred standards—a cargo for a test case. In 1921, Russia exported forty thousand standards, in 1922 two hundred thousand standards, while in the year 1923 our plans are to export four hundred thousand standards, and in all probability, given normal conditions, these figures will be exceeded. Exports, which in 1921 amounted to not more than 3 or 4 per cent of imports, are quickly overtaking the latter and, in the last quarter of 1922, already constituted about 60 per cent of the imports. For the first four months of 1923 the value of the exports has actually been larger than that of our imports. Of course, it may be a little early as yet to speak of a positive Russian trade balance, but there can be no doubt that Russia is progressing rapidly on the way to establish a balance between exports and imports.

The nature of our exports is an important consideration for Europe. In addition to timber, flax, bristles, hides, and furs, there are oil products, and quite recently Russia has begun the export of grain and oil cakes. Finland already covers her deficit in grain during these last months, chiefly by imports from Soviet Russia. Germany has received considerable quantities of rye, barley, oats; oil cakes were sold to Scandinavia. The total value of Russia's exports, from £2,000,000 in 1921, has grown up to £8,000,000 in 1922. The anticipated value of ex-

ports in 1923 will be not less than £30,000,000 to
£40,000,000. Thus we are keeping up a rate of increase in this sphere of 400 per cent per annum.

Of course, all these figures may be insignificant by
themselves, and represent only a small percentage of the
pre-war export. But it must not be forgotten that Russia emerged from a state of war three years later than
any other European country, and that during the European war she bore much heavier sacrifices, both economically and in loss of life. Within the next few years,
however, Russia unquestionably will speedily restore her
pre-war position on the world market as a source of supply of grain, agricultural products, and raw materials.

PROSPECTS IN RUSSIA [1]

A grey dawn is setting in over Russia after a long
spell of darkness. There was a time when a great Tsar
might have gathered all the nations of his Empire around
him in the struggle for freedom and justice, but a weak
and misguided Tsar squandered the treasure of popular
trust which was at his disposal in the opening of the war.
There was a time when a coalition between patriotic socialists like Kerensky and patriotic military leaders like
Kornilov might have prevented the shameful disruption
of the state, but Kerensky and Kornilov fought one another for the benefit of fanatical adventurers. Indeed,
the history of Russia during these last years reminds one
of the legend of the Sibyl, who offered to sell her book
of prophecy to the Roman authorities. They declined the
offer because of the high price. After great disasters the
Sibyl appeared again with half the pages torn out, and
yet asked the same price for the remnant. Her offer
was again rejected; when she came a third time there was
only one leaf of the prophetic text left, but the price was
the same.

[1] By P. Vinogradov. Contemporary Review. 115: 606-12. June, 1919.

Even so in Russia—it is not victory nor glorious re-generation that her statesmen have to bid for now, but existence, the re-establishment of the bare foundations of political life. But even in this task it is not enough to discover the right course: the people must find strength to steer such a course. The object lessons of the Bol-shevik experiments are bringing enlightenment to the most obdurate experimentalists. Advanced students in Marxian economics have begun to realize that a country cannot live without exchange, transport and credit, as a human being cannot live without circulation. Industrial workmen are coming to the conclusion that it is not in their interest to revert to natural husbandry; peasants have learnt that it is not enough to seize the land of the neighboring squires, that bread comes from the distant south to the north and boots come from the distant north to the south. Nor can the paradox of an army led by terrorized officers be upheld much longer. Bolshevism is dying, but who is to bury it and to succeed to its ruined estate?

A military dictatorship is a necessary stage, but only a transitional stage. All the leaders have declared em-phatically that they want to liberate Russia, and not to enslave it. Besides, as Napoleon said long ago, one can conquer with bayonets, but not sit on bayonets. There are some generals and officers in Russia whose range of political vision does not extend further than to the estab-lishment of a military dictatorship. But shortsighted cynicism would merely create another entanglement, and delay the development of the main action for some time without preventing the ultimate settlement. It is clear to all thinking patriots that it would be fatal to fall back under the sway of a political system which has produced the monster of Bolshevism with its ideal of self-destruc-tive hatred.

The real danger to be faced is the immense difficulty of erecting a solid structure on the ruins of old Russia.

In its simplest form the difficulty will face the Constituent Assembly which must meet sooner or later to reconstruct the state. Is new Russia to be a monarchy or a republic? There is a question, which, though put in general terms, points to a series of other knotty problems.

Monarchy can be neither created nor rejected at will. Monarchy certainly appeals to the inarticulate feelings of the people as the embodiment of the state in a living person. The heathens gave their gods human shapes, because the human form helped them to approach the forces of nature; even so elemental *demos* is inclined to personify power. But the monarchical myth does not arise at random. It wants a peculiar soil for its growth—the soil of more or less successful historical achievements. There may be monarchical feeling still alive in the consciousness of the people. The work of Peter the Great, of Catherine, of Alexander I, of Alexander II, had formed a capital which it was not easy to squander. But the last generations of the Romanovs have done everything possible to desecrate traditional authority. The humiliations of the Berlin Congress and of the Japanese War, the experiences of the wretched "Kids" armed with sticks and sent to the trenches to face Mackensen's machine guns, the insolent corruption of Rasputin, prepared the revolution in people's minds, and there are no personalities among the surviving scions of the old dynasty capable of inspiring the nation with renewed confidence.

The question of a possible attempt to revive a monarchy on a different dynastic basis remains open, but it would be useless to speculate on the chances of such an adventure. I should like merely to remark that the events of 1613 when the Romanovs, an aristicratic family of second rank, were raised to the throne formerly occupied by descendants of Rurik, cannot be regarded as a historical precedent in this connection. This act of the reconstruction of Russia was a natural one in the atmosphere of three hundred years ago. In the political thought of the people there existed no other mould of government except that of Tsardom. All the usurpers and pretenders of the "Troubled Times" set up claims to that title and power. Needless to add, the range of possible combinations has been substantially extended since then: even in the darkest corners of the country they know now that there are other means of governing the state. The notion of a commonwealth is by no means unfamiliar or repugnant to the people, while, on the other hand, no claim as to monarchical succession would remain unchallenged or could be put forward with any measure of traditional authority. The political education of the Russian nation has been slow, and in some respects it has taken an unfavorable turn, but three hundred years have not passed without leaving their mark on political consciousness.

Another form of monarchical settlement is, however, more than a subject for fanciful speculation. I mean an attempt to turn the military dictatorship arising out of the death struggle with Bolshevism into a permanent Empire on the Napoleonic pattern. Such an eventuality is not to be ruled out as fanciful or substantially improbable. The disillusionment as regards liberal theories, the craving for rest and order, the demand for retaliation and punishment which is sure to follow the collapse of the Bolsheviks will provide a good deal of material for a "counter-revolution," and the chief who succeeds in putting an end to the present trouble will naturally form the center of political movements directed toward the restoration of personal government on imperial lines. Let us, however, express the hope that the recoil in this direction will not result in irretrievable errors of judgment. An imperialistic counter-revolution would mean the reopening of the fatal struggle between authority and freedom to which the present ruin of the country must be ascribed. Authority is a necessary element in the constitution of a state, but it would be the greatest misfortune if authority were set up in reconstructed Russia as the one and absolute principle of government. Authority has to be combined with law and justified by law, that is, by an order of rights, and no order of rights can be maintained if the life of the state depends ultimately on personal discretion.

The recognition of this interdependence between authority and right is the essence and the common trait of all constitutions, and the wisdom of statesmen in civilized countries has consisted in ascertaining the conditions and proportions in which these two elements of stability have to be combined in particular cases. Any violation of this fundamental formula would give rise to continuous unrest and struggle, to a state of things similar to that prevailing in China or in Persia after the downfall of their traditional political systems. Apart from that, a counter-revolutionary empire would find itself entirely out of touch with the general progress of democracy in the civilized world. There can be no doubt that many difficulties have been created for the cause of national reconstruction in Russia by the distrust of western democratic opinion in regard to the aims and policy of the military leaders. Koltchak's *coup d'état* of Omsk may have been necessary from the point of view of the creation of an effective force and of an efficient administration, but it was a grievous set-back from the point of view of international cooperation, and future historians will probably examine very carefully the possibility of arranging a working compromise with the anti-Bolshevik socialists represented by Avkertiev and his colleagues. The fact that these men, when displaced and banished, remained staunch in their denunciation of Lenin's tyranny shows at any rate that there was no lack of patriotism on their part, even if some of their views and measures may have been trammeled of rapid and decisive action.

I am mentioning this rather antiquated episode only because it presents a warning against much more ambitious
schemes in the future. A permanent estrangement between reconstructed Russia and the progressive democracies of the west would be an irretrievable disaster for
both sides. Russia, in any case, is bound to derive immense advantages from the support and good-will of the
west: to steer a course leading into German harbors
would be to steer toward enslavement. According to the
parable in the Gospel nothing is to be more dreaded than
the return of an evil spirit who has been temporarily
driven out from the command of one possessed: he would
come back armed with increased violence, and the latter
state of the conquered would be worse than the former
one. There may have been attempts to negotiate with the
hereditary enemies of the Slavs, and the stupendous
blunders of the entente, such as the Prinkipo project or
the desertion of Odessa, have lent plausible pretexts for
such attempts, but the vital interests of Russia require
her to join the circle of western civilization, and any
swerving from the fundamental principle is bound to
lead to mischief in the end.

This being so, the leaders of Russia ought to strive
for a democratic settlement of Russian constitutional
problems. The task of ensuring such a solution is not an
easy one. The deplorable state of ignorance and political
inexperience of the Russian people is putting serious
obstacles in the way of such a solution. Our chief aim
is to educate the nation for self-government and political
activity. But this cannot be done in a few years, and the
constitutional settlement cannot wait. It will have to be
taken in hand as soon as the country has been liberated
from the incubus of Bolshevism.

The problem of organizing the democratic mainstays
of government is not less ominous. The unpractical idealists of 1905 thought they had discovered a simple formula
to solve all difficulties. Let the country be governed by

assemblies elected by means of universal, equal, direct, and secret suffrage. This famous formula "with four tails" was proclaimed from every platform and any attempt to introduce some modifications in the sacramental demands was condemned as a device of aristocratic and bureaucratic reactionaries. The sacramental formula was put into practice after the upheaval of 1917, with the result that crowds of uneducated people swamped the elections in the wake of unscrupulous demagogues and wire-pullers. Persons who had sat in the four Dumas of Nicholas II were *prima facie* handicapped by the fact that they had had some experience of affairs of state. The naïve theory that a modern commonwealth can be ruled by a supposed sum total of all the wills of its individual members is a curious survival of the rationalistic conception of society prevalent in the eighteenth century. We know by this time that votes must not only be counted, but ought to be weighed; the fiction of equality in experience and aptitude, when applied to politically undeveloped communities, is simply an excuse for sleight of hand and log-rolling. The best that can be said for universal suffrage is that it is difficult to substitute for it a reasonable and just scale of citizenship. One qualification, at any rate, can be imposed without any derogation to democratic principles. Let men and women vote without any regard being had to property or class, but let it be recognized that at least elementary education is required from those who are entrusted with a decisive function in the government of their country. If a modest test of literacy were required, somewhat on the lines of the tests used in the United States and contemplated in Canada, possibly one-third of the population of Russia would receive the vote at once, and the expansion of the franchise would depend automatically on the spread of education. This seems a sufficient guarantee both against the blundering of electoral mobs and against the sinister interests of plutocratic and oligarchical groups.

But whatever may be the details of constitutional arrangements, it must be borne in mind that a great social revolution has taken place, and it would be more or less futile to try to revert to the limitations and privileges of the old régime. A government attempting to restore the former status of landed proprietors would be submerged before long in another upheaval of the peasantry. It is not mere greed that has incited the village communes of great Russia and the small peasant proprietors of the Ukraina to grab the land of the squires. The fundamental reason for the social catastrophe was a congestion of the working population hemmed in by the privileged land-holding of the few. The first condition for a return to social peace is to recognize the expropriation of the squires, to indemnify them as far as possible, and to regularize the new distribution of the soil among the peasants. Napoleon, and even the Bourbons of the restoration recognized the force of the *fait accompli* in similar circumstances, and the rulers of new Russia are prepared to do the same, if one may judge from their solemn declarations.

We have been concerned with institutions and with the machinery of government, for the single reason that calculations as to this side of the process admit of some probability. But it is evident that there must be a background of moral evolution to all these institutional changes. It is not only knowledge and experience that are required for the building of a commonwealth, but a certain spirit of devotion, of self-control, of belief. The most terrible aspect of the Bolshevist mania is the "despair of the state," as General Smuts has put it, the disgust of the millions as regards political ties and duties. This despair is at the back of the bestiality and fiendish cruelty of the struggle. *Homo homini lupus* is, indeed, the right word for this terrible crisis. Is there any reason for supposing that the Russian people are about to overcome this attack of bloodthirsty rage? After all, the prophets of Russia—Tolstoy, Dostoyevsky, Vladimir Solovyëv, have revealed to us the psychology of the Russian people not only in the power of darkness, the frenzy of the "possessed," the despair of the "dead house," but as a mysterious and beneficent force, capable of sincere charity, and most sensitive in its conscience of truth and justice. It is difficult to speak of these things otherwise than in poetical terms, but I should like to point to one sign of the returning consciousness of right and wrong. I mean the revival of religion. In the sad years of the old régime, religion had been debased like everything else by the idolatry of absolutism. The clergy, instead of acting as spiritual teachers, were performers of ceremonies, submissive to the episcopal bureaucrats and to the *Procureur* of the Synod, helpless in their dealings with the intellectuals and with the common people. The upheaval of 1917 brought a crisis in this respect. For a time the Bolshevists seemed successful in their war against religion; the despairing people were carried away by a mania of sacrilege. But the orgy of godlessness did not last long. The persecution of priests and of the faithful has purified the moral character of the Christian community and recalled it to a sense of the unconquerable power of the spirit. The patriarch had the strength to anathematize the oppressors and to hold them at bay by his moral prestige. Everywhere confessors died for their faith and thereby vindicated the sincerity of their religion. It would be impossible to express the force of this movement in exact terms, but of one thing there can be no doubt; the degradation of Bolshevism has already secured a truer and loftier conception of the church than could have been achieved by a more peaceful development. Russian orthodoxy cannot fall back into the slavery of the Holy Synod after having been regenerated by its martyrs. The revival of a pure church in Russia means in truth the first step toward the moral and political education of the people. Men live not only by bread, but by the word of God.

Looking back on the wide range of questions raised in this paper, I should like to emphasize that it is neither prediction, nor a concerted plan, nor yet a set of doctrinal affirmations, that I am submitting to the public. The matters discussed are too important, the events expected are too complex, to admit of any treatment on dogmatic lines. And yet those who love Russia cannot help speculating on the best means of raising her again to the rank of a civilized nation. Perhaps some of the thoughts expressed in this article may find sympathy and approval on the part of those who will be responsible for the reconstruction of the country.

THE GREAT NARCOSIS [1]

On May first of the past year, there appeared in Moscow in the so-called Soviet Russia, which had, by that time, reached the zenith of its glory, a book intended to crown that glory—the first number of the *Communist International*. On the cover of the book is the usual gaudy picture, the terrestrial globe with iron chains all around it, and a figure of a workman with an uplifted hammer. The workman, of course, is naked, wearing only a leather apron, and his muscles are those of a Hercules. And in the text of the book itself, one may read among other things the declaration of Maxim Gorky to the "proletariat of the world," that Russia "is now performing her great, planetary deed." And by the side of this shockingly shameless declaration one may find the following lines that are heart-rending in their cynic crudity:

The Tsars and the priests, the former masters of the Kremlin, never dreamt that in its gray walls would gather the representatives of the most revolutionary part of modern mankind. And yet it has come to pass. The mole of history has dug well under the Kremlin wall.

[1] By Ivan Bunin. Living Age. 306: 502-5. August 28, 1920.

These lines were written by one of the chief representatives of the "workman-peasant" government, which
now reigns in the Kremlin. Good Lord, what farce of
a government it is! What an unimaginable absurdity!
What a peal of mocking and sneering laughter over nar-
cotized Russia that has sold her soul to the devil! These
lines were written by Trotsky, and they have a ring of
overwhelming confidence. Yet Trotsky is right only in
one thing. The blind and vengeful beast, crafty and
sharp-clawed, has indeed dug well under the walls of the
Kremlin, the ground under which is still so soft. But in
the rest Trotsky is mistaken. The old masters of the
Kremlin, its legitimate owners, its parents and its children, the builders and the upholders of the Russian land,
would have turned in their graves if they could have
heard Trotsky's words, and if they could have known
what he and his followers have done to Russia. Inexpressible would be their pain and their agony at the sight
of what is taking place in the walls of the Kremlin and
outside of them, where, according to the merry expression of one of the modern Moscow poets,

> Blood, blood gushes forth,
> As water in a bathhouse
> Out of an overturned bucket.

Unimagined horror would have seized those "Tsars
and priests" at the sight of the gigantic and bloody hurly-
burly into which Russia has been transformed. And
yet, it seems to me that they could and should have foreseen the manifold new misfortunes and disgraces which
might and would overtake again their unfortunate land.
They knew and they remembered the fearful recurring
periods of civil dissension when, in the words of a
chronicler who might have been speaking of our own
days, "the earth was sown with seeds of internal dis-
cords and fattened by their fruit"; when the voices of
those tilling the soil were heard but seldom, but the ravens

croaked all over the land, dividing the corpses among them; for one brother said to another "This is mine, and this is mine, also," while pagan outsiders fell upon them from all sides, winning victories over them, and Kiev and Tchernigov groaned under the invader's yoke.

"The Tsars and the priests" could foresee much, knowing and remembering their people's changing hearts and unstable minds, their tearfulness and their cruelty; the country's illimitable steppes, impassible forests, endless marches, historic destinies; and its neighbors, "so greedy, crafty, and merciless," its youthful immaturity before those neighbors, its backwardness, and its fatal peculiarity of always moving forward in circles. They knew all that made Ivan the Terrible once exclaim: "I am a beast, but I reign over beasts." They knew that all these things have changed but little down to our day, and really could not change overnight in our steppes and forests and bogs, or during that short period of time during which the Russian people have been a conscious nation.

The Tsars and the priests! But did we foresee what was bound to happen? And what has come to pass is really that Russian rebellion, "cruel and senseless," which Pushkin foretold and about which we only now begin to think. What has come to pass is merely what has happened before. And yet many are even now confused by that vulgar and absurd word, "Bolshevism," and believe that something unprecedented has taken place, something that has no example in the past. They feel that it is something that is connected with the changing psychology of the race, with the evolution of that European proletariat which speaks of bringing into the world a new and beautiful religion of the highest humanitarian ideals, and at the same time demands that we witness without protest the filthiest and cruellest crimes of history, occurring in the Christian Europe of the twentieth century.

History repeats itself, but nowhere, it seems, does it

repeat itself as it does with us. And its very elementals afford us so slight a foundation for future hope! Moreover, we have forgotten even those elementals.

A peasant from Orel said to me two years ago:

> We cannot allow ourselves freedom. Take me, for instance. I am good and kind until I start going. And then I become the first murderer, the first thief, the first drunkard around.

But what is this if not the first page of our national history? Do you remember how it reads?

> Our land is great and plentiful, but there is no order in it. Drag us apart or we shall cut each other's throats. Bring peace into our midst, for we are too cruel in spite of our good nature. Lead us into the shafts of the plow and force us to draw the furrows, otherwise our land, which is the richest in the world, will become overgrown with weeds. For we are temperamentally indolent, despite our physical capacity for work. In short, come and rule us. Everything in us is unstable and unorganized. We are greedy and extravagant, capable of the most beautiful and highest, and yet of the lowest and meanest. We are possessed of a diabolic mistrust and yet, by means of the most flimsy lies we can be led into any trap with marvelous ease.

That is our beginning, and what follows it? To illustrate the next step, take the famous robber, Vaska Buslayev, who when an old man, bitterly repents his crimes and weeps because during his youth he murdered and robbed. Then we have the "great Russian revolutions" the eternal struggles among principalities before Moscow became supreme, the endless internal troubles in Moscow itself, the false leaders and pretenders to the throne, recruited from the lowest ranks, before whom we first grovelled on our knees to frenzied shouts of joy and the pealing of the bells, and later in equal frenzy mocked and sneered over their mutilated bodies. Then the numberless massacres in the Ukraina, the bloody tyrant Razin who was literally worshipped by whole generations of the *intelligentsia,* which waited so eagerly for his second coming; for the blessed time when "the people shall awake." And so through our whole history. The swinging of minds and hearts from side to side, self-looting, self-annihilation, thefts and fires and murders, the floods that flowed from the destroyed taverns, in whose fiery fluid madmen were literally drowned at times; and on the following day attacks of sentimentalism, tears and contrite repentance before holy relics, and parades in front of the red steps of the Kremlin bearing the bloody heads of decapitated false tsars and false atamans. Remember, remember all this, oh you, "the most advanced of revolutionary mankind," now so strongly entrenched in the Kremlin!

I have just lived through what took place yesterday and is taking place today in the Ukraina, in that cradle of the Slav soul, and involuntarily I recall the story of Hmelnitsky and his followers. Read again your history.

The serfs gathered in bands and destroyed the homes of the rich and poor, razed whole villages to the ground, robbed and burned and murdered and mocked the dead and tore the skin from the backs of their victims, sawed them into halves and quarters, roasted them on coals, threw hot water over them, and were cruellest in their treatment of the Jews. They danced and drank on their holy books, they tore the intestines out of small children and showing them to their parents, asked with laughter, 'is this kosher or not?'

This is what happened. And Hmelnitsky himself "fasted and prayed at one time, and drank without stop at another. At times he sobbed, kneeling before a holy image, and sang songs of his own composition. At times, he was tearful and mild, and then suddenly became wild and haughty."

And how many times did he change his "orientations!" How many times did he violate his oaths taken on the cross! How many times did he change his allies and his friends!

And remember Emelyan Pugatchëv and Stenka Razin, whose rebellions we at last begin to compare with what is taking place today, and still do not dare to draw the obvious conclusions. Read again what you read in your history perhaps inattentively at the time:

Stenka's rebellion caught the whole of Russia like wildfire. Everything pagan rose up.

Yes, let Trotsky and Gorky stop boasting about their Red Bashkiria. This "planetary deed" was done already, long before the "Third Internationale."

The Zyrians, the Mordvians, the Tchuvashi, the Tcheremisi, the Bashkirs rose with Stenka and burned and murdered everything in sight, without knowing what they were fighting for. All over the Moscow realm and even to the shores of the White Sea, Stenka's letters were circulated and in them he declared that he "came to destroy all the Boyars, the nobles, and the officials, to sweep away all authority, and to establish equality for all." All the cities which were captured by Stenka were given to the mercy of his Cossacks. The property of each city was divided among Stenka's "warriors," and he himself was drunk every day. Everyone who had the misfortune of displeasing him was doomed to death. Some were cut to pieces, some were drowned, Stenka himself was a "self-willed and changing man, now sombre and cruel, now easily excitable, now humble and contrite, ready to make a pilgrimage to the uttermost monasteries, now rejecting the mysteries of the church, mocking religion, murdering priests. Cruel and bloodthirsty, he came to hate laws, society, and religion and everything that stood in the way of personal desires. Mercy, honor, humanity were unknown to him. His whole being was imbued with vengeance and envy. And his whole army consisted of fugitive thieves and vagabonds, of all that riff-raff which called itself Cossacks, but was not recognized as Cossacks by the people of the Don. Stenka caught this mob into his net by promising them complete freedom and complete equality, but in reality he enslaved them all. The slightest disobedience was punishable by the cruellest death. He called them all brothers, and yet forced them to crawl on their knees before him."

Good Lord! what an amazing similarity there is between this description and what is taking place now in the name of the Third Internationale! Although, of

course, Stenka's authority was a thousand times more
natural than the present "workman-peasant" authority,
that most unnatural and most absurd "absurdity" of
Russia's history; although, of course, that "government"
of Stenka Razin was a hundred times better than the
"workman-peasant" government which reigns in the
Kremlin!

CHAPTER III

POLAND

POLAND, THE LAND AND THE STATE[1]

[The Polish alphabet has a number of letters not occurring in English. They are pronounced as follows: ą = *an*, in *swan;* ę = *en*, in *even;* ć = *ti*, in *tune* or *literature;* ł = *ll*, in *mellow* or *yellow;* ń=*ni*, in *onion;* ó=*o*, in *wolf* or *woman;* ś=*sy*, in *sure* or *sugar;* ź=*si* in *fusion* or *vision;* ż= *zh* in *seizure*—THE EDITOR.]

The foundation of the historical life of nations is laid down in the relatively unchanging features of the earth. Strong and organized human wills can temporarily deflect national life from the course favored by nature, but sooner or later, life flows back into natural channels and its return is almost invariably marked by some upheaval in customs, character, or national life.

Let us glance at the relationship between historical life and its natural foundations in the Vistula region. Along this river led the route followed by the Phenicians in their trading voyages to the Baltic for amber, as is evidenced by cowry shells in the form of amulets which have been found in prehistoric tombs along the Baltic littoral. In the fourth century of our era, as one of a series of racial migrations, a Slavic wave appears for the second time, driving the Goths against the Roman Empire. *Pulsae a superioribus barbaris,* says Julius Capitolinus, referring to the Goths. The Slavs continued to push onward, until the limit of their westward expansion was set by Charlemagne, whose name stood for power among the western Slavs.

[1] By E. Romer. Geographical Review. 4: 6-25. July, 1917.

What were the peoples whom Ptolemy called by the general name of *Venedae*, and Procopius by that of *Sclaveni* or *Slaveni?* Already differentiated, they formed numerous groups in the Frankish period. The eastern of these tribes, nameless at first, were destined to play a prominent part in later history. In the southwest the Bohemian-Moravian group settled down in a hilly country, so situated that it was alike protected from hostile neighbors and accessible both to Roman and Byzantine influences. No wonder, then, that this particular Slavic group made the earliest entry upon the arena of history. Through their German neighbors we happen to know the names of many of the tribes that resided in the western lowlands, such as the Abodrites (Obotrites), the Liutizians, and the Sorbs, all of them belonging to the group of the Polabs, or Slavs of the Elbe. The history of all these tribes has but one tale to tell; the alternative of extermination or Germanization. To the east of the Polabs resided the Lekhs, or Poles, among whom Nestor, an early chronicler, counts the Polians, Mazovians, Pomeranians, and Liutizians. From Nestor's account one must conclude that the Liutizians and probably the entire group of the Polabs belonged, in tribe and language, to the Poles (Lekhs). This historical inference is confirmed by linguistic research. [1] A further inference of importance is to be derived from linguistics. If we cast a glance upon Nitsch's map showing the present distribution of the various forms of Polish, it will be seen that the section where the language is the most homogeneous, where it possesses the smallest number of peculiarities of dialect, and where it most closely approaches the accepted literary form, is located on the westernmost edge of Polish linguistic territory. Is not this extreme peripheral position of the main body of the Polish tongue a proof that Germanization has not been limited to the Polabs alone?

[1] Rozwadowski: The Relationship Between the Polish and Other Slavonic Languages. Polish Encyclopedia. Vol. 2. p. 379. Academy of Science. Cracow. 1915. [In Polish.]

Germanization went hand in hand with Christianity, for, as the eminent historian Potkanski puts it, together with the cross the German apostles carried into Slavdom the boundary posts of the German state. This movement had its good side, however. It stimulated the Slavs to political organization and, consequently, to an apostolic propaganda of their own as a shield for national independence.

We are not concerned here with historical processes but with the relationship existing between them and the land. Christianity radiated across Slavdom from both Roman and Byzantine sources. It penetrated through various channels. The movement reached its greatest intensity in the tenth century. In the direction of the Baltic, Christianity met the same or even greater obstacles than did Slavdom in the Frankish period. Just as Slavdom had, at that time, avoided the gorge of the Nieman between Grodno and Kovno, so Christianity came to a standstill before this obstacle. In the east Christianity extended farther in the year 1000 than Slavdom did in the time of Charlemagne. Its victorious advance was only stopped on the lower Dnieper where the rapids caused by the passage of that river through the south Russian granite threshold form an obstacle to navigation.

At the end of the tenth century the now fully developed Polish state becomes an historical factor. The political expansion of this state during the reign of Boleslav the Great (992-1025) strikes the keynote of the nation's forthcoming development as conditioned by its geographical setting. If we eliminate the districts which had succumbed to early Germanization, we are immediately struck by the likeness existing between the extent of Slavdom in 800, of Christianity in 1000, and of the Polish state at the beginning of the eleventh century. When we remember that Poland occupied, under Boleslav's predecessor, in 962, an area of only forty thousand square miles, while it increased fifty years later to over one hundred and seventy thousand square miles, it becomes evident that the sword of Bolesłav had found a powerful ally in the individuality of the land.

The topography favorable to eastward racial pressure has attained its climax of development in the basin of the Vistula. That the term *Drang nach Osten* is identified more especially with German history is due not to a greater suitability of the German region to this tendency, but, on the whole, to the way in which the German people have utilized it. This tendency has expressed itself quite differently in Poland's history. In order fully to understand the difference, it is necessary to take into account yet another feature of the Polish region and compare it with the history of Russia. Poland, limited on the south by the Carpathians, is not a plane gradually sloping from there to the sea: it is a broad depression leading from west to east, into which the rivers flow in a concentrated direction and out of which they flow into both the Baltic and the Black Sea through deeply cut gorges or winding ravines, across the lake-dotted uplands of the Baltic heights and the broad plateaus that slope down to the Black Sea. The affluents of the Vistula, more numerous from the east than is the case with any of the other river systems to the west, would indeed seem to have assigned to Poland an eastward expansion on a scale impossible in the west, where the lowland belt is narrower. How different the map of Europe might now be had not the Poles been a people whose social and political institutions were directly opposed to the spirit of conquest!

Rivers not only were decisive factors in determining the direction and extent of Poland's expansion as a whole, but also in determining her subdivisions. For, in the lowland area that is Poland, the configuration of the land is in great part dependent on the drainage system. As a consequence there developed a division into the longitudinal zones characteristic of the Polish state.

The first zone is the broad belt of the great east-and-west valleys, the cradle and center of Poland, including Great Poland, Cuyavia (Kujawy), and Mazovia. The second is the zone of moderate relief which includes Polish heights within the arc of the upper Vistula and the foothills of the Carpathians and Sudetic Mountains, that is, Silesia, and little Poland, and, in prolongation thereof, red Russia the transition ground between Poland and the Ruthenia of Kiev, as Silesia had been the link between Poland and Bohemia. Finally, the third zone is the coastal region, including Pomerania and Prussia.

These political subdivisions, based on the physiognomy of the country, again reflect the fundamental fact that the main waterways were always the axes, never the border lines, of vital parts of the Polish organism. This is true even for Poland's first period of weakness, when she had fallen apart into numerous separate sections and the rulers of these petty states were fighting one another. Never even in this period did a great river become a border line, not the Vistula or the Warta, nor yet the Notetz or the Pilitza.

Furthermore, just as the division and organization of the territory were based upon the character of the land, so did the nation itself draw its racial and spiritual characteristics from the soil. Pomeranian, Polian, Mazovian, Cuyavian (Kujawski), Silesian, etc., are not names derived, as some think, from political terminology; they are the names of Polish tribes, differentiated among themselves by slight peculiarities, but all of them stamped by the individuality of the land. A novel and conclusive argument in this respect has been furnished by the researches of Nitsh, who has demonstrated that the dialectical peculiarities of the Polish language correspond exactly to the division into provinces at the time of the Piast dynasty, and also to the primitive divisions into eparchies.

The dependence of even the smallest units of Poland's political structure on the physiognomy of the land is so close that the calamity of the partition appears all the more painful to Polish minds. It not only struck a deadly blow at the state, but, by tearing up the frontiers of districts and autonomous provinces, shook to its innermost foundations the social and economic life of the nation. The boundaries which the various partitions of Poland have introduced into the political map of Europe have been destructive and not constructive. Rivers which once pulsated with life have now become merely dead border lines.

The actors in the crime perpetrated upon the Polish nation separated themselves from one another by boundary lines that followed rivers. Assuredly strife would not be long in breaking out again. One can hardly refrain from quoting the words of the poet, who foresaw the part to be played by the river frontier:

> The Niemen separates the Lithuanians from their foes:
>
> On this side throngs of Lithuanian youths
>
> On the other, in helmet and armor,
> The Germans on horseback stand immovable.
> Each party watches the crossing.
> So the Niemen, once famed for hospitality,
> That linked the realms of fraternal nations,
> Now for them has become the threshold of eternity:
> For none without loss of life or liberty
> Could cross the forbidden waters.
>
> (Adam Mickiewicz, *Konrad Wallenrod*)

Poland from the first extended to the Moravian Gate. As early as the seventh century the region was politically organized. The first rays of Christianity penetrated through that gate along with Byzantine civilization. But though the Moravian Gate afforded an easy path across the Carpathians, it led up to an almost inaccessible way to the Adriatic, the passage through the rocky wilderness of the Karst. As a gateway between the northern and southern seas, the Moravian Gate could never compare, even in Roman times, with the convenient passes leading across the Alps. The Brenner Pass, especially, was superior and caused the Adriatic lands to become a region of German political expansion under the Hohenstaufen.

This insufficiency of the Moravian Gate as a southern outlet and the eastward trend of the main affluents of the Vistula undoubtedly account for the impetus given to Poland's political expansion in the direction of the Baltic-Pontic isthmus. The position of Poland in an area unobstructed by mountains and her equipment with a system of natural valley highways are the basic physical facts which have affected Poland's political existence and development.

It seems pertinent to close this discussion with an explanation of the causes by which Poland, rather than Lithuania or Ruthenia, became the bridge between the two seas. The ice of the glacial period never held Ruthenia in its grip, and consequently this province remained a shelter for all life, including man. Nowhere in Poland are there any remains of paleolithic culture such as are found in Ruthenia. The dawn of history greeted Ruthenian lands, and perhaps the people, earlier than it did Poland. Moreover, it was easy for Byzantine influences to stream into Ruthenia, as the channel was broad and free. Many obstacles, however, had to be overcome by the Romans before they could reach the Poland of the Piasts. Thus for centuries Ruthenia towered culturally above its neighbors, Poland and Lithuania. But in Ruthenia power to organize did not go hand in hand with culture. The reasons were many. The greater part of Ruthenia consisted of steppes. Material life, therefore, absorbed most of the energy of its inhabitants. Meanwhile the steppe remained open to the incursion of organized hordes. But the steppe culture of Ruthenia lacked the strength for a defensive organization. Wooded Poland and Lithuania, however, were able to take the initiative in freeing and defending their countries from invasion—a normal occurrence in the steppe. Although Ruthenia brought culture to Lithuania, especially along the valley of the Dnieper, and although Lithuania remained receptive of Ruthenian culture for centuries, still it was Lithuania that furnished the impulse and took the lead in Ruthenia's political organization.

In addition internal weakness was not wanting in Ruthenia. This country, a level land of steppes, was characterized by a sameness of climate, of natural productions, and of material culture that is uncommon over so large an area. This general uniformity was one of the causes of economic dependence, a feature which was strengthened by the lack of communications. For Ruthenia lies mostly in the region known as the Pontic or Ukrainian plateau, a strongly dissected oldland from which waters flow in all directions. At the time when Poland and Lithuania, as well as the larger part of Europe, were buried under ice, the Ukrainian crest of land was gradually rising. Under this slow but steady process, the Ukraina reached an elevation of three hundred to six hundred feet, while its rivers cut their channels to a corresponding depth. Cut by wild and deep ravines the land became a roadless labyrinth. It is not strange that Ruthenia, though from time to time consolidated by the will of some strong ruler into a single state, should always have relapsed, because of its lack of communications, into many independent principalities.

Totally different were the conditions determining the fusion and physiognomy of the lands belonging to Poland even as early as the time of the Piasts. During the glacial period, the ice-cap, as it receded northward across Poland, would halt from time to time; then a deluge of waters would spring forth from its margin and stream down to the North Sea and the Black Sea. This process created not only the east-and-west valleys in Poland's central zone, but also the peripheral highways of the unglaciated region.

It is not strange then that Ruthenia, linked to Lithuania by the artery of the Dnieper, submitted to her politically, even if, at first, she dominated her culturally. Nor is it strange that later cultural centers of Ruthenia, located upon the Ukrainian plateau, felt the influence of Poland. A wilderness led to the Dnieper, while the fringing ways of communication, such as the Bug, the Pripet, and the Dniester, were all part of the network of Poland's east-and-west valleys.

It is not strange, therefore, that Poland, physiographically varied, should ultimately have attained the highest degree of culture. In control of all the natural highways of Lithuania and Ruthenia, Poland was predestined to become the territorial link of these three parts of a physical unit.

IMMORTAL POLAND[1]

In the eighteenth century the Polish state was one of the most important in Europe. For centuries the most serene republic had been the bulwark of Christendom against Turk and Tatar. It was John Sobieski at Vienna gates who had saved Europe from the Saracen, like Charles Martel at the gates of Tours a thousand years before him. Cracow and Warsaw were the twin homes of culture in eastern Europe long before Berlin was heard of or St. Petersburg built. The Poles were famed as the most tolerant and chivalrous of peoples. But the state was ill-governed. The constitution was an anarchical hotch-potch of republic and monarchy, with all the vices of one and none of the virtues of the other; a witless mixture of democracy and aristocracy, and worse than either. The republic was weak, uncovetous, and over-tolerant of strangers. She was encircled, for her undoing, by neighbors who were strong, covetous, and intolerant of all scruples. The strong plotted together, swooped down upon the weak, and robbed her

[1] By G. Dennis. Hibbert Journal. 15: 113-24. October, 1916.

of a large portion of her lands and people. It was stark, unqualified brigandage. But the kings were shameless. Frederick (styled the Great) chuckled, and rubbed his bony hands. Catherine (styled the Great) said, "Poland is my door-mat"; and in her gentle, womanly way hanged noblemen, priests, and little children high on the same gallows with dogs, to teach the Poles the price they should pay for daring to resist the enemies of their country. As to the philosophers, who were supposed to wield the sceptre of European public opinion in those days, they fawned upon the evil-doers. How do otherwise? Had not the king-philosopher of Potsdam shown himself a staunch adept of the new ideas? Was he to be scolded for a mere peccadillo such as the ruin of a nation? Why make so much fuss about a stupid people like the Poles? as he said to his crony Voltaire. And the Semiramis of the north,—she was so discerning as to talent, so up-to-date in her ideas! She wrote such charming letters! she made such splendid plans for the happiness of all humanity!—why boggle if she chose to treat one small section of it as she did her own husband! One only of the monarchs wavered. "It is a great stain upon my name," said Maria Theresa to the Count de Barck, the Swedish Ambassador at Vienna. "Madam," said he, taken aback, "sovereigns have only to account to God." "Yes," replied the Empress, "it is Him I fear." And to her signature on the Treaty of 1772 she added these strange and prophetic words: "*Placet,* I consent to it, since so many great and wise persons wish it to be so; but, long after my death, men will see the result of having trampled under foot all things that up to now have been held to be just and sacred." For protest from the philosophers, there was one light word of Rousseau's. "They can swallow Poland," he said, "but they will never digest her." Jean Jacques and the Empress-Queen were little heeded, for 1772 showed the princes that if they succeed force and cunning may take the place of right. The Partition "shook the political system, lowered the public morals, and weakened the public law of Europe, for it was an example of strong powers conspiring to plunder a feeble power, with less regard for honor, or honesty, or the mere decency of appearances, than is shown by a burglar or a footpad." We may deplore the revolution in that it fought the old faiths, trampled on the old traditions, and let loose upon men and spirits of vain reason of vainer unrest and unbelief; but we must in justice remember that it was the kings and not the Jacobins who first mocked at the old morality and tore up the public law of Europe. When the monarchs upbraided France for her aggressions their words recoiled upon themselves, who were the prime disturbers of established right and order. For the first partition was but a beginning. In 1772 the three powers solemnly declared that they guaranteed what remained of the republic as free and independent for ever. In 1793 and 1795 they gave themselves the lie. This was the plea: "Convinced of the absolute incapacity of the republic of Poland to give itself a firm and strong government, have recognized that it is of an indispensable necessity to proceed to a total partition." Mark well. Then consider the facts:—(1) The basis of Russo-Prussian policy toward Poland was the secret treaty of 1764, by which the two states agreed to oppose, *if necessary by force,* any attempt on the part of the Poles to render the throne hereditary, to strengthen the government, or to abolish the *liberum veto*, which was a main source of the republic's political weakness; (2) Poland at last put her house in order, and by the constitution of 1791 made the throne hereditary, strengthened the king's power, abolished the *liberum veto*, and improved the condition of the peasants. If the partitioners had put their true reasons on paper, they would, therefore, have said: "Convinced of the now unfortunately proved capacity of the republic of Poland to give itself a firm and strong government, which it has been the bedrock of our policy at all costs to prevent, have recognized, etc., etc." They acted on the words they dared not write and Poland disappeared in blood and terror from the comity of nations. Yet when Kościuszko fell on the dolorous field of Maciejowice and Poland with him, I will never believe, as his enemies tell, that "Finis Poloniæ!" escaped his lips. For he knew that a house whose foundations are watered with the blood of sacrifice abides and is not destroyed.

A few words must suffice here to bridge the gulf between 1795 and 1914. The hopes of the Napoleonic era were vain, and the Treaty of Vienna in "liberating" Europe confirmed the doom of Poland. The Tsar promised certain liberties to the conquered people, but the promise was not kept. Hence the great rebellion of 1831. The Poles fought with all their ancient valor; but Russia was stronger, and she took the vengeance of the strong. Poland was henceforth ruled by the sword and the knout. Men who used their own language in public or women who wore the national costume were whipped until they bled. Little children, from seven years old, were taken from their families in thousands to serve as the tragic "enfants de troupe" in the Russian armies. These were the years of the Great Dispersion, when Mickiewicz and Chopin and Słowacki established in western Europe the cult of the martyr-nation. It is hard to read of the Polish exiles (as you may in Edgar Quinet) and to read dry-eyed: of penniless nobles, who had lost their lands and their homes because they had obeyed the call of duty and fought for their country, begging their bread in the streets of Paris; of exiles who risked all to see Poland once again and paid for a few hours in their native land with a lifetime in Siberian chains; of Adam Mickiewicz lamenting, prophet-like, at the Collège de France, "God has chosen my people to bear the evangel of patriotism to the world," till the

French youth stood up and cheered him till they wept, crying, "Vive la Pologne Immortelle!"—"and," adds an eye-witness rather quaintly, "even an Englishman who was present half-shamefacedly wiped his eyes." All that was best in France responded to the sufferings of Poland, if not her governments, which are often all that is worst. Vernet, when court painter at St. Petersburg, was once at work on a series of historical pictures for Nicholas I. "Can you paint me one on Poland?" asked the Emperor. "No, sire," replied the Frenchman, "I have never learned to paint Christ upon the Cross." . . .

If the lot of the exiles was hard, those who stayed behind fared worse. Misery came to a head in the last desperate rebellion of 1863. It failed, failed utterly; though Mazzini cried aloud for pity on "poor brave Poland," and poor brave Napoleon III tried vainly to stir the conscience of Europe. There was no pity, and no conscience. Orgies, floggings, massacres, torture; wild Cossacks shooting and sabring in the streets; a vast crowd, men and women and children, kneeling in the snow before the palace and praying to God for Poland, till the last of them was mowed down by the cannon or crushed to death under the horses' hoofs, and the snow was scarlet; while Prince Gortchakov played whist at the palace window (though he died soon after, as God knows, haunted by spectres of black-clad women, and sick with fear); and the waters of the Vistula were foul with corpses;—thus it was that "order reigned in Warsaw." It leaves one puzzled with human wickedness: why do men treat each other like this? Nor was the fate of the nation much better under her other oppressors. Neither fulfilled in the smallest degree the solemn promise of self-government made in 1815. Austria had sudden qualms of conscience; but by raising the horrible *jacquerie* of 1846 she decimated the great families who were the chief repositories of the national tradition, and by annexing the city-republic of Cracow stole the last inch of free Polish soil. Prussia set to, qualmless and unabashed, at a truly Prussian scheme of systematic denationalization, which later on culminated in the expropriation laws, the Hakatist campaign—and gaol for little children who pray to God in the tongue of their mothers. Thus in that same generation which witnessed the victory of the national principle throughout Europe, which saw the triumphant entry of Victor Emmanuel into the Eternal City, a German Emperor crowned at Versailles, the Turk beaten and the Balkans freed—Poland sank maimed and miserable, finally from the sight of men.

POLAND, THE CRIME OF PARTITION [1]

Some clever person has said that it is always the unexpected that happens, and on a calm and dispassionate survey the world does appear mainly to one as a scene of miracles. Out of Germany's strength, in whose purpose so many people refused to believe, came Poland's opportunity, in which nobody could have been expected to believe. Out of Russia's collapse emerges that forbidden thing, the Polish independence, not as a vengeful figure, the retributive shadow of the crime of partition but as something much more solid and more difficult to get rid of—a political necessity and a moral solution. Directly it appeared its practical usefulness became undeniable, and also the fact that, for better or worse, it was impossible to get rid of it again except by the unthinkable way of another carving, of another partition, of another crime.

Therein lies the strength and the future of the thing so strictly forbidden no farther back than a few years of the Polish independence expressed in a Polish state. It comes into the world morally free, not in virtue of its sufferings, but in virtue of its miraculous rebirth and

[1] By Joseph Conrad. Fortnightly Review. 111: 657-69. May 1, 1919.

of its ancient claim for services rendered to Europe. Not a single one of the combatants of all the fronts of the world had died consciously for Poland's freedom. That opportunity even was denied to Poland's children. And it is just as well! Providence in its inscrutable way had been merciful, for had it been otherwise the load of gratitude would have been too great, the sense of obligation too crushing, the joy of deliverance too fearful for mortals, common sinners with the rest of mankind before the eye of the Most High. Those who died east and west, leaving so much anguish and so much pride behind them, died neither for the creation of states, nor for empty words, nor yet the salvation of general ideas. They died neither for democracy, nor leagues, nor systems, and not even for abstract justice, which is an unfathomable mystery. They died for something too deep for words, too mighty for the common standard by which reason measures the advantages of life and death, too sacred for the vain discourses that come and go on the lips of dreamers, fanatics, humanitarians, and statesmen.

Poland's independence springs up from that great immolation, but Poland's loyalty will not be rooted in anything so trenchant and burdensome as the sense of immeasurable indebtedness, of that gratitude which in a worldly sense is sometimes called eternal, but which lies always at the mercy of weariness and is fatally condemned by the instability of human sentiment to end in negation. Polish loyalty will be rooted in something much more solid and enduring, something that could never be called eternal, but which is, in fact, life-enduring. It will be rooted in the national temperament, which is about the only thing on earth that can be trusted. Men may deteriorate, they may improve too, but they don't change. Misfortune is a hard school which may either mature or spoil a national character, but it may be reasonably advanced that the long course of adversity of the most cruel kind has not injured the fundamental characteristics of that nation which has proved its vitality against the most demoralizing odds. The various phases of the Polish sense of self-preservation struggling amongst the menacing forces and the no less threatening chaos of the neighboring powers should be judged impartially. I suggest impartiality and not indulgence simply because, when appraising the Polish question, it is not necessary to invoke the softer emotions. A little calm reflection on the past and the present is all that is necessary on the part of the western world to judge the movements of a community whose ideals are the same, but whose situation is unique. This situation was brought vividly home to me in the course of an argument more than eighteen months ago. "Don't forget," I was told, "that Poland has got to live in contact with Germany and Russia to the end of time. Do you understand the force of that expression: 'to the end of time'? Facts must be taken into account, and especially facts such as this, to which there is no possible remedy on earth. For reasons which are, properly speaking, physiological, a prospect of friendship with Germans or Russians even in the most distant future is unthinkable. Any alliance of heart and mind would be a monstrous thing, and monsters, as you know, cannot live. You can't base your conduct on a monstrous conception. We are either worth or not worth preserving, but the horrible psychology of the situation is enough to drive the national mind to distraction. Yet under a destructive pressure, of which western Europe can have no notion, of forces that are not only crushing but corrupting, we have preserved our sanity. Therefore there can be no fear of our losing our minds simply because the pressure is removed. We have neither lost our heads nor yet our moral sense. Oppression, not merely political, but affecting social relations, family life, the deepest affections of human nature, and the very fount

of natural emotions, has never made us vengeful. It is
worthy of notice that with every incentive present in
our emotional reactions we had no recourse to political
assassination. Arms in hand, hopelessly or hopefully,
and always against immeasurable odds, we did affirm
ourselves and the justice of our cause; but wild justice
has never been a part of our conception of national man-
liness. In all the history of Polish oppression there was
only one shot fired which was not in battle. Only one!
And the man who fired it in Paris at the Emperor Alexander II, was but an individual connected with no
organization, representing no part of Polish opinion.
The only effect in Poland was that of profound regret,
not at the failure, but at the mere fact of the attempt.
The history of our captivity is free from that stain; and
whatever follies in the eyes of the world we may have
perpetrated, we have neither murdered our enemies nor
acted treacherously against them, nor yet have been
reduced to the point of cursing each other."

I could not gainsay the truth of that discourse. I
saw as clearly as my interlocutor the impossibility of
the faintest sympathetic bond between Poland and her
neighbors ever being formed in the future. The only
course that remains to a reconstituted Poland is the
elaboration, establishment, and preservation of the most
correct method of political relations with neighbors to
whom Poland's existence is bound to be a humiliation
and offence. Calmly considered it is an appalling task,
yet one may put one's trust in that national temperament
which is so completely free from aggressiveness and revenge. Therein lie the foundations of all hope. The
success of renewed life for that nation whose fate is to
remain in exile, ever isolated from the west, amongst
hostile surroundings, depends on the sympathetic understanding of its problems by its distant friends, the western powers, which in their democratic development must
recognize the moral and intellectual kinship of that dis-

tant outpost of their type of civilization, which was the
only basis of Polish culture.

Whatever may be the future of Russia and the final
organization of Germany, the old hostility must remain
unappeased, the fundamental antagonism must endure
for years to come. The crime of the partition was committed by autocratic governments which were the governments of their time; but those governments were
characterized in the past, as they will be in the future,
by their people's national traits, which remain utterly incompatible with the Polish mentality and Polish sentiment. Both the German submissiveness (idealistic as
it may be) and the Russian lawlessness (fed on the corruption of all the virtues) are utterly foreign to the Polish nation, whose qualities and defects are altogether
of another kind, tending to a certain exaggeration of
individualism and, perhaps, to an extreme belief in the
governing power of the free assent, the one invariably
vital principle in the internal government of the old republic. There was never a history more free from political bloodshed than the history of the Polish state,
which never knew either feudal institutions or feudal
quarrels. At the time when heads were falling on the
scaffolds all over Europe there was only one political
execution in Poland—only one; and as to that there still
exists a tradition that the great Chancellor who democratized Polish institutions, and had to order it in pur-
suance of his political purpose, could not settle that
matter with his conscience till the day of his death. Poland, too, had her civil wars, but this can hardly be made
a matter of reproach to her by the rest of the world.
Conducted with humanity, they left behind them no an-
imosities and no sense of repression, and certainly no
legacy of hatred. They were but an argument in a political discussion and tended always toward conciliation.

I cannot imagine, in whatever form of democratic
government Poland elaborates for itself, that either the

nation or its leaders would do anything but welcome the closest scrutiny of their renewed political existence. The difficulty of the problem of that existence will be so great that some errors will be unavoidable, and one may be sure that they will be taken advantage of by its neighbors to discredit that living witness to a great historical crime. If not the actual frontiers, then the moral integrity of the new state is sure to be assailed before the eyes of Europe. Economical enmity will also come into play when the world's work is resumed again and competition asserts its power. Charges of aggression are certain to be made, especially as related to the small states formed on the territories of the old republic. And everybody knows the power of lies which go about clothed in coats of many colors, whereas, as is well known, truth has no such advantage, and for that reason is often suppressed, as not altogether proper for everyday purposes. It is not often recognized, because it is not always fit to be seen.

Already there are innuendoes, threats, hints thrown out, and even awful instances fabricated out of inadequate materials, but it is historically unthinkable that the Poland of the future, with its sacred tradition of Poland and its hereditary sense of respect for the rights of individuals and states, should seek its prosperity in aggressive action or in moral violence against that part of its once fellow-citizens who speak Ukrainian, or Lithuanian. The only influence that cannot be restrained is simply the influence of time, which disengages truth from all fact with a merciless logic and prevails over passing opinions, the changing impulses of men. There can be no doubt that the moral impulses and the material interests of the new nationalities, which seem to play now the game of disintegration for the benefit of the world's enemies, will in the end bring them nearer to the Poland and unite them sooner or later by a spontaneous movement toward the state which had adopted and brought them up in the development of its own humane culture—the offspring of the west.

THE POLISH QUESTION [1]

There is no problem of European politics on which such conflicting and misleading views are expressed as on the Polish question. This is chiefly due to the complete ignorance of Polish history in western Europe. Such accounts of Polish history and politics as exist are either written by Polish enthusiasts or are drawn from German sources, and are naturally colored by the undying antagonism between Pole and German. The whole history of Poland is one long struggle against Germany. After the absorption of the western Slavs on the Elbe and the Oder by the Germans, the young kingdom of Poland waged a fierce struggle for existence with the border states of the empire, especially the Mark of Brandenburg. On the break-up of the unity of the mediæval empire, the Teutonic order established itself on the Baltic seaboard to the north of Poland. The order was conquered by Poland in 1466, but it left the German Duchy of Prussia which later on united with Brandenburg to form the Kingdom of Prussia, a state which could only realize its political unity by the annexation of the mouth of the Vistula. This involved the disintegration of Poland and was actually carried out by the three partitions, which gave West Prussia and Poznania to Prussia. But the ethnographic frontier of Poles and Germans remained where it had been in the Middle Ages.

With Russia Poland had relatively few relations, because Russia was not an aggressive power and, falling under Tatar rule in the thirteenth century, was cut off by distance and civilization from central Europe. But the bulk of the White and Little Russians fell to the

[1] By A. B. Boswell. Sciencia. 22: 294-302. October, 1917.

Lithuanians in the fourteenth century by the Union of Poland with Lithuania in 1569, these peoples became part of the Polish state. As Moscow grew up and began to reunite the Russian lands, she came to regard the east of Poland as a *Russia Irredenta* and from the seventeenth century aimed at their conquest, so that Catherine II joined Frederick the Great in his scheme for the partition of Poland. But by this time many of the Little Russians had come under Polish and Catholic influence, and though the majority of the peasants were reconverted to the eastern church, the whole of the gentry had become Catholic; so that a great struggle ensued between Moscow and Poland for national and cultural predominance in these provinces, a struggle which has not yet ended.

In the days of her independence, Poland was a Catholic state in close touch with western culture, especially with Italy and France, with a great literature and educational system with its center in the great University of Cracow. She was thus divided by religion from Lutheran Germany and Orthodox Russia. She was territorially one of the largest states in Europe and as a great military power, waged successful wars with Sweden, Austria and Moscow. She was the bulwark of Europe against the Turks and the Tatars. Her form of government was a crowned republic and she held the highest ideals of freedom and religious toleration. But her power declined in the seventeenth century for internal and external reasons. Internally her power declined because her free constitution depended on the enlightenment of the individual citizen, and after the Reformation her educational system passed into the hands of the Jesuits who preferred religious orthodoxy to moral enlightenment and patriotism. The loss of the eastern trade routes through the Turkish conquest of the Near East, led to the ruin of her commerce, and Poland became a purely agricultural community based on serf

labor.   Her one outlet was Danzig, which was largely
in the hands of German merchants.   Further, the union
with Lithuania where the gentry, whether of Polish or
Little Russian origin, formed large estates among the
Lithuanian and Little Russian peasantry, overthrew her
social and political equilibrium.   It might be said that
Latifundia perdidere Poloniam, since the ambitious mag-
nates of the Eastern provinces—the Radziwiłłs, Potockis
and so forth—quite overshadowed the more patriotic
gentry of Poland proper.   Externally she declined because her loose, free constitution was unfitted to maintain her independence against her more powerful neighbors.   Poland preferred liberty to order and security at
a time when powerful centralized, bureaucratic . states
with hereditary diplomats and large standing armies had
grown up at Vienna, Berlin and St. Petersburg.   Moreover, she lacked cohesion, as she was a federal state
comprising, besides Poles, large masses of Little Russians, Lithuanians and Jews.

By the middle of the eighteenth century, Poland was
hopelessly weak.   But the important fact in her history
is that she experienced a great revival political, social
and intellectual, culminating in the great reforms of
1791, which gave her an excellent constitution on the
British model, a large army and an educational system
second to none in Europe.   These changes with a reasonable political equilibrium in Europe should have secured her independence.   But the balance of power in
Europe was overthrown by the French Revolution, and
Prussia and Russia were able with impunity to abandon
their crusade against France in 1792 and 1794, for more
immediate gains in Poland.   All honor is due to the Polish gentry who voluntarily renounced their social and
political privileges at a time when the French *noblesse*
were not only leaving their country *en masse,* but were
even fighting against her in the ranks of her enemies,
and when the Magyar nobility were forcing Joseph II

to withdraw the measures he had passed to free the serfs of Hungary.

The Polish state fell, but the intellectual revival left the nation stronger than before. Throughout the nineteen century the Poles played a great part in the national revivals, because not only were the Poles a large nation with great traditions like Germany and Italy, but they had only recently lost their unity and independence, and were only waiting for a favorable political situation to regain them.

The first half of the nineteenth century is known in Poland as the romantic age. The Poles not only produced their great romantic literature, the poetry of Mickiewicz and the music of Chopin, but they carried their romanticism into politics. They were the upholders of the tradition of parliamentary government and national freedom in central Europe, and in the age of Metternich they could only realize these ideals by war and rebellion. They formed legions to fight for Napoleon in Italy. In the Grand Duchy of Warsaw and the Kingdom of Poland 1807-1830, the spirit of Polish freedom was reincarnated. The revolutions of 1830 and 1863 against Russia and of 1846 against Austria, were the leading events in this struggle, but every national leader, Mazzini in Italy, Kossuth in Hungary, German Liberals and French Republicans, found in the Poles their staunchest supporters. But the failure of armed resistance brought about a change of attitude. The peasant emancipations of 1848 and 1864, and the rise of Polish industry, brought fresh social problems; and a gospel of work and organization took the place of the former romanticism.

This new period saw a tremendous strengthening of the social cohesion and internal resources of the Polish people, the attainment of social unity by the growth of her middle class, and the transformation of her politically indifferent serfs into patriotic peasant proprietors.

The peasant now took his place alongside the squire as the upholder of the national traditions. The grant of autonomy to Galicia in 1867 gave Poland a center for her political and intellectual development with its two universities of Cracow and Lwów, and its Polish Viceroy and administration. Galicia became a sort of Piedmont round which was to grow the greater Poland of the future. At the same time a great industrial development made Warsaw and Łódź one of the great manufacturing areas of Europe, and together with the coalmines of Silesia and the oilfields of Galicia, gave Poland a firm economic basis.

Together with this reaction against romanticism there grew up a new political philosophy expressed by the Cracow school of historians, who regarded the past history of Poland as a failure owing to the lack of a strong administration. They regarded it as essential that the three parts of Poland should rally to the support of the three governments and draw from them concessions by counciliatory methods. This current of opinion was strongest in Galicia, the most conservative part of Poland, which had taken no part in the reform movement in 1791; and it became crystallized there by the grant of autonomy to Galicia in 1867. But it also existed in Russian Poland in the program of Wielopolski and his successors. Toward the end of the century, however, a strong reaction against this pessimistic outlook and passive policy grew up, chiefly in Lwów and Warsaw. Professor Korzon in history and Sienkiewicz in fiction, revived the glories of the past of Poland; and a new party, the National Democracy, was formed which was Pan-Polish, aiming both at the unity of all parts of Poland and at the closer cooperation of gentry and peasants. This school of opinion soon became predominant in Russian and Prussian Poland, and formed in eastern Galicia a strong opposition to the conservatism of Cracow. But the latter remained closely bound to

the Hapsburg monarchy and gave many ministers to
the Austrian government.

When the World War broke out, the Manifesto of
the Grand Duke Nicholas won over Russian Poland to
the Russian side, and the majority of the Poles have
been fighting willingly in the Russian army.   It was
even possible at one time that the Polish Legions in the
Austrian army might come over to the Russian side.
But as the result of the tactless administration of conquered Galicia by the Russian civil authorities, and of
the dilatory methods shown by the Russian government
in realizing the promises of the Manifesto, this enthusiasm was considerably damped.   The Russian revolution of 1917 has for the first time given to Poland a
real hope of unity and independence.   The causes of the
failure of a Russian-Polish compromise in the past no
longer exist for the following reasons:

1.   The question of cultural and political domination
over Lithuania and the Ukraina, was the rock on which
all attempts at agreement split in 1830 and 1861. Now
that the Little Russians and Lithuanians have their own
national movements, this is no longer a question as between Russians and Poles.

2. The Kingdom of Poland formed in 1815 was a
small liberal state situated in the heart of reactionary
Europe, and bound by a dynastic union to Russia, the
most reactionary state of all.   Its failure was not due
to any weakness on the part of Poland, or malice on the
part of Russia, but simply to the incompatability between the autocratic and liberal institutions under the
same dynasty.   Russia is now a modern progressive
state, and has no reason to check the rise of democracy
in Poland.

3.   Russia's influence on the other Slavs was always
weakened by her oppression of Poland. She came into
the war to help Serbia, and now that she intends to let

Poland alone, her moral influence over the Slavs will be enormously enhanced.

4. The Russian national antagonism to the Poles was not natural, but was inspired by German political ideas. All reactionary German influence over Russia has now gone.

5. The Russian oppression of Poland was at best a temporary policy and failed to absorb or assimilate the ten million Poles under her rule. Not only was a change of policy inevitable, but the union of all the Poles in one state was greatly in her interests, as it would form a bulwark against Germany.

Externally then, the Polish question has become simpler. But there are great internal difficulties in Poland itself, such as the Jewish question, and the Ukrainist question. The Ukraina, Lithuania and eastern Galicia, formerly belonged to the Polish state, and still contain a great number of Polish landowners, while Wilno and Lwów are almost purely Polish cities. But the Little Russian peasants have remained orthodox in religion and anti-Polish in social and racial sentiment. They have now in the Ukrainist idea a strong national movement in Galicia, which tends to spread into south Russia. Are the Poles willing to renounce their historical claims to these vast Little Russian lands whose culture is still largely Polish, and where a great part of the land is still owned by Polish gentry? If they make this concession, Poland would be a compact state, confined to her own ethnographical boundaries with a small German minority and a large Jewish population in the cities, but with no deep racial division among its people as was so fatal to her in the past. The thorny Ukrainist question would become a question for Russia alone, and be no longer complicated by German and Polish intrigues. Under the new Russia that is arising, a complete solution of this question should be possible. The Polish state so revived would be smaller but more compact than in the past, but based on firm foundations and able to

uphold its old traditions of toleration and liberty, and
free to develop the great social and artistic ideals which
the Poles have so notably upheld in their days of adversity.

It is often stated by the enemies of Poland, and generally believed, that the Poles are a nation of aristocrats,
who resent any concession to the other classes within
the Polish community. Whatever truth there may have
been in this statement as regards the past, it is utterly
untrue today. The emancipation of the serfs in the nineteenth century has made the peasant the chief figure in
Polish life. It is to the peasants that Poznania owes
the success of its extraordinary resistance to German
colonization. The peasants have given a large number
of writers and artists to modern Poland, and many of
the political leaders of Poland are of peasant origin.
This sturdy democratic element is fusing with all that
is best in the gentry who hold the best traditions of the
national past, to form the Polish nation today, and the
economic revival of the last fifty years has given Poland
that middle class element that was so lacking in the
eighteenth century. It is characteristic of Poland today
that besides her old friend and ally France, she has
formed deep bonds of friendship with Italy and Great
Britain, and time will doubtless heal the old feud with
Russia. Moreover, the great migration of Poles to
America, where there are now between one and two
millions, has created close bonds between the republic
of the past and the great republic of the modern world.
Poland will take her place as an illustrious member of
the Grand Alliance which is to mould the Europe of the
future.

POLAND REBORN [1]

I

Poland rose from out "the smoke of fires and the
waves of blood," according to her national hymn, and

[1] By A. H. Debski. Asia. 18: 1010-14. December, 1918.

now from the maelstrom of the World War, she is emerging once more toward an independent existence. We are facing the era of social justice. The readjustment of national frontiers in accordance with national ideals will wipe out the injustices of centuries. Poland will be a land for the Poles instead of a milch cow for the world's autocracies, now breathing their last.

Already in the tenth century Poland stood as an independent nation on the banks of the Vistula, Oder and Wartha, a nation that subsequently outgrew in power the other kingdoms of Europe. For long centuries her frontiers stretched from the Baltic Sea on the north to the Carpathian Mountains and the Black Sea on the south; on the east she extended to the rivers Dnieper and Dvina. During the thousand years of her independent existence under the continuous rule of forty kings she attained as high a degree of culture as any country in Europe.

In the Europe of that period Poland stood between Christian Europe and the Mongols and Tatars, who made periodic excursions across the plains of the Ukraina. For five centuries the barbaric waves from the east broke against her frontiers. The struggle against the barbarians was initiated by King Pius Henry in 1241 at the Battle of Lignica in Silesia. The death blow to Ottoman supremacy was delivered by King John III Sobieski in 1683 under the walls of Vienna. If it had not been for this impenetrable barrier established by Poland, Europe would have been unable to develop as she subsequently did. It was Poland that, at the end of the Middle Ages, christianized Lithuania, the last of the pagan nations in Europe.

The seventeenth century was the period of Poland's rapid rise. The first university of eastern Europe, the precursor of similar institutions at Wilno, Warsaw, Lwów (Lemberg) and Zamość, was opened in 1364 at Cracow. From its walls emerged Copernicus. In the sixteenth

century great poets, like Sarbiewski, crowned triumphantly at the Capitol of Rome, eminent writers and
scientists, like Andrew Frycz and Modrzewski, made
their appearance, and masterpieces were created under
the inspiring influence of ideals of tolerance, fraternity
of nations, and individual rights. Toward the middle of
the eighteenth century the first Ministry of Public Education in Europe was created in Poland under the name
of the "Commission of Education." The reforms introduced by this commission were many centuries ahead
of the educational ideas of the time. Moreover, during
this period Poland developed a complex political organization far in advance of that of other European nations
—an organization which has left its indelible mark on
Polish character.   While Europe was in the grip of
oppressive autocracy, Poland was rapidly developing into
a republic. The Polish Habeas Corpus Act was granted
in 1430; the inviolability of the home was secured in
1588; freedom of speech and of the written word were
granted in the fifteenth and sixteenth centuries. In many
countries it was only the nineteenth century that saw
torrents of blood shed in the same cause. The Diet, or
Congress, of Poland was established in 1493 on the principle of a parliament with two chambers, the senate and
the chamber of deputies, a form of government copied
by England at a much later date and still to be attained
by many modern nations.   This form of government
reached the height of its development in the sixteenth
century and lasted until the fall of the republic, two
centuries later. The principle of a free union between
free people was first formulated in 1569 at the union of
Poland and Lithuania: "The free with the free, equals
with equals." The law stood above the king, and if the
king persisted in ignoring the wishes of the people there
were means whereby he could be forced either to sub-
mission or to abdication (*lex de non praestanda obedi-
entia*). The Polish nobility, jealous of its privileges,

prevented the kings from becoming all powerful, and as a result of this understanding between the ruler and the ruled no Polish king was ever assassinated or jealously guarded every time he left his palace.

Nevertheless, one hundred and twenty years ago Poland fell a victim to her powerful and united enemies. Since that time the country has been torn by one bloody revolution after another, led by one fiery patriot after another, men whose names have become historic, such as Thaddeus Kościuszko, Henry Dombrowski, Josef Poniatowskí and today Josef Piłsudski. To these men the freedom of Poland was the sole and only ideal. Every generation has followed them valiantly into battle; for, though divided, Poland has always preserved strong unity of spirit—a characteristic that has made her unconquerable. During the century of triple servitude to Russia, Austria and Germany, the Polish people have maintained their individuality, not only successfully resisting all attempts at cultural suppression, but even adding to the world's treasury of human culture. The genius of Mickiewicz in poetry, of Sienkiewicz in prose, Chopin in music, and Matejko in art will always remain the possession not only of Poland, but of the whole world. When the present war broke out the Polish Legions, under the leadership of General Josef Piłsudski, marched fearlessly into battle for what they considered the right. During the German occupation of Poland the struggle has been bitter and ceaseless, for the Pole does not easily give in.

Russia imposed heavy tariffs on the Kingdom of Poland and did all in its power to discourage commercial development; the territory grew into one of the most congested industrial centers of the old Russian Empire. This does not imply that the land was not under cultivation. On the contrary, for the last twenty years the peasants have been buying up the big estates both there and in Austrian Poland, but agricultural production was insufficient to supply the demand. Cattle were imported from the Ukraina, flour from Russia and Germany, butter from Siberia. Tobacco came from the Caucasus, cotton from the Far East—Tashkent and Persia—flax from Lithuania. The exports were directed to Russia and the Far East. The sugar refineries of Poland rivaled those of the Ukraina; in 1912 there were, according to German statistics, four hundred and seventy-nine mines and glass works, the production of which was valued at 601,394,419 rubles, or, according to the *ante bellum* rate of exchange $300,697,209 per annum; there were sixteen hundred and sixty-six textile plants, and the linens from Lódź found a market in the remotest corners of Russia. The country has unlimited natural resources, among them vast coal deposits, naphtha, salt, iron ore, and phosphates.

In Galicia, where the Austrian government succeeded better in stilling all industrial development, the country naturally turned to agriculture. The export of farm products was heavy; horses, eggs, cattle, butter and grain were but a few of the necessities exported to Vienna. Although the country is undoubtedly undeveloped, it has shown the same vitality as the Kingdom of Poland in struggling against adverse conditions. Thus, in 1913, there were fifteen hundred and eighty-seven industrial and farm cooperative societies, with a membership of 1,160,264 and an invested capital of $17,319,457.

Posen has also been kept as an agricultural country by the policy of the German government. But although the struggle was between three and a half million Poles and the power of Germany, still before the war there were two hundred and eighty-seven commercial enterprises and factories, with property worth $6,797,689, and a reserve capital of $3,883,815. Silesia escaped the fate of both Galicia and Posen, for its coal and iron deposits made it one of the liveliest industrial centers of Austria.

Poland is now facing the most difficult of all problems, that of reconstruction in a country completely ruined by successive invasions. First Russia marched through, devastating and requisitioning, and taking with her, when she retreated, all the available machinery. Then Germany laid hands on all that Russia was unable to take. In Łódź, vast stores of raw material—railroad equipment, steel products, linen, cotton and sugar fell into her hands. Nothing was left that could be transported. I was in Poland from February, 1915, to February, 1917, and had ample opportunities to study the plans and methods by which the Poles were already then preparing for the work of reconstruction. As a member of a Special Commission organized by the Agricultural Society, I had an opportunity to see not only what the Agricultural Society was doing but to follow the work of several other large organizations as well.

The old policy of the manufacturers was to produce goods only for export purposes, ignoring the local demands and depending upon cheap Russian imports to satisfy the needs of the Polish peasants. It was owing to this established method that Germans were so fearful of Polish competition in Russia, for the Poles not only understood the market well but had already many established branches throughout the country. The German aim is to eliminate Polish goods from the Russian market at any cost. Although the Poles are certainly going to do all in their power to forestall any such action, nevertheless the entire industrial program of Poland has been fundamentally changed. All the numerous commissions and organizations with which I was in touch aimed first to supply the local market with machinery connected with all forms of agricultural work, railroad material for the rebuilding of the ruined railroad system, bridges to replace those that were destroyed, roads, flour mills, and all other necessities for the upbuilding of a country that for four years has been overrun with foreign troops.

All plans have laid particular stress on government aid, since the precedent for such action has already been established. Before the revolution of 1830, the Polish Minister of Finance founded a Polish Bank, which not only subsidized a number of industrial undertakings, but even operated smelting works of its own. No trouble is foreseen in getting the government to undertake the operation of the railroads, the postal telegraph and the mines, which will constitute the first step toward easing the financial situation and to a great extent stabilizing the financial market. The commissions working on these projects, however, have looked beyond. Foreseeing the collapse of Austria, they have already made plans to extend the Polish market to the south, especially to the Balkans, where the Slavonic origin of both Poles and Bulgars may be a great aid in establishing permanent business relations.

The thoroughness of organization and the definiteness of program in all reconstruction work struck me with peculiar force. Committees of the Agricultural Society were working out irrigation schemes, especially with reference to the irrigation of peasant holdings. The Technical Society was collecting and analyzing at headquarters all the statistics relating to labor conditions in the country. After seeing the methodic and efficient work of this organization, I realized thoroughly that the great undertaking of reconstructing Poland already had a good start, and that all that was needed was the execution. The dream of a free and independent Poland has always found concrete expression, either in revolution or in industrial reconstruction.

II

The legitimate optimism regarding the future of Poland's industrial life cannot be applied, however, to financial conditions, for these are complicated and have been altogether outside the reach of Polish workers. It will need the efforts of an International Congress to settle the various difficulties involved. The first of these is that Poland lacks a national currency, having made use in the past of rubles, kronen and marks. The Russians took away what was available in gold. Each conqueror, upon entering the country, has followed the practice of buying up the enemy coin at a low valuation and then carting it off, until both values have dropped almost to nothing and coins have ceased to exist. The country's exchange has had to confine itself to paper currency. Meanwhile, debts and mortgages cannot be repaid, for there is no standard rate of exchange. German efforts to settle this puzzle have been neither sincere nor honest. Moreover, the country is flooded with receipts for requisitioned horses, cattle and other property. The Russian and Austrian governments, it is true, undertook to liquidate these, but neither power exists any more. Who will pay the Polish peasant for his losses?

Given the opportunity, the Poles will reestablish rapidly, but help will have to be extended from an outside source. When the financial tangle is theoretically settled there will still remain the need of meeting current obligations and only a foreign loan can satisfy that demand. Germany will probably bid for the honor, but Poland fears her, for back of her money looms the Junker; political supremacy stalks in the shadow of economic aid. The United States is the only country from which the Poles could accept the loan with pleasure, knowing that it would be given without ulterior motives.

Poland has always been the scene of recurring revolutions, for the secret organization against the three powers that have held her in bondage has been active and unfailingly efficacious. At the time of the Russian revolution of 1905, the Poles also had their upheaval, and soon after, one of the greatest revolutionists that Poland has ever known, Josef Piłsudski, conceived the idea of building up a secret military organization, a revolutionary army that would be trained and armed in readiness when the opportune moment for striking for freedom should come. When the European war broke out in 1914, Piłsudski and his forty thousand men turned their arms against Russia, for Tsarism was Poland's most immediate and active enemy. With the Russian autocracy overthrown, Piłsudski planned to turn on the central powers and to wage a defensive war against them. The entire plan had the support of the radical and peasant organizations, in strong opposition to which stood the conservatives, representing the landowners and clericals, who had always supported the Tsar. The fall of the Russian bureaucracy was foreseen by Piłsudski as early as 1915, at which time he disbanded the Polish Legions stating that there was no need for them, since they could not wage open war upon the central powers.

It was at his request that I organized the National Central Committee, composed of the peasant parties, the socialist party and the progressive parties, thus forming one vast organization, purely civilian in character, wielding the majority power. Its purpose was the establishment of a solid defensive front against the Germans. It organized schools, evening classes, lectures; it printed and circulated quantities of educational material. Josef Piłsudski took charge of a parallel organization among the soldiers, and this was called the "Polish Military Organization." Both bodies were secret and their power was so widespread that the Germans were unable to cope with them or suppress any of their activities.

At the same time a demand for a definite Polish government was made. Germany, having had many previous unpleasant experiences with Poland, granted a provisional government in January, 1917. But she attempted to control the membership, whereupon each of the Poles who received an invitation to participate in the Council

refused the honor and referred Germany to the existing political parties for the prospective Council. Germany accepted the reprimand and the elections were
held. Piłsudski, who was one of those returned, immediately declared war on German methods. The abolition
of the Austro-German frontier in the Kingdom of Poland, and the establishment of a regency as a symbol
of supreme power were promptly demanded. Piłsudski
and the radicals insisted that since there was no supreme power in Poland, temporary representatives
should arrogate the power until a proper representative
of the people could be duly elected. Germany feared
to agree, whereupon Piłsudski and six other radicals in
the Council resigned. The German government, dread-
ing that he might put forward even more energetic measures, arrested and imprisoned him in the Fortress of
Magdeburg.   This only rendered the situation more
desperate; for the Polish Legionaries, when they heard
of the treatment accorded their leader, refused to serve
on any of the fronts. Some surrendered to the enemy,
and one hundred and forty were shot in Hungary for
insubordination. The central powers were forced into
a compromise, and on October 5, 1917, the regency was
granted, a Ministry formed, and a Great Council, or
Parliament, promised. But the regency, when elected,
represented only the Polish conservatives.

After the Brest-Litovsk treaty, the regency and the
Ministry declared that both the German and Austrian
Emperors had been false to Poland, and the Ministry
resigned. The regency could not do so owing to the
oath of tenure of office that it had taken. In May, 1918,
a Council of one hundred representatives was granted
by the central powers, in which the radicals would not
take part because it was not elected on a democratic
basis. Nevertheless they agreed to support the conservatives in all the measures directed against the Germans.

Partisanship has been carried over even among the

Poles of the United States, which has been the center
of a bitter fight between the conservatives, represented
by the Polish National Committee, with Ignace Paderewski as the representative in America in opposition to
the Polish National Defense Committee, organized by
me at the request of Piłsudski. The National Council
is also responsible for the Polish Legions organized in
opposition to the policy of the Polish National Defense
Committee, which maintained that if Poles found a good
home in the United States, the United States army was
"good enough to fight in." When the Mid-European
League was formed, the Polish National Defense Committee refrained from joining on the ground that American Poles had no right to try to dispose of the fate of
Poland. That is in the hands of the elected representatives of Poland. That the Poles would uphold the
establishment of a number of independent states, however, there was no doubt, for Ignace Daszyński publicly declared himself for an independent Bohemia.

With the revolution in Germany and the disintegration of Austria, the regency gave the supreme power
over to Josef Piłsudski as the representative of the
people until such time as the elections could be held.
Ignace Daszyński, Polish deputy in the Vienna parliament, a prominent radical and the most brilliant orator
in the parliament, was proclaimed temporary premier.
The situation is almost without parallel. A group of
men, representing the conservative party, has elected to
give over its supreme power to a socialist. Our enemies usually accuse us of partisanship. Can there be
a more conclusive refutation of this accusation than the
action of the conservative regency? The union with
the socialists proves that in the decisive moment, Poland stands first. Our party struggles are forgotten. We
are willing to grasp hands with our enemies, for it is
only by united action that the Poles will be able to build
up a free Poland.

THE INSPIRATION OF POLAND [1]

I have had the fortune to be associated since 1914
with many of the men who are now comprised in the
government of Poland. It is truly an inspiring thing to
witness thirty millions of people of one race and one
language emerge from one hundred and fifty years of
foreign military dictatorship into a free country. It is
doubly inspiring to an American to see a new nation
founded on the inspirations and ideals that we of the
United States hold as the very basis of liberty.   The
sympathies of the American and Polish peoples are not
an over-night creation. There is not a school child of
the United States who does not know of the great service to our own war for freedom through those great
military leaders, Kościuszko and Pulaski. There is not
a Pole who does not know the service these same men
gave to free Poland for which they gave their lives.
Further, during this one hundred and fifty years there
has been a constant migration of Poles to the United
States in an endeavor to find freedom. There has been
a constant return of these Poles to Poland and an interpretation of American hopes and ideals among the Polish people. The American sympathy for the struggle
of Poland to secure her independence has been constant
from the days of our own freedom. It was President
Wilson who first enunciated the absolute stipulation
that the complete independence of the whole of the Polish people was a fundamental condition of the peace.

The Polish citizens of the United States have, out
of sympathy for their mother-country, been constant in
contribution and moral support to those leaders for Polish independence who entered Warsaw in triumph in
January, 1919. They have contributed, not only their
resources, but their sons to this great thing. America
has still another great link of sympathy with Poland.

[1] By Herbert Hoover. National Review. 75: 278-84. April, 1920.

One of these two great Poles who now lead the Polish people lived many years in the United States, and his visionary inspiration of government arises from our institutions. Thus it comes that one of the two great men who have been the builders of the freedom of Poland is practically an American citizen. These two great men, Paderewski and Piłsudski, are today two of the greatest figures that have emerged from the war. They have the abilities, the courage, and resolution of constructive statesmanship.

It requires but a short review of the situation that existed a few years ago within the present boundaries of Poland, in contrast to its position today, to appreciate the gigantic strides that have been made in the making of the great edifice of the independence of Poland. Poland has been for one hundred and fifty years under subjugation of foreign military government. The Polish people were given no opportunity for the development of political experience. Their only training as a statesman lay in political sabotage and in opposition. This same opposition has maintained alive the spirit of Poland for over one hundred and fifty years and, ripening at times into bloody revolution, finally secured the Polish people their independence. Yet political opposition is a poor school for constructive government. The world feared that the Poles would fail in this emergency—but they have not.

During the war Poland was ravaged by four separate invasions—parts of it by even seven invasions. The destruction of property and civilian life was greater than all the destruction of property and life on the western front. Between three and four millions of Poles died of starvation or disease during the war. The Russians ruthlessly destroyed thousands of square miles and drove the entire population from home in an endeavor to create a desert that might retard the advance of the German armies. This shocking barbarity, the literally hundreds of thousands who died as refugees at the road-side, is itself perhaps one of the curses that fell on the military oligarchy of Russia. The Germans also systematically abstracted at the point of the bayonet every resource of Poland, scraping away such minor surpluses of food as existed in the more prolific sections of Poland and leaving other regions to starve. This, together with the destruction of her farms and the looting of every bit of agricultural machinery, at the armistice left millions of Poles threatened with starvation. There is a greater exhaustion of work-animals in Poland than in any other part of Europe.

At the time of the armistice, approximately one-quarter of Poland was in the hands of the Austrian army, approximately one-half in the hands of the German army, something over one-quarter in the hands of the Bolshevik army. The armistice called for the evacuation of certain undoubted Polish territory by the German and Austrian armies. With the German withdrawal hordes of Bolsheviks invaded a large part of Poland, perpetrating indescribable crimes in every village and city. Even in the east, north, and south the armistice provisions left Poland completely surrounded with enemy territory. She had no outlet to the sea, and could not send a letter or a telegram except through enemy hands. I do not know in history of so appalling and disheartening a situation as faced that great soldier and patriot, Piłsudski, when, escaped from a German prison, he laid the first stone of the Polish government at Warsaw.

Here was a country of thirty millions of people in a state of total anarchy; in the midst of a famine such that the children had ceased to play upon the streets; a country with thousands dying daily from typhus and contagious diseases; a large part of the country in the terrible grip of Bolshevik invasion; the Bolshevik army advancing behind a cloud of conspirators; and disintegrated by one hundred and fifty years of separation, a population incapable of paying taxation; a people absosultely without the means for preserving order or repelling invasion; a people without even the rudimentary machinery on which to build a great administrative government. The railways and telegraph lines had been greatly destroyed and had practically ceased to function. The rolling-stock had been destroyed or removed from the country.

Yet, eight months after the arrival of Piłsudski in Warsaw, I found in Poland a vigorous government, functioning with Ministries of Foreign Affairs, of War, of Food, of Finance, of Railways, of Labor, of Education, of Agriculture, and of Public Health. An army of five hundred thousand well-drilled, well-equipped, and spirited troops. Order established throughout the entire area. The Bolshevik driven out of Poland. A general election had taken place under universal franchise. A Congress had been set up, and from the moment that it was convened the government of Poland ruled, responsible to this Assembly. Local government had been established in every quarter. Land reform had been inaugurated by law. A public-school system had been established. Poland, after ten months, was a democracy with a government for the people and by the people, in a country that had had no government for one hundred and fifty years but the government of foreign oppression. Railways had been rebuilt. Abandoned cars and locomotives had been repaired and brought into use. Regular, though deficient, train services were being maintained over thirty thousand miles of railways. Canals were opened and in operation. Coal-mines were running. Fields, abandoned for years, were being steadily replanted. Post and telegraph services had been re-established. Typhus was being brought under control. The fundamental functions of government were being steadily extended. Poland had gained at the

Peace Conference her critically necessary boundaries and
her outlet to the sea. The people had been fed, and
children were again playing in the streets.

I am proud that the United States should have had,
through her organized representatives in Poland, a material part in the making of this great miracle. I am
proud to have been appointed by the American government to direct this service. American assistance was
given to Poland in ships, in opening the route to the sea
through Danzig, in railway material and skill, in fighting famine and typhus, in financial assistance to the
government, in charity to the poor. Beyond this, devoted and disinterested Americans have participated in
the building of her economic and political government.
This service marks the final repayment of a debt of the
American people of one hundred and fifty years' standing.

LITERATURE AND NATIONAL LIFE IN MODERN POLAND [1]

The catastrophe of the insurrection of 1863 was as
overwhelming as that of 1831 had been, but its effects
were widely different. It produced no compact body of
emigration in one foreign center, like Paris after 1831.
Poland itself is henceforth the principal stage of all
Polish endeavor, and the very real difficulties which all
Polish activities encountered from the governments
of the three partitioning powers gave a tinge of *realism*
to national thought, as contrasted with the project-
mongering and windy talk of the old Parisian days.

Besides political conditions, the atmosphere of the
epoch developed realism in the Polish mind: the air of
Poland was stirred by the breath of triumphant scientific discovery from the west, and positivist ways of attacking intellectual problems became the watchword of

[1] By R. Dyboski. Slavonic Review. 3: 117-30. June, 1924.

the day. Not only has Poland ever since been producing an increasing number of brilliant names in science,
but the spirit of the age was manifested in a critical
attitude toward Polish history too. There arose the Cracow school of historians, which devoted its attention
chiefly to the inward causes of decay and fall in the old
Polish commonwealth, and made even too much, by way
of warning lessons, of its moral and social defects. And
criticism was not slow in exercising itself on the revolutionary methods of recent political activity too: the desperate and unhappy insurrections were condemned by
it, and poetry, which had fed the exalted sentiment and
impulsive rashness of youth, came in for its share of
blame.

Poetry itself at this time, as everywhere in Europe,
receded before the growing tide of the novel. What
there was being produced of it, busied itself with the
intellectual problems common to all modern humanity,
as does the poetry of Adam Asnyk, the representative
poet of the period. And in the works of a representative novelist like Bolesław Prus the social tendencies of
the age—such as the emancipation of women, the rise of
the middle class and the claims of the proletariat in the
industrial towns, the decay of landlordism and the growing strength of the peasant in the country—are selected
in preference to the old national issue which had occupied so exclusively the minds of the emigrant poets in
Paris, and which it was next to impossible to write about
at all in Warsaw.

And as those poets, after 1831, had made "a virtue
of necessity" by turning political degradation into glorious martyrdom, so these writers at home made a virtue
of necessity in their way: the new realism imposed upon
the chivalrous and romantic Polish nation, mainly by
outward forces, was raised to the dignity of a complete
program of national life. "Organic work" is the name
by which this realist system of ideas has been known

since. It was based on the principle of resigning for the immediate future all hopes of sweeping and violent political change, and of devoting all the nation's energies to the slow and gradual increase of wealth and the spread of enlightenment, as foundations for social improvement and for such minor political gains as would in course of time secure a strong position and a satisfactory measure of self-government to the three sections of the Polish nation, each within the empire to which it belonged.

In literature, the bookshelves of the age were filled with numberless historical novels of the inexhaustible Kraszewski, covering almost the entire field of Polish history. And one greater than he came after him— Henryk Sienkiewicz—who in his memorable *Trilogy* of historical novels gave a vivid picture of that most critical period in the seventeenth century when Poland, flooded by foreign invaders on all sides, emerged safe through the heroism of its fighting men. Once more, in later years, when the struggle in Prussian Poland had reached its acutest stage, Sienkiewicz comforted the hearts of his countrymen by recalling, in another great novel, the mighty check inflicted by Poland early in the fifteenth century to the rising power of the Knights of the Cross, the forerunners of modern Prussianism.

It was chiefly by these stirring novels from Polish history that Sienkiewicz earned in the eyes of the nation the proud privilege of becoming the spokesman of Poland on many an international occasion, when all the world willingly listened to the well-known author of *Quo Vadis.* Mickiewicz had been the international herald of Poland before: now again it was a great writer who represented the living interests of the nation before the European forum.

But all this was obviously not yet enough. Sienkiewicz, the illustrious herald of Poland, was not a leader in actual political endeavor, as Mickiewicz had been in

his later days. Neither his novels nor Matejko's paintings were a call to action. True, the triumphs of the
past now became, chiefly through these two men, a subject of frequent and demonstrative commemoration, but
they were still a holiday thing, and the idea of emulat-
ing them by a new rising in arms still appeared absurd
to the vast majority of the Poles. In fact, that majority was settling down more and more into conciliation
with the political *status quo*, and the national program
of "organic work" was narrowed in practice to mere
selfish individual money-making. Even Sienkiewicz
glorified the commonplace new type of Pole—the clever,
laborious, and politically short-sighted business man—in
his novel, "The Polaniecki Family." The ancient militant
spirit seemed quite gone from a nation whose citizens
had taken an active and often leading part in all European revolutions of the earlier nineteenth century. That
some of this militant spirit would again be needed in
a coming world-conflict which would give Poland its
chance, began to be realized about the turn of the century by far-sighted Polish patriots. And again, writers
were well to the front in perceiving and expressing the
demands of the historical moment. It was with a view
to re-arousing the old war-like spirit of Poland that the
leading novelist of the younger generation, Stephen Żer-
omski, in a grandiose three-volume story called "Ashes,"
gave a picture of the wanderings and battles of Polish
soldiers in all parts of the world during the heroic age
of Napoleon. He also revived all the national sentiment that had clung to the desperate attempt of 1863,
by commemorating the fiftieth anniversary of that insurrection in his novel "The Faithful River." Nay, even
Sienkiewicz in his old days, on the very eve of the war,
paid all his tribute to the new active spirit by beginning
to write a historical novel on the Polish legions of
Napoleonic times.

But these were vague expressions of a growing tend-

ency rather than definite statements of new and more
worthy political aims. The crystallization of these in the
national consciousness was once more, after 1831, effected
in the work of a great poet. He came when times were
ripe, in the person of Stanislas Wyspiański. Poet and
painter in one, he has more of the Titanic impetus of
Michelangelo in him, than almost any figure in the history of Polish art. His stained-glass windows for
Cracow churches breathe all the majesty of medieval
Polish history, which had from earliest days inspired
one who grew up in the shadow of the ancient Royal
Castle on Wawel Hill, that "Polish Acropolis," as he
called it in one of his works. It was by his poetic
dramas that Wyspiański truly shook the slumbering national conscience "as with the sound of a trumpet." In
a play called "The Wedding," occasioned by the fantastic marriage of a young poet with a village girl, he un-
sparingly laid bare the utter unpreparedness of modern
Polish society for the united, active effort which would
be required for it in the coming hour of crisis.

The constructive sequel to this trenchant criticism
of the generation was given in Wyspiański's next play,
"Deliverance." Here he boldly attacks the national gospel
of the great nineteenth century poets. His hero defies
the genius of Mickiewicz in the audacious words:
"Hence, Poetry! thou art a tyrant!" What this strange
utterance means in the mouth of a poet becomes clear
when Wyspiański's hero prays to God on Christmas Eve
that He may let him live to see "sword and punishment
sent in fulfilment of God's promises"; that the nation,
long homeless, may at last have a "roof of its own above
its head, as other nations have"; that its strength may
burst forth in inspired action; that "a kingdom may
come which will no more be the kingdom of crucifixion,
but of salvation"; that, in fine, the people, impatient of
longer subjection, may victoriously "build up *a state*
again on Polish ground."

It was for such an ideal, then, that the gospel of the older poets, the gospel of redemption by suffering, was to make room now. Here were new vessels indeed for the old wine of patriotic feeling. The saving word *state* had been uttered: only in the material shape of a united and independent political body could Poland become a living force in human civilization again.

That the road to this lay through armed effort, Wyspiański foresaw, and it was, therefore, that he devoted no fewer than three of his dramas to the national war of 1831, and one to the glory of Mickiewicz's Polish Legion in Italy in 1848.

When examining these dramtic homages of Wyspiański to armed national action in the past, the foreign observer is likely to be puzzled by one ever-recurrent feature in the treatment of the themes. "Victory *or* Death!" is the war-cry we should expect a poet to raise when possessed by the idea of a national rising. "Victory *through* Death!" is the cry that meets us in Wyspiański's pages.

Thus, in "The November Night," the youthful initiators of the 1830 insurrection, on the very point of beginninig their fateful work, behold in a vision the figure of Persephone taking leave of her mother Demeter, to descend with an eagerness of joy into the darkness of her husband's kingdom. And the moral of the pageant is pointed in the ominous words: "All that is to live, must die!"

Death as the condition of national regeneration and achievement: what a strange and supremely unfit *motto* for a new era of national action it would seem! And yet this is neither sterile mysticism, nor romantic paradox, nor suicidal exaltation. To a generation of selfish seekers after worldly success, to those "eaters of bread" of whom Słowacki, in his poetical Testament, had said that the poet's word must "torture and transform them into angels"—to these, Wyspiański's harping on death

simply and sternly brings home the tragic truth that
only through another great sacrifice can the national
cause be attained, that the nation must shed anew some
of its best blood if Poland is to rise again, that the task
must, when the hour comes, be attacked in a spirit of
bitter and desperate determination.

And in this spirit it was attacked by those who, during the World War, under various banners, fought and
fell for Poland on all battlefields. They died with Pis-
gah sights of the Promised Land before their eyes, and
their graves, scattered over many countries, are the
foundations on which the fabric of the new Polish state
rests.

THE ART AND ARTISTS OF POLAND [1]

In his book on Poland, Mr. Louis Van Norman calls
the people of that country "a race of artists by birth."
In making this statement he gives utterance to a truth
which unbiassed students of history and ethnology generally concede. Seldom has a nation been endowed with
such artistic ability and temperament as the Poles. Indeed, there is scarcely a department in the whole realm
of art in which this people has not gained distinction
and world-wide fame.

In literature the names of Mickiewicz, Krasiński,
Słowacki, Zaleski, Ujejski, Wyspiański, Konopnicka,
Sienkiewicz, Prus, Madam Orzeszkowa, Reymont, Żer-
omski, Conrad (in England), Klaczko and Wyzewa (in
France) are as great as any that the world boasts of.
The names and works of Chopin, Moniuszko, Wieniaw-
ski, Leszetycki, Moszkowski, Paderewski and Hoffman
are familiar to students of music the world over. Jean
and Edward Reszke, Bandrowski, Mierzwiński and
Madam Sembrich have charmed large audiences with
the beauty and sweetness of their song. Madam Mod-

[1] By J. P. Wachowski. Arts and Decoration. 12: 6-7, 46-7. November 15, 1919.

jeska was one of the world's greatest actresses. Sculpture, too, has its representatives in such men as Cyprian Godebski, Gadomski, Laszczka, Popiel, Raszka, Szymanowski, and Weloński; while Wit Stwosz is a unique figure in wood-carving throughout the world.

Painting was one of the last branches of art to be cultivated in Poland. The reason lies in the fact that the Poles found little time for activity in this field during the early years of their political career. It is to their greater glory and credit, therefore, that they have accomplished so much in so short a time. Through the genius and the indefatigable efforts of its numerous representatives, Polish painting occupies an exalted position in the world of art today.

By her culture and religion Poland belongs to the western group of nations. Owing to her geographic position—she was the most eastern outpost of western civilization in Europe—Poland was of necessity the connecting link between the east and west. It was her mission to defend European culture against Asiatic barbarism. While the other nations of Europe were active in developing the arts and sciences, Poland was for a greater part of her political existence busy warding off the savage hordes of Mongols, Turks and Tatars who made continuous inroads into Europe, and threatened Christianity and civilization with destruction.

Although the Poles were themselves hampered in cultivating this branch of art, they nevertheless contributed very much toward its development through the appreciation they showed and the support they gave in that respect to the other nations of Europe. Polish kings and nobles were among the most liberal patrons of art in their time. They invited painters from Italy, France, Germany, Spain and even England into their realm, and encouraged their work in every possible way. The Jagiellos, Sigismund I, Sigismund III, Sobieski, Leszczyński, Stanislaus August Poniatowski were all great patrons of native and foreign art.

Nor were the nobles behind their rulers in supporting artistic activity in their country. The numberless private galleries scattered throughout the land, containing countless works of the best Italian, Flemish, Dutch, Spanish and French masters, give eloquent testimony to the nation's innate artistic temperament. After the partition of the country most of these treasures were stolen and carried off to Petrograd, Berlin and Vienna.

The interest which the higher classes in Poland showed in art could not but exercise a beneficial influence upon the entire nation. In the fifteenth century there arose in Cracow a school of religious painters, who, though under the influence of the School of Cologne and later of the old Flemish masters, did splendid work in that department.

Polish religious and portrait painters of the sixteenth century imitated the style of the School of Nuremberg and the Cranachs. In the seventeenth century, Italian mannerism and the style of the painters of Flanders, particularly Rubens, was followed, especially by Lexycki and Semiginowski. Later on, toward the end of that century and in the beginning of the following, the influence of Dutch genre painting was plainly in evidence in the works of the two Lubienieckis.

In the eighteenth century Italian baroque invaded Poland, and later on, by way of Vienna and Dresden, the affected French style of the period of Louis XIV. Simon Czechowicz and Thadeus Konicz are its chief exponents.

The accession of Stanislaus Augustus to the throne of Poland gave a new impulse to artistic activity in the country. Stanislaus was one of the most cultured men of his time. His court was the rendezvous of literateurs, poets, musicians, sculptors and painters from every country of Europe as well as from Poland itself. He took particular pains, however, to cultivate and encourage home talent more than any other. Among the painters who enjoyed his protection and patronage were Kosiński, Smuglewicz and a host of artists of lesser fame who produced works of no mean worth in Poland at that time. Contemporaneously with these Kucharski gained considerable fame in Paris as a finished and powerful portrait painter.

Despite the fact however that many Poles were producing works of great merit, there was as yet no distinct school of painting in Poland. As one Polish art critic strikingly puts it: "There was art in Poland but Polish art did not yet exist."

It was left to a Frenchman (Jean Pierre Norblin de la Gourdaine) to establish the first national school of Polish painting, based on the observation of all classes, particularly the townsfolk and peasantry. From this school in Warsaw (1772-1804) issued the first representatives of Polish national painting. Orłowski, the first and ablest of the national school; Płoński (1782-1812), a genre painter and engraver known also outside of Poland, and Rustem (1770-1835), whose influence contributed much toward uplifting the later pseudo-classic school of Wilno in the period of its decline.

The example of Norblin was soon followed in other cities of the kingdom. In Cracow, a group of artists headed by Peszka and Joseph Brodowski founded a distinctive school of their own. In 1831 (the year of the second Polish insurrection against Russia) the schools of Warsaw and Wilno were closed. The school of Cracow was also on the decline. It was later revived by Adalbert Stattler (1800-1882).

The second half of the nineteenth century witnessed the greatest development of Polish painting. In 1854 the Society of the Friends of Art was organized in Cracow. The exhibitions conducted under its auspices brought new names to the public notice. Chief among these was that of Julius Kossak (1824-1898). Kossak studied drawing with Maszkowski in Lwów. He traveled extensively, lived in Paris six years where he continued his studies under Vernet. In 1870 he settled in Cracow, where he lived for the remaining part of his life.

Kossak was one of the most prolific of Polish painters. It would be difficult indeed to enumerate all his works. But apart from painting, Kossak was a master with a pen and pencil. His highly finished illustrations of literary works were scattered throughout the land. In this way Kossak popularized art more than any other of his countrymen. Poland produced artists who possessed greater talent and technique perhaps, but few who enjoyed a greater popularity. He exercised a strong influence on the younger generation of Polish painters who came into prominence after the tragic year of 1863, a year so disastrous to Polish political aspirations.

Heretofore, Polish art was but little known outside of Poland and the surrounding countries; the time had at length arrived in which the productions of Polish genius were to receive the recognition of the entire world. Two bright stars appeared almost simultaneously. The advent of Grottger and Matejko marks a new era in the history of Polish painting, which reached its highest development during this period.

Arthur Grottger is an unusual phenomenon in the world of art. Born November 11, 1837, he received the rudiments of painting from his father, and made farther studies, first under Maszkowski and Kossak and then in the Academy in Cracow, in Vienna and Munich (1852-1858). He died on December 13, 1867. In the last years of his life (1864-1867) he gave to the world his "Lituania" (six charcoal drawings), "War" (eleven drawings), "March to Siberia," and many other works principally of a historico-patriotic character. Grottger is to Polish painting what Chopin is to Polish music—a poet of high inspiration and of sublime and forceful expression.

Jan Matejko is the glory of Polish painting. Born in Cracow in 1838, he received his first lessons in painting in his native city. He also studied in Vienna and Munich, but only for a time. The originality of his genius could not be fettered too much by the conventionalities and academic rules of any particular school.

Matejko is above all an interpreter of Polish history. With his magic brush he has immortalized the most important epochs and incidents of Poland's great past. To him art was a medium for accomplishing a great national mission. Like Sienkiewicz, who wrote his great historical novels "for the strengthening of hearts," Matejko painted the glory of Poland's past to buoy up the drooping spirit of his countrymen and to infuse new hope into their despairing breasts.

He left two hundred and forty oils (seven of these are panoramic size), a countless number of aquarelles and sketches, and thousands of studies from nature and from life.

Decorated with medals seven times in Cracow and in Paris; created member of the French Academy; made honorary Doctor of Philosophy by the University of Cracow, he received from his own nation the golden scepter of Polish art.

Matejko was director of the Cracow Academy of Fine Arts and from this school came such painters as Lipiński, Moniuszko, Piwnicki, Krzesz, Krukowski, and the great Jan Styka (1858), whose famous panorama "Golgotha" is well known in America.

Apart from the School of Cracow the foreign Academies of Petrograd, Vienna, Munich and Paris exercised a powerful influence on the development of Polish art in that period.

From Petrograd came a group of history and genre painters of a cosmopolitan character, who gained international reputation. Among these are: Roztworowski (1858-88) and Henryk Siemiradzki (1843-1902). The latter became famous for his large classic pictures from the life of ancient Greeks and Romans.

The School of Munich gave forth Joseph Brandt, painter of history and war episodes. His compositions are full of life and action. He is a master of color and technique. Next to Brandt, Kowalski and Czachórski have gained recognition outside their native land. Kowalski's name is well known even in the United States. His "Lone Wolf's Nightly Watch" is familiar to nearly everyone through its numerous reproductions. Czachórski (1850-1910) is a painter of beautiful women and fine portraits.

Polish landscape painting likewise has its representatives in the Munich School. Alex and Max Gieryniski, Bendykowicz, Gedorowicz, Kochanowski, Maslowski, Sokolowski, Rapacki, Wywiorski, Witkiewicz, Ruszczyc (the Ploughshare), and the greatest Polish exponent of Western impressionism, Josef Chełmoński.

At the head of the present-day School of Polish painting stands Malczewski, in many ways a unique figure in the world of art, often called "the Polish Boecklin." He is a painter of symbolism and mysticism. His "Death of Ellenai," "Two Generations," "The Enchanted Circle," "Poisoned Well," etc., insure him a very high position in Polish art.

The number of contemporary Polish painters is legion. A few of them deserve special mention. Adalbert Kossak (1857), son of the famous Jules, for a time court-painter to the ex-Kaiser, is Poland's greatest living battalist. He is an artist of bold conception and forceful expression. There is a boldness and dash to his style, charactistic of himself. Okuń paints beautiful portraits; John Falat is an incomparable landscapist. And Joseph Mehoffer, the famous designer of the stained-glass windows in the cathedral of Fryburg in Switzerland, and decorator of the interior of the Wawel in Cracow. In the United States Polish painting is represented by Chełmiński, W. Benda and Iwanowski, whose illustrations are familiar to all readers of our magazines.

When we consider the high standard of excellence which they have attained in their works, we must acknowledge that the Poles have been eminently successful in the domain of art. Their success is all the greater because it came to them during a period of national depression. Now that Poland has once more become a free country may we not expect still greater things from her artists? No doubt they will labor with renewed energy to bring Polish art to still greater perfection and they will give to the world and to humanity many more valuable products of their inexhaustible genius. The painters of Poland have not yet spoken their last word.

THE POLISH LANGUAGE [1]

The Polish language is spoken by some twenty millions of people in central Europe. Since the suspension, more than a century ago, of the political independence of the Poles, the Polish language has been the chief bond of Polish nationality.

So well has it fulfilled this function that the population of Poland is today as homogeneous as ever in the past. In western Poland the western neighbors of the Poles, the Germans, have as land-owners in small numbers encroached on Polish territory. In the Middle Ages large numbers of German Jews emigrated to Poland; while the upper class of these is now fairly well Polonized, the great mass still constitutes a foreign population. In compensation, the Poles have spread eastward and northward: in eastern Galicia, where the peasant population is Ukrainian ("Ruthenian" or "Little Russian"), the city-dwellers and land-owners are Polish, and in Lithuania, similarly, from 2 to 16 per cent of the inhabitants—the proportion varies by districts—are Poles.

[1] By L. Bloomfield. Open Court. 31: 372-5. June, 1917.

The popular speech of the Polish territory divides itself into a number of dialects, which, however, are not very divergent. The book-language, and with it that of the schools and of the educated class, is derived originally from the Great Polish dialect (spoken in the district of Posen); from an early time, however, it has been influenced by the Mazurian dialect (which centers round Warsaw) and by the Ukrainian dialect. Adam Mickiewicz (1798-1855), the most popular and perhaps the greatest of Polish poets, was a Lithuanian Pole; through him the Polish of Lithuania has influenced the literary language.

Although Latin was the chief written language up to the time of the Reformation, Polish possesses a number of vernacular documents from the medieval period. The Reformation, though in the end unsuccessful as a religious movement, succeeded in making Polish instead of Latin the language of books and polite intercourse.

By the end of the sixteenth century Polish was classed with Spanish and Italian as one of the three most elegant book-languages of Europe. The two following centuries were a period of decline in this respect, but at the end of the eighteenth century there came a revival; since this time there has been unbroken progress, and today Polish stands in the first rank as a literary medium.

In its general structure, and to some extent even in its native vocabulary, the Polish language will not seem utterly unfamiliar (as would, for instance, Chinese or Malay) to the English-speaking student.[1] The reason for this lies in the fact that Polish and the other Slavonic languages (Bohemian, Wendish, Russian, Ukrainian, Slovene, Serbian, Bulgarian) form a branch of the great Indo-European family of languages to which belong also the Germanic languages (English, Dutch, German, Scandinavian) and Latin, Greek, Sanskrit, Persian,

[1] Thus the "parts of speech," the cases, genders, numbers, persons, tenses, and the general syntactic structure are like those of English, German, or Latin; such word-stems as *sta-* "stand," *da-* "give," or the feminine ending *-a* will be familiar to the student of Latin.

and others. All these languages are divergent forms of
a single prehistoric language, from which they have inherited many common features.

Among the Slavonic languages Polish is distinguished
by a number of features. The most striking of these is
the use of nasalized vowels, that is, of vowels like those
of the French words *pain* and *pont*. At one time all the
Slavonic languages possessed these, but Polish alone has
retained them. Another feature peculiar to Polish is the
almost universal rule that words of more than one syllable are accented on next to the last syllable. The accent
in Polish does not invovle (as in English or in Russian)
a weakening or slurring of the vowels of less-stressed
syllables; on the contrary, these latter are pronounced
with their full value; the syllables are all brought out
distinctly, as in French: "a string of pearls" is the
metaphor that has been used to describe this manner
of speaking.[1]

A striking feature, present to some extent in all the
Slavonic languages but most widespread in Polish, is
the "palatalization" or "softening" of consonants. A
palatalized consonant is pronounced with the middle of
the tongue pressed against the front part of the palate.[2]
Almost every consonant has in Polish two forms, plain
and palatalized. The extensive use of the latter gives
the language a soft and rather graceful sound, for there
is, even for the foreign ear, an endearing quality about
these "softened" consonants.

Polish goes even farther than the other Slavonic
languages in the clearness and freedom with which words
are derived by means of affixes of the most varied and
delicate shades of meaning. Almost every syllable of
a word contributes its distinct share to the significance

[1] Technically it is known as "open-syllable-stress without vowel-weaken-
ing."—Of the phonetic beauty of the Polish language the following story
is told. A celebrated Polish actress was asked to recite in her native
language to an American audience. She brought her hearers to tears
by counting from one to a hundred.

[2] In English *ch* and *j* are palatalized sounds; for *ch* is not the same
as *t* plus *sh* (as in *it shall*), but differs from this combination by being
palatalized.

of the whole. A single example may not be amiss: *pan* means "Mr., sir, master, gentleman," but there are also the derivatives, *panek* "lordling," *panicz* "young gentleman," *paniczyk* "pretty little gentleman," *panoczuszek* "little dandy," *panisko* "poor dear master"; the feminine is *pani* "Mrs., madam, mistress, lady," with such derivatives as *paniusia* "little lady" and *paniuńcia* "dear little madam"; another derivative is *panna* "Miss, young lady," with its own further derivatives, such as *panienka* "little miss" and *panieneczka* "dear little miss,"—and so on, including adjectives, adverbs, and verbs, as well as nouns.

Other striking features of Polish are the six cases of the noun, the "aspects" or "manners" of the verb, and the peculiar gender-inflection of the preterite; they are, however, not peculiar to Polish and their description would take us far afield.

While all the Slavonic languages have in common certain traces of the superior civilization of their German neighbors, yet Polish, more than any other Slavonic language, has become in the course of centuries, a western European *Kultursprache*. Among the Slavonic languages Polish is the torch-bearer of western European civilization. This is true of its syntactic and stylistic modes of expression, but is most striking in its vocabulary which differs from that of the other Slavonic languages by the great mass of western European words which it has adopted. Most of these are Latin, some are French and some German. Such terms as *determinacja, kombinacja, komunikacja, platform, balustrada, wagon* (railroad carriage), *lokomotiwa, dentysta, sens, ton,* etc., etc., are immediately intelligible to any European, and are as significant as, in the opposite sense, the many and common words which the Russian has taken from the speech of the Tatar.

Two other features less immediately bound up with the language itself, deserve mention in this connection. Polish employs the Latin alphabet, and uses it more

wisely than English or French, for the spelling of a
Polish word uniformly and precisely indicates its pronunciation. The rhythm and cadence of Polish verse are
entirely within the western European tradition, and, indeed, at the very forefront of it in beauty, dignity, and
pathos—as those will attest who have heard such
masterpieces of poetic form as the "Sunset" of Mickiewicz or Kraszewski's "Youth."

If two Slavic peoples, the Russians and the Poles,
are to emerge from these years of suffering with new
liberty and hope, we shall perhaps do no injustice if we
look to the Poles rather than to their eastern neighbors
for the more immediate fecundation of our cultural life.
The Russian will have to learn much before he becomes
a European, and he may decide, wisely perhaps, to grow
in a different direction; the Pole is already one of us,
and needs but the opportunity to give of his best. From
our national standpoint we may hope that the million
Poles in America (Chicago has one of the largest Polish
populations in the world) will receive a new encourage-
ment toward the preservation of their inherited language
and culture, for it is thus that the American who re-
members his foreign birth or descent can best serve our
country. [1]

[1] As people are often at a loss to pronounce Polish names, the following suggestions may not be amiss. They give a key for a very rough
imitation or rather Anglicization; to acquire the native pronunciation
would, of course, be a serious task. Palatalized consonants are indicated
either by an accent-mark over the consonant or by an *i* written after it;
for English purposes a consonant plus *y* (as in *yes*) may be substituted
for the Polish palatalized consonant, e. g., *miara*, really beginning with
palatalized *m*, may be pronounced as *myara*.

Words are accented on next to the last syllable. The vowels are all
short but distinct, and have the German or Italian (*continental*) values;
y is roughly like *i; ó* with an accent-mark over it equals *u; a* and *e* with
a small hook beneath, are, respectively, like the vowels of French *bon* and
bain.

c is pronounced *ts; cz* and palatalized *c* may be roughly represented by
English *ch;* Polish *ch* is somewhat like the German sound in *ach*.

g is always "hard" as in English *get; j* is the English *y*-sound, as in
yes; l is French or German *l,* the same letter with a cross-line through it
may be roughly reproduced by American English *l*.

rz is English *z* in *azure*, except after *p* or *t,* where it is English *sh; s*
is English *s* as in *so; sz* and palatalized *s* may be rendered by English *sh*.

w is English *v*.

z with a dot over it and palatalized *z* are, roughly, like English *z* in
azure.

(*See also* the Editor's note in the first article on Poland. p. 203.)

THE FUTURE OF POLAND [1]

The Polish nation is today living through solemn moments. I suppose that in its eventful history there was never a time more solemn, more fateful than the present. The fate of our country is at stake; powerful people holding in their hands the destiny of the world, are building a framework for our independent existence. Violent bursts of hope and of joy and anxiety are strongly shaking our national spirit. From every side, from every corner of our former commonwealth, people are coming to Warsaw and going to Paris, in frock coats and smock frocks, in old-fashioned country dress, in mountaineer costume, and they cry aloud and implore that their distant provinces should be united to the Polish state. The Polish eagle does not seem to be a bird of prey, since people are gathering themselves under its wings.

In the course of one hundred and twenty-six years of Prussian oppression and systematic Germanization many Poles have forgotten their native tongue, and there are many real Germans settled in Gdansk. However, the former will soon remember Polish, and the others will soon learn it. Gradually Gdansk will tend to become what we wish it to become, if we show seriousness and common sense, enterprise, and political understanding. All Polish state property is returned to Poland absolutely, without any burdens or expenses. On the whole, I consider that Poland may be grateful for the verdict. If we are not obliged to shed more of our blood, I say that this is a great and fine gift from God.

True to the national spirit, we shall never wage a war of conquest or gain. We sacrifice our lives in defense of the lives and property of our countrymen, and in the conviction that our great sacrifice will insure the preservation of order and will protect Europe from

[1] By Ignace Paderewski. From a speech before the Polish Seym (National Assembly). Living Age. 301: 779-82. June 28, 1919.

the threatened ruin of the world's civilization. In
defending the borders of our former commonwealth, the
life and property of the inhabitants, without discrimina-
tion between religion or language, we are at the same
time protecting the west from the invasion of the east.
We are doing the same as our ancestors did seven hundred years ago. We are not seeking new glory for the
Polish arms. We are not boasting of our victories; but
we cannot shut our eyes to the chivalrous virtue and
civic merits of our incomparable soldiers. We express
our admiration and gratitude to the commanding chief
for the liberation of Lida, Swięciany and Wilno from
the Bolshevik hordes, for the liberation of Sambor,
Drohobycz, Borysław, Stryj, Żołkiew, Brody, and Zło-
czów from the demoralized, merciless, and cruel Ukrainian troops. We express our warmest thanks and highest
recognition to our heroic, brave, and devoted army.

The foreign press and different political parties
abroad sometimes accuse Poland of having an imperialistic policy. One of our most prominent deputies
eloquently stated that there is a general prejudice abroad
against Poland, and, at the same time, said that the
responsibility for this falls upon certain classes of our
community. I do not go so far. I cannot blame any
party for this. I must, however, remark that this
prejudice actually exists, and is even spreading. The
reproach of imperialism was made against us very long
ago by the very three empires that robbed us and divided
us. Today this reproach is made by just those people
who are stretching out their greedy hands for Polish
territory, and its wealth.

We never conducted a war of conquest, and we have
no intention of doing so. We do not want what belongs
to others; we do not want to conquer anybody else's
territory. Poland does not deny the right of Lithuania
and Ukrainia to be independent, nor the right of the
White Ruthenian people to individual development.
Poland is ready to help them heartily and effectively.

Food always follows the Polish soldier. We are sharing with the border peoples the supplies we get from America. In order to establish autonomy in these border countries.

We have very much to be grateful for from America and its President. Without the powerful support of President Wilson, whose heart the best friend of the Polish cause, Colonel House, was able to win for us, Poland would no doubt have remained an internal question for Germany and Russia, at best confined within those frontiers which were assigned to her by the Germans in the Act of November 5, 1916. America gave us food, America gave us clothes, boots, linen, and munitions of war, and other supplies, on very easy terms, and with long credit.

Just before my departure from Paris, I received a letter from Mr. Hoover, promising Poland effective financial and economic help. President Wilson, recognized the necessity of our defending ourselves against the Bolsheviki, but did not wish for further war on any front. Mr. Wilson expressed this wish repeatedly and very firmly. Could a Polish Prime Minister, director of the Polish government, a man upon whose shoulders falls the really dreadful responsibility for the fate of his people in the near future, could such a man wave aside such demands? I did as my conscience prompted me. I acted as my love for my country and my honor as a Pole demanded. I said that I would do all I could to satisfy these demands, and I have kept my word.

An armistice was demanded. I agreed in principle to that. It was demanded that Haller's army should not fight against the Ukrainians. It was withdrawn from the Ukraine front, and finally it was required that the offensive should be stopped. Law and order will quickly be introduced there by every possible means. We are, at least for the moment, strong there, but we shall not abuse this strength. None of us think of retaliation or revenge, nor would Polish sentiment ever permit such a thing. There should be liberty, equality, and justice for everybody. And in this spirit and with this wish I ask the honorable Seym to vote in favor of autonomy for East Galicia, and at the same time I ask for powers for the Polish government to open peace negotiations with any government in Ukraina that shows moral strength and inspires confidence.

CHAPTER IV

CZECHOSLOVAKIA

CZECHOSLOVAKIA AND ITS PEOPLE [1]

[In the present and following articles on Czechoslovakia the names are spelled in the Czech form. Thus: ě = ye, in *yes* or *yet*; ů = ou, in *soup* or *route*; ň = ny, in *canyon*; č = tch, in *ditch*; š=sh, in *fish*; ž=zh, in *azure*; ř=rzh, in *Kramář* (read: *Kramarzh*). Other vowels and consonants are pronounced as in continental Latin. The accent ′ makes the letter long.]

The aspirations of the Czechoslovaks to be regarded as a distinct people, with national traditions and ideals peculiar to themselves, have been formally acknowledged by most European states. Their claims are incontestable and are only disputed by those who fail to distinguish between what is meant by self-determination and the question whether or not a nation is fitted to take charge of its own destinies. Few people in Europe have proved more resistant to efforts toward assimilation than the Czechs and the Slovaks, who have suffered the double disadvantage of forming part of a corrupt and stagnant empire. They have been cut off during the past three hundred years from all contact with western Europe and have lived in a constant state of instability and insecurity on the very fringe of that empire, which though strong enough to encompass them, was not strong enough to subdue them. After the centuries of sufferings under foreign domination, the race which gave birth to Hus, Comenius, Kollár, and Palacký, and which has justly earned a reputation for courage, industry, and integrity, has come into its own.

[1] By Milivoy S. Stanoyevich. Geographical Review. 8: 31-6. July, 1919.

The Czechoslovaks, or Čechoslováci, as they are proud to call themselves, live in a compact mass in Bohemia, Moravia, Silesia, and Slovakia, from the Böhmerwald on the west to the Danubian city of Bratislava on the south and to the upper Tisza on the east. There are about thirteen and a half millions of these people altogether. This extensive region, about the size of the state of Pennsylvania, is, as a whole, mountainous, except for the Danube plain, and is richly endowed with forest. This forested mountain land offered to the western Slavs a natural refuge against the invading hordes of Magyar, Mongol, or Turk, which, throughout the centuries, swept across the great, open Hungarian plain of the Alföld only to be halted by this obstacle in their onward sweep.

Under pressure of invasion from without, the Slovaks of northern Hungary and the Czechs of the Bohemian plateau were thrown together and shared a mutual life, especially since the rolling Moravian country constituted no barrier. They had the same language, the same interests, the same enemies, and the same religion. In fact the only obstacle to their unification was the policy carried out by the Austro-Hungarian monarchy. But to understand better the claims of the Czechoslovaks, the elements of their history should be briefly reviewed.

After the rise of the Holy Roman Empire, which, in the name of the Roman Catholic Church, Germanized the Slavs of central Europe, Bohemia succeeded in maintaining her national integrity and Slav character under the rule of her native princes. In the eleventh century the independence of Bohemia as a kingdom was recognized by the Roman emperors, and the kings of Bohemia became electors of the Holy Roman Empire. In the thirteenth century the Bohemian King Přemysl II began aggressive warfare against Rudolph Hapsburg, which ended in his defeat.[1] Rudolph's position was thus

[1] See Ottův: "Slovník Naučný." Vol. 6. p. 215. 1893.

strengthened to such an extent that he became emperor of the Holy Roman Empire and laid the foundations of the Austrian Empire. During the fourteenth century there arose a movement in Bohemia against the luxury and demoralizing influence of the Catholic Church and of the emperor personally—a movement directed toward a purification of life and morals. Jan Hus, head of the University of Prague and a disciple of John Wiclif, became the exponent of this new doctrine, which opposed the authority of Rome. This movement was in reality the germ of the Reformation. The burning of Hus and his friend Jerome of Prague by the Council of Constance, with the silent consent of the Emperor Sigismund, was the cause of the Hussite wars, those implacable struggles of the Czech nation against the Holy Roman Empire and the Latin Church.[1] The battle of the White Mountain (Bilá Hora) in 1620 wiped out the Bohemians as a nation and almost exterminated them as a people. The Hussites also disappeared as a political power but continued to exist as the Bohemian Brethren. Later they were included in the more general name of "Protestants" borne by the adherents of the Reformation.

The religious wars had weakened Bohemia to such an extent that she was obliged to recognize the Hapsburgs as her rulers. The despotic rule of the Austrian emperors led to many rebellions and revolutions in the seventeenth and eighteenth centuries, but they were always suppressed by terrorism and persecution. In such acts of oppression the Hapsburgs were assisted by the Jesuits, who took revenge on the "heretic" Czech nation by burning hundreds of thousands of Bibles and religious works written in the vernacular. It seemed at one time as if both the nation and its language were destined to

[1] The Hussite wars lasted for many years. When they were finally brought to an end, the Czechs found that they had lost two million two hundred thousand men. (Cf. "Czechia i Czechi." *Russkaya Beseda,* January, 1896. p. 107; cf. *also* E. Denis: *Huss et la Guerre des Hussites.* Paris. 1878.)

be exterminated under the Germanizing system of the foreign rulers.

But in the beginning of the nineteenth century there came about an entirely opposite result, namely the revival of the national consciousness of the Czech nation. It was due partly to the humanitarian revolutionary movement that spread from France over all Europe and partly to the efforts of a few Czech and Slovak patriots to revive the almost forgotten Czech language and literature. Jan Kollár (1793-1852), a scholar and poet, was the first to seek to inculcate in the Slavs the sentiment of Pan-Slavism. He compared the Slavonic culture to dawn; the German culture, to day; the English, to midday; the French, to afternoon; and the Spanish, to night. His collection of poems "Daughter of Slavdom" (Slávy Dcera) inspired the Slavonic race with great hope and confidence. It is regarded as the gospel of Pan-Slavism. Another Slovak who played a great rôle in the revival of Bohemia was Paul Josef Šafařík (1795-1861), author of "Slavic Antiquities" (Starožitnosti Slovanské), "Slavic Ethnography" (Slovanský Národopis), and numerous philological works. The third member of the triumvirate of the Bohemian renaissance is František Palacký (1798-1876), author of "The History of the Bohemian People" (Dějini Narodu Českeho), a work based on wide research into original sources. He is the greatest of the Bohemian historians, and the Czechs call him "Otec Naroda" (Father of the People).

The iron despotism of Metternich and the Hapsburgs utterly failed to stop the revival of Bohemian literary, social, and political life. The new generations, with L. Štúr, K. Havliček, Svatopluk Čech, Jaroslav Vrchlický, Masaryk, Kramář and Beneš as their leaders, continued the struggle of their predecessors against the Hapsburg rule, or rather misrule. To reconcile Bohemia with Austria was the work of a Sisyphus. The Czecho-

---

[1] That is, the past of Europe belonged to the Latins, the present belongs to the Anglo-Saxons, and the future will belong to the Slavs.

slovaks were deceived by the Austrian statesmen not once but many times. They have often been imposed upon by the emperor himself. That is the reason why they never gave up the struggle all through the reign of Francis Joseph. But it is necessary to add that throughout the war they still persisted in supporting their juridical case. It was in view of this case that the Reichsrat was convoked on May 30, 1917, for the first time during the course of the war. On that occasion the Czech deputies solemnly proclaimed the independence of their country. It is by virtue of this juridical case that similar proclamations have been made since that time, at every sitting of the Reichsrat. The united Czechoslovak parties declared before the entire world that they accepted this program. The most resounding acclamation of these ideas took place in Prague, when the Czech deputies of the Reichsrat and the Diets, finding themselves in accord with the Slovaks of Hungary, came together on January 6, 1918, in a Czech constituency and voted a declaration to this effect. Such a declaration had been violently suppressed by the Austro-Hungarian government. The Austrian government, however, was not able to put down the determination to act expressed by those Czechoslovaks who remained outside the Hapsburg monarchy.

On October 18, 1918, the Bohemian National Council, recognized by the Allied and American governments as the provisional government of the Czechoslovak state, issued a new declaration of independence signed by Professor T. G. Masaryk, as Prime Minister of Finance, General M. Štefánik, Minister of National Defense, and Dr. E. Beneš, Minister of Foreign Affairs and the Interior. This declaration was issued simultaneously in Paris, London, Rome, and other European capitals, and in New York.[1] Its significance consists in the fact that it influenced the other Slavs, especially the Yugo-

---

[1] For the complete text of the document in English see the New York Times of October 19, 1918.

slavs, to resist the Austro-Hungarian empire and to accelerate its dissolution. The acceptance of the terms of the armistice, as framed by the Allies, meant the fall and the dismemberment of the dual monarchy. What the future will be of this former mighty empire, which is now a small mid-European state, will depend largely upon the effectiveness of the League of Nations.

As to the Czechoslovak republic, its future will depend on the skill with which its boundaries are drawn. Expediency, and not strict justice, has always ruled the decisions of the great powers, who are the final court of appeal in such matters. But if a mistaken idea of what seems to be the easiest way is allowed to prevail, and if the land greed of the neighboring states is permitted to supplant the claims of natural and ethnical frontiers, then the central European question, far from being settled, will only be directed from Scylla toward Charybdis.

Provided Czechoslovakia is assured the possession of the geographical and ethnographical frontiers that are her due, she has no reason to despair of a prosperous and even brilliant future. The Czechoslovak has many of the sterling qualities that make for success. He has known how to utilize the resources with which nature has lavishly endowed his country. Agriculture is highly developed. Oats, rye, barley, wheat are the chief grain crops. The potato, which forms the staple food of the people, is extensively grown. The cultivation of the sugar beet has become of great importance. Flax and hemp are also grown; also fruit, especially plums, which constitute an article of export. Although not so well developed as agriculture, the rearing of sheep, horses, and cattle and poultry and bee farming are also extensively carried on. The unusually rich coal and iron resources of Bohemia and its water power point to a high degree of industrial development. Indeed, the country in the last half of the nineteenth century has become one of the greatest manufacturing centers of Europe. The glass industry, introduced from Venice in the thirteenth century, is of great importance. The manufacture of porcelain is extensively carried on. The textile industry also stands in the front rank. Silver and leather work have a long history as local industries. Such industries exhibit the Czechs' delicate artistic sense and are capable of considerable development.]

If there are any grounds for pessimism at all, they lie in the departments of administration and finance. Much money will have to be expended before the economic resources of the country can be properly made available. The opening of communications and the construction of roads and waterways will absorb the ordinary machinery of government, of schools, hospitals, and other institutions.[1] The reform of the system of land tenure, which entails the breaking up of huge feudal estates, is an absolutely necessary political measure which should be undertaken before the country can look forward to any agricultural progress.[2] The government, of course, will have no easy task in overcoming local prejudices against changes and in combating the power of vested interests. Taxation, too, is another difficult and intricate problem for the administration to solve. However, hope lies on the one hand in the patriotism of the people, particularly in that of the richer manufacturers and local leaders, and on the other hand in the fact that, whereas every other state in Europe resumes its normal life after the war burdened with an unprecedented debt, Czechoslovakia starts clear of lia-

[1] In Czechoslovakia there are now about seven thousand elementary schools, one hundred and ninety-four secondary schools and junior colleges, seventy-five agricultural schools, forty-six commercial and industrial schools, four polytechnic institutes, and five universities.

[2] Recently it has been announced that the National Assembly has already ordered expropriation of all estates in Czechoslovakia of more than three hundred and seventy-five acres under cultivation and two hundred and fifty of woodland. Under this law the state will take altogether three million two hundred and fifty thousand acres of cultivated land and seven million five hundred thousand of woodland, sufficient, according to estimates, for maintaining four hundred and thirty thousand families.

bilities excepting those which she voluntarily incurs for the development of her resources. If Europe is in earnest in her intention to create this new republic and is careful to go about the undertaking in a spirit of frank and painstaking justice, she may rest assured she will not be disappointed with the result of her labor.

BOHEMIA AND THE CZECHS[1]

I

The Czechs are the westernmost branch of the Slavs, their name being derived, according to tradition, from that of a noted ancestral chief. The term Bohemia was applied to the country probably during the Roman times and was derived, like that of Bavaria, from the Boii, who for some time before the Christian era occupied or claimed parts of these regions.

Nature has favored Bohemia perhaps more than any other part of Europe. Its soil is so fertile and climate so favorable that more than half of the country is cultivated and produces richly. In its mountains almost every useful metal and mineral, except salt, is to be found. It is the geographical center of the European continent, equally distant from the Baltic, Adriatic, and North seas, and, though inclosed by mountains, is so easily accessible, because of the valleys of the Danube and the Elbe rivers, that it served, since known in history, as the avenue of many armies.

Beside Bohemia, the Czechs occupy Moravia and adjacent territory in Silesia. The Slovaks, who show merely dialectic differences from the Czechs, extend from Moravia eastward over most of northern Hungary.

The advent of the Czechs is lost in antiquity; it is known, however, that they cremated their dead, and cremation burial in northeastern Bohemia and in Mo-

[1] By Aleš Hrdlička. National Geographic Magazine. 31: 163-87. February, 1917.

ravia antedate 500 B.C. Their invasions or spread southwestward, so far as recorded in tradition or history, were of a peaceful nature, following the desolation and abandonment of the land through wars.

Like all people at a corresponding stage of development, they were subdivided into numerous tribes which settled different parts of the country, and the names of some of these clans, with remnants of dialectic, dress, and other characteristic differences, persist even to this day.

Their documentary history begins in the seventh century, at which time they already extend as far south as the Danube. They are agricultural and pastoral people, of patriarchal organization. Their government is almost republican, under a chief, elected by an assembly of representatives of the main classes of the people. Later this office develops into that of hereditary kings, whose assumption of the throne must nevertheless be in every instance ratified by the national diet. The nation possesses a code of formal supreme laws, and the people are noted for their physical prowess, free spirit, love of poetry, and passionate jealousy of independence.

In the ninth century the pagan Czechs accept Christianity, with Slav liturgy, which becomes at once one of their most cherished endowments, as well as a source of much future hostility from Rome. The various tribes become united under the Přemysl Dynasty, begun by the national heroine Libuša, with her plowman husband, and lasting in the male line until the first part of the fourteenth century.

Under their kings the Czechs reach an important position among the European nations. They rule, in turn, over Hungary, Poland, and Galicia. But their fortune varies. From the time of Charlemagne they struggle, often for their very existence, with their neighbors, irritated by their presence, their racial diversity, and their riches.

The first recorded war with the Germans dates from 630, when the Frank, Dagobert, endeavors by force of arms to impose vassalage on the Czechs, but suffers defeat; and from this time on the Bohemian history is replete with records of fighting with the Germans. How the nation escaped annihilation must remain a marvel of history. It is sometimes reduced to almost a German vassal; yet it is never entirely overcome, and rises again and again to assert its individuality and independence.

Some of the Bohemian kings, under political and other influences, permit, and even invite, settlements of Germans on the outskirts of Bohemia. This is the origin of the German population of the country, which has played and still plays such a large part in its politics.

The latter part of the thirteenth century is a most critical period of Bohemia. Under Otakar II, one of its ablest kings, the country has reached the acme of its power. It extends from Saxony to the Adriatic, and Vienna is its second capital. Many of the German principalities are its allies and the king comes near to being called to head the Holy Empire.

But Rudolph of Hapsburg is elected to his office, and from the moment of the advent of the house of Hapsburg commence Bohemia's greatest misfortunes. The only offense of the Bohemian king is that he is Slav, but that, with the jealousy of his power, the democratic institutions, and the wealth of his country, which contains the richest mines of silver in Europe, is sufficient. Great armies, German and Hungarian, are raised against him; finally he is treacherously slain in battle, his kingdom torn apart, and Bohemia is ravished and reduced almost to a "possession" or a fief of the empire.

Yet the wound is not mortal, the nation is too strong; it rises again, and within a few decades, under Otakar's son, regains its independence and much of its former power. In 1306, however, the last Bohemian king of the great Přemysl family is slain by an assassin, and there begins a long period of dynastic difficulties, which become in time the main cause of Bohemia's downfall.

The next Bohemia ruler of some note is John of Luxembourg, married to Elizabeth, the last princess of the Přemysl house, and killed, fighting for France, at the battle of Crecy, on the Somme (1346). The knightly John does little for Bohemia, but he gives it Karel (Charles IV), his and Elizabeth's son, who proved a god-send to the country.

In Bohemian history he is known as "the father of his country." Under his long, wholesome, patriotic, and peaceful reign (1347-78) the whole nation revives and strengthens. Independence of the country, except for the honorable connection with the Roman Empire, is fully reestablished. Education, art, and architecture thrive. The University of Prague is founded (1348) on the basis of the high seat of learning established a century before by Otakar. The medicinal waters of Karlovy Vary (Carlsbad) are discovered and the city of the same name rises on the site; and Prague, as well as other cities are beautified.

Charles is elected Emperor of the Romans in 1348, and Bohemia stands "first in the world in power, wealth, progress, and liberty." The excellent relations of the country with England culminate in 1382 in the marriage of Richard II with Anne of Bohemia.

But Charles is succeeded by a weak son, and it is not long before Bohemia suffers again from its old enemies.

A great national and religious leader arises in the person of Jan Hus. But Rome excommunicates Jan Hus and accuses him of heresy. He is called to report to the Council at Constance and leaves with a written guarantee of safe conduct from Sigismund, the king and emperor, which, however, proves a "scrap of paper." Hus is not permitted to adequately defend the truth, nor to return; he is thrown into prison; his teachings are condemned; and July 6, 1415, he is martyred by being burnt at the stake. The very ashes are ordered collected and cast into the Rhine, lest even they become dangerous.

The shock of the death of Hus and of his fellow-reformer, Jeronym, burnt a little later, fire Bohemia with religious and patriotic zeal and lead to one of the most wonderful chapters in its and the world's history, the Hussite wars. A military genius arises in Jan Žižka, and after him another in Prokop the Holy; a new system of warfare is developed, including the use of some frightful weapons and of movable fortifications formed of armored cars; and for fifteen years wave after wave of armies and crusaders from all Europe, operating under the direction of Rome, Germany, Austria, and Hungary, are broken and destroyed, until religious and national freedom seem more secure.

As an eventual result and after many serious internal difficulties of religious nature, another glorious period follows for Bohemia, both politically and culturally, under the king George Poděbrad (1458-71). One of their enemies of this period, Pope Pius II (Æneas Sylvius) cannot help but say of them: "The Bohemians have in our times by themselves gained more victories than many other nations have been able to win in all their history." And their many other enemies find but little more against them.

No inquisition, no evil of humanity, has ever originated in Bohemia. The utmost reproach they receive outside of the honorable "heretic," is "the hard heads" and "peasants." Few nations can boast of as clean a record.

The fateful period for Bohemia comes in the sixteenth century. The people are weakened by wars, by internal religious strifes. A fearful new danger threatens central Europe—the Turks. In 1526 the Bohemian king, Ludvik, is killed in a battle with the Turks, assisting Hungary; and as there is no male descendant, the elective diet at Prague is influenced to offer the crown of Bohemia, under strict guarantees of all its rights, to the husband of Ludvik's daughter, Ferdinand of Hapsburg, archduke of Austria.

Hungary, too, joins the union, and the beginning of the eventual empire of Austria has been effected. Continuous wars with the Turks and a terrible plague further weaken the Czechs.

Ferdinand proves a scourge. Religious persecution and then general oppression of Bohemia follow. The freely chosen king becomes tyrant and before long the greatest enemy of Bohemia. Backed by the rest of his dominion, by Rome and Spain, he tramples over the privileges of Bohemia; depletes its man-power as well as treasury; by subterfuge or treachery occupies Prague and other cities, and follows with bloody reprisals and confiscations, which lead to an era of ruthlessness and suffering such as the country has not experienced in its history. The weakened state of the country allows of no effective protest, and of its former allies or friends none are strong enough to offer effective help.

Yet even worse was to come from the Hapsburgs, the association with whom for Bohemia was from the beginning of the greatest misfortune. During the reign of Ferdinand's immediate successors there is a breathing spell for the Czechs; but in 1616 another Hapsburg, Ferdinand II, again under force of circumstances, is elected king of Bohemia, only to prove its greatest tyrant. Within two years the Bohemians are in open revolt, and in another year the king is deposed.

The stranger elected in his place, Frederick of the Palatinate, son-in-law of the King of England, however, proves an incompetent weakling. The Czech armies are disorganized, and November 8, 1620, the main force of twenty thousand is defeated at Bilà Hora, near Prague, by an army of Germans, Spaniards, Walloons, Poles, Cossacks, and Bavarians.

The following part of the Bohemian history should be read in detail by all its friends—by all friends of humanity. It is a most instructive, though most gruesome, part of the history, not merely of Bohemia, but of Europe, of civilization. In Bohemia itself it is a period of concentrated fiendishness under the banner of religion, and of suffering, of thirty years duration. Beginning with wholesale executions, it progresses to the forced exile of over thirty thousand of the best families of the country, with confiscation of their property, and to orgies of destruction of property and life.

Under the leadership of fanatics, every house, every nook, is searched for books and writings, and these are burned in the public squares "to eradicate the devil" of reformation. Rapine reigns, until there is nothing more to burn, nothing to take, and until three-quarters of the population have gone or perished—a dreary monument to the Hapsburg dynasty, to the status of mankind in the seventeenth century.

Had not Germany itself been ravaged by the religious wars thus kindled, this period would probably have been the last of the Czechs; as it was, there were not enough Germans left for colonizing other countries. Yet many came in the course of time, as settlers. German becomes the language of commerce, of courts, of all public transactions; the university is German, and in schools the native tongue finds barely space in the lowest grades.

Books have been burnt, educated patriotic men and women driven from the country, memories perverted. It would surely seem that the light of the nation would now, if ever, become extinct. And it becomes obscured for generations—yet is not extinguished. The roots of the stock prove too strong and healthy.

The people sleep for one hundred and fifty years, but it is a sleep of rest, not death—a sleep healing wounds and allowing of a slow gathering of new forces.

Toward the end of the eighteenth century the Czech language is almost wholly that of the untutored peasant.

But the time of quickening approaches. First one cell, one nerve, one limb of the prostrate body revives; then others. The history of the nation is resurrected and proves an elixir of life; to learn it is to a Czech enough for a complete awakening. But the awakening period becomes one of constant struggle against all the old forces that would keep him down; yet step by step he advances, over prisons and gallows.

Literature, science, art arise again; journalism begins to develop. The university is regained; Prague, the "mother" of Bohemian cities, is regained, and others follow. Education reaches a higher level ultimately than anywhere else in Austria. A great national society of Sokols ("Falcons") is formed to elevate the people physically, intellectually, and morally.

Bohemian literature, music, art, science come against all obstacles to occupy again an honorable position among those of other nations.

Agricultural and technical training progresses until the country is once more the richest part of the empire. Finally journalism has developed until, just before the war, there are hundreds of Czech periodicals. The Czech language is again heard in the courts, in high circles, in the Austrian Reichstag itself; and, though still crippled, there is again a Bohemian Diet.

Such is the very brief and imperfect abstract of the history of the Czech people, who see once more before them the dawn of liberty which they so long cherished.

II

As to the modern achievements of the nation, they follow largely in the footsteps of the old. Notwithstanding the most bitter struggle for every right of their own, the Czechs have extended a helpful hand to all other branches of the Slavs, in whose intellectual advance and solidarity they see the best guarantee of a peaceful future. They have extended their great organization Sokol, which stands for national discipline, with physical and mental soundness, among all the Slavic nations, and they are sending freely their teachers over the Slav world, and this while still under the Hapsburg.

To attempt to define the characteristics of a whole people is a matter of difficulty and serious responsibility even for one descended from and well acquainted with that people. Moreover, under modern conditions of intercourse of men and nations, with the inevitable admixtures of blood, the characteristics of individual groups or strains of the race tend to become weaker and obscured.

Thus the Czech of today is not wholly the Czech of the fifteenth century, and to a casual observer may appear to differ but little from his neighbors. Yet he differs, and under modern polish and the more or less perceptible effects of centuries of oppression, is still in a large measure the Czech of the old.

He is kind and with a stock of native humor. He is musical, loves songs, poetry, art, nature, fellowship, the other sex. He is an intent thinker and restless seeker of truth, of learning, but no apt schemer. He is ambitious, and covetous of freedom in the broadest sense, but tendencies to domineering, oppression, power by force over others, are foreign to his nature. He ardently searches for God and is inclined to be deeply religious, but is impatient of dogma, as of all other undue restraint.

He may be opinionated, stubborn, but is happy to accept facts and recognize true superiority. He is easily hurt and does not forget the injury; will fight, but is not lastingly revengeful or vicious. He is not cold, calculating, thin-lipped, nor again as inflammable as the Pole or the Yugoslav, but is sympathetic and full of trust, and through this often open to imposition.

His endurance and bravery in war for a cause which he approved were proverbial, as was also his hospitality in peace.

He is often highly capable in languages, science, literary and technical education, and is inventive, as well as industrial, but not commercial. Imaginative, artistic, creative, rather than frigidly practical. Inclined at times to melancholy, brooding, pessimism, he is yet deep at heart forever buoyant, optimistic, hopeful—hopeful not of possessions or power, but of human happiness, and of the freedom and future golden age of not merely his own, but all people.

Every nation has its local heroes, local geniuses, but these mean little for the rest of the world. Bohemia had a due share of such among its kings, reformers, generals, and especially writers; but it also gave the world many a son whose work was of importance for humanity in general and whose fame is international. Not a few of these were exiles or emigrants from the country of their birth, who, having settled permanently abroad, are only too readily credited to the country that gave them asylum. Germany and Austria, as the nearest geographically and with a language that the Czech youth were forced to learn, received most of such accessions; but some reached Holland, France, England, and even America.

One of the most honored names in the universal history of pedagogy is that of the Czech patriot and exile, Jan Amos Komenský, or Comenius (1592-1671), the last bishop of the Bohemian Brethren.

Driven away, in 1624, after all his books and manuscripts were taken and burnt, he settles for a time in Poland, then in Holland. His pedagogical writings constitute the foundations of modern education. His best-known works in this connection are "Janua linguarum reserata" (1631), "Labyrinth of the World" (1631), "Opera didactica magna" (1657), and "Orbis pictus" (1658). This latter work is the first children's picture-book. He condemns the system of mere memorizing in school, then in use, and urges that the scholar be taught to think. Teaching should be, as far as possible, demonstrative, directed to nature, and develop habits of individual observation.

All children, without exception—rich or poor, noble or common—should receive schooling, and all should learn to the limits of their possibilities.

They should learn to observe all things of importance, to reflect on the cause of their being as they are, and on their interrelations and utility; for the children are destined to be not merely spectators in this world, but active participants.

Languages should be taught, like the mother tongue, by conversation on ordinary topics; pictures, object lessons, should be used; teaching should go hand in hand with a happy life. In his course he included singing, economy, politics, world history, geography, and the arts and handicrafts. He was one of the first to advocate teaching science in schools.

The child should "learn to do by doing." Education should be made pleasant; the parents should be friends of the teachers; the school-room should be spacious, and each school should have a good place for play and recreation.

Such were, during one of the darkest periods of European history and when schooling was so debased, the notions of this great exile whose life-long desire was to return to Bohemia; he was not permitted to do so and died at Amsterdam, Holland, predicting the fall of the Hapsburgs and the future freedom of his country.

The year 1798 sees the birth of the greatest Bohemian historian, František Palacký (1798-1876). Writing in Czech, as well as German, he edits the Bohemian Archives, publishes what has been saved in Europe from the old Bohemian historians. His historical works, as well as his statesmanship and other important activities, bring him the name of the "father of the nation." He is regarded as the foremost Bohemian of the nineteenth century; and his monument in Prague is one of the most remarkable works of art in Europe.

In the line of invention this earlier period gives Prokop Diviš (1696-1765), the discoverer of the lightning rod (1754), and Josef Ressel (1793-1857), the inventor of the screw propeller.

In science and medicine there stand foremost Jan (Purkyně) Purkinje (1787-1869), founder of the first physiological institute in Germany and father of experimental physiology; Karel Rokytanski (1804-1878), the most deserving pioneer of pathological anatomy; Josef Škoda (1805-1881), the founder of modern methods of physical diagnosis of disease; Edward Albert (1841-1912), the great surgeon of the Vienna University; Ant. Frič (1832-1913), the noted paleontologist.

The Bohemian pantheon is particularly rich in composers and musicians. Of the former one of the best known to the world is Bedřich Smetana (1824-1884), the founder of the modern school of Bohemian music and the composer, among many other exquisite works, of the "Prodaná Nevěsta" (The Bartered Bride), a national opera which has appeared repeatedly within the last few years at the Metropolitan Opera House, New York. The great cycle, "My Country," with the "Libuše" and "Dalibor," are a few other of his compositions.

Anton Dvořák (1841-1904) was admittedly the greatest composer of his time. His "Slavonic Dances" and his symphonies are known everywhere. Invited to this country, he was for several years director of the National Conservatory of Music in New York City, during which time he made an effort to develop purely American music based on native, and especially Indian, motives.

Among musicians the name of Jan Kubelik and Kocian are too well known in this country to need any introduction, and the same is true of the operatic stars Slezák and Emmy Destin.

Of poets the two greatest are Svatopluk Čech (1846-1910) and Jaroslav Vrchlický (1853-1912). They are not as well known in foreign lands as the Bohemian composers and musicians only because of the almost unsurmountable difficulties which attend the translation of their works. In novelists and other writers, of both sexes, Bohemia is rich, but as yet translations of their works are few in number and they remain comparatively unknown to the world at large.

The above brief notes, which do but meager justice to the subject, would be incomplete without a brief reference to a few of the most noted Bohemian journalists and statesmen of more than local renown. Of the former at least two need to be mentioned—Karel Havliček (1821-1856), martyred by Austria, and Julius Grégr (1831-1896), the founder of the *Národni Listy,* the most influential of Bohemian journals.

The most prominent modern *statesmen* of Bohemia are T. G. Masaryk, E. Beneš, and K. Kramář.[1]

It seems a far cry from Bohemia to this country, yet their relations are both of some import and ancient. The man who made the first maps of Maryland and Virginia, introduced the cultivation of tobacco into the latter state, and for these and other services became the lord of the "Bohemia Manor" in Maryland, was the exiled Bohemian Jan Heřman, as were the parents of Philip, lord of the Philip's Manor on the Hudson, one of whose descendants came so near becoming the bride of Washington. Not a few of the Czechs came into this country with the Moravian brethren; and Comenius was once invited to become the President of Harvard University.[2]

The immigration of the Czechs into this country dates very largely from near the middle of the last century, when, following the revolutionary movements of

[1] Those who may be more closely interested in the more recent and still living men of note of Bohemia should consult Narodni (National) Album, Prague, 1899, which contains over thirteen hundred portraits, with biographies.

[2] "The Bohemians." By E. F. Chase. New York. 1914.

CZECHOSLOVAKIA 287

1848, from which Bohemia was not spared, persecution
drove many into foreign lands. During the American
Civil War many Czechs fought bravely in the armies
of the north.

The Czechoslovaks are found in practically every
state of the American union, though the majority live in
the central states. Many are independent farmers or
artisans, and it is only fair to say that they are everywhere regarded as desirable citizens. They take active
part in the political and public life of the country. Two
United States congressmen, a number of members of
state legislatures, and numerous other public officials
are of Czech descent.

In American science the names of men like F. G.
Novy (University of Michigan), B. Shimek (Iowa
University), A. Zeleny (University of Minnesota), John
Zeleny (Yale University), and Charles Zeleny (Univer-
sity of Illinois), are well known and honored; while
the number of university students of Bohemian parent-
age is exemplified by the "Federation of Komenský
Educational Clubs," with its many branches, and by the
fact that the Bohemian language is now taught at the
Universities of Nebraska, California, Texas, Columbia
University, and several other institutions of higher learning.

THE CZECHOSLOVAK REPUBLIC [1]

Of all the so-called "succession states," by which the
former Hapsburg monarchy has been replaced, Czechoslovakia has unquestionably made the most rapid progress in the first years of independence. It, of course,
enjoyed certain great initial advantages. Unlike Serbia
or Rumania, its territory had not been invaded or plundered, and though during the war it had shared Austria's
food shortage and consequent privations, it is now

[1] By R. W. Seton-Watson. Contemporary Review. 119: 310-21.
March, 1921.

known that the connivance and passive resistance of the Czech officials saved the population of central Bohemia from the worst hardships. But, above all, it had a large and active educated class, brought up in intellectual traditions as old as Hus, disciplined by such movements as the famous Sokol gymnastic societies, proud of the distinctive standards of Czech art and music, and ready to give brains and music to the new state organism. The anti-national part played by the great nobles and the Catholic hierarchy had long ago placed the political leadership in the hands of the small *bourgeoisie*, and furthered the latter's working alliance with the peasant masses, who in Bohemia are keenly national and free from illiteracy. The radical tinge thus acquired by the Czech national movement was strengthened by the steady growth of an industrial proletariat: and when independence came, nationalism and an advanced social program almost necessarily went hand in hand.

There were several reasons why a republic was the only possible form of government for Czechoslovakia. The House of Hapsburg was universally hated by the Czechs, who quite rightly held it to be mainly responsible for their national misfortunes from 1620 onward, and denounced Francis Joseph for his double perjury and lifelong hostility. The aristocracy, with a few rare exceptions, was entirely out of touch or sympathy with the rest of the nation, which for that very reason was the more averse to the idea of a Court, where the big families might come once more by their own (or rather by what they owed to Ferdinand II's wholesale expropriation of a nation in favor of their alien ancestors). Above all, events had provided a natural leader in Professor Masaryk, who had organized the cause of independence abroad, and who personifies to a peculiar degree the democratic ideals which date back to Hus and Comenius. Not merely is Masaryk true to type, not merely does he illustrate in his own person the essential unity of Czech and Slovak; but the position which he, the philosopher and student of history, has won for himself, is what might be expected of a nation whose most cherished national leaders have been thinkers and scholars no less than men of action. The author of a new realism in politics which is the very antithesis of the old *Realpolitik,* he had already found in exile an unusually apt pupil in Dr. Beneš, who has held the portfolio of Foreign Affairs in successive Cabinets since the birth of the republic. While Yugoslavia and Rumania had as yet only partially rid themselves of the old political gangs which exploited them before and during the war, the Czechs were able to make an almost entirely new start, with the most honest and progressive elements in the nation at their head. Best of all, the socialists—unlike their Yugoslav and Rumanian comrades, who sacrificed immediate results to a doctrinaire and obviously unattainable program, and thus provided the reactionaries with a plausible excuse for repression—took a prominent part in the coalition governments of 1919 and 1920, and so have left their mark upon the constitutional development of the new state.

In the very nature of things the first National Assembly was an emergency body, hastily summoned to direct affairs during a period of revolutionary transition; but though not the product of elections, it was composed of delegates from all existing parties, in proportion to the number of votes polled by each at the last Austrian elections, under universal suffrage. The Slovak delegates had to be selected more arbitrarily, for the simple reason that till the revolution the Slovaks were virtually unrepresented in the Hungarian Parliament, and the existing franchise did not provide the basis for a general appeal to the people. But no one who knew the first assembly will attempt to deny that no national leader, even of the second and third rank, was omitted, unless otherwise employed, and that its decisions accu-

rately reflect the overwhelming opinion of thinking
Czechoslovaks. The constitutional charter, which was
its main work, declares the people to be "the sole source
of all state power" in the republic. It provides for the
septennial election of a President, who has power to dissolve, but is powerless to prevent the automatic sum-
mons of Parliament, and whose right of suspensory veto
on any law can be overridden by a fresh vote of both
houses in favor of the enactment in question. The legis-
lative power is vested in the Chamber of Deputies and
the Senate, both elected on the basis of universal suffrage for both sexes, proportional representation, and
a triple scrutiny. The term of election and the qualify-
ing age are respectively six and eight years, and twenty-
one and thirty years. The Lower House can override
the Senate's opposition by a 50 per cent majority, while
the government is free to order a referendum on bills
rejected by Parliament. The existence of a Constitutional and an Electoral Court, and of a standing
Parliamentary Committee elected by proportional representation among the various parties, provide further
democratic guarantees. Other important enactments
provide for the equality of all religious confessions, civil
marriage, divorce (rights hitherto successfully resisted
in Austria), freedom of the press, association, and
assembly (the two latter non-existent under Hungarian
law). Titles have been abolished, and so far the modern leprosy of civil decorations has been avoided. The
confiscation of Hapsburg landed property and the expropriation of all large estates have been enacted, subject to compensation according to pre-war prices: but
the grave blunders in the land question committed in
Bosnia and Transylvania have in the main been avoided,
the actual subdivision of land having been made over to
a special Land Office, and applicants for land having
been assigned only what they can prove their ability to
cultivate, and *on lease only,* until the plans of subdivision can be worked out.

Meanwhile the rights assured by the Treaty of Versailles to racial and religious minorities were still further elaborated by a special law of February 29, 1920. The language of the minority must be accepted in the courts and by the administrative officials, wherever it is spoken by 20 per cent of the inhabitants, and the state is bound to support schools whose language of instruction is that of the nationalities. But an even better guarantee lies in the adoption of proportional representation for both the parliamentary and municipal elections, and in the measures taken to ensure secrecy and purity of elections. Great efforts are being made to make good the neglect of education in Slovakia under Magyar rule, and special classes are being organized for adult illiterates, and for the instruction of recruits by civilian teachers. Conscription has been reluctantly adopted, pending general schemes of disarmament. The separation of church and state has been accepted in principle, but the first onset of the anti-clericals has given place to the wiser decision to work out the details by private negotiation with the Vatican. This fact is perhaps symbolic of the improving position of the Catholic Church, which before the war had shared the discredit of the hierarchy—mere creatures of the Hapsburg Court, sometimes instruments of Germanization, and generally slack in tone and over-endowed with worldly goods. Its salvation has been the parish clergy, who if not exactly Puritans in standard, were at once good priests and keen patriots. In the first days of the new era anti-clericalism was rampant, and in several cases the mob destroyed monuments of the Immaculate Conception, or even insulted officiating clergy. While this was mere froth on the surface of the stream, the movement for church reform—whose four points were, a national liturgy, election of Bishops by their clergy, abolition of celibacy, and reversal of the sentence upon Hus—seemed for a short time to develop into a real Hussite revival. But its leaders, instead of pressing for constitutional reform from within the church—a policy which would have rallied support from other Slavonic countries and might easily have forced Rome to concessions similar to those enjoyed by the Ruthene and Rumanian Uniates—soon plunged impatiently into session; and although they have carried two hundred and fifty thousand adherents into the new "Czechoslovak National Church," and have established relations with the Serbian orthodox episcopate, their ill-considered tactics have lessened the chances of a real religious reform. The Curia, relieved at its temporary escape from this danger, has sent a Nuncio to Prague, and is playing a "safe" and waiting game. In its appointments to vacant sees it has carefully eliminated all ecclesiastics of real eminence in the republic, and (save in one case where the Prague Foreign Office insisted) has selected worthy but pliant nonentities. But disappointing as are the omissions, the coming of a new and national hierarchy has had an immediate and beneficial effect, especially in Slovakia.

The Germans complain loudly of Czech interference with their schools. But while I would not venture to deny that there have been cases of tactlessness or even unfair treatment, I have failed to discover grievances such as justify the outcry. The Germans retain their University in Prague (amply subsidized by the state), two technical colleges (i.e., as many as the Czechs themselves possess for double the population), seventy-two out of the one hundred and ninety-four middle schools of Bohemia, nine industrial schools, as compared to thirteen Czech, and in Slovakia have acquired three middle schools which the Magyars had not tolerated. The Czechs point out that the average number of children in a Czech school are one hundred and sixty-seven, in a German school only one hundred and forty-two; and, while admitting that in certain instances German schools have been closed, maintain that in each case this was due to the very scanty number of children attending, who could be accommodated in neighboring German schools.

The German-Bohemian leaders have for a whole generation past been conspicuous for their lack of vision, tolerance and sincerity; and the bankruptcy of their intransigent policy seems to have left them for the moment in a political *cul-de-sac*. On the other side, the Czech authorities cannot be acquitted of a weak and negative attitude in the German question. It is too often assumed that it is for the Germans to make the first step, and that the road to a settlement lies through Canossa. In reality, it is from the victor in a quarrel that the first overtures should come; and the Czechoslovaks will have provided the "acid test" of constructive statesmanship when they make it possible for the Germans to enter the government and take their due share in the conduct of political affairs.

An unsolved internal problem of such magnitude is bound to react upon the republic's foreign policy, especially since the German minority borders on three sides with its kinsmen in Germany and in Austria, which may ere long form part of Germany. Fortunately, this merely reinforces the already strongly pacific leanings of President Masaryk, and of the Foreign Minister, Dr. Beneš, whose diplomatic skill, both before and since the Paris Conference, has secured him an unique position in the counsels of Europe. His policy, resting on the sanctity of treaties and on loyalty to the Allies, is none the less the very reverse of negative. Obviously the first essential was to secure the new frontiers and to paralyze subversive propaganda in Allied countries; the next was to win the Entente's public recognition of the view that the restoration of the Hapsburg dynasty in Hungary or elsewhere is an international, not a mere internal question. But paper assurances to this effect have a solid backing in the Little Entente, which is Dr. Beneš's peculiar creation, and which consists of a close defensive alliance between Czechoslovakia and Yugoslavia, and of a parallel understanding with Rumania on all matters Hungarian. So long as this triple combination is free to act, Hungary is clearly impotent; but Dr. Beneš rightly felt the need for further steps to ensure that diversions or complications in other directions may not leave one or other of the three allies face to face with Hungary.

The extension of the Little Entente to include Poland has sometimes been advocated from Bucharest, but hitherto without success. Neither the bad blood left by the Teschen affair nor the intrigues of the Polish aristocracy with Budapest are the real hindrance to a Polish-Czech entente, but far rather the fundamentally Russophil attitude of every Czechoslovak and Yugoslav, and their resolve to endorse no territorial settlement in the east, such as the future Russia—in whatever form she may emerge—could not honorably accept. But there is good reason to hope that as Poland gradually settles down after her terrible trials, and as her democracy consolidates, she will come to realize the advantages of friendship with Prague as the natural mediator in the Slav world—between Russia and Poland no less than between Serbia and Bulgaria. Meanwhile Czechoslovakia goes forward on her path as the most pacific and the most constructive of the new democracies bred by the war.

THE BOHEMIAN SOKOL [1]

To the vast majority of English people the word Sokol will convey no meaning. It is only those who happen to have read, and who remember, the few accounts which have appeared in the newspapers, or the slight references to be found in books about Bohemia, or those who have visited the country, and more particularly those who were in Prague in the summer of 1907 or of 1912, to whom the word will convey anything of its real significance. Primarily, the word means in the Czech language a falcon, but it has gained a secondary

[1] By W. Jerrold. Fortnightly Review. 100: 347-58. August, 1913.

and deeply significant meaning from having been adopted as the distinguishing word for one of the most remarkable patriotic organizations in history.

The Sokols form, no doubt, a great force for the moral and physical uplifting and organizing of a nation; but secondarily, from the point of view of the onlooker, it is not fanciful to find in them a manifestation of the undying spirit of nationality; to realize that in them we have the hopes and aspirations of the Czech people working consciously along lines of self-preservation, and in a manner with which we should have the greatest sympathy, seeing the way in which we have for generations made something of a cult of games and sports, have claimed to find physical and moral good even in boxing. The noble art of self-defense by means of fisticuffs was supposed to enable a man to hold his own against attack; was, as it were, an individualistic art, but that same noble art of self-defense may have the result of producing bullies—the Sokol produces patriots; stands, indeed, for a triumphant attempt at self-conscious nation-building.

An advance post, as it were, of the Slav races, almost surrounded by Teutons, the Bohemians have resolutely fought against Germanizing influences, and in this great gymnastic organization have built up a force the full significance of which it is not easy to gauge, though it is not difficult to read in it a fervid declaration of nationality, of the right to claim that nationality, and of the determination, should it be necessary, to uphold it. Visitors who were in Prague in 1912, had some indication of the extraordinary extent to which this gymnastic organization—the Sokol movement—has grown, both on the plain of Letna, where the massed drill was displayed, and in the square before the Old Town Hall in the ancient city, where about thirty-five thousand men Sokols formed up in a compact mass, with an array of banners which showed that the loyal Bohemians, banded together under the sign of the falcon, included many who had come from several centers in America, from London, from Paris, Berlin, Dresden, and other European cities, and that with them were Sokol contingents from Russia and all the Slavic countries of south-eastern Europe.

It was a remarkably picturesque sight, this massed gathering of the "Falcons" in the Town Hall square. It was a deeply impressive one on the Letna plain where successively eleven thousand men, and then six thousand women, Sokols went through their gymnastic exercises. These thousands making their successive movements as one in accord with the music of a great band gave an impression of sureness and strength simply astounding. It was, as it were, an army of peace that possessed a significance far more touching, far more inspiring than could have been realized from any display of a similar number of soldiery. Here, one could not help thinking, was the young manhood and young womanhood of a nation—the parents of the next generation—dominated by a passionate loyalty, giving itself up to a strenuous but ordered physical education; and the more one inquired into the matter the deeper became one's admiration, not only of the thing accomplished, but of the underlying idea. It was, indeed, a sight to set the observer thinking and inquiring—thinking of how fine a result was to be obtained by systematizing the gymnastic energy of a people, and inquiring as to how the present pitch of excellence had been attained in Bohemia.

The answer to such an inquiry can only be given by stating, though briefly, the story of the Sokol—a story which the Bohemians are, not unjustifiably, proud of repeating. It was one of the grievances of the people in the days of their worst oppression that they were not permitted to form themselves publicly into any such associations as serve to foster and preserve the spirit of nationality. Thus it came about that when the first days of comparative liberty dawned upon the ancient Kingdom of Bohemia, little more than fifty years ago, one of the first uses—one of the most significant and valuable of uses—made of the reacquired privilege was the formation of a Gymnastic Union. This was done under the energetic leadership of Dr. Miroslav Tyrš, an able and far-sighted young man of nine-and-twenty, who would seem from the first to have appreciated the patriotic value that such an organization might come to possess.[1]

Today we find the Sokol writ large throughout Czechoslovakia. In many of the provincial towns one of the most striking buildings will be seen to have carved in bold letters across its front the inspiring word, and inquiry elicits that it is the gymnasium of the local Sokol. This wide-spread training must have a cumulative effect, as every year brings fresh thousands into the movement—an effect not only on the physique but on the *morale* of the people. Indeed, it is not fanciful to recognize something of the result of fifty years of Sokol training on many of the men and women whom we see in Prague and other centers of Sokol activity.

The closer we study the great organization, the story of the development of which has here been sketched, the more fully do we understand the thoroughness with which it has been planned, the sincerity and strength of the national attachment to the ideals which it postulates. The drilling Sokols, whom we may see in their hundreds in their halls or drill-grounds, or in their many thousands at a great quinquennial Congress, form but a part of the whole scheme which is so planned as to include all. The practising of gymnastics is made to begin early. Thus the 1911 statistics show that there were in Bohemia nearly twenty-seven thousand juveniles under the age of fourteen receiving the Sokol training, and nearly as many again lads and girls between the ages of fourteen and eighteen, while the Czechoslovak

[1] Miroslav Tyrš (pronounced Teersh), born on September 9, 1832, was Professor of Esthetics at the University of Prague, but as an ardent Bohemian patriot gave himself up largely to the idea of training his nation more or less upon the lines of ancient Greek gymnastics. He died in the Tyrol on August 8, 1884.

Sokol Union included over eighty thousand men and fifteen thousand women members. Particular care, it may be said, is taken regarding the training of young people leaving the compulsory schools, to ensure that they shall not go adrift. They have already been grounded in gymnastics and have been inspired with the desire to become full Sokols. Every facility is given them to continue the training until they can take full membership of one of the Sokol societies. Such membership is not, however, an end, but only a means—a means toward fuller self-realization in the best sense as part of a community; and membership, as has been pointed out, is no light thing to be lightly undertaken, for it is not play in which the Sokols indulge, but strenuous work with the object of fitting themselves in the most complete fashion to take their places as well-equipped men and women, as representative Czecho-slovaks.

The training has not only its physical value, but it has its moral importance also. These young men and women on the threshold of responsible life have to give up three evenings of each week to their gymnastic training, and, as a Bohemian gentleman who had himself been a drilling Sokol suggested, the drill keeps them out of mischief or seeking after idle forms of amusement; for after an evening's exercising the Sokol is glad to get to bed. Nor are the intervening evenings given up to idleness either, for the moral and intellectual training of the Sokols is no unimportant part of the scheme, and they attend lectures, visit places of interest, or by debates and discussions are exercised in the arts of oratory. It should also be emphasized that the whole organization is maintained on the most democratic basis. All Sokols are equal—the son of a mechanic may be the drill companion of a son of a professor at the university. The son of the wealthiest man and the son of the poorest meet as friends on the common ground of their Czech nationality, and thus is fostered that fraternal spirit which is by no means the least important or the least significant part of true patriotism.

The spirit which gave birth to the Sokols, the spirit which has made it grow to a power the full influence of which it is not easy to foresee, seems to be the spirit of the whole Czechoslovak race today. Though Tyrš is justly honored as the man who found the passionate enthusiasm and the means of organizing and fostering that spirit, it is possible to trace the inspirations of their work in the writings of the great Bohemian historian, the father of his people as he is fondly termed, František Palacký (Frantishek Palatsky). It was Palacký who roused the Bohemian nation in the days of its depression to a sense of its glorious past, and the ideals of the Sokol are the ideals which the historian formulated with vehement eloquence. It was, therefore, only fitting that the Sokol gathering should have been made the occasion for unveiling the grandly impressive monument which the Bohemians have erected to the memory of Palacký, and that at the foot of the statue of the historian one of the leading Czechs of today, Dr. Karel Kramář, should have reaffirmed for the Czechs of the present the ideals to which Palacký denoted his life:—

That is the great legacy of our forefathers—the legacy of a noble, just democracy, which, if we will remain true Bohemians, will give us a notable place in the ideal strife of humanity— the strife, that is, for the victory of truth and right, for liberty and justice for all. . . . The main thing is always the central idea of the whole movement, and this was to Palacký, and is to us, equal justice to all individuals, to all classes of society, and to all nations. But as Palacký was, we are enemies of demagogy; we must refrain from any misuse of the democratic idea in the way of a mere rule by numbers and material strength; for a truly noble democracy, just to all, guided by the desire to improve not only the material conditions, but also the moral ones, to get culture and enlightenment, to raise the moral level of the whole nation, that is the democratic program in Palacký's meaning, in the spirit of our great history.

And that, it may be added, is the ideal in forming and quickening one of the most remarkable idealistic and

practical patriotic organizations of the modern world—
the Bohemian Sokol.

THE YANKEES OF CENTRAL EUROPE [1]

No achievement since the war is of greater significance in preserving the rule of democracy and of order
among the central European powers than that which
produced the "Little Entente." This combination of
small nations, completed during the summer of 1921,
strictly speaking, represents three separate understand-
ings between Czechoslovakia and Yugoslavia; between
Czechoslovakia and Rumania and between Yugoslavia
and Rumania. The foundation for these agreements
was economic as well as political.

The combined population of the three nations is forty-
two million. Together they have standing armies numbering six hundred thousand and in case of necessity are
able to mobilize an additional ten million men. Besides
purposing to maintain the treaties which were the outcome of the war, eliminate existing conflicts, create an
atmosphere of conciliation, and stimulate among the
nations of central Europe that spirit of cooperation
essential to the lasting peace of all Europe, one of the
avowed principles of the Little Entente is to prevent any
Hapsburg from again ruling in central Europe.

It is of the rôle of Czechoslovakia in this little league
that I wish to write. It was my good fortune to be a
visiting professor at Prague, and while there the vital
significance of this new republic impressed me with
greater force month by month. In his address before
Parliament, October 18, 1921, the prime minister, Dr.
Edward Beneš, outlined the policy of the new cabinet.
He presented a plan for insurance and old-age pensions,
discussed the problems of land reform, housing, and
unemployment; promised prompt attention to the con-

[1] By J. A. James. Century Magazine. 104: 857-64. October, 1922.

sideration of the separation of church and state; declared that the policy of making economic and political treaties with all the neighboring states would be continued; and closed with an appeal for the cooperation and support of all.

This program, merely sketched, is the more surprising when it is recalled that the independence of Czechoslovakia was recognized by the government of the United States, by France and Great Britain; that on October 14, 1918, a temporary government was organized, with Dr. Masaryk as president and Dr. Beneš as foreign minister; and that on October 28, following what is called the "bloodless revolution," an independent republic was set up in Prague. After fourteen months' labor on the new constitution, that document was accepted by the Constitutional Assembly. Following its provisions, on May 27, 1920, the National Assembly by unanimous vote elected as president Dr. Masaryk.

This constitution, undertaking to deal fairly with the outcome and social problems of the nation, probably has no superior among the constitutions of the nations of the world. In principle it reflects the American and the French constitutions, but on questions of governmental organization it resembles the constitution of France. The creation of a democratic republic in central Europe, with the people as the "sole source of all state power," and the success of that government under the most trying circumstances are due in large measure to the vision and labors of President Masaryk.

In the remaking of Europe at Versailles, Czechoslovakia, a name which still sounds strange to most Americans, was made an independent state. Its territory of fifty-five thousand square miles, with the exception of a small area, was carved out of the former Austro-Hungarian dominions and comprised 28 per cent of the landed possessions of that monarchy. The constitution provides for a unified rather than a federated state. A special treaty between the Allied powers and Czechoslovakia provides that Carpathian Russinia (Ruthenia), although an integral part of the republic, shall be granted certain public rights not accorded the other provinces, such as having its own governor and its own diet, which has the power of legislation on linguistic, educational, religious, and other matters of domestic administration. The governor is appointed by the president of the republic, but he is also responsible to the diet.

The population of the republic is thirteen million, five hundred and ninety-five thousand. Of this total, nine million are Czechs and Slovaks; three million, Germans; nearly one million, Magyars, and the remainder are Russian and Polish. Czechoslovak immigrants have gone in large numbers to other countries, and it is estimated that there are five hundred thousand within the bounds of the Austrian Republic; nearly the same number in Hungary; over two hundred thousand in Yugoslavia and Rumania, and one million five hundred thousand in the United States. In general, the German population in the northwestern part of the state and the Magyar population along the southern border of Slovakia constitute the real problem of the republic. Clashes between groups of these diverse elements have not been infrequent, but the liberal treatment accorded the racial minorities by the government will in time, I believe, bring about real national solidarity.

Prague is the intellectual center of Czechoslovakia. The university, the oldest of German universities, was one of the leading institutions of higher learning during the medieval period. Toward the middle of the eighteenth century and at the close of the first quarter of the next century, Czech science and literature again received attention by native scholars. In 1882 the establishment of an independent Czech university (Charles University) was permitted, and notwithstanding the lack of physical resources, it has been an important factor in the development of a national spirit and culture. The study of philosophy, especially that of the Slavonic languages, and the realist movement in philosophy and sociology under the leadership of Professor Masaryk have been emphasized. The study of English is now receiving considerable attention.

At Prague and the two other universities, at Brno and Bratislava, there are twenty-eight thousand students. Three-fourths of this number are in Prague, and are devoting themselves primarily to the study of law, medicine, engineering, chemistry, and to the philosophical, commercial and agricultural courses. That students are flocking to the universities in such numbers is attributed to the fact that thousands of the middle class were, under the old régime, prevented from attending the institutions of higher learning. The education of large numbers was interrupted by the war, and over four thousand students from other near eastern countries are receiving instruction at Prague. "The Free Ukrainian University" was opened on October 23, 1921, for students of Ukrainian birth.

Marked interest is manifested in all Slavonic nations on the part of President Masaryk, whose *Russia and Europe* is one of his best literary contributions. This interest is shared by other leaders and especially those in the university, who are ambitious to make Prague once more the leading center for all Slavonic studies. To that end, in addition to instruction given by professors in the Czech and Slovak languages and literatures, some fifteen other well known professors are offering courses in fields such as the comparative study of Slavonic languages and literature; phonetic study of Slavonic languages; Yugoslav languages and literature; Russian language and literature; Polish language and literature; the history of the Slavonic races; Slavonic archæology; Slavonic ethnography; and Slavonic law. Seven journals and reviews are devoted to these studies, and in the curricula of the new universities Slavonic studies are likewise emphasized. Prague University library. among its five hundred thousand volumes, has a good collection of Slavica, and the library of the National Museum contains among its three hundred thousand volumes the richest collection of Slavonic works to be found in central Europe. In addition to the universities, provision is made for state, technical, commercial, agricultural, and special trade schools.

No account of the development now taking place in Czechoslovakia would be complete without some mention of the provisions which are made for elementary and secondary schools. In no other way is the characteristic energy and perseverance of the people more manifest, despite their struggle for centuries, than in carrying out the ideals of their great educational reformer, Comenius. In Bohemia, Moravia, and Silesia, only 2.5 per cent of the population is illiterate. In Slovakia, under the dominance of the Magyar government, no instruction in the Slovak language was permitted in the schools, and the percentage of illiteracy was 28. During the first year of the republic twenty seven hundred elementary schools for Slovak children were established by the government. One hundred and two higher elementary schools, thirty-seven gymnasia; six *real*-gymnasia, a number of *lycées* for girls, thirteen teacher's training colleges, and the Comenius University at Bratislava have also been opened in Slovakia. A law providing for the opening of libraries in every community came into force on January 1, 1922. Provision is made whereby all persons may come to know native art, music, and objects of historical interest by visiting the galleries, the opera, and the museums.

The influence of American philanthropic and social agencies in European reconstruction is to be seen in no other country to better advantage than in Czechoslovakia. The tributes to America heard on all sides are due in part to the belief in American democratic ideals and to the insistence by some of our leaders that the rights of small nations shall be preserved. But they are also expressions of gratitude for the timely aid given to them in their first months of national existence by the American (Hoover) Relief Administration, the American Red Cross, the Rockefeller Foundation, the Young Men's Christian Association, and the Young Women's Christian Association. But this is a story space will not permit.

Located in the very heart of Europe, Czechoslovakia has been acquiring the best in western civilization, and has, as no other nation, an inherent understanding of the great Slavic world to the east. May it not be said that this nation, viewed from its four years of development, will become under normal conditions the chief force in bringing the Slavic peoples into complete cooperation with the western world?

SOCIAL LIFE IN PRAGUE [1]

Prague is seen at its best on an evening in the spring-time, when a mist gently envelopes its towers and the humped roofs of its old houses, investing with indefinable mystery the strange bundle of palaces and churches that crowns it. Far in the distance the islands rise like stumps upon the calm immensity of the river. All is silent, but with a singular silence which one knows to be heavy with life. Happy is he who can abandon himself to this charm and let it conquer him little by little.

But the Prague of today is no longer in this poetic condition, nor yet does it live in the memory of past ages. Open stores, cafés, walls plastered with bills, modern streets furrowed by carriages and motor-cars, send up joyously and sonorously the news of the capital rising anew. The people of Prague in earlier days held very high the culture and the honor of their city. With

[1] By G. Bouchard. La Revue Universelle. 6: 731-5. September 15, 1921.

fury in their hearts, they endured three centuries of German domination, and now they are again liberated and have their free city in their own hands, the center and the head of a state greater than their realm of yesterday. Too grand, too big, too great, perhaps—from the mountains of the Böhmerwald to the Carpathians.

Their happiness is justified. From Prague the appeals of the nation have gone up for seventy years. It is at Prague that so much generous blood has been spilled for the Czech cause, until the recent day when, after the Austrian officers had fled, the fall of the Hapsburgs and the liberty of Bohemia were proclaimed as heralded in the peace. The glory of the past and the distinction of the present are going to the head of the citizen of Prague, intoxicating him. He is hospitable and easy of approach. He is delighted to meet a Frenchman, for he has a profound respect for France. But he thinks it necessary to dress up his welcome with all the solemnity of a pope. He is dignified, serious; he insists upon the great honor which he has done France in learning the language of that country. He adds the majesty of a German to the simplicity of a Slav. I still have in my ears the "Welcome, I hope you will enjoy yourself. Do you forget Bohemia. Why do you speak German?" which fell about my ears with the gravity of an insincere chorus.

The Czechs often compel themselves, in our presence, to a protestation of faith in Prague and in republicanism. They curse Austria and cast anathema toward Rome. Then they follow the reply of the Frenchman to whom they are talking, after the fashion of a good student who would like to profit by an English lesson. What a false impression! When that husk of gravity has burst, I have known Czechs who were perfectly witty with a spirit which was satiric to the verge of malice, never very really gay or jolly, but very good comrades and serviceable to the last degree.

As intimacy increases, one discovers among them the Slavic charm—famous, much praised, and puzzling—of their Russian brothers. Emotionalism dominates these artist souls, emotionalism and sensuality, and yet their capacity for friendship is large. They possess the delicate secret of proving their friendship by testimony which pleases, and which comes at a happy time. Have they the sturdy will and the firmness that make strong friendship? As the soul of a people reflects that of individuals, will the Czech people be for France, the ally which it promises to become?

The man of Prague is tenacious in his friendships, but his fidelity is not always free from feebleness, and great are the difficulties of the young republic. I remember a brilliant discourse in which M. Ribot congratulated the Belgians on having only a few political parties. Since the Czechs have not taken Belgium as their model, to what can one compare their state? Already a great number of parties divide the country. Social questions and religious quarrels—deadly, alas, to the Bohemia of Jan Hus—tear and divide the citizens. No doubt the socialist processions of the first of May do not seem very ferocious at Prague; tranquil promenades of a flower-crowned throng, who carry threatening banners. But the tone of the newspapers is bitter, the political speeches violent, and in more than one simple soul, as the wounds of the war are not healed and the cost of living continues high, there grows up a regret for the golden time of his slavery.

One day a Czech friend of mine gave an old woman a theater ticket that he could not use. They were playing *L'Aiglon* that evening. The next time he saw the recipient of his bounty, my friend asked what her impressions were of the celebrated French play.

"O, it was lovely! And there was one thing that gave me great delight."

"What was it?"

Then lowering her voice, with tears in her eyes, the old woman confessed: "The Austrian national hymn! I thought that I would never hear it again!"—for the reader will remember that in the second act of *L'Aiglon* one hears the Austrian hymn above the cannonade.

Nothing but a stray remark of an old woman, some one may say; but all the same, there stuck in my memory certain frolicsome remarks which I had overheard. From the chaos of today, from the uncertainty of tomorrow, certain Czechs have drawn so painful an impression, one so agonizing, that it deprives them of courage. Slovakia is expanding, but tomorrow she will be threatening to secede. Her representatives, it is true, protest their fidelity to the republic. They understand the difficulties and unfriendlinesses, which are involved in the sudden fusion of two peoples who, although brothers in race, have been separated for eight centuries. Will the mountaineer of the Tatras and the bourgeois of Bratislava understand one another and have nothing to regret?

Yet the gravity of the Slovak question is not to be compared with that of the German problem. The Czechs say that the Germans of Bohemia are more furious than those of Berlin. One might believe it when, in the regions of the west, the most insignificant street porter assumes an arrogant, haughty attitude, and ostentatiously replies in German to any question that may be put to him in Czech. An active pan-Germanist progapanda is at work in these regions.

The Czechs, who are undergoing their apprenticeship in democracy, have not yet attained to the republican spirit. Of their own free will, they seek refuge in a single man. Their President, Thomas Masaryk, seems to be the keystone of the arch of the new edifice, exactly as Emperor Francis Joseph made certain the stability of the old, undermined scaffolding. Installed in the Royal Palace, treated like a sovereign—they even stop work to celebrate his birthday—President Masaryk is generally beloved. In Prague you see his portrait everywhere; behind the windows of the stores his short-sighted eyes smile out from the shelter of his glasses above the professorial white beard. A Slovak by birth, a Czech from having passed all his life at Prague, distinguished for his sociological study, attracting the attention of the learned men of Europe ever since 1895, devoted to his patriotic efforts with Woodrow Wilson, he well deserves his popularity. He pacifies the feuds of the parties; he calms their quarrels; with his prestige he covers this or that unpopular minister. If he is not exactly a Washington, as some people suggest, at least he fills the place very acceptably. Close at his side, masculine in her mannerisms and temperament, with a proud carriage and a pair of spectacles planted on her imperial nose, Alice Masarykova, Ph.D., expends her activity in good works. She once achieved the title of Minister of Social Welfare.

Prague still holds dear Karel Kramář, the former chief of the National Assembly. His quarrel with M. Beneš swept him from power, for the radical parties accused him of reaction. Calm and smiling behind his white moustache with a big neck and high shoulders, M. Kramář lets them talk. He is the king of the bourgeoisie. Married to a Russian lady of high birth, he pins his faith to the speedy resurrection of a sound and liberalist Russia. He is rich and he lives in his own house, which is a great privilege. He is just waiting. His is a great and noble character. While I am talking of a friend of France, how shall I forget the President's neighbor, the Abbé Monsignor Zavoral, who, in his monastery at Strahov or at his senatorial desk, expresses the most generous and wisest judgments and induces the Czech clergy to model themselves on French clergy, who have been able nobly to unite respect for religious laws with the holy duty of patriotism?

The old German methods are still in force at the

universities, but the Czechs do make appeal to the resources of French science. The dullness of German books is compared with the force and clearness of works by men of Latin race and especially those of the one Frenchman who forms the link between the Czechs and the French people, and devotes his sincere spirit to the service of this cause, Ernest Denis. I ask pardon of the modesty of Professor Pekař for writing his name here. He is a prominent historian and has taken upon himself too much disinterested labor, both of patriotism and of faith to permit me to be silent. He is, I know, a true friend of French ways and French history.

These are the great, energetic, worldly figures that honor a country in spite of obstacles and troubles. They provide the best approach for the French colony. Before the war, what Frenchman, except Ernest Denis and Louis Leger, did anybody know at Prague? Since the armistice the number of French compatriots have grown steadily in Bohemia, and France has become the teacher of this reviving land. The task was hard. Quite aside from the faults and the sensitiveness of the Czechs, German ideas have a tenacity, and it is no small task to uproot them. The list of the difficulties overcome by the military and university missions would be long. The results are far from complete and efforts are by no means slackening. It is even necessary to urge the French as far as possible, to take an interest in this task. The labors which French compatriots have begun over there, conferences, charities, even business affairs, have been for the Czechs a means of instruction and an example.

General good-will, native intelligence, sympathy for France—certainly there is all that at Prague; and in order to obtain the best results constantly, we must make an unremitting appeal to these qualities, for the Czechoslovak republic, in spite of its old civilization, is a young state. It ought to take up its education anew. It ought to feel keenly the importance of such a task. It is for Prague, more visited by foreigners than any other part of Czechoslovak territory, richer and more accessible in everybody's opinion, to give to the whole land its impulse, and to establish the proper standard. Firmness and restraint are more necessary in the liberty that has been attained than efforts toward liberation.

ART IN CZECHOSLAVAKIA [1]

I

THE HISTORY OF CZECHOSLOVAK ART

In speaking of art among modern peoples of the white stock, we can hardly do so any more in the comprehensively subjective sense and say American, or English, or even French, Russian or Czechoslovak art; it is, rather, art in America, England, France, Russia, Czechoslovakia. The pristine time, when a people such as the Egyptians, Assyrians or Greeks, could develop an art realm of their own, is past, and the more modern nations must be content with a more or less secondary rôle. For art, however broadly we take it, is after all limited. It is limited by our resources, but especially by the scope of our senses and our intellect. Once the available field is fairly covered and the main possibilities have been utilized, there remains not much more for art than amplification and refinement. Later historic nations develop details, styles, peculiarities, "schools," but, in the main, upon already well known principles.

However, as each people differs more or less in mentality from all others, so will their art differ. Given the same ideological proposition, no two scholars will achieve the same literary production, and the same applies to art and to nations. It is thus that art in

[1] By Aleš Hrdlička. Art and Archaeology. 11: 179-83, 213-19. May, 1921.

America will some day be shaded "American," that art in France is tinged by something distinctly "French," and that art in Czechoslovakia has acquired and is developing the flavor of "Czechoslovak," which might be difficult to define in so many words, but which is well appreciated by those of developed art knowledge and sense in other countries.

Artistic tendencies are inborn in all peoples, they are a pan-human quality, but they differ from group to group in volume, warmth, color, directions and effects. Again, as with individuals, there are peoples in whom artistic tendencies on the whole are poorly developed, or at best remain quite secondary to the routine mental manifestations, the routine life; in others they are well represented in the mental complex, but yield readily to a cool coordination with the rest of the intellectual pursuits; and then there are those in whom the love of beauty, of form, of live color, of sound, of rhythm, are of the strongest life attributes, and in whom art in some form or other is a constant efflorescence, at the expense even sometimes of the more utilitarian functions. These are the favored of the muses to whom appreciation and love of beauty in its whole gamut are soul essentials. Such people create in art, and in all directions where creation is still possible; with nature's tools they embellish and intone more sober nature, and if general conditions are not forbidding, they give from their plentiful cup to the rest of the world; they produce painters, sculptors, architects, musicians of world reputation.

The Czechoslovaks must belong somewhere near this last category of peoples. With the rest of the Slavs they are people of sentiment, of natural and pious idealism, of predominating love of beauty in all its forms. Their villages blossom irrepressibly with folk art; their cities reflect the best arts of modern Europe; while music, a higher than ordinary music, from ancient poetic folk song to modern powerful hymns and opera, pervades everything. As a witness to their riches in just one direction—there is now in press a collection of their folk chants, to the number of twenty thousand. They have given the world, notwithstanding their relatively small numbers and their débacle during the Thirty Years' War, with the subsequent three paralyzing centuries under Austrian subjection, many a composer, musician, painter and others in art, not to speak of poetry and literature, of more than local and in some cases of truly world reputation. Names like Dvořák, Smetana, Fibbich, Ševčík, Kubelík, Destinn, Mánes, Brožík, Mucha and others are well known wherever art is cherished.

The innate qualities of the Czechoslovaks in relation to art are an inheritance of the far past, and have their source doubtless in the original Slav stock from which these tribes during the earlier part of the first millenium B.C. began to separate. In the course of their subsequent existence however, the Czechs in all lines of intellectual pursuits are subjected to considerable outside influences, especially in Bohemia; but the effects of these influences may always be traced and discounted. They merely give another direction now and then, and usually a general impetus, to the art pursuits in the country. There are noticeable in Bohemia in turn strong Byzantine, Roman, Dutch, Italian, as well as French and German influences. These influences introduce the classic styles and modernized art, and at times prevail; in the end, however, their results are essentially always but a stimulation and strengthening of the native qualities; the new is largely assimilated rather than grafted on. As soon as the pressure of circumstances relaxes, the native artists and the native bred art begin to reassert themselves. Moreover the foreign influences remain limited to the cities and their spheres of influence, the country, in the main, remains as it was. That there was never respite enough, outside of folk art, fully to develop the native tendencies, was wholly a matter of the vicissitudes to which the country was subjected.

The history of art in Czechoslovakia may be roughly

divided into (1) the Early Historic; (2) the Medieval; and (3) the Modern. The early period is that before the Christianization of the rulers of Bohemia in
874; the Medieval may well be conceived to begin with
the year 874 and to end with the Thirty Years' War and
the long prostration that followed it; while the Modern
period, though beginning properly with the commencing
reawakening of the nation toward the end of the
eighteenth, does not actually set in before the middle of
the nineteenth century.

The art of the Early Historic period was the Czechoslovak art proper; but it was perishable art which left
little if anything to posterity, except in survivals. It
was the art of the frame dwelling, of the carved statue
of the pagan diety, of possibly some carved or painted
utensils and furniture, and of the woven, embroidered
or painted decoration. There was also some art in pottery, weapons and jewelry, but this was probably less
truly native, and belongs also more to the field of archaeology. There were surely abundant folk dances and
folk songs with poetry and mimicry. Survivals of much
of this can be traced, and that in wide distribution, to
this day, but records are very fragmentary.

The christening of the Czech Duke Bořivoj in 874,
by the Macedonian apostles, Cyril and Methodius, which
was soon followed by the Christianization of the whole
nation, makes a sharp boundary in art development.
Under Byzantine and then Byzantine-Roman influence,
characteristic church and later on monastery and con-
vent structures arise, remnants of which may be found
in Czechoslovakia to this day; and architecture is soon
followed by church painting, sculpture and carving. In
the course of time as cities grow there is also a development of lay architecture with decoration and artistic
work in metals. The dukes and then kings, the nobles,
the wealthy merchants, foster art in all directions. Where
native training does not suffice, they call in temporarily
renowned architects and other artists from other coun-

tries. The transitional or old, and then the true Gothic, follow upon the Byzantine and Roman, exerting a profound and widespread influence. Prague the capital, other large cities and the country, become studded with remarkable churches, castles and mansions, many of which (some still well preserved, some in ruins) exist to this day in the "hundred-towered" city above the Vltava and elsewhere in Bohemia. And the smaller towns, then as later, reflect the prevailing art in the facades of their houses, in their roofs, their causeways and ceilings, their furniture, and in other particulars. Even the better class of rural houses show the changing tendencies. The prosperous period of art lasts from the thirteenth to the fifteenth century. The time of Karel IV (1333-1378), in particular, is the "golden age" of art in all branches, in what then represented the Czech countries.

The fifteenth century, however, brings a serious reversion. It is the time of the stern spirit of early Reformation, and engenders the terrible Hussite wars (1419-1436) which are attended with vast destruction. Many of the castles are ruined, churches burned, much in all forms of art destroyed, and but little constructed.

The main work for many decades after the Hussite wars is that of repairs. With the gradual advent of more peaceful times art, however, reasserts itself, and that with the so-called Vladislavian or late Gothic, and then with the Renaissance (1510 onward). But the nation never fully recovers. It is beset with increasing internal as well as external difficulties of religious and political nature, which forciby pre-occupy the minds and which eventually, in 1620, culminate in the abrogation of Bohemia's independence, in the scourge of the Thirty Years' War, the exile of nearly thirty thousand of the best Czech families, the systematic destruction under Jesuit-Austrian guidance of the literature of the "rebel," "heretic" people, with a vast loss of life and material ruination.

It is long after the Thirty Years' War that art in

the Czechoslovak countries really begins again to prosper, and little wonder that once more it is the subject at first of considerable outside assistance, favored by the enriched enemies whom indebted Austria has rewarded at Bohemia's expense. Only slowly do the innate qualities of the people begin again to reassert themselves. Some of the damage is repaired and some new work furthered. The baroque and rococo, introduced by the now dominant Catholic Church, are adopted, and are greatly modified into more pleasing forms which gain a wide dispersion. History, literature, poetry, painting, especially painting *al fresco,* and sculpture begin again to be cultivated. But on the whole, the nation is recuperating, and preparing for its future cultural as well as political liberation.

The revival or modern art period is delayed until the nineteenth century. When it finally comes, it is characterized in Bohemia as everywhere by a variety and mixture of styles, with adaptation to modern requirements and resources. Painting, which hitherto has been almost wholly church, portrait or decorative and illuminative painting, extends now predominantly into the natural and humane spheres, to culminate in the beautiful wall paintings of Ženíšek and Aleš in the National Theatre, the sceneries of Marak, the portraits of Svabinsky, the exquisite sketches of Marod, and the great historic tableaux of Brožík and Mucha. The old "Fraternity of Painters," established in 1348, is succeeded (1796) by the "Association of Friends of Art," which exists to this day. Art work in metals and carving rejuvenates, only however almost to yield later to modern machinery. Sculpture assumes a healthy, virile progress, and has reached already some striking composites, such as Palacký's, St. Vaclav's and the Jan Hus monuments in Prague.

Aroused by Mánes the national spirit finds increasing favor and for a time it seems as if at last it would be permitted to develop fully—when at the very end of the century it is temporarily no doubt, but seriously blighted once more by the "official," made-to-order, art "regulations" of Austria. Austria, increasingly jealous of its provinces, and controlling absolutely all art as well as other instruction, abused its position for the introduction of regulations which did away on the part of the Czech art scholars with national originality or tendency, replacing it forcibly by a banal, cold art of the Austrian "empire." This results in a progeny of "ex-nationalists" whose art is out of sympathy with the warm national Slav tendencies. Only the masters have escaped, but their whole example and influence, as well as time, will be required for undoing the harm done. Austria has left to Czechoslovakia many a burden of malheritage, of which that in art is not the least.

Notwithstanding all, today art in every branch, in the purely aesthetic as well as in the applied and the industrial arts, is once more fully alive in Czechoslovakia, and as in the past so now, it is willingly or unwillingly modifying the foreign, the weak "internationalistic" and the abnormal "hypermodern" tendencies, in accordance with the inherent poetic, sensitive individualism of the people. If times are propitious, a rapid and fruitful development in all lines may confidently be predicted, and it will not be long before, in painting and sculpture particularly, the Czechoslovak artists may give to the art world new classics, radiating the pure spirit of the nation's individuality.

Czechoslovakia is rich in art instruction, and rich in museums devoted exclusively or partly to art. It is a country of museums, for there are over three hundred and fifty of these scattered over the larger and smaller cities, and established mainly for the preservation of local folk art and artistic antiquities. At the head of these stand the Modern Art Gallery with the older Art Gallery "Rudolfinum," in Prague, the Art Industries Museum in the same city, the National and Ethnographic Museums in Prague, and the State Museum of

Moravia in Brno. As to art schools, Prague has the Academy of Arts, the Schools of Architecture and Industrial Arts, the Conservatorium of Music, and a School for Organ Music; in addition to which there are the Government School for Sculpture, the Government School for Ceramics, a Government School for Arts in Metal, a School for Art Industries in Bronze, etc., and additional ceramic schools also in other large cities. Besides with Czechoslovak students are to be found in all the most renowned art schools in Europe.

America itself is not wholly a stranger to Czechoslovak art, even if we omit music. There are several of Brožík's pictures in this country; there have been exhibited here a series of those of Mucha; and there exist here already a number of noted young native-born or naturalized painters and sculptors of Czechoslovak derivation.

II

Painting in Czechoslovakia

The history of the art of painting in Czechoslovakia has really but two subdivisions, the old and the modern, the latter beginning strictly only with the later part of the nineteenth century.

The long old period is characterized especially by church art. The first painters mentioned in Czech history are the first two abbots of the Sázava Monastery. The art is partly ornamental, partly representative; and the latter appears for a long time restricted or almost so, to paintings on cloth, wall or wood, or religious scenes, of saints and of madonnas. Of the earlier productions but very little remains to our day, and we are unable to judge of their standards.

As for all arts, so for painting in Czechoslovakia, the "golden days" are those of the nineteenth century. In 1348 the painters are already numerous and important enough to associate into a fraternity. It was, also, during this time that painters and other artists were elevated to a special dignity at the court. It is of interest to note that the Painters Fraternity embraced painters in general and the heraldry painters, between whom there was kept a clear distinction which is not now fully understood. The patron saint of the fraternity was St. Lucas. During this century there is an influx into Bohemia of painters from Germany, some of whom remain temporarily, while others settle permanently in the new country; and with these newcomers are brought in German and Dutch influences which are very perceptible in the Bohemian art remains of the period. In conformity with the spirit of the time, and the piety of Karel IV, the sphere of painting remains still very largely religious, but there is also some portrait and "worldly" painting. There is a marked development of painting *al fresco*.

The survivals of painting from this period are quite numerous and afford interesting material for study. Besides the western there are noticed some Italian and even still some Byzantine influences. The quality of work reaches in some instances a high standard without, however, constituting masterpieces which would equal the best Flemish or Italian. It is plain that circumstances have as yet not been sufficiently propitious to develop a school of characteristic painters of Bohemia itself.

Simultaneously with the development of painting at large, a very considerable progress has also been realized during these earlier centuries in the development of miniature paintings and especially in the illumination of bibles, breviaries, psalters, and books of the gospels. An effort was also made during the reign of Karel IV in art mosaic. During this period the painting of church interiors reached its maximum development, and there are accounts of whole series of churches and castles that were filled with paintings in this manner. Unfortunately a large majority of this painting has, in the course of time, been destroyed. Some good examples have been accidentally recovered in recent times during repairs to old churches.

During the reign of Václav IV, the son of Karel, the favorable period for the development of art and painting continues, but the latter is now marked by more boisterousness and less restriction. The art of illumination has progressed extensively, and has left a series of valuable examples. The Reformation and the Hussite wars of the fifteenth century not only stopped art progress, but resulted in widespread destruction. What this produced follows very largely old traditions. The art of illumination, however, shows a decided advance still further, as witnessed by the number of precious remaining examples, some of which begin already to show the influence of the Renaissance.

In the sixteenth century painting is especially favored during the reign of Rudolf II. As a Hapsburg, Rudolf called in a number of Dutch and German masters, the foremost of whom is Bartholomew Sprangher of Antwerp, who eventually settles in Prague for the rest of his life. The new impetus given to the art of painting extended, however, all over the country and resulted in the appearance of a series of native painters, some of whom become especially noted.

The seventeenth century and the Thirty Years' War were on the whole a most unfavorable period for the art of painting in the Bohemian territories. A number of the foremost native artists were among the exiles from the country; and there was no incentive for the development of others. In addition to which there was a wide destruction. After the Thirty Years' War the new nobility and new rich owners, mostly of foreign extraction, in repairing the partly ruined and in building new mansions, called in again numbers of foreign painters, the foremost of whom was Peter Brandl, whose paintings were characterized by unusual power The art which showed the most rapid advance toward recovery was painting *al fresco,* represented by a new progeny of native painters, among whom excelled especially Václav Reiner (died 1745). The development in this direction is such that it is possible to speak of a Czech school of fresco painting of the eighteenth century. The subjects of the paintings were partly religious, partly battle scenes, either historical or allegorical, besides which there appear also landscapes, paintings of flowers, etc.

The reign of Joseph II, as a complete antithesis to that of Rudolf II, directly interfered with all progress in art, including painting. By the decree of 1782, the Painters Fraternity was dissolved. Rudolf's art gallery, and many privately owned pictures were sold abroad; and nothing was now produced. This curious state of affairs can only be regarded as one of the manifestations of abnormality which here and there have been observed in the different Hapsburgs. Fortunately, in 1796 conditions have so changed that the establishment of an "Association of the Patriotic Friends of Art" became possible, which was soon followed by the foundation of a permanent Art Gallery and Art School. This, properly speaking, was the beginning of the modern period of the art of painting in Bohemia, though for a long time yet the art was laboring under foreign influence.

The rest of the history of painting in Czechoslovakia is that of a steadily accelerating development toward the best of modern standards and an equally augmenting emancipation from traditional and foreign influences. The main pioneer in this direction is J. Mánes (1821-71), whose excellent studies of the native types and illustrations from old Czech history have exerted a strong influence on a line of followers. Jaroslav Čermák (1811-78) devotes himself to scenes from the life and environment of Slavs in the Balkans. F. Ženíšek and Mikuláš Aleš follow ingeniously and originally in the same direction (in Bohemia and Moravia). It is these two who produced in the main the exquisite wall paintings of the National Theatre.

Historic painting is represented foremost by Václav Brožík (1851-1900), known the world over by his great tableaux "Jan Hus before the Council of Constance," "Columbus before the Court of Isabella," etc.; and at the present time by A. Mucha who, since 1880, is working on twenty great tableaux that are to illustrate the main events of Slavic history. Eleven of these huge tableaux, 18 by 28 feet, have been completed and a number of them have, within the last two years, been shown in the Art Institute of Chicago and the Brooklyn Museum. Scenery in all its forms, genre, and all other forms of the art of painting, have today in Czechoslovakia able and noted representatives.

The older national collections of art are housed since 1882 in the beautiful and extensive "Rudolfinum" in Prague, while the more recent art treasures are housed in the "Modern Gallery." Also, there are a number of important private collections, and, taking the arts together, the great old churches and mansions of Prague, and the old churches, monasteries, castles and mansions scattered over the country, are similarly as in Holland, Belgium, France and Italy, so many parts of one vast art museum.

CHAPTER V

YUGOSLAVIA

YUGOSLAVIA'S RESOURCES AND BEAUTY[1]

The new state, generally known in the United States
as Yugoslavia, is made up of the old Kingdoms of Serbia
and Montenegro and the Austro-Hungarian provinces
of Slovenia, Croatia, Slavonia, Bosnia-Herzegovina,
Dalmatia, and what is now known as the Voyvodina,
which includes the several small provinces north of the
Danube between Slavonia and the new Rumanian
boundary. The population of the kingdom is practically
all Slav, with a small admixture of Turks in southern
Serbia, a few Italians in some of the cities along the
Adriatic, and groups of Hungarians, Austrians and Germans in some of the other provinces. Aside from the
Turks in southern Serbia and the Hungarians and Germans in the Voyvodina, the non-Slav population is confined almost entirely to the cities and towns. This is
especially true along the Adriatic, where even the hinterland of Trieste, which has been given to the Italians,
is almost entirely Slav, while the city itself has a large
Italian majority.

The northern portion of the old Kingdom of Serbia
was partially liberated from Turkish rule about one
hundred years ago, but the Macedonian or southern portion was freed only in 1912, and the transportation system for the kingdom had not been perfected at the time
of the beginning of the World War.

The industrial development was very limited. There

[1] By W. G. Atwood. Current History. 13: 278-86. February, 1921.

were a few sugar, silk and cotton mills, some minor manufacturing, and a very limited mining development. While the country is mountainous, there are a number of large valleys of fertile land, and before the war there was a considerable export of foodstuffs, principally wheat, hogs and hides. Practically all the factories were destroyed by the retreating enemy, and most of the mines were destroyed or badly damaged.

Almost the entire area of the kingdom north of Skoplye (Uskub) is underlaid with minerals, but there has been very little mining for many centuries. The Romans knew and operated a number of the mines, principally those of copper, gold and silver, and the locations of many of their workings can still be found. In addition to these metals, there are large coal deposits of all grades, from a poor lignite of 3,000 calories to coals containing over 8,000 calories. There is also a great quantity of lead, antimony, chromium and iron, together with some cinnabar. One copper mine containing considerable gold and silver values, in addition to the copper, had a record up to the beginning of the war of practically continuous production for over eighty years, but this and one other copper mine of more recent date are practically the only developed mines in the entire old Kingdom of Serbia.

The only standard-gauge railroad in operation before the war extended from the Danube at Belgrade and Smederevo (Semendria) to Nish, from which place one line crossed the Bulgarian border and led to Sofia and Constantinople and the other followed the valleys of the Morava and Vardar to Skoplye and Salonika. An unimportant branch ran from Skoplye to Mitrovitsa. The construction of a new line was under way in 1914 from Prahovo, on the Danube, in a southwesterly direction toward Nish. This was the Serbian section of the so-called "All-Slav" railroad, which was a stragetic Slav line projected from Odessa, in Russia, to one of the Albanian ports of the Adriatic, thus forming a check to the Pan-German Berlin-to-Bagdad road. Only a comparatively small section of this line was completed prior to 1914. A considerable narrow-gauge system (2 feet 6 inches) existed in the northern part of the kingdom, partially acting as a feeder to the standard-gauge line and partially constructed for the development of the mining industry—principally coal. At the time of the German evacuation the entire railroad system suffered almost complete destruction. The shops were entirely stripped of tools, and many of the buildings destroyed. Practically all bridges of over one-meter span were blown up, together with most of the switches; only about a dozen locomotives, all in bad condition, were left, and cars were destroyed or rendered useless.

The barren mountains of the Kingdom of Montenegro, whose name fairly well describes the character of the country, have never produced enough food for the inhabitants, although the large flocks of sheep and goats herded among the rocks have assisted in a measure to clothe as well as feed them.

The province of Bosnia-Herzegovina, seized by Austria in 1875, contains quantities of coal, enormous deposits of iron, and many of the more valuable minerals which exist in Serbia. Several of the coal mines had been opened, and others were opened during the war. There was some development of the iron industry not far from Sarayevo, but at Lyubiya the largest deposit of iron in the new kingdom and probably one of the most important in Europe had not been touched. This deposit consists of a range of mountains almost entirely of high-grade ore. Development was commenced by the Austrians at the northern extremity of the range toward the end of 1915, and before the armistice about nine hundred thousand tons had been shipped, most of the ore being used in the famous artillery plant of Skoda at Pilsen. This mine, physically, is similar to the mines of Minnesota, and is operated by steam shovels in the same manner. Local tradition avers that the ore from which the Damascus steel was made came from this mine, and there are old slag dumps and other evidences of still more ancient workings to be seen.

The principal reason for the lack of industrial development in a territory so rich as these provinces was the lack of transportation. The two provinces were served with a system of narrow-gauge railroads which were not adequate for the needs of the country and did not permit any great industrial development. The only standard-gauge line was a military road which passed near the iron deposits of Lyubiya and reached the coal mines near Banya Luka.

Bosnia-Herzegovina is a country of high mountains, and, except in the northern part, has a comparatively small amount of agricultural land. It is a country of wonderful scenery, easily comparable to Switzerland, and, if advertised and exploited as Switzerland has been, would become a favorite playground for tourists. Many medicinal and hot springs exist of as great value as the better-known watering places of Europe. In Sarayevo, Mostar and other cities there is an exceedingly beautiful and picturesque blending of the Orient and Occident. The brilliantly dressed peasants are among the most picturesque in Europe, and their handiwork in both textiles and metal is of a very attractive character. There is also a great amount of timber land, and while there is quite a little lumber produced, the industry is far from being developed to the extent which is easily possible.

Slovenia, for many centuries under Austrian rule, is a mountainous territory, with beautiful scenery, but little agricultural land, so that it does not produce enough food to support the population. It contains a number of mountain resorts, and, being on the edge of Tyrol, is perhaps better known to Americans than any other part of the kingdom. There are several important coal mines and a considerable amount of minor manufacturing. The main railway line between Trieste and Vienna passes through this province, and when both these cities were under the same rule the transportation was adequate for the requirements of the province.

Croatia and Slavonia were formerly under the Hungarian crown and contained large areas of agricultural land, with a well-developed lumber industry, some coal mines, a prospect of future oil development and a considerable amount of small manufacturing. The transportation requirements were fairly met under the old conditions, but the railroads fitted for heavy traffic crossed the provinces from north to south, principally in the western end of Croatia, connecting Budapest with the Adriatic at Trieste and Reka. The east and west lines were of minor importance and not constructed for heavy traffic.

In the Voyvodina is some of the best agricultural land in Europe, producing a large surplus of foodstuffs —wheat, corn, cattle and hogs—for export. Its railroads, of which there are several, were constructed with a view to the shipment of all this surplus to or toward Budapest, either by rail or by water.

In addition to its existing railroads, the kingdom has a large mileage of navigable waterways in that portion of the Danube within its boundaries, together with two tributaries, the Sava and Drava. The Sava River is much better located to serve the transportation needs of the kingdom than any of the existing main line railways. The railway in the valley of this river must become one of the main traffic lines for export and import, but it was built as a second-class line and requires complete reconstruction before it will become adequate for the present traffic requirements, to say nothing of the needs of the future.

It is a recognized fact that a political unit of the size of the new kingdom—some fourteen million people—requires adequate outlets to the outside world in order to maintain itself, and that if these outlets are not available a condition will arise which is almost certain to cause war. The only port accessible during the Fiume controversy was Salonika. This port is in Greece, about fifty miles south of the southern border of the former Kingdom of Serbia. Under old treaties it was made a free port for Serbia, but many difficulties are put in the way of its free use, and the capacity of the port itself is insufficient for the new kingdom. The railroad from Belgrade to Salonika was never a high-capacity line, and the fact that its almost total destruction during the war has not been entirely repaired still further reduces its capacity. A large expenditure is required to put this route in reasonably good condition, and even then it will be useful only for the export of products of mines and agriculture of Serbia itself, together with the import of a part of her requirements.

The Danube offers a transportation route for the export of the products of Slavonia, the Voyvodina and northern Serbia, but on account of the difficulties of transportation upstream through the "Iron Gates" it is not so valuable for import business. The mouth of the river is in Rumanian territory, but under the Treaty of Versailles the river is internationalized. As in the case of many other provisions of the treaty, it is very difficult to say just what this means or what effect it will have on the traffic of the river. The products most readily exported by this route are foodstuffs, of which the Black Sea littoral has a large surplus, so that, on the whole, the importance of the Danube as an export route is not much greater than its value for imports.

The principal markets of the kingdom must be to the west. Her food is needed in Austria, Italy, France and England, and her metals and coal will find a market in these same countries. The location of the future markets necessitates the development of the western ports of the kingdom, all of which are located on the Adriatic, as well as the development of transportation lines connecting the producing sections of the kingdom with these ports.

The important ports of the Adriatic for the kingdom are those of Reka (Fiume), Split (Spalato), Dubrovnik (Ragusa), and Kotor. There are other minor ports which may some time be developed, but the need of them, with the four above mentioned, is not pressing enough to require the immediate expenditure of the large sum necessary for their development. In this class are such ports as Zadar (Zara), Shibenik (Sebenico), etc., which would be locally important were it not for the Italian occupation, but are not of great value to the country as a whole. The Adriatic also has a number of small ports of great importance to their immediate hinterland for the importation of food and other supplies to a barren country. The coastal region is not fertile, and produces little export tonnage except olives, oil and fruits. The ports in this latter class are Bakar (Buccari), Novi, Seń, etc. During the recent controversy Bakar was much in print as a port which could be substituted for Reka. Statements to this effect are intentionally misleading or are made without knowledge of the conditions. The bay is perfectly protected from the wind, has a large area and considerable depth. Mountains rise directly from the water's edge to a height of one thousand feet or more, with 45-degree slopes, and there is, consequently, no room for the construction of railroad terminal facilities or even for the housing of the population; nor is there a practicable route for a railway from the existing line to the bay. As this was the only place on the Adriatic near a standard-guage railroad still in the control of the government, it was proposed to construct an aerial tramway from the nearest point on the railway to the bay, in order to get the necessary food supplies for the coastal population to the sea. An idea of the physical conditions can be formed from the fact that this tramway will be about two miles long, while the present highway, which is as short as it can be and still keep an 8 per cent grade, is about eight miles long.

As a harbor, and because of its comparatively easy access by rail, the most desirable port is that of Split (Spalato), with the adjoining bay of Kastelski. This bay formed the harbor for the ancient Roman city of Salona, many of whose walls are still standing. There is on the shore of the bay sufficient level land to permit the construction of proper railroad facilities at reasonable cost. There is already developed considerable hydro-electric power in this vicinity, much of which is used for the manufacture of Portland cement and carbide. The harbor of Split itself is good on a small scale, but there is not sufficient space for development here of wharves or railroad terminals. The city has about fifteen thousand population, approximately one-fourth of whom live in the Palace of Diocletian, constructed in the third century. A standard-gauge railroad connects Split and Shibenik with Knin on the western slope of the Dalmatian Alps, and it is proposed to extend this railroad to a connection with other lines in the interior. This work was commenced before the war by the Hungarian government, but neither of the projected lines was completed. One passes within a short distance of the great iron mine of Lyubiya, and its early completion is very desirable for the successful operation of this property. There is at present a narrow-gauge line connecting Knin with Lyubiya, but it was constructed mainly for the development of the lumber industry, and is not suitable for heavy traffic.

When one of these projected railroads can be connected with the existing line at Knin, Split will become the principal port of the kingdom. A new railroad from the vicinity of Belgrade, across Bosnia, is being planned and will probably terminate either at Split or in the Bay of Kotor. This route, when constructed, will form the principal traffic route for the kingdom, but since the country through which it passes is very mountainous, construction will be slow and expensive, and until it can be completed it will be necessary to depend on the reconstructed line in the Sava River valley with the connection to be constructed to Split.

Kotor is one of the great harbors of the world. It has a shore line of approximately sixty miles and has been an important harbor since the days of the ancient Phoenicians. There is sufficient level land suitable for terminal construction, and it is thought that a practical railroad route can be secured within reasonable financial limits. The bay is almost entirely surrounded by mountains reaching elevations of six thousand feet, and in many places the shores are so precipitous that the highway which follows the shore line is built out over the water on timber. This is especially true of the inner sections of the bay. If it is found that the proposed main line railroad can be constructed to the harbor as readily as to Split these two points will become equally important.

Dubrovnik (Ragusa) is an ancient walled city which was for centuries the commercial and shipping rival of Venice. Practically unchanged for the last four hundred years, this city is one of the most picturesque and attractive spots in Europe. The old port, formed by a recess in the walls, is too small and too shallow for modern commerce, but the village of Gruzh, about two miles distant, has an excellent natural harbor, though it is not equipped with cargo-handling devices or adequate warehouses. It is connected to the interior via Sarayevo by a narrow-gauge railroad with 6 per cent maximum grades and eleven miles of rack and pinion. Manifestly, this railroad is not practicable as a traffic route of importance, and the port of Gruzh is not susceptible of any great amount of future development. The railroad, however, does offer a most attractive tourist route, as the country through which it passes is very rugged and beautiful, and the population contains many interesting types of beautiful and picturesque peasants.

The recovery and reconstruction of the Yugoslav state as an economic entity of strength will require much time and a large amount of capital, but unless another war be forced on it the recovery is certain. Large quantities of food supplies can be exported at present, and much greater amounts when the capacity of the transportation system will permit. The development of the mineral wealth is largely dependent on capital and transportation, although a sufficient coal production to permit of some export can be reached without large capital investment. The population as a whole is industrious, and, while the men do not work rapidly, the rate of pay is low and the production costs are reasonable.

The mineral resources of the country are of great value, but cannot be developed without the entrance of a large amount of foreign capital. The country itself has very little liquid capital, and the government finances are not in good condition. The treaties require that the new states assume a proper proportion of the pre-war debt of the old Austrian Empire and that they also assume specific debts which are a lien on railways and other utilities taken over from the former empire. The amounts to be assumed are to be established by commissions. The taxation is heavy, and the policy of the government is to develop the country so far as possible by local capital and government aid. There is, however, a great opportunity for investment of foreign capital, not only in the development of minerals, but also of manufacturing.

There is a large amount of water power available, very little of which has been developed, and there are numberless commercial enterprises, such as the establishment of tourist hotels and routes for the exploitation of the beautiful scenery and medicinal springs found in many parts of the country. The roads in the entire kingdom are excellent for automobile traffic.

The problems of Yugoslavia are similar to those of Rumania and Poland, which, with their present frontiers, have been formed in a similar way. It is probable that Yugoslavia has more undeveloped mineral resources than either of the other two, and it offers more attractive conditions to tourists. The feeling of the people and the government toward the United States is of the most friendly character. In fact, it is frequently stated that the United States is the only friend of the new kingdom, and, therefore, the opportunities offered for American investment are on more favorable terms than those of other nations. There is no part of Europe which will better repay both the tourist and the capitalist for their study and interest than the new kingdom of the Serbs, Croats and Slovenes.

THE NEW ADRIATIC STATE [1]

The "greater Serbia" plot, and the growing power and national consciousness of the southern Slavs, had become an ever-increasing danger which at length impelled Austria to the repression that provoked the war. Dr. Wekerle asserted—though his authority had been disputed—that the "plot" had made necessary the disturbing and precipitate action of Austria in her annexation of Bosnia and Herzegovina. Be that as it may, the evil was done, and great efforts were made to crush any demonstrations of sympathy with Serbia. Croatia, though, under the treaty of 1868 with Hungary, she had secured independence as a separate nation within the lands of St. Stephen, was sternly governed; taxes were raised; strict censorship was established; and the coun-

[1] By J. Leyland. Nineteenth Century. 88: 787-96. November, 1920.

try was treated almost as if under martial law. Out of
this harsh rule surged the rebellious spirit, the new impulse, which made possible the unified nation of the
Kingdom of the Serbs, Croats, and Slovenes. To them
—and to the Czechoslovaks also—has come the ripest
fruit of "self-determination." Unlike the Arabs, they
are ruled by no unwelcome self-donated mandate; unlike
the Koreans, they are crushed by no iron heel of
tyranny. Yet a malign fairy was there to cast an evil
spell about the cradle of the new nation, which wise
statesmanship has forestalled in its working, and which,
with good judgment and moderate counsels, we may
hope will never be permitted to work its disastrous end.

The Yugoslavs are virile people, awakened to a new
destiny, their country rich in resources of timber, coal,
lignite, iron and copper ore, all to be developed; of
wheat, barley, oats, maize, and rye; of leather, dyes,
tobacco and silk cocoons. Their railways are few, and
their roads indifferent, but they have old industries
which are developing and will rapidly expand. They
demand many things that Europe and America can give
them—railway material, agricultural machinery, machinery for many trades, machine tools, manufactured
goods of every kind, fabrics, clothing, boots, and all the
requirements of a prospering people. Their commercial
agents are active in England and in the countries of
the continent, in Scandinavia, and in the United States.
After long pleading and earnest argument, extending
over many months, they are obtaining, through the
Maritime Service of the Reparations Commission, the
means for extending further their old advantage of the
carrying trade at sea.

It must be realized that these Yugoslavs—those of
them who live on the long coastline and in the islands
of the Dalmatian Archipelago and at Kotor and
Ragusa—are pre-eminently a maritime race. For centuries they have been great Adriatic seamen. The circumstances of their geography, and in a chief degree

the wonderful configuration of their coastline, with its
sheltered waters and admirable anchorages, made them
seafarers. They possess geographical advantages which
are in strange contrast to the long bare coastline of Italy
in the Adriatic. The proud Venetians knew them as
pirates and marauders long ago. They slew the Doge
Pietro Candiano the First in an expedition he led against
them. Pietro Orseolo the Second subjected them, and,
being made Duke of Dalmatia, the ceremony of blessing
the sea was instituted in commemoration of his prowess.
"O Lord," intoned the bishop as they moved out to the
Lido, "grant this sea unto us!" and thereafter Venice
became wedded to the sea. She was from first to last
the great sea power of the Adriatic and the Levant; but
it may be questioned whether her domination gave to
the Dalmatians any greater advantage than that of
fostering and developing their prime qualities as seamen,
which the valiant captains and hardy sailors of Dubrovnik and Kotor, with a larger degree of freedom—"Lib-
ertas" was the word on the flag they flew at their mast-
heads—showed more prominently. There has never
been a better seaman than the pirate turned trader.
When the Venetians grew opulent, and lost their civic
virtues, and their liking for personal adventure in the
risks of navigation, they entered Slavs in their fighting
and merchant marines, and often entrusted their trading
vessels to the command of Dalmatian captains. It was
a lament of Benedetto Pesaro, the Venetian Admiral
against the Turks, in the fifteenth century, that his
galleys were not fully manned with these fine fellows
and prime seamen rather than with the "Lombardi"
whom he despised. At the time when, under Article
XCIII of the Treaty of Vienna, 1815, Vienna and its
possessions, the Venetian Islands, Istria, Dalmatia, the
Boka Kotorska, and, indeed, the whole eastern side
of the Adriatic, passed to the House of Hapsburg, the
vessels plying in Adriatic waters were very largely
Slav.

The dominant position which Austria-Hungary thereafter assumed as a maritime power, the menace of her small but highly efficient navy, bearing the prestige of the victory of Lissa—in which Tegetthoff, in the *Ferdinand Max*, defeated Persano and sank his Flagship, the *Ré d'Italia*, July 1866—and the loud claim for the "Vorherrschaft in der Adria," the very waters which Italians called *il mare nostro*, created the Adriatic question. The Congress of Berlin, 1878, left bitter memories in Italy. The Irredentists claimed the incorporation in the Italian Kingdom of Trieste, Istria, and Dalmatia. The position of Italy in the Triple Alliance became almost intolerable, and she was deeply wounded by the action of her German Ally in supporting the forward policy of the Dual Monarchy. *Delenda est Austria* Mazzini had cried, and it needed only the annexation of Bosnia and Herzegovina in 1908, followed by Count Montecuccoli's great plan of expanding the Austro-Hungarian navy, to bring into active existence the fiery Italian nationalist movement, which, through a clamorous press, led by the *Idea Nazionale*, lost no opportunity of fomenting hostility to the rule of Francis Joseph.

When the war was at an end Austria had been destroyed, as the Italian nationalists desired, or, at least, had broken up into the elements of which the Empire was composed. But there were many in Italy who feared a recrudescence of the old danger. A new state would arise on the other side of the Adriatic, a country nearly as large as Italy, though more sparsely populated, possessing all the maritime advantages of its predecessor. What might that forebode? The secret Treaty of London was an attempt to exorcise the peril. Published to the world by the Bolsheviks, it was a revelation of the fears and ambitions of Italian statesmen and of the complaisance of their British colleagues. Italy had rendered signal service during the war by bearing the weight of the Austrian blow, and by her strong support of the Allies, and she complained that she was promised but a small reward for all her great sacrifices. The Allies had covenanted with her for a price, which had to be paid, but they were invested with no right to make it good by giving her what was not theirs to bestow. There was grave danger at the time of creating a "Yugoslavia Irredenta"—the very counterpart of the "Italia Irredenta" which the war had redeemed.

The peril which the Italians foresaw lay deep at the root of the theatrical exploit of D'Annunzio at Fiume, and of the attitude of many Italian naval officers, led by Admiral Millo. There was real danger in these strange unofficial adventures, and in the activity of the legionaries of the poet-patriot in the islands which the Wilson line left to the Yugoslavs. The Italian occupation of Dalmatia caused extreme bitterness among the population there. Can the new nation endure for ever the presence of the Italians at Fiume and in the islands of the Quarnero and Quarnerolo, the inclosed waters between the Croatian coast and eastern Istria, islands, perhaps, yet to be fortified? No answer will be attempted to this question. Only good-will, international amity, and moderate policy can prevent the Adriatic problem from raising its threatening head again. D'Annunzio and his like are firebrands, who may yet enkindle the flame. Exceeding bitterness followed his first astounding offense, and the support which Admiral Millo gave to him. The South Slav press become almost hysterical. Thus wrote the *Epoca* of Belgrade in November 1919:

We do not forget benefits, neither do we remember evil. If you wish it, Italians, we will not forget that you let us die at San Giovanni di Medua, at Durazzo and Avlona in 1915-1916; we will not forget that you took away from us Istria and Gorizia: that you tried to instil Bolshevism in our country; that you ill-treated, tortured, and deported our Adriatic population; that you took the Yugoslav fleet, made our Fiume suffer, enslaved our Zara; closed our Adriatic ports, and were contemptuous of our ills. We will not forget, and we will recall them to your mind one day, for evidently you do not want us to forget.

Articulate thought in Italy, though not always expressed with the crudeness of this outburst, was inspired generally by the same or like ambitions. There was, it is true, a cleavage in public opinion, and a moderate party existed. But Signor Bissolati, who dared to express his views through an English paper, and afterward declared them in a great oration delivered before the Italian Society for a League of All Free Nations in the Scala at Milan on January 11, 1919, was overthrown. He pleaded that Italy should be true to the spirit in which she had waged the war, and with regard to the new trans-Adriatic state, recognized existing facts:

Yugoslavia exists [he said], and no one can undo this. But to the credit of Italy be it said, the attainment of unity and independence for the Serbs, Croats, and Slovenes was and must be alike the reason and the certain issue of our war. The factors that determined the European War were the attractive force exercized by Serbia upon the Slav elements in Austria-Hungary, and the design of that empire, under German and Magyar influence, to absorb Serbia and open up the main routes to the East. Italy felt that if Serbia had been swallowed up by that monstrous empire—itself the vassal of the German Empire—her own economic expansion and political independence would have received a mortal blow. And so she was on Serbia's side, first in neutrality, then in intervention. And now, with the victory of Italy and the Entente, the duel between Austria-Hungary and Serbia ends as it was logically bound to end; the Yugoslavs of Serbia are uniting with their brothers of the empire. Those who only see, in the formation of the Yugoslav State, a sympathetic or antipathetic episode of the war, or a subsidiary effect of it, have failed to detect its inner meaning.

Transport and movement are to a nation what the circulation of the blood is to an individual. National life is impossible without them. High hopes have been formed of the kingdom of the Serbs, Croats, and Slovenes, but it must have freedom of movement by sea and land. It suffers from some internal maladies which it is to be hoped will not open the way to disruptive intrigue, and it is threatened with dangers from without. Much is due to it from the great powers which brought it into being. Yugoslavia became a contracting party to the Treaty of Versailles as an Allied state, and the League of Nations must be its safeguard. Its great internal riches will be developed with the growth of imports and exports and the extension of means of communication. More and more it will look to the sea. Its navigation must be unrestricted and unthreatened. It seeks no conflict with Italy. The ambition of its officers to possess themselves of the Austro-Hungarian fleet, which in a large degree they had made the efficient organization it was, must not be regarded as indicating a national determination toward sea-power. All experience does indeed show that a great mercantile marine, which Yugoslavia may yet possess, will demand protection, but it will be long before the country aspires to create such forces as the Peace Conference has dispersed. The friendship of Italy and not her enmity— not the explosive tactics of D'Annunzio and his like— are necessary for the peace and prosperity of Yugoslavia. The fears of Italy are explained by the map of the Adriatic shores. She claimed Dalmatia and the islands despite nationality, mainly on strategic grounds, but if she should take anything that rightly belonged to Yugoslavia, there could be no certain hope of continued peace between the Latins and the Slavs.

ITALIAN AND YUGOSLAV PSYCHOLOGY [1]

The nations demanding control of the lands of the Adriatic are on the one hand the heirs of the traditions of Mazzini and of Garibaldi, on the other, a struggling people of peasant origin who have tasted of the bitterness of oppression. Both are ardent advocates of liberty, and firm believers in the righteousness of their claims. Both are hurt in their deepest feelings, and feelings

[1] By M. Montgomery-Campbell. Nineteenth Century. 86: 889-98. November, 1919.

play a serious part in the lives of the Latin and Slav races. The eternal feminine, the Psyche, is always with them. Poetry and passion are living realities to them, and in them one finds the fervor of the Catholic or the mysticism of the orthodox. The abstract appeals to them as it does not to more phlegmatic natures, and a treasured quotation, the recollection of a popular hero, and a combination of colors, set their emotions vibrating passionately. Thus far these two antagonistic races are akin, and this very kinship accentuates their differences. It is not fire and water, it is two fires that meet, and here the similarity in their psychology ceases. Beyond this, without pressing the comparison too closely, the difference between them may be likened to that existing between the persistent, stolid Ulsterman and the captivating, mercurial southern Irishman. Or one may be said to represent the rugged Karst of the hinterland, and the other the smiling Littoral. The Yugoslav is not gifted with the ingratiating manners, the sunny charm, and the quick wits of the Italian, he is more deliberate, more uncouth, though not unkindly, and his wrath is the awful wrath of the slower nature. But he is striving and fond of learning, although in the country districts geographical conditions have rendered him often unlettered. From all over the world Yugoslavs have sent money to support their home schools. Only perhaps amongst the Scottish peasantry could equal eagerness to acquire knowledge in the face of hindrances be found, and the Yugoslavs have produced eminent writers, poets, and scientists under difficulties with which no Scot has had to contend. Students of the native University at Agram have been forced by the authorities to complete their studies at some Austrian university, this being part of the plan to suppress the national language and to establish *Deutschtum*. To receive subsidies for primary schools instruction had to be given in the German language, that the children might grow up to look at it as their mother tongue. It was for that reason that the Yugoslavs made so great an effort to have their own schools, holding it, as they did, to be of paramount importance. The Italians also complain of the treatment they received regarding schools, although the Yugoslavs consider that they were favored.

The literary language of Serbs and Croats is identical, the language of the people varies according to local dialects. In Dalmatia, as elsewhere, the Serbs belong almost entirely to the orthodox church, whilst the Croats are Catholics. Istria is largely Catholic, and by special Papal permission, in many places, including the islands, Mass is said in the old Slav tongue, as it is always in the orthodox churches. The preservation of their ancient language is very precious to the Yugoslavs, and any interference with it would prove a source of trouble. Undoubtedly they are a devout people, but the Italians charge them with having used religious processions as an occasion for political demonstrations, and there have been unfortunate incidents when mutual abuse, and even violence, have marred the solemnity of festivals. Images of Saints have been borne through the streets adorned with national colors, and, if all tales be true, hymns were sometimes made the medium of insulting the Italians. One can only accept that, as opportunity makes the thief, so also it makes the disturber of the peace, and that it would be reasoning from the particular to the general to quote such occurrences as a general indication of the character of the Yugoslav, who is tenacious, knowing what he wants and meaning to get it, but is not naturally domineering or agressive. His character may not unfitly be summed up in the words of Coleridge:

> God gave him reverence for laws,
> Yet stirring blood in freedom's cause,
> A spirit to his rocks akin,
> The eye of the hawk and the fire therein.

The Yugoslav is a man of the mountains with the hardiness of the mountaineer and the deep love of home of the highlander. He is patriarchal in his ideas, and *clannish*. The *Zadruga* which continues in many Slav centers puts every member of the family under one recognized head, under whom he works and to whose authority he submits. Family ties and hospitality take a large place in his life. He will gladly set before you what he has, and you will be introduced to a large circle of his cousins, who will ask you to dinner and take it ill if you refuse. The fare may be of the simplest but the welcome will be lavish.

On the Italian character it is unnecessary to dwell in detail. Italy is known to most of us, and many of us share the Brownings' love for her, and in these days, which are so pregnant with anxiety for Italy, we echo Mrs. Browning's query:

> Can she live and be strong,
> Or is it another dream
> Like the rest we have dreamed so long?

Only, it is impossible not to recognize that, even if the wishes of the irredentists are not wholly fulfilled, the Italians will still have their own country, the heritage of a great historic past, to fall back upon, whilst the Yugoslavs have no choice but emigration if things become impossible for them in the land where Slavs have suffered and struggled for a thousand years, and where they have dreamed dreams of a great Serb kingdom which should realize their yearnings for solidarity.

Had it not been for Austrian machinations, there seems little reason why the two nationalities should not have dwelt side by side as neighbors, their diversities of character complementing each other instead of engendering strife, and the monarchy's own wealth increased by their industries. Austria herself frustrated this. Shortsightedly she made the lands that might have enriched her the mere dumping-ground of her own wares; being timorous, she played a double game, and, finally, she subserviently obeyed her Potsdam masters, who only looked on her as a "milch cow to graze on Balkan lands, and when she had grazed enough to be killed for the benefit of Germany." Of Austria, it could be truly said, "If thou hadst known, even thou, at least in this thy day, the things which belong unto thy peace." But she did not. She had to deal with two independent spirited nationalities, who might have been wooed, but whose spirit could not be broken, and by her misrule she only succeeded in making both her enemies. The patriotism of the Italians and Yugoslavs was fanned into flame, a jealous hatred was aroused between them, and the imperial and royal government played the part of Mr. Punch and made the puppets fly at each other's throats. The similarity of their complaints prove how cleverly they were tricked. Each in turn looked on the other as the Benjamin of Austria, and both had the same tale to tell of harsh treatment, and of unfairness regarding education and municipal and imperial representation, whilst each was made thoroughly mistrustful of the other. And all the while Austria, wire-pulled from Berlin, laughed in her sleeve and schemed to her own undoing, whilst furthering pan-Germanism.

To keep the inhabitants of the Littoral in subjecton, their industries were discouraged, and despite of heavy taxation little or no help was given for fighting disease amongst the olives and vines, for irrigation, drainage of land, or increasing production by improving on antiquated methods. The very considerable water power of the falls of the rivers of the Adriatic provinces was also but little developed. Oil produced on the littoral, even under primitive conditions, has been preferred to that of Lucca, and many a cask of Dalmatian wine was shipped to France in the past, and sold as "best Bordeaux."

Another Austrian folly was the obstruction caused to salt extraction, which was lucrative and provided much employment. The land laws were not equitable, and the peasants of Istria and Friuli had often to content themselves with 2 per cent of the profits of co-operative farming, a system which when well worked, as in France, has brought prosperity to many an agriculturist. On the Adriatic, the ground landlord was allowed to pocket the larger share of gain. In Dalmatia the whole expense of the police and *gendarmerie* was borne locally.

The laying down of railways, which would have increased the commerce and incomes of the dwellers on the coast by connecting them with their hinterland, was also systematically neglected. It says much for the inhabitants of the Littoral, that trade and agriculture were not wholly destroyed in many places, and it gives promise of almost moribund industries being revived and expanded under happier conditions. This would not be only of local advantage, but would supply exports much needed by other nations. The artistic talents of the Dalmatians and Istrians are shown in their productions in embroideries, weaving and goldsmithing. The climate of the seaboard, despite the inroads of the boisterous Bora, lends itself to extensive horticulture, and the abundance of fish in the waters of the Quarnero allows for the curing of anchovies, sardines, and tunny fish, on a large scale. Besides this, the distilling of perfumery and liqueurs, and marble quarries suggest industry.

In the few years of the beginning of the last century during which Napoleon ruled the Illyrian provinces, he introduced juster laws—which the Austrians revoked —caused good roads to be constructed, and permitted newspapers to be printed in the language of the people. There was no liberty of the press under Austrian rule, and if a man dared to tell the truth in public he had to leave the country or hide in the *macchie,* the dense scrub of the coastal background. During the war, whilst politicians wrangled, the people were actually starving. It

is little wonder that up to the time of the outbreak of
hostilities the working class emigrated in large numbers.
In some of the villages there are only boys and decrepit
old men, the young manhood had gone to seek its fortune overseas. Yet under juster conditions there might
have been a living for all at home.

THE SERBIAN PEOPLE IN WAR TIME [1]

My own first impressions of Serbia were formed
when, as a prelude to settling down there for five
months, I accompanied Sir Thomas Lipton through the
country on a fourteen days' hustle. Not every man can
claim that he has been personally conducted on a lightning Cook's tour to see war at first-hand.

We no sooner reached Belgrade than what practically amounted to free tickets were given us for what
the citizens jokingly termed their "bombardment performances." Shells no sooner bust forth from the
picturesque little town of Zemun across the river, than
we could, if we chose to brave the risk, mount to the
top of the fortress in order to view the firing with
more realistic effect. And in the *entr'actes* between
these performances—which, curiously enough, had a
knack of repeating themselves at fixed hours on
appointed days of the week like theatrical matinées!—
we had official permission to wander by the river's edge,
where, looking through powerful binoculars, we could
see thrifty Austrian housewives bartering in the market-
place while the rest of the straggling populace sauntered
up and down Zemun's main street. How near war then
seemed to us! And, if the truth must be known, how
ludicrous, too, was the main effect produced! In building their capital on a site which the enemy could shell
so comfortably from his own door-step, the Serbians
had obviously made a big initial mistake. The result

[1] By S. Naylor. Scribner's Magazine. 59: 368-80. March, 1916.

was much as though the city of Liverpool were waging deadly conflict with her friendly neighbor across the Mersey, Birkenhead, or as though Long Island were at war with New York.

In the brief but crowded space of those first days we spent in Belgrade; several elaborate "war excursions" were planned in our honor. We began by inspecting the various batteries and intrenchments erected round the city. On mounting to the more prominent gun positions, some of us felt a trifle staggered to be told, with so little concern that we might have been examining marble statuary in the Louvre or the British Museum, how narrowly these guns had been missed by Austrian shells just half an hour before. "But our casualty list was not at all heavy," our guide, a Serbian officer added consolingly. "Only two sparrows killed and one lizard wounded.

It was again our coveted distinction to be let into the then secret movements of a set of plucky young English naval men who, disguised in the uniform of Serbian officers, had come to Belgrade to manage a dashing little picket boat known as *The Terror of the Danube*. With Lieutenant-Commander Kerr—he has since been awarded a D.S.O.—at their head, these jolly sailors were having the time of their lives, for on dark nights it was the *Terror's* habit to dart into mid-river and play pranks with the fleet of Austrian monitors assembled majestically on guard near Zemun. This fleet was two hundred times the strength of the little picket boat. Any one of the monitors would have made very short work of her, if given half a chance. But dignity opposed to impudence does not always win the day. The *Terror* had a way of springing up unawares just when she was least expected. And that sometimes she could torpedo with the best of them was shown in the unmistakable evidences of wrecked monitors floating about the Danube for all Belgrade to see.

Our passports, as we traveled, proved to be equally
elastic all along the line. No matter where we went—
to the military headquarters at Kraguyevats, to the mis-
erably overcrowded, disgustingly dirty, and dishevelled
city of Nish, where the seat of the government had been
transferred from the capital, to the more comfortable,
sleepy-eyed Skoplye, formerly Uskub, which, Serbian-
ized though it had been, obstinately retained the eerie
eastern charm of its old-time Turkish setting, or to the
picturesque group of villages clustering round the Bulgarian frontier—always the curtain was lifted on persons, places and things that would have been carefully
screened from us had we been unknown wayfarers,
journeying alone. And yet there was a reverse side to
all these advantages.

Serbia, it is true, had turned the handle of her war
kaleidoscope very generously for our benefit. We knew
how irretrievably bombardment and invasion had spoiled
the fair face of Shabats, hitherto one of the wealthiest
of her townships—how all the churches and public
buildings in this district had been completely destroyed
while the sufferings of the inhabitants hardly yielded
in frightfulness before those of Belgium. We knew,
again, how great was the havoc wrought to Belgrade,
that once beautiful city which had been every Serbian's
pride—a sort of miniature Paris, the only one of his
cities which could boast any claim to enlightenment and
progress; incidentally, too, the only city rich enough
to have installed an adequate system of sanitation. We
knew that the mass of ruins at Belgrade now included
the royal palace, the museum, and, above all, the university, with which had perished a century of research
work, to say nothing of a world of thought. And we
knew that the pinch of poverty was now felt there so
acutely that thousands of citizens were living on three-
pence a day.

Happily, it is of the finer rather than the sordid side

of Serbia we all now think. Today the whole world has
nothing but wonder and praise for the splendid fight the
little nation put up when she was attacked by three
fronts in that cataclysm of 1915. The Serbs then made
a stand which, as an epic of bravery, is more Homeric
than Homer. Wonderful is a big word, but it is not
too big to fit them. And even before this great onslaught
they had proved themselves wonderful many times over.
They had been wonderful, first of all, in the stoicism—
one had almost said, gayety!—with which they had
borne the heat and burden of war. They were wonderful, again, when in that first moment of the European
conflict they successfully drove five hundred thousand
Austrian invaders from their territories and took sixty-
two thousand of them prisoners into the bargain. And,
perhaps, they were most wonderful of all when, before
Bulgaria declared her hand in October, and Germany
and Austria still refrained from striking a decisive blow,
they "stood like greyhounds in the slips waiting for"—
well, they knew not what.

Toward the end of these ten months of masterly in-
activity there was to me something impressive and grand
in the picture of these stout-hearted men of Serbia—
massed round the little nation's borders—waiting, always
waiting. Several hours daily for nearly a year many a
Serbian private soldier had known what it was to stand
there rigidly on guard, glued like an automaton to his
post, his face stolidly inscrutable, but his heart yearn-
ingly aflame to be once more up and doing. "I'm dead
sick of having to wait," a private told me when I talked
with him while off duty, through an interpreter who,
having lived in America, was able to translate very
racily. "If only we could have another whack at 'em!
I'm just longing for the war to end. You see, I haven't
seen my wife and children for three years. My home
is so far away and we have been so everlastingly fighting or expecting to fight that I have never had a chance
to go back."

And if such was the lot of some of Serbia's first-line soldiers still in their prime, what of those veterans of the third and fourth lines to be found guarding the remoter places less liable to attack? These grizzled warriors were generally cheerful. Yet for them, also, life held more than its fair share of irony. "Of course, I'm only scrap-iron—too old for the firing line," one of them confessed to me. "I'm fifty, and I've been in the army thirty-three years. In Serbia, you know, we start serving at seventeen and finish at fifty-five." "Then in another five years you will be free?" I ventured encouragingly. "Yes, in another five years I shall be free all right," he replied; "but please don't forget, sir, *I shall also be fifty-five!*"

But not for nothing has the Serb been called "the Irishman of the Balkans." His temperament is mercurial and his moments of depression soon slip away. One of his most charming characteristics is a complete freedom from malice. Hard fighter though he is, it seems constitutionally impossible for him to bear hatred for long; and although he far from loves his enemy on the battle-field, any animosity he feels toward him vanishes like lightning as soon as he takes him prisoner. To strangers traveling through the land nothing was more amazing than the sense of comradeship which existed between the Serbs and their Austrian captives. Captives, forsooth! Some of them openly gloried in their chains.

That the lot of a private in the Serbian army, no matter how far he might be from the firing line, was often worse than that of an Austrian prisoner, first struck home to me at Belgrade when in the main street I saw a peasant soldier bargaining with a prisoner for a loaf of bread. The soldier had just reached the city, weary, worn, and more than a trifle footsore, after a long cross-country march. The one solitary loaf, which was all his daily ration comprised from the military authorities, had long since been devoured. The poor fellow was obviously hungry and in need of another. The Austrian prisoner, on the other hand, with a cigarette between his lips, looked sleek and well-fed. Yet the bargain between the two was completed in the friendliest spirit, and cash down was paid for that extra loaf.

When I asked a Serbian soldier why prisoners of war were treated so leniently by his country—being left to wander at large unmolested like one of themselves —he replied that the great majority of the captured Austrians were of their own kith and kin. They were of Slavonic origin and had no heart in this war. With them it was simply a case of Hobson's choice. They had either to fight for Austria or be shot. Evidence of their curious detachment in the struggle was given in that, since the opening of hostilities, many of these so-called "Austrians" had fought valiantly and well *on both sides!* On being taken prisoners, they had at once re-enlisted under the Serbian flag!

But while this explanation held good in the case of Slav prisoners, how came it to pass that throughout the country one constantly met German-Austrians and Magyar Hungarians who were almost equally fortunate in the treatment meted out to them? Consider the generosity shown to that small minority of prisoners who were considered too dangerous to be allowed at large. The big internment barracks in which these enemy officers were quartered at Nish were a veritable *hôtel de luxe.* The accommodation provided for the officers of the Serbian army was not nearly so lavish. Separate kitchens were run, so that the Germans, Hungarians, and Croats could each have their food cooked in the style most pleasing to their respective fastidious palates. And there were several acres of beautiful grounds in which the prisoners could rove at will. They played tennis and other outdoor games while, escorted by a Serbian guard, they often went on picnics and excursions in the surrounding countryside. Some of them, well-known Hungarian artists, were daily to be seen with Serbian soldiers in attendance, sketching the landscape in and around Nish. And as with the interned officers, so with the interned men in the ranks: they were infinitely better housed and better fed than the Serbian troops in training a stone's throw away.

Although openly hostile to the Serbian cause, prisoners were frequently found again in civilian occupations at good rates of pay and, except that they had periodically to report themselves to the authorities, they were allowed to live practically as free men. Many Londoners visiting the leading restaurant in Nish were surprised to recognize installed there as *maître d'hôtel* an Austrian who for many years had been a waiter at the Carlton Hotel. This old-time friend seemed as happy and cheerful as ever. He was just as well-groomed as in his palmy Carlton days. Looking at him, you would never have judged him to be an Austrian prisoner out on "ticket of leave." "When the war is over, I hope to meet you all in the same old spot," he told his English customers hopefully.

Common sense, of course, was at the root of Serbia's policy in placing her prisoners in occupations to which they were peculiarly fitted. At a time when the country was denuded almost entirely of her male population, the flower of her manhood being away with the army, why should not the trained services of her sixty-two thousand odd able-bodied Austrians be turned to profitable account? So, no doubt, Serbia argued, and therein lay one explanation of the humanity and kindness she showed to every prisoner who was willing and able to fill a definite place in the working life of the community. And so, too, it followed that all over the country one found Austrians, skilled at their business, who were employed on a fair financial basis as mechanics, engineers, tailors, and bakers—in fact in well-nigh every con-

ceivable trade; while, without the aid of prisoner order-
lies, it is now universally admitted that most of the war
hospitals in Serbia could never have been run.

So far as possible each prisoner was given the job
that suited him best. There was somehing Gilbertian in
the situation that nightly at Nish and Skoplye sweet
music was distilled in the open air, quite as though the
fashionable German and Austrian spas had been trans-
planted to Serbia, by those captives who happened to be
professional musicians. But not unnaturally among so
many thousands there were occasional human misfits. It
appeared to be rather a hardship, for instance—although
it may strike some minds as ironically appropriate—that
the gentleman who in peace time had been professor of
mathematics at Prague University was mainly engaged
in counting the dirty linen at a big hospital in Kraguyevats. And a Vienna merchant, who informed me his
normal income had never been known to amount to less
than the equivalent of three thousand English pounds
sterling a year, fulfilled the duties of bootblack in the
same institution.

I happened one afternoon to be in a little town when
a young German aviator literally dropped down from the
skies. In charge of what were believed to be important
papers bearing on the Dardanelles campaign, this flying
Teuton had come from Mehadia, near Orsova (on the
Hungarian side of the Danube near where Serbia, Hungary, and Rumania meet). His intention was to fly to
Bulgaria and then go on to Turkey by train. But his
proud hopes were dashed. At first, all went swim-
mingly. According to his own story he flew high over
Nish at a height of six thousand feet. Then, two hours
later, when near the Bulgarian frontier—so near that he
cocksurely imagined he had crossed the border-line!—
his engine gave out and he came down to earth with a
thud, only to find himself still in Serbia and soon in the
custody of two stalwart frontier guards, who marched
him off to this nearest wayside town.

In almost any other country but Serbia this dramatic *débâcle* of an enemy airman would have meant a bitterly hostile demonstration. To say the least, there would have been frantic hisses and boos. But the Serb, when once he has captured his prey, is good-natured. The advent of this unexpected visitor hardly aroused more than the ripple of laughter with which most country people greet the arrival of a traveling showman or clown. Among other things, his equipment included a plentiful supply of visiting cards, and these were clamored for as souvenirs by the amused townsfolk. Otherwise, there was little excitement.

The authorities had doubts as to what kind of hospitality to give to so unusual a guest; and it was eventually decided to accommodate him for a night or two in the town's best hotel—where, as luck would have it, I too was quartered. After the evening meal in the little inn restaurant this German captive seemed thoroughly to have recovered his equanimity, if he had ever lost it. Stolid in his exterior, he was voluble enough in his talk. Gradually the company gathered round his table and a merry evening was spent. For the nonce the Serbs were disposed to bury the hatchet. They treated the intruder with the utmost friendliness, as one of themselves.

Side by side with these side-lights on the innate chivalry of the Serb place the irrefutable proofs that abound of his bravery on the battle-field, and you soon realize that, despite many black pages in Serbian history, he springs from a stock of which heroes are made. Difficulties do not daunt him. Instead, they went on fighting —for the unification of all Serbian-speaking peoples, for what is known in Serbia as the Yugoslav ideal. To them the thought that Serbia should be vanquished was simply unthinkable. Patriotism, an all-consuming love of the land of their forefathers, was practically the only religion they knew and understood. Provided they held fast to their faith in the salvation of Serbia, they felt

all would be well.   Inevitably their enemies would go
to the wall.

Next to the love of his country the peasant soldier
places his love of a woman—or, perhaps, it would be
more accurate to say, all women. In the famous folk-
songs which he composes extemporaneously, and is
heard singing day and night, his theme is invariably
either the glories of war or the charms of some fair
maid. In Serbia the lad who has not been deeply in
love by the time he is sixteen is reckoned to be, indeed,
a fool. The Serbian peasant places woman on a ped-
estal—*until he marries her*. Then she who was his divinity quickly becomes his drudge.

"And this—God forgive me!—is my wife," is the
habitual formula used by a peasant if forced to introduce the woman of his choice to you. He is, however,
passionately fond of his children. In Serbia the humblest child is an *enfant gâté*. One day, while I was stay-
ing at a hospital at Vrnyatchka Banya, a wounded soldier, whose leg had been amputated, was visited by his
wife and child. The father greeted the little one rap-
turously, while his wife, her face full of the tenderest
solicitude and sympathy, stood meekly aside. At length,
turning from the child to the woman, he seized her by
the hand and said gruffly: "Well, Milka, my girl, have
you brought something nice to eat? How's the cow?"

The Serb, in his whole conception of womanhood, is
unblushingly Oriental.   It seems, then, to be a comic
stroke of fate whereby feminism has lately scored a notable triumph in his midst. The women most vital in
nursing wounded peasant soldiers back to health and
strength have been in many cases suffragettes—women
of an emancipated view-point in direct antithesis to that
of their patients. Several of the most efficient war hospitals in Serbia have been conducted by feminists as all-
women institutions, no man being employed where a
woman will do.

EARLY YUGOSLAV CIVILIZATION [1]

The geographic position of Yugoslavia is one of the best in the world, especially from the point of view of commerce, but it has been at the same time the source of all its misfortunes and disasters, because it excited, as no other country did, the covetousness of imperialistic nations. It is like a bridge for the armies between the south and the north and between the Orient and the Occident and vice versa. Innumerable inroads of Francs, Cumans, Germans, Magyars, Bulgarians, Tatars, Saracens, Venetians, Byzantines and Turks, have hindered and almost completely destroyed Slavonic civilization and for five centuries made impossible any cultural progress. The Turkish invasion especially was fatal to the Slavonic race. The Turks destroyed innumerable magnificent monuments and left nothing but bare mountains and desolation. It would be impossible to calculate the immense damage inflicted by foreign invasions and dominations. All these invaders marred our progress. In my opinion there is no question as to why the Yugoslavs did not develop their culture equally with that of France, Italy or England. But how was it possible for our nation, in such a geographical position to save itself from complete destruction and be able to shake off the yoke of the Magyars after eight centuries of tyranny and the yoke of Austria, Venice and Turkey after more than four centuries of subjection.

Every time the nation could breathe a little more freely it developed a civilization worthy of a free people. The best example of this is the Republic of Dubrovnik (Ragusa) which, in spite of its precarious position, always menaced by the Turks, Venetians, and Hungarians, developed an admirable culture. The same can be said of the other towns of Dalmatia though in a lesser degree,

[1] By A. T. Pavitchich. Yugoslav Review. 2: 2-7. March, 1924.

because they were under the domination of Venice, Byzantium or Hungary.

Dalmatia always marched at the head of Yugoslav civilization. It may sound paradoxical, but I dare to maintain, that Dalmatia has given more to Italian civilization than Italy has given to Yugoslavia. Italy has given us very few poets and writers as for instance, the poet Cavagnini (Yeronim Kavanyin) and the two brothers Appendini, both philologists and sincere admirers of the Yugoslav language, which they praised above all other languages. We can, however claim that we gave a very great impulse to the Italian Renaissance. I shall name only a few names of great artists and writers of Slavic blood who became illustrious in Italy: F. Vrana (Francesco Carcano) called Schiavone (1425-1500) the delightful sculptor and painter; L. Vrana, (Luciano Carcano) Bramante's teacher; George Culinovich (1450-1511) called Gregorio Schiavone; A. Medulich (1522-1582) called Andrea Schiavone; Julius Glovich (Clovio) the greatest miniaturist of his time, and V. Carpaccio, the famous painter of Venice. The Latin poet Cervinus, crowned with laurel on the Capitol of Rome, was a Tsriyevich or Cerva from Dubrovnik. Dalmatia further gave innumerable professors to the Italian universities. Lyubich in his *Ogledalo* asserts that the single island of Hvar (Lesina) gave more than a hundred professors to the University of Padua. It would take me a long time to enumerate all the Yugoslavs who won celebrity in Italy and who pass as Italians in the history of civilization.

Dalmatia is the cradle of Slav civilization. She developed navigation, commerce, architecture, sculpture, painting and literature almost at the same time as the most progressive states of Europe. No one can calculate what degree of progress Dalmatia would have attained had she not had the Turk under the very walls of her towns. Towns like Shibenik, Trogir, Split, Omish, Hvar, Kortchula, Dubrovnik, Kotor and Perast bear admirable witness of the native genius of Yugoslavia. The cathedral of Trogir, the work of the architect Goykovich and that of Shibenik, the work of the illustrous architect Matiyevich, are admirable monuments of the Yugoslav, worthy to rank with the finest creations of Italian architecture.

The modern Yugoslav literature began to develop in Dalmatia toward the end of the fifteenth century. The first of our poets of that time was Marko Marulich of Split. He was also a Latin poet and a philosopher whose reputation spread all over Europe. His philosophical works were translated into many languages. Hvar (Lesina) gave birth to two great poets Hektorovich and Lutchich, the town of Nin to Zoranich, Zadar to Karnarutich and Barakovich, all writers of the sixteenth century.

But the Athens of the Slav nations is Dubrovnik (Ragusa), the little republic, built on a rock on the Adriatic Sea, which aroused the admiration of Machiavelli. It was a school of diplomacy, navigation and many other forms of human endeavor. All the arts flourished in this small but very wealthy city, until the earthquake (1667) destroyed the treasures gathered during long and busy centuries. After the earthquake a terrible fire broke out and, raging for three days, completed the work of annihilation. One of the most beautiful cities of that age became a mass of ruins. But though earthquake and fire may destroy the arts it cannot harm literature and so the glory of the "Yugoslav Athens" was safe.

It would be a long task to enumerate all the pleiade of the poets of Dubrovnik, many of whom show great originality of talent, quite independent of Latin or Italian influence. To the very beginning of our national literary renaissance at the end of the fifteenth century they sought inspiration in our national poetry. This is what gives a higher value to the works of George Derzhich and Shishko Mentchetich. I shall make no mention

of the innumerable poets who initiated the classic and
Italian poets but only of such as improved the native
tongue by their original creations. In this category in
the sixteenth century we find Dinko Ranyina, Mavro
Vetranich and especially Andriya Tchubranovich who in
his *Yedyupka,* created a marvellous and thoroughly
original erotic poem. Dinko Zlatarich, although influenced by his classic models improved the language
and the literary taste. Marin Derzhich, a century before
Shakespeare and Molière, made Plautus and Terence
popular in Dubrovnik, not as a servile imitator but as a
very original and clever writer of comedies, taking his
subjects from the national life and borrowing from
Plautus only the scenic apparatus, just as Hanibal Lutchich, the author mentioned above, dramatized episodes in
our national history especially those from the Turkish
invasion and the imminent danger to which it exposed
Dalmatian towns.

The golden age of the literature in Dubrovnik was
in the seventeenth century which gave birth to the very
great poet Gundulich (1608-1665) to Palmotich, Bunich,
Vladislav Mentchetich, etc. Gundulich, called *rex Illy-
rici carminis* is thoroughly national and was certainly a
genius who marked a forward step in epic and dramatic
poetry and may be compared to Torquato Tasso, not
only because he is more classic, sober, deeper, with equal
poetic imagination but because he is more modern in
his ideas and feelings. The time of the religious epic
had passed and Gundulich felt that a new era was coming, the era of nationalism. In his chief work *Osman*
he sings the past glories of the Yugoslavs and the Poles
while in his pastoral drama *Dubravka,* a work that
need not fear comparison with the *Aminta* of Tasso
or the *Pastor Fido* of Guarini, he allegorically lauds
his beloved city and the delights of liberty which had its
sacred temple in the little republic. Gundulich seems
like a modern poet, a bard who could say of himself,

like Horace, *crescar laude recens.* To the same century belongs Mavro Orbinich the great Yugoslav historian.

The eighteenth century was the century of decadence in Dubrovnik but it gave birth to a great lyric poet Ignyat Dyordyich and to the great philosopher and mathematician Rudyer Boshkovich, a genius of the first rank whose name will be known in years to come and of whose works in English translations have recently been published. The Reformation had also its influence among the Yugoslavs. Primozh Trubar, a Slovenian, was its most strenuous propagator. The literature of this period was furiously persecuted by Austria and the Jesuits.

The other Yugoslav countries could not compete with Dubrovnik in literary production. For the most part they produced religious works. In Croatia the two martyrs to the cause of national liberty, Count Peter Zrinski and his brother-in-law the Marquis Francis Frankopan, the brother of Count Peter's beautiful wife Katarina Zrinska, cultivated literature. Count Zrinski sings the high exploits of his ancestor Nikola Zrinski, the hero of Siget. Both Zrinski and Frankopan were treacherously lured to Wiener Neustadt under a *salvum conductum* by the Austrian Emperor Leopold and there beheaded as traitors (1671). After the fall of the Austrian Empire their ashes were solemnly transferred to Zagreb, the capital of Croatia.

In the eighteenth century Dalmatia gave birth to the most popular poet of Yugoslavia, Andriya Katchich Mioshich, who was one of the first to imitate the national poetry and to propogate the sentiment of national unity among the Yugoslavs. Another popular poet from Dalmatia, Filip Grabovats, finished his days in prison in Venice, because in his poems he praised the benefits of liberty and exposed the miserable slavery of the Dalmatian people under the Venetian yoke. In Slavonia the poet Matiya Relkovich (1772-1798) followed in the footsteps of Katchich using the national

decasillabic verse in his *Satir* in which he describes all
the misery of his fatherland under the Austrian yoke.
In Bosnia the Franciscan monks cultivated religious literature and occupied themselves with the grammar of
the language. The best writer of this province is Div-
kovich (1563-1631). The Serbs concentrated their literary effort in the convents of the Frushka Gora in the
Batchka and in the Banat as no literary work was possible in the territory under the Turkish yoke. The pious
monks cultivated, as their predecessors in the Middle
Ages had done, religious literature, history and chronicles.

The most important historians of the seventeenth
century are Lutchich of Trogir in Dalmatia and Pavle
Vitezovich (1652-1715) of Croatia. In the eighteenth
century the Serbian Yovan Raich promoted the cultivation of Serbian history (1726-1801). The father of
all modern Serbian literature, Dositiye Obradovich was
born in the year 1742 at Tchakovo in the Banat. He
died in Belgrade in 1811.

The traditional literature has done incomparably
more for the civilization of the Yugoslavs than the written word and is much more beautiful and original. It
is morally and esthetically sublime. The Turks not only
devastated the national treasure of the Serbian people
but also every possibility of developing their civilization
by literary labor. They destroyed all the cities, towns
and convents even to the burning of the ashes of the
great promoter of Serbian civilization St. Sava. The
vilas, the beautiful fairies of the national folk-lore, re-
tired before the barbarous invader to the high mountains
where they taught the lonely shepherds to hope for a
better future and to prepare for the redemption of their
down-trodden nation. They gave to the blind bard
the *gusle* and taught him to sing of the great achievements of the heroes of Kosovo and thus spur the youth
of the country to emulate their exploits and to dream
always of the hour of vengeance and their liberation.

The *vilas* flying secretly on their white wings over the high mountains and the immense plains visited every cottage and sowed the seeds of those gorgeous flowers in every heart whispering in every young ear the sacred entreaty of the Emperor Lazar, who perished on the battle-field of Kosovo, charging that none should remain at home if ever again the voice of their Emperor should call them once more to the battle-field of Kosovo to rescue the sacred ashes of the heroes who died there for Christendom, civilization and liberty.

MODERN YUGOSLAV LITERATURE [1]

During the nineteenth century Yugoslav literature passed through four phases, which took place roughly speaking in the first, fifth, eighth and tenth decades. Between 1800 and 1850 occurred the first romantic revolt known in Yugoslavia as Illyrism or the Illyric movement; between 1850 and 1870 we have practically the same literary movement under the name young Serbia or the times of *Omladina* (Youth). The period from 1870 to 1900 is characterized as realism or naturalism, and the authors from 1900 up to the present are often called the symbolists or modernists, who attempt to strike out altogether new lines in art and poetry.

I

The leadership of the romantic period in Yugoslav literature belongs to three great pioneers: Yerney Kopitar, Vuk Stefanovich Karadzhich and Lyudevit Gay. This triumvirate of literary reformers was followed by the poets and romantics proper: Stanko Vraz, Ivan Mazhuranich, Branko Raditchevich, Petar Petrovich Nyegosh, France Preshern, and Petar Preradovich.

[1] By Milivoy S. Stanoyevich. North American Review. 217: 96-106. January, 1923.

The most brilliant, influential and infinitely versatile of all the Yugoslav authors was Vuk Stefanovich Karadzhich. He was born in Trshich, a village near the river Drina. As a boy he learned to read and write in a monastery, using a reed instead of a pen and a solution of gunpowder for ink. In lieu of writing paper he was happy if he could get cartridge wrappings. Throughout that whole region there was no regular school at that time and his father at first did not allow him to go to Austria. Meanwhile the Serbian insurrection had broken out in 1804. Vuk was made a scribe in a military company. When the Turks plundered and burned his native village, he betook himself to the city of Karlovtsi and studied there privately the Latin, Germanic and Slavonic languages. Later on he was for a certain time in the civil service of the Serbian government. In 1813 he was forced to leave his country, which had again been conquered, and went to Vienna. Here chance brought him into contact with Yerney Kopitar, the well known Slavist, who was the first to write a scientific "Slovene Grammar" and to recommend the popular tongue for the literary language. He encouraged Vuk to write also a "Serbian Grammar" and "Serbian Dictionary," and to introduce the vernacular speech into literature. This program was adhered to by the latter, who all his life acknowledged gratefully what he owed to his mentor. His future life was devoted to the reformation of the Yugoslav language and gathering of traditional songs, legends, proverbs, riddles, customs and usages.

In 1814-1815 Karadzhich published two volumes of *Srpske Narodne Pesme* (Serbian National Songs), which afterward increased to four, then to six, and finally to nine volumes. In enlarged editions, these admirable songs drew toward themselves the attention of all literary Europe. Goethe characterized some of them as "excellent and worthy of a comparison with Solo-

mon's "Song of Songs." Jacob Grimm found in them
a link between "Oriental and Occidental Lyrics." He
compares them with the noblest flowers of Homeric
poetry, and the "Zidanye Skadra na Boyani" (Building
of Scutari on the Boyana) he says that it is "one of the
most touching poems of all nations and all times." The
founders of the Romantic School in France, Charles
Nodier, Prosper Mérimée and Lamartine, translated a
goodly number of them, and they also attracted the attention of some English men of letters, Walter Scott,
Owen Meredith, and John Bowring. In recent days we
find a few collections of translated Serbian songs in
both English and American literature. Especially good
renderings were made during the World War and after
by J. W. Wiles, H. Rootham, and D. H. Low.

Karadzhich's great merit for Yugoslav letters is
threefold. First, he revised the written speech; secondly, he collected the national poetry; and thirdly, he
created a new basis of literary taste. His reform was
founded on a phonetic principle, which is today known
as simplified spelling (Write as you speak, and read as
it is written). By this rule he introduced one sign for
each sound, and one sound for each sign. Except the
Spanish, perhaps, hardly any other nation in the civilized world has such a simple, logical and precise spelling system as this. His volumes of the popular ballads
and lyrics were a discovery in the true sense of the
word. They served as a standard for other similar collections in Slavonic literatures, and with their simple
structure, their vision and breath of beauty, they inspired men of genius. A whole generation of Yugoslav poets was reared and educated in the spirit of the
national poetry. And this was due to Vuk Stefanovich,
to his invincible diligence and his ardent enthusiasm for
lore and literature.

The champions of Illyrism, instrumental in securing
the triumph of Vuk and Gay, were Vraz, Mazhuran-

ich, and Raditchevich. Stanko Vraz was one of the principal stars in the Illyric (Yugoslav) firmament. He wrote love poems entitled *Dyulabiye* (The Red Apples) and several other collections of sonnets, ballads, verse-romances, and political satires. Ivan Mazhuranich is generally known by his classic epic *Smrt Smail-Age Tchengicha* (The Death of Ismail-Aga Tchengich), published in 1846. This exquisite epopœia, written in the meter of the heroic Serbian ballads, gives a vivid description of life in Herzegovina under Turkish rule, and of the hereditary border feuds between Christians and Moslems. The style of the poem is natural and noble, the diction nearly always correct and elegant, and the verse as a rule sonorous and full of harmony. In later life Mazhuranich gave up poetry and, plunging into the vortex of politics, distinguished himself as a statesman.

Another writer, Branko Raditchevich, within a brief space of time contrived to enhance Yugoslav literature with several perennially attractive poems. *Dyatchki Rastanak* (The Students' Parting) is the best of his works. Nothing is lovelier in this remarkable poem than those passages in which he pictures the life of college students. For a time he gives himself up to the fleeting impressions of the moment. He greets the gently rolling hills and the changing scenes of the landscape. He revels in the calm and coolness of the forest and delights in the view of the Danube valley below with its widening rivers and vistas. In *Put* (The Road), a magnanimous allegory, Branko has shown unusual skill in satirical nomenclature by stigmatizing Vuk's adversaries who disapproved the reform of language and orthography. In the epic *Stoyan* he dared to measure himself with Byron, imitating "Lara," and naturally came off as poorly as Belial might have done from a contest with Raphael. However the lyrics of this talented man display extreme tenderness, beauty, originality and delicacy of fancy. Some of his shorter pieces are adapted to national melodies and are sung by younger people all over the country. His poetry is small in bulk and slight in body, but it endures, and will endure, in Yugoslav literature, because it is the embodiment of the spirit of immortal youth. Branko is the poet of spring, and those who have not read him before the meridian of their lives may abandon all hope of perusing him when the snows of time are on their heads.

II

More perfect in their construction and technical execution than the above mentioned poets were Nyegosh, Preshern and Preradovich. Petar Petrovich Nyegosh, the "Magnus Parens" of modern Yugoslav poetry, was a native of Montenegro. He commenced a career of literary exertion by the publication of a small collection of national songs. In 1845 he wrote *Lutcha Mikrokosma* (The Light of the Microcosm), a poem of great energy and sublimity of sentiment, founded on an episode of Milton's "Paradise Lost." After two years appeared *Gorski Venats* (The Mountain Wreath), a dramatic masterpiece of magnificent conception, in which are described the virile qualities of his race. It is often called the "Serbian Iliad," and really there are in it some verses condensed into epigrams more concise than the Greeks ever uttered:

> Merchant plays you with a smile beguiling,
> Wife beguiles you with her tears bestreaming,
> But the lie of Turk is far more monstrous . . .
> * * *
> No one ever drained the cup of honey,
> Without bitter taste of gall enduring,
> Cup of gall requires a cup of honey,
> By the mingling one makes light the drinking . . .
> * * *
> Wolf has right to undefenceless lambkins,
> As the tyrant has o'er feeble subjects,
> But to trample mercilessly the tyrant,
> And to bring the righteous law to conquer,
> Is a duty most humane and holy. . .

Besides writing *Gorski Venats,* Nyegosh is also the author of *Stepan Mali* (Stephen the Little), a drama without dramatic action, the theme of which was drawn from local history. Stephen the Little, the Montenegrin Rasputin, was a monk and adventurer who presented himself as the escaped Peter III, the murdered husband of Catherine II. After a few years this impostor of the Perkin Warbeck type was recognized and put to death. The mystery which generally surrounded the early Slavonic rulers, particularly marked in this case, gave Nyegosh good material which he handled in a masterly manner.

France Preshern was in certain respects a votary of classicism, especially in his collection *Sonetni Venets* (The Sonnet Wreath). In his epic *Krst pri Savitsi* (Baptism on the Savitsa) he manifested a clear tendency toward Romanticism. He was an apt, though not a servile, disciple of Byron, the brothers Schlegel, Bürger, and other "poets of full moon." The romantic love for medieval traditions has complete expression in two dramas, *Marko Kralyevich* and *Vladimir i Kosara* of Petar Preradovich. But this man achieved widespread popularity with his lyric poems. His pensive melancholy expressed itself in the allegory *Putnik* (The Wonderer), which hides a whole life of homelessness and isolation. The same note of sadness and longing is felt in his songlet "Miruy, miruy, srtse moye" (Be still, my heart, be still). Some lines of the latter remind one of Musset's "Tu te gonfles, mon cœur" although it is quite different in melody of words and structure:

> Who has stirred thee, heart of mine,
> That thou art so restless now?
> As a bird in cage thou longest,
> In the heavens to wing thy way.
>   Be still, my heart, be still! . . .

In most of his poems Preradovich upheld a mystic patriotism in the manner of the Polish messianists and

Czechoslovak panslavists. But being too reflective, and not so keen as his progenitors, he did not exercise any decided influence on his successors.

The younger romantic movement is represented by Lyuba Nenadovich, Dyura Yakshich, Yovan Yovanovich Zmay, Yosip Stritar, Yanko Yurkovich, August Shenoa, and Laza Kostich. Nenadovich was an author of considerable reputation and ability. His travels, in the form of letters, describe the sundry manners of western European people in their private and social life. He edited for several years a literary review *Shumadinka*. He also wrote lyric poems, but they did not bring him high fame so much as his versified *Zapisi* (The Inscriptions). The ease, elegance, and humorous mirth of these aphorisms have made many couplets pass into the memory and language of society. Dyura Yakshich, a king in heroic style, was a painter, educator and author. He may be considered the ideal representative of the age of "Omladina" (Youth.) Into his "Stories" he infused creations of his own romantic fancy free from all external influences. His dramas "The Migration of the Serbs" (1864), "Elizabeth" (1868), and "Stanoye Glavash" (1878) are soaked with the essence of his nationality. They are lacking in technique, but they are full of inspiration. His song "Na Liparu" (On the Lipar Hill) is tender, and rises at length into a strain of grandeur and loftiness, which later poets have never been able to surpass. Some of his poems are marked with pessimism. A gloomy trait is particularly noticeable in his incantation "Ponoch" (Midnight) ending with a deeply sad tone:

> The door creaked . . .
> Oh, ghostly spirit! Oh, dear shadow!
> Oh, my mother, happy am I now!
> Yet have passed me many, many years
> With their bitter and still bitter truths;
> Many times my breast has trembled,
> And my heart was fain to break,
> Because of people and their errors.

> Yet I consoled myself with death;
> Many bitter cups I quaffed of,
> Many loaves with tears I melted. . . .
> Oh, mother, mother! Oh, dear spirit!
> Since I last saw you, mother darling,
> No good has come near to bless me,
> And perhaps even now you are thinking:
> "It is well with him that he hears not
> Spider weaving o'er the blackened ceiling!
> He is midst the people, neighbors!" . . .
> Yet it's bad to be amongst the rabble:
> For malice stalks apace with vice,
> With them envy shakes fraternal hands,
> And the lie is always to be found
> There where baseness leads them,
> Flattery and treason court and serve them,
> Escorted by unfaithfulness as well. . . .
> Oh, mother, mother, malicious is the world,
> Life, oh, my mother, is full of sorrow.

Of the same bent is Yovan Yovanovich Zmay, the poet of sympathy. In his lyric songs under the collectives titles *Dyulichi* (Little Red Roses) and *Dyulichi Uveoci* (Faded Little Red Roses) he touches the highest point of his creative genius. There are six large volumes of his *Pevaniya* (The Book of Songs), and several smaller collections including the satires, epigrams, and children's songs. To the American literary world Zmay is known partly through the rendering of Mr. Robert Underwood Johnson. In the following we have the poet's definition of poetry that few would think of contending for even in these modernistic days:

> Where is Pain and dire Distress,
> Songs shall soothe like soft caress;
> Though the stoutest courage fails,
> Song's an anchor in all gales;
> When all others fail to reach,
> Song shall be the thrilling speech;
> Love and friends and comfort fled,
> Song shall linger by your bed;
> And when Doubt shall question, Why?
> Song shall lift you to the sky.
>   (Johnson's translation)

Of the above authors the three are novelists: Yanko Yurkovich, Yosip Stritar, and August Shenoa. From

their earliest years these three men of letters had been
laying up from French sources impressions which were
to be definitely useful to them in the creations of their
interesting and suggestive prose-romances.   Yurkovich
deserves notice for his satires and dramatic compositions. Stritar was the founder and editor of a literary
paper *Zvon* (The Bell), and wrote novels of which
the most popular are *Zorin,* the Yugoslav *Werther,*
and *Gospod Mirodolski* (Mister Mirodolski), a sort
of "Vicar of Wakefield."   Shenoa edited the review
Venats (The Wreath) and wrote the novels *Zlata-
revo Zlato* (Goldsmith's Gold), *Selyatchka Buna*
(The Peasant Revolt), and *Diogenes.* He is credited
also with many short stories. Laza Kostich may be characterized as an eccentric but with a spark of genius. His
writings abound in coined words, and in devious turns
and twists of expression. He was the first to introduce
iambic meter into the dramatic poetry, and the first
translator of Shakespeare into Yugoslav. He also composed three original dramas: *Maksim Tsrnoyevich*
(1866), *Pera Segedinats* (1875), and *Gordana* (1890).

III

In the eighth decade of the nineteenth century ap-
peared in Yugoslav literature Svetozar Markovich and
Yasha Ignyatovich, the founders of the Realistic
School. It is from this time on that reaction against
Romanticism may be said to date.

The second half of the last century was under the
domination of science. The scientist was commonly believed to be in possession of the means whereby the
riddle of the universe might be explained, and the whole
future of humanity shaped. All the great writers of that
time were under the irresistable spell of this prestige of
science. Each sought to utilize as much as possible the
facts and theories of science, and to make of the novel
or drama an instrument of scientific observation and

discussion. The realists purported to create a school of "applied literature." The ultimate goal of the school was, first, exact and almost photographic delineation of the accidents of modern life, and secondly, non-suppression of the essential features and functions of that life which are usually suppressed. There is no doubt that Markovich and Ignyatovich belonged to this school.

Svetozar Markovich was a publicist and critic who first introduced the doctrine of social reform among the southern Slavs. He exerted tremendous influence on his contemporaries, recommending them to be positivists in science, republicans in politics, and realists or rather utilitarians in literature. He subscribed to the realistic novels of Ignyatovich, who did not hesitate to draw largely on his own personal adventures and who professed to portray human life, not as a fairy-tale, but as "stuff on which to try the soul's strength." Among Yasha's best romances may be reckoned *Patnitsa* (A Miserable Woman), *Vasa Reshpekt* (Basil the Respectable), *Vetchiti Mladozhenya* (The Perennial Bridegroom), *Trpen Spasen* (The Suffered Saved), and *Milan Narandzhich*. All these novels form a prominent landmark in the development of Yugoslav prose fiction.

Of the novelists following Ignyatovich there stand out a galaxy of story-tellers of whom the foremost are Yosip Yuritchich, Milovan Glishich, and Yanko Kersnik. The novels and sketches of country life of these authors are highly appreciated by the critics. In the same class are placed Eugen Kumitchich, Yanko Veselinovich, and Svetolik Rankovich, who tinged their picaroon romances with the spirit of revolt against established moral and political arrangements. And contemporary with these came writers of the social novel, Yosip Kozarats and Lyubomir Babich Dyalski, who in their short tales described the beauty and scenery of their homeland with much skill.

The fiction of psychological analysis was cultivated by Laza Lazarevich, who is still finding readers mostly because of his impeccable style, and Sima Matavul, who employed his skill in holding up to ridicule the peculiar foibles of the Dalmatian Slavs. Of about the same date as these there are two other novelists of note, Stevan Sremats and Radoye Domanovich. Sremats is one of the best Yugoslav humorists. His remarkable novels include *Ivkova Slava* (Ivko's Patron Saint), *Pop-Chira i Pop-Spira* (Priest Chira and Priest Spira), *Zona Zamfirova* (Zona of Zamphir) *Tchitcha Yordan* (Uncle Jordan), and *Vukadin*—all characterized with local coloring. *Ivkova Slava* was dramatized and is far more successful in this new form. Domanovich is the diminutive Yugoslav Swift. During his short literary career he succeeded in developing the great powers of the satirical novel, although some of his stories are distorted by pessimism and grime.

Succeeding these leaders we have the younger group comprising Fran Meshko, Borisav Stankovich, Fran Govekar, Velko Petrovich, Ivo Chipiko, and Milosh Stanoyevich. All these promising *litterateurs* with slight exception adhere closely to the earlier established realistic school. With their followers and contemporaries, of whom many are omitted here, they accept realism as a practical method, not as an ultimate result and consummation. They never go down too deep and too low into the unclean mysteries of modern humanity. Their works abound in fertile imagination and vision. But these young men have an artistic distaste for experimental naturalism and all that is repulsive and unseemly.

More celebrated as playwright than novelist is Branislav Nushich. His incident novels and journalistic *feuilletons* are not always of moral and polished type, but they are lively and amusing sketches of life. He is more prolific in historical drama and comedy. Of his plays the most popular are *Protektsiya* (The Pull),

Obitchan Tchovek (A Usual Man), *Iza Bozhyih Ledya* (Behind the Back of God), *Prince of Semberia* (English translation by Luka Dyuritchich and Bertha W. Clark), *Putchina* (The High Sea), *Hadzhi-Loya* and *Rastko Nemanyich.* Before him the comedy of characters was fostered by Yovan S. Popovich, and the comedy of intrigue by Kosta Trifkovich.

The historical bent given to drama by Nushich was continued by the versatile Ivo Voynovich and Ante Tresich Pavitchich. Apart from his dramas and songs, the latter is also the author of an intensely interesting book entitled *Preko Atlantika do Pacifika* (Across the Atlantic to the Pacific), in which he gives his clever and striking observations on American politics, literature and social life in general.

The Yugoslav "Parnasse," representing the last quarter of the nineteenth century, exhibits a remarkable transition between the old and the new poetic schools. To this group of poets belong Anton Ashkerts, Voyislav Ilich, Silviye Krantchevich, and Aleksa Shantich. The last named poet is one of the most engaging figures in Yugoslav literature. He is noted for his sincerity and appealing depth of sentiment. In the following verses we have an illustration of the genuine touches of his poetry :

> O, my night, when will thy shadows vanish?
> —Never!
> O, my dawn, when shall I see thee coming?
> —Never!
> O, my joy, when will I greet thy advent?
> —Never!
> O, my heaven, when will blaze thy glory?
> —Never!
> O, my darling, when our wedding banquet?
> —Never!
> O, my weeping, when will cease thy flowing?
> —Never!

These poets paved the way for the modern symbolistic school, of which the most noteworthy representatives in prose composition are Ivan Tsankar and Yosip

Kosor. In poetry and drama the symbolists or modernists are represented by Milan Begovich, Yovan Dutchich, Vladimir Nazor, Milan Rakich, Dragutin Domyanich, Sima Pandurovich, Oton Zhupantchich, and Svetislav Stefanovich.

It would be too rash to dogmatize about this new movement, and yet more rash to prophesy. The Yugoslav symbolists, like their fellows in other countries, stand for the exclusive, the delicate, and the mystic beauties of the supernatural. The enigmas of metaphysic, mythology, and music are the favorite subjects of their poesy. In common daily life when they lack wealth they despise it, but when they get money they hold on to it, and become supreme egoists. In most cases they nurse a grudge against the world and attack all things with which they are discontented. But in certain of their works they discover at least some glimpses of the ideal world. If in their art they abstain from search after the unusual, abnormal, and deliquescent, it is possible that they will attain some distinction, and may have a future in the new country of Yugoslavia.

MODERN YUGOSLAV ART [1]

Modern Yugoslav art moves along lines which give it the characteristic traits of youth, the product of a youthful civilization. In it also are reflected the main distinctive features of the Yugoslav people and of their distressing and singular fate. That this statement is true will be apparent if we glance over the efforts of the Yugoslavs in the field of art since the year 1870, about the date at which this movement started.

What at first is most striking about this movement is the almost complete lack of native artistic tradition. Being separated from the Golden Age of the Serbian medieval past (thirteenth and fourteenth centuries) by

[1] By Branko Popovich. Art and Archaeology. 17: 233-40. May, 1924.

a long interval of national bondage, modern Yugoslav art in none of its forms shows any link with the high traditions of that great era. Even the fine and flourishing Dalmatian Renaissance, of more recent date, did not succeed in making this new movement, which was unsteady from the outset, fruitful. Nor had the various forms of foreign influence any marked success in this respect. In the last decade of the nineteenth century the influence of Austria and of Hungary (in Slovenia, Croatia and Voyvodina), of Italy (in Dalmatia), of Germany and of France (in Serbia), though frequently evident, has been unable to get the ascendency over Yugoslav taste to the extent of imposing prevalent traditions of those countries upon Yugoslav artists. This movement, therefore, was from the first condemned to uncertainty.

Evidence of this unsettled condition was found in the lack of any schooled or trained guidance of a consistent character. There being no center in the country for the systematic cultivation of art, no well-organized schools, no public sense of art, while the artists had all studied abroad in different art centers, the movement necessarily could not be steady or uniform. It lacked a more generalized discipline. The very spirit of the people, who had become united only a short while before, was opposed to it and underwent a rapid and hurried process of formation.

The applied arts were hardly developed in Yugoslavia, as the handicrafts were not very long ago in a primitive state. Consequently, here also was no stimulus nor basis for the organic and systematic development of art. The only thing, apparently, the youthful Yugoslav art could still avail itself of, was that natural course of action and development which it did accept and which perhaps is not wholly disadvantageous individualism. As a result, there has evidently been very little uniformity thus far.

However, the movement at the same time is proving very interesting. Possibly in no country do the natural talent of the artist and the general value of his moral and intellectual qualities play such a decisive part in the production of a work of art, and thus to such an extent, as in Yugoslavia. Technical ability, freedom of conception and execution, and a good school have never proved sufficient for the production of a work of art. The initial efforts of all the better Yugoslav artists have been made in a period of great stress. In more favored cases the academic mode of expression, or in less favored cases the local manner, which had been introduced from various places, could hardly ever suit their temperament; nor could it be applied to the nature of the subject as some undertook to treat and others hoped to visualize it. In the case of the more gifted artists, moreover, this crisis occurred at the time when they were pursuing their studies.

Ivan Meshtrovich, a sculptor of the first rank and the greatest living artist in Yugoslavia, when but nineteen years old was the best student at the School of Fine Arts in Vienna and yet had already come into violent conflict with the discipline of the school. He courageously endeavored to find an expression of his own in art and that naturally led him also to look for an individual manner of artistic expression. There was no predecessor in his country to whom he could have looked for support. Carrying with him the grand vision of the national epos which he was desirous of representing in plastic form, an impersonal academic mode of expression could not satisfy him. At one time he found help in the great Rodin. A formal inspiration came to him in some measure, but only for a brief time, from Metzner. But that was all. For the execution of his very mighty statues, so full of expression and so very peculiar, with which he desired to perpetuate the glory and the tragedy of Kosovo, he was obliged to have

recourse to the spirit that characterized him as a child of
the Yugoslav nation and to his natural talent. And then
he started to create wonders. While working on his
Kralyevich Marko, the national legendary knight and
defender of justice with the iron will, in whom he
wanted to represent the type of the Yugoslav hero,
Meshtrovich, then quite young, nearly collapsed under
the tremendous strain. Before Meshtrovich the same
had happened to George Krstich, a painter endowed with
the greatest qualities, an artist who was passionately
fond of the national type and whose soul was, like that
of his nation, full of deep feeling and emotion. A
similar situation was faced by Ivan Grohar, Ferdo
Veseli and Rikard Yakopich—that refined impressionist
—at about the time they saw their work crowned with
success (beginning of this century); all of them being
fanatically devoted to colors, to Slovenian scenery and
to their homes. The same is true, though to a less extent,
in the case of Rista Vukanovich with his first portraits;
of Nadezhda Petrovich and, especially, of Marko Murat.

In short, a similar fate befell all those artists who
were possessed of a feeling of individuality, native pride
and national consciousness. A whole series of gifted
young artists passed through this seemingly unavoidable
crisis. To unfold one's personality in an artistic interpretation of the admirable ethical ideals of the nation,
as embodied in and magnificently reflected by the
national epos and knightly exploits; to impress one's
personality on the work of art in which one has mater-
ialized that strangely complex Yugoslav soul, that is
both archaic and classic, romantic and rustic, but always
of great depth and profoundly human; to express one's
personality in representing the national type and temperament and the beauty of one's beloved country—that
is the natural wish of all gifted Yugoslav artists, which
until today has manifested itself in various forms, fluc-
tuating between the extreme differentiation of indivi-

dualism and the normal equilibrium of the general type of man.

There are, it is true, a large number of Yugoslav artists, chief among them those who lived abroad, who were not subject to these struggles and crises. In accepting at once the academic or prevailing mode of expression these artists mainly had to face the question of the degree to which they were capable of modification or adjustment. They changed their manner and even their whole palette, not according to their conviction, which would have its source in their conception of the world and their sentiment of nature, but according to the prevailing fashion, whether it originated in the Academy or in the Salon. Some of them have become good technicians, others reputable illustrators of national manners and customs, a few even undertook to illustrate the country's history and religious life. Most of them, however, have continued to make an eclectic imitation of works of art and modes of execution of which they approved. With the execption of Paya Yovanovich and Vlaho Bukovats, most of the modern painters belong to this group, viz.: Nikola Mashich, Urosh Predich, Tchikosh Stoyadinovich, Tselestin Medovich, Oton Kovatchevich, Klement Tsrntchich, Robert Frangesh, Sima Roksandich, Dyoka Yovanovich, Rudolf Valdets and also a pretty large number of younger painters and the very youngest. For the sake of precision some distinctions and remarks should be made here. Nikola Mashich and Urosh Predich, by reason of some of their works, stand apart from this group of artists, which may conveniently be called that of impersonal technicians. Because of the sincerity of their realistic interpretation, and of the accuracy of their observation—as evidenced in some of their paintings ("Girl Guarding Geese" by the first artist; "The Jolly Brothers" by the second)—these two conscientious and intelligent artists have succeeded in reaching the height of true creation,

to the like of which Paya Yovanovich and Vlaho Bukovats, though greater as virtuosi, have never been able
to attain. Then, in addition to this, the fact should be
mentioned that Paya Yovanovich has produced most of
the illustrations of folklore (of Montenegro and of
Albania) and of history, some of which are realistic
and fairly good, and others technically clever; but all
these illustrations, as indeed all his paintings, lack sincerity; they are cold and expressionless.

Lastly, it should be noted that Vlaho Bukovats had
a marked sense of colors, though he did not develop and
refine it, and that at one time his work approached very
closely that of the French impressionists, though only in
its form. Before Ivan Meshtrovich and in spite of the
meritorious efforts of R. Frangesh, S. Roksandich, D.
Yovanovich, P. Ubavkich, R. Valdets and others, Yugoslav sculpture did not excite more than local interest.

Generally speaking, although this group of impersonal technicians strenuously strove to call into being an
artistic atmosphere, it could not do much toward the
formation of a real Yugoslav art. It contributed in no
way to the conception of original artistic work and had
no share in the search for, and creation of an expression
and manner of expression, of its own. It might, therefore, belong to any art movement whatever.

It is the individualists who have contributed to the
creation of an original Yugoslav art. Their forerunners were romanticists Dyura Yakshich and George Krstich, and their first representative to meet with complete
success was Ivan Meshtrovich.

Independently of Meshtrovich, there are Ferdo
Veseli, Ivan Grohar, Rikard Yakopich and Mateya
Yama who work with success in Slovenia and who, in
that beautiful mountainous country, are creating a
naturalist and impressionist genre of painting, very
refined and very colorful. This group might also be
referred to as the Slovenian school, for the bonds of
art which drew those painters together have been of an

intimate and evident nature. They approached the
French impressionists in their conception of nature, but
their technical ability was weaker while their sensibility
was stronger. Other Slovenian painters: Tratnik, Vav-
potich and Sterner, though evidently moved by other
tendencies (Tratnik is above all a graphic artist; Vav-
potich is inclined to the academic manner; Sterner is
attracted more and more by solid and naturalist material
and coloring), are more closely related to any one of
those first four painters than to any other Yugoslav
artist. Thus the first signs of a greater uniformity of
work characterized by naturalistic impressionism may be
recognized in Slovenia. Those most intimately identified with this group are: Nadezhda Petrovich, with a
strong inclination toward romanticism; Marko Murat,
who, after his brilliant success in outdoor painting, suddenly plunged into literature and restricted himself to
schematization; and Milan Milovanovich who kept to
impressionist scenery with some inclination to neo-im-
pressionism.

With the appearance of Ivan Meshtrovich, Yugoslav art, particularly sculpture, is given a wonderful
impetus with wings of genius. Meshtrovich, dissatisfied
after the production of his Kralyevich Marko, continues
a still more energetic search for expression. But he had
then already achieved the consolidation of his power of
spontaneous conception as a sculptor, his exceptional
facility and virtuoisity in handling the material he works
with, his extremely well-developed sense of tentative
methods, and his admirably developed feeling for plastic
form of a grand and expressive character. His development has been so rapid, his production so abundant, that
his eighteen years' career as a sculptor may be compared to a giant's prolonged and impetuous attack;
which, moreover, still continues and the like of which it
would be hard to find in the history of art. As in the
case of the unknown Egyptian masters, the ancient classical masters, and Michaelangelo, Meshtrovich conceives

the idea of a superb work in the form of a gigantic plastic symphony, in which a final synthesis of his conception as an architect would result from the association of architecture with sculpture and painting. Thus the Temple of Kosovo or Temple of Sacrifice (monument of the battle of Kosovo, 1389) is to incarnate and glorify the heroism, sufferings and sacrifice of his people in the struggle for justice and liberty. Meshtrovich's model of this temple is done in wood and on a large scale. In the same spurt whole sets of plastic visions of the tragedy of Kosovo were executed by him to people his temple. His work then approaches most closely that of the Greek masters. Around him assemble a large number of gifted young artists: Toma Roksandich, Tomislav Krizman, Mirko Ratchki and later Yoyo Klyakovich and others. It was the time when a great and important concentration of Yugoslav artistic talent apparently began to show about the national epos and about Meshtrovich. A rapid development of Yugoslav art and a uniform and continuous action were expected from this concentration. And that is indeed what happened, though on a far smaller scale. Hardly had Meshtrovich and his companions been welcomed by Serbia when this country became involved in great wars. Concurrently with the wars came numerous changes and perturbations, and then the rather unwholesome condition following war. Meshtrovich himself is changing, laboring always hard and with success. At the time he was in exile (1916-1919) the thought of the national epos and the idea of the Temple of Kosovo were abandoned by him. He left his companions and isolated himself. After a short period devoted largely to technical exercise and to endeavor, a period of approach to Egyptian, Assyrian and Indian art and to the art of the Middle Ages, he gave himself entirely over to Christianity and to religious sculpture and became eclectic in the grandest style. Today it is the Christian and the Catholic who speaks by his mouth: a profound change all along the line. The national sculptor creating grand monuments has become an eclectic Christian, exalted and refined; a stylist; at times even a miniaturist. Meshtrovich also in this genre produces works of inestimable value. Besides, this change that has occurred is possibly for the better. The concentration referred to above may have come somewhat too soon; the country's general state of civilization and the stage of development which art had reached there, evidently were not yet on the level required for the realization of so grand an enterprise.

Yugoslav art is relapsing into a phase of ferment and individual, disorganized effort. This time, however, the movement is attended by much more success and much more method in research. Meshtrovich, isolated, introduced a new note, a religious one. Toma Roksandich, freed from the influence of Meshtrovich, returns to nature, to the wholesome form and the classical conception of plastic art and produces a number of extraordinary wooden statues. And there appears a whole phalanx of new and young artists of naturalist and extremist tendencies, lending a new impetus and fresh vigor to the national art. Finally, all the virtues and failings of modern European art are penetrating here. But order is being gradually restored by the regulating influence of the native artist's wholesome conception and sincere as well as profound sensibility. The national soul and the Yugoslav type have not yet reached their highest expression. Among this number of sedulous artists we may note: Branko Popovich, Miroslav Kralyevich, Branko Deshkovich, Vladimir Betsich, Lyuba Babich, Petar Dobrovich, Sava Shumanovich, Palavitchini, Krshinich, Yovan Biyelich, Tartalya and many others. Every one of these artists is perfecting his means of expression. Painters diligently study problems connected with the art of painting; sculptors, problems of plastic art. Literature, history and archaeology are excluded from the realms of painting and sculpture. A gifted artist dares to give expression only to a purely artistic conception. The value of his work does not depend upon the perfection and purity of the expression. That this expression is inseparable from the artistic vision and its reproduction, has never been seriously contested. With Yugoslav artists this fact is quite evident, and this even in perhaps too large a measure.

CHAPTER VI

BULGARIA

BULGARIA'S PAST AND PRESENT HISTORY [1]

Bulgaria was the first of the central powers to ask for terms of surrender, and although these were declared to be unconditional she at once accepted them. In this she showed an independence which has characterized the nation since it existed. Every well-wisher to the peasant state was glad that she was out of the war. She ought never to have been in it. The blundering of diplomats had much to do with her entry, but King Ferdinand of Coburg had more. Ferdinand's abdication was the best thing he ever did in the interests of Bulgaria. Whether his son Boris will satisfy the people over whom Ferdinand, acting upon the bad old conception that a king has the right to dispose of his subjects, reigned, remains to be seen.

The immediate cause of her exit was notably weariness of the struggle in which her enemies were obtaining steady success. But the sturdy obstinacy of the Bulgars would not have permitted such an exit except for other and entirely different causes. The national heart was never in the war. The people never forgot that Russia was their deliverer from the Turkish yoke. Even after many reasons for distrusting Russia they willingly consented in February, 1912, to leave the settlement of their differences with Serbia to the arbitration of the Tsar, and until the collapse of Russia they claimed that these should be so settled. There were other causes which influenced the exit of Bulgaria.

[1] By E. Pears. Contemporary Review. 114: 484-8. November, 1918.

As I am concerned here mainly with Bulgaria's recent action I pass lightly over her early history after 1878. I note, however, three facts which ought not to be overlooked as contributing to her recent action.

1. Russia was the deliverer of Bulgaria and both deserved and received the gratitude of the Bulgarian people. The Russian war party made it transparently clear that their intention was to make of Bulgaria a Russian province. That party was both obstinate and persistent in carrying out this design.

2. That Austria acquiesced in this project, but apparently always on condition that she should be allowed to do what she liked with Serbia. The two great powers plotted one against the other for many years, and in 1897 an understanding was come to between them that Bulgaria should be left within the sphere of influence of Russia, while Austria was to have a free hand in Serbia. As early as 1885, while Prince Alexander was still on the princely throne, an incident occurred which illustrates both the statements I have made. Russia, irritated by the constant opposition of the Bulgars who, under their first great Minister Stambulov, raised the cry of "Bulgaria for the Bulgarians," determined to bring the people to heel. Every officer in the army above the rank of lieutenant was a Russian. Russia in one day ordered all these officers to return home. Prince Alexander was absent at Varna. Then the news came that a Serbian army had invaded the country. Without superior officers a fierce soldiers' battle was fought (November, 1885) at Slivnitsa, the Serbians were badly beaten and were pursued to the frontiers of the country. There the Bulgarians had to stop because Austria announced that if they entered Serbian territory they would have to deal with her. In other words, the two most despotic powers in Europe had agreed that Bulgaria might be forced by the Tsar to become a Russian province. Each wished to employ

a small Balkan state as a pawn for its own purpose. The next quarter of a century saw a long diplomatic and selfish struggle between Russia and Bulgaria.

3. The third fact to which I call attention is that Bulgaria had reason to believe in the desire of England, France, and the United States to do her justice. War weary, led into the struggle against her wishes, called on to fight side by side with her traditional enemies, she was anxious to get out of the war and having confidence in the three powers named, especially in America, she made an unconditional surrender. The story of Bulgaria since her creation as a nation in 1878 is a clear-cut one, and furnishes a valuable illustration of the injunction. "Put not your trust in princes."

The essential features of Bulgaria's history must be briefly recalled. A people long oppressed under the tyranny of the Turks attempted, in 1876, to rise against their oppressors. The knowledge that such an attempt was contemplated led to Moslem atrocities in which sixty villages were burned and twelve thousand men, women, and children were massacred in cold blood. It was the only method which the Turk had learned of suppressing risings or answering calls for better government. When the news reached England popular indignation drove the government to enquire into the truth of the reports which had been sent. Two commissions, the first American, the second British, were sent into Bulgaria. They each found that the above statements were not exaggerated. Russia, quite unprepared for war, became even more completely aroused than was England; for her people had long claimed to be the protector of the Christians under Turkish rule. A conference met in Constantinople in December, 1876, in which every power in Europe was represented. Its object was to persuade the Porte to adopt reforms for the benefit of Bulgaria and Serbia, and prevent the recurrence of massacres. Its members were unanimous in pressing for such reforms;

but Abdul Hamid had now been girt with the sword of Osman and refused all reforms or suggestions of reforms. The conference broke up at the end of January, and Lord Salisbury, the representative of Great Britain, was hounded out of Turkey by the subsidized press. Lord Salisbury remarked to me and others the last evening he was in Constantinople, "We have tried to save Turkey, but she refuses salvation." Russia declared war on April 24th, 1877, and after a year's hard fighting Turkey was beaten. Bulgaria was established as a principality by the treaty of San Stefano which was revised by arrangement between Great Britain and Russia and the treaty of Berlin took its place.

The Bulgars were to choose a prince. They chose Alexander, a good but weak man. Then a struggle began which vitally altered the relations between Russia and Bulgaria. The war party in Russia, as already stated, determined to have its own way. There was no pretence of "self-determination" of the people. Russia was "the Deliverer and the Conqueror." Bulgaria should become a Russian province. During ten long years the struggle went on. An infamous Russian intrigue expelled Alexander in 1887. Then it became necessary to choose a successor. Russia put forward her candidate. But the people would not have him. A deputation was appointed by the Sobranye, the Bulgarian Chamber, to find a prince. They selected Ferdinand, as yet an unknown Austrian officer. Russia was once more disappointed, and from that time onward she became the enemy of Bulgaria.

Two influences must be noted as having great importance from that time up to the present upon Bulgarian history, the first is that England steadily supported the independence of Bulgaria and opposed the Russian intention to force its people to accept her yoke. England never has had a design for a foot of Bulgarian territory and her diplomacy was used solely for the

benefit of the people. The influence to which I allude is
that of the United States. As my readers have probably
noticed the United States has never declared war upon
Bulgaria, the explanation is that Bulgaria has received
from America more aid in finding her soul than from
all other countries. This influence came mainly from
the great American institution known as Robert College
in Constantinople. The late Dr. Washburn, the Principal of that College for nearly forty years, was a man
of magnetic influence resembling that of Arnold of
Rugby. Every year saw a number of graduates of various races in the College, but notably Bulgarians, who
were hard students and whose minds had been trained
to accept the ideals of America. Stambulov, though not
himself there trained, spoke in very high terms of the
value of his work. His successor Stoilov was a graduate and a man greatly respected both in Bulgaria and
in England. He was one of the earliest graduates and
with him was Mr. Panaretov who since the commence-
ment of the World War has been the able representative
of Bulgaria in Washington. Clear-headed and thoughtful but strictly straight in his diplomatic and private
conduct, he has earned the respect of all in America
who take an interest in eastern politics. The only other
Robert College Prime Minister who may be mentioned
was Mr. Geshov whose conduct in refusing to continue
in office when King Ferdinand, probably at the dicta-
tion of Austria, sent new terms to be added to those
already settled between him and Mr. Pashich, the Serbian Premier, gave him a notable place in the history of
the Bulgarian people. If the story as told by various
writers, largely confirmed by Geshov himself, be true,
then King Ferdinand was responsible for the second
Bulgarian war and for her entry on the side of Germany and Austria. Pashich, the Serbian Premier and
Geshov who occupied the same position in Bulgaria,
were authorized to arrange the difficulties between their
two countries. They had virtually completed their task

when Geshov received an order from his King to await
the arrival of Savov. When the latter arrived he produced new terms and on reading them Geshov indignantly threw down his pen and declared that as they
meant war he would have nothing to do with them.
Mr. Geshov emphasized the fact that no meeting of
ministers had taken place and that the new terms were
those of King Ferdinand alone. Efforts were made to
retain the services of Geshov, but within a month he had
resigned. War ensued. The intention of Ferdinand
was to surprise Serbia but he had miscalculated, and
in the war, which was due to his interference, the Bulgarian army was deservedly beaten to its knees. Even
before that event the King had forfeited the confidence
of the best men of his country and especially of the
large section of the educated class that had been trained
at Robert College. He was regarded as the tool of
Austria and subsequently of Germany.

When in August 1914 war was declared, Ferdinand
found the sentiment of his people favorable to the
Allies. Bulgaria, as it appears to me, had a real grievance in the refusal of the powers to carry out the
arrangement which had been entered into in February,
1912. The British government, several months after the
World War commenced, was approached with the suggestion that the Allies should promise that if Bulgaria
remained neutral this grievance should be redressed. A
promise was given and the Bulgarians asked for it in
writing. Time was lost and the Bulgarians claim that
representations which they made to our minister at
Sofia were never transmitted to England. When the
answer came it is said to have been different from the
promise which had been made. One power was against
the suggested arrangement. I believe that power was
Serbia herself. A well-informed observer, Mr. Noel
Buxton, who was in Belgrade in December, 1914, states
that it was his impression that Pashich was waiting to
be ordered by the powers to make the concession

demanded. If such an order were given he could have
told his constituents that it was in their interests to
comply with it, but as it was never given, the war party,
urged constantly at Sofia by the representatives of Berlin and Vienna, decided that Bulgaria should throw in
her lot with the central powers. Finally, partly as a
result of the vacillation of diplomacy, the King had his
own way, but the feeling in the army as well as in the
country generally was in favor of England and the
Allies, and it soon became recognized that if they could
get rid of their king who had never been popular, their
best course would be to act as they already did.

THE BULGARIANS, A SIMPLE FOLK WITH A HEART [1]

It is in Tchirpan, a small town of thirteen thousand
inhabitants, in the south of Bulgaria, that I am reaching
nearer to the heart of this people, whom one cannot help
but love once inside the rough outer shell. All the
streets present the aspect of having broken out in a stone
rash; they curl unceasingly in between the low whitewashed houses and rubble fences, to the vast annoy-
ance of the only architect in town. "No building is ever
square," he confided to me recently, "and the plans are
fearfully difficult to make."

The tiny wooden shops present openings with an
elevated platform on which sits the merchant, his buyer
remaining in the street. Of course there is progress in
Tchirpan, and many merchants own real little shops
with a real counter. It is every man's ambition to
order such a plan and build a modern building, and then
stand behind the counter. The houses are whitewashed,
presenting endless rubble fences to the street and a large
wooden gate, the frontier which separates the dusty
street from the oasis within. And what an oasis!

[1] By N. de Bogory. Outlook. 135: 536-9. November 28, 1923.

Once inside the gates, it is the home; several small whitewashed houses cluster around, serving as living quarters and summer kitchens. There is always a grape arbor, from which there now hang blue clusters of grapes, often a foot in length. Around the buildings the ground is laid with large flat stones, and beyond is the garden—fig trees, pears, plums, mulberries. But the housewife's great pride is her flower garden. Nasturtiums, tobacco plants, dahlias, grow in the ground, while most of the plants are potted in anything from an old kerosene can to a packing-case. The solid mass of plants can be thus moved from the burning sun in summer and in winter protected from the extremes of cold.

During a visit I had been admiring one especially lovely garden. My hostess's remark was:

I can have it because there's a well in my yard; others have to carry their water from the nearest fountain.

And I realized why the housewives are so tender with their plants. It takes a great deal of feeling for a plant to be willing to water it from buckets slung on a pole and brought from a fountain, often many blocks away. The rain rarely falls here through the summer months; even the grass withers into yellow wisps. "We do the best we can, but life is primitive." Such is the answer one gets most often; self-criticism is the rule and the desire for something better is a national characteristic. I think it is this special mental trait which makes the Bulgarian the most intelligent and most advanced of the Balkan peoples.

I met an old acquaintance whom I had known during my previous visit, and we started discussing the condition of the town. I remarked:

Your streets are fearful. I suppose two wars with Stambulisky on top just about bankrupted you.

His answer was:

No. I don't think it's a question of money; it's our Bulgarian way. We spend a lot of money fixing up a street, and

then we economize by refusing to keep it repaired. It takes
Western culture to understand the value of upkeep.

Personally I think he was exaggerating, but there
is no doubt that this is the general attitude of mind,
and the educated people are doing their best to fight
this Oriental acceptance of things as they are and to
introduce the go-ahead spirit of cultured countries. The
Bulgarian mother, with no special education, and tied
solidly to her household duties by the fact of complexity
due to utter lack of any improvements, worries about
her children. She knows that the public schools leave
much to be desired, but there is little other choice, and
except for the Samakov School run by the American
Board of Commissioners for Foreign Missions along
American lines, there are no good schools. As a result
the entire weight is laid on the university education,
which is preferably given abroad, to pay for which the
family at home economizes and often almost starves.

However, life in Tchirpan is almost city life compared to that of the surrounding villages. I went to one
of them, six kilometers from Tchirpan, to a mill run by
several Russian refugees. The villagers all seemed to
own sparkling new whitewashed homes with red-tiled
roofs and balconies which gave them a chalet-like appearance. From a distance the entire village was a mass
of green trees, with just the houses peeping out. The
mill stands on the main road leading to the village fields,
so before noon, wagons, donkeys, and horses went by,
heavily laden with produce, the pick of that morning;
corn, beans, melons, watermelons—it was an endless
stream.

But not one passed us by; as each neared the mill
he stopped, called out, and handed a picked melon. One
of Russian owners explained:

A village custom. They do this every morning—every one
of them. Why we get it, we can't decide. Perhaps because
we are Russians, for whom there is a great sympathy, or perhaps
because they know we have nothing. But in the village those

who own land always give to the poor. It is customary for children of poor families to sit beside the road, simply collecting what the peasants give them.

This is probably an old Turkish custom which has remained because of its compatibility with the national character; there is a rough kindness among the people here. Nobody ever starves. The spirit of giving is much developed, and it is done not as a charity but as a due; those who have naturally give to those who have not. And yet it was in this same village that another Russian refugee was beaten to death for taking a watermelon.

Strange contrasts, difficult for a European or American to seize. Here, where nobody, man or beast, starves, children are beaten and animals are so roughly treated that one's nerves are constantly on edge. Dogs swarm everywhere, and, while there is always a hand to throw them something to eat, the stone often follows just as readily. Bulls, goats, buffaloes, donkeys—all get good food and lots of kicks. A village boy I met, who is studying medicine in Vienna, gave me an interesting side-light on the simple peasant's reaction to our civilization.

"I don't like it," he explained, rather plaintively, "probably because I don't understand it. Your luxury, your manner of living, your love of dogs. I simply feel strange to it all." Which is undoubtedly true; this man will become an excellent physician because he spends his time studying, and not amusing himself, but he will remain a villager and our culture will make no dent on him.

However, this state of mind is by no means a general one, and most Bulgarian students imbibe a great deal from their university courses not included in the official curricula. But a great deal of impetus for good is wasted when it comes in contact with, to my mind, one of the most retrograde elements in Bulgarian life— public opinion. There is no doubt that it is a very necessary thing in society, but there comes a time when it begins to hamper progress, and as I get glimpses of real Bulgaria I feel that it is a handicap. Public opinion is the small-town mentality, the state of mind which fears to do anything new, anything which neighbors might not approve. Women here, for example, are doing nothing to organize the sport activities of their children because they are afraid they might be laughed at, and as a result their boys are brought home with broken arms while playing rough football. But as public opinion does not condemn dirty politics and graft while in office, it is an accepted fact that those in power steal public money; public opinion is like a capricious woman with little logic.

In a village I saw this public opinion in full sway. It was a Sunday afternoon, and on the green were gathered all the young girls of the village. The young men floated around vaguely, dodging behind trees—I caught glimpses of their brown pants and pale-blue shirts. Before them, as far away as possible, stood three couples, one of which was holding hands. A Bulgarian friend explained:

The village courtship. No young man can visit a young woman in her home; he has to court her here, and woe to him who once having made his choice tries to change his mind.

It was a pathetic sight—these couples—but perhaps the publicity was more painful to me than to them. Public opinion had worked out this method of courting and of protecting its young women; and later I was told tales of village life, of peasant cupidity and criminality, and I understood the scene on the green. It is natural that with such strict customs, murders over women are common among men. But an even stranger thing is the kidnapping sport, practiced by peasants; if a girl pleases a young man either for her beauty or for her money, and his advances have been repulsed, it is not infrequent for half a dozen young men to come together and to kidnap her for their friend. She is taken to a neighboring village and kept there practically prisoner for a few weeks. By that time she is either willing to marry the man or to be more determined than ever not to do so; she sometimes escapes, and there have been cases of murder at the altar. It is a primitive country with primitive people, and there is a great deal of reason for many of the customs which appear so utterly barbaric.

I thought of our immigrant girls, living in numbers in one room in the crowded East Side of New York, and a sense of pity rose for them; unprepared and utterly defenseless, they land in the United States in the care of questionable relatives, and then are allowed to shift for themselves. Small wonder that so many sink to the bottom. They are never given even a fighting chance. The wonder is that so many develop into decent and honest women.

In an office in Tchirpan where some of the "intellectuals" often foregather to discuss politics and philosophy I met one afternoon a fair-haired man who eloquently attacked materialism and proved that the world was going through a spiritual awakening. As there were several Russians present, the conversation shifted easily from Bulgarian to Russian and back, and his Russian speech showed that he had lived in Russia.

"You've been in America?" he suddenly asked during a lull in the discussion.

"Yes—just come from there," I answered.

"Perhaps you would like some books to read?" he said in clearest English.

Needless to say, I was surprised and pleased. He told me he had been in the middle western states for ten years, going through high school and working in the telephone company. Then he had gone to Russia, and now he kept a little store in Tchirpan. I admitted that books were what I missed most, as I had brought none.

"I have Emerson, Thoreau, Ruskin. Please come and visit my wife and select what you want. I love

American writers, who are little known here, and I have
many of their writings." He told me that he had not
continued his university studies in the United States
because he realized they would not give him what he
needed for his life; but he was always reading, receiving American magazines and carrying to Tchirpan a
message of practical Christianity and spirituality. He
stood out to me as an apostle of our finest European
and American thought, and yet he, too, had been a
simple peasant. His philosophy of faith, contentment,
and progress was refreshing, and as I listened to his
attack on materialism I felt a sense of thankfulness that,
after all, here at least was one man who had come
through the test of Americanization with brilliant results; he could compare with some of our clearest
thinkers. Then I looked around at the Bulgarians, lis-
tening to him with understanding and sympathy, and I
felt that there is a big future in the country where such
a question can take up men's time.

EDUCATION IN BULGARIA [1]

In talking about Bulgaria, one should bear in mind
that she is one of the younger states on the Balkan
Peninsula and in Europe. Prior to 1878, Bulgaria was
a simple Turkish province and its inhabitants were deprived of all political rights and privileges. They were
downtrodden Turkish subjects ruled by a government
whose chief concern was to oppress them and to drain
the country of all its material resources. No help or
incentive was afforded them for material, intellectual,
moral, or any other advancement. Commerce, industry,
education, and other enterprises which make for the
progressive civilization of a nation were not encouraged,
nay, were quite impossible under existing circumstances.
Even under these adverse and discouraging conditions

[1] By Stephen Panaretov. National Education Association. Journal of
Proceedings and Addresses. 1915: 190-3. August, 1915.

however, the people were keen on education for they felt strongly that in education lay their future salvation. Communal schools were maintained without any state help by the people, who, in addition to the taxes they had to pay to the government, voluntarily and cheerfully taxed themselves with a special school tax.

Up to 1835, Greek was the language of the schools of the country, for Bulgaria had the great misfortune to become politically subject to the Turks and spiritually and ecclesiastically subject to the Greek patriarch in Constantinople. The bishops and archbishops in whose hands the spiritual welfare of the people was placed were Greeks, alien to their flock in language and race, and inimical to its nationality. It is difficult to say which of the two yokes that the Bulgarians had to bear was the most galling and pernicious. While the Turk was satisfied with getting out of the country as much as he could through taxation and extortion, leaving supremely alone its nationality and language, the Greek bishops not only mulcted the people but were intent upon denationalizing and Hellenizing it. The Bulgarian language was proscribed from the schools as well as from the churches. It was really in the early sixties of the last century that Bulgarian schools with the Bulgarian language as a medium of instruction began to spread and multiply.

But since 1878, when Bulgaria was liberated from Turkish rule and erected into a semi-independent principality, education has progressed by leaps and bounds. Its management and direction are in the hands of the state under the guidance and supervision of the ministry of public instruction. According to the Constitution of Bulgaria, primary education is free and obligatory, while for the instruction received in the colleges and the university, a small fee is charged. Every village that has forty houses or more must have a school, while smaller units are grouped together with a common school. Wherever you see in a Bulgarian village a nice-looking building standing prominently in view, you may be sure that it is the schoolhouse.

In the primary and in the high schools, as well as in the university, coeducation exists. Attention is paid not only to the education of the boys but to that of the girls also, and both the boys' and the girls' colleges or gymnasia are full to overflowing. In some of the larger towns, the government is obliged to maintain more than one high school and college in order to meet the ever-increasing demand for education. Illiteracy is diminishing year by year, and Bulgaria stands today as one of the Balkan states with the least percentage of illiterates. In the University of Sofia, the capital of Bulgaria, with its three faculties of law, philosophy and mathematics, one-third of the students are women.

Besides these institutions Bulgaria has made provision for commercial and professional schools. Under the Turkish régime no such schools existed, nor were there any agricultural schools. There are now two such schools, where young men are given opportunities to learn better methods of agriculture, dairy farming, stock breeding, etc. During the summer vacations, the students are sent out among the villagers to instruct them in these various methods. It is surprising to see how ready the peasants are to profit by this instruction. The introduction of modern and improved agricultural implements, as ploughs, reaping, threshing, and winnowing machines, to replace the primitive implements is an evidence of the progress that has been achieved in many parts of the country.

Normal or pedagogical schools have also been established to prepare teachers, both men and women. In the capital of the country, there is an art and musical school, in both of which good and creditable work is being done. Classes for teaching, cooking, sewing, dressmaking, and domestic economy have been started in Sofia for the girls. Kindergartens are to be found in some of the principal towns, and one of them in Sofia is under the management of an American woman.

Bulgaria is one of the Balkan countries where America and American institutions are best appreciated and valued. Through Robert College in Constantinople, and other American schools in Bulgaria, where hundreds of Bulgarians have studied, as well as through the education which many Bulgarians have received in the United States, the spirit of American institutions has found entrance into the country. The graduates of Robert College have been prominent in various pursuits of life as political leaders, teachers, merchants, etc., and have had a large share in molding the destiny of their country. Whatever defects critics of American education may see in it, it cannot be denied that it does impart to those who have been brought up in it certain characteristics which are lacking or are not so prominent in the graduates of the educational systems of Europe and especially of those in the Near East. American education stands for independence of thinking, for self-reliance, self-help, and self-control, for the honor and dignity of honest work and for the inculcation of morality and spirituality as the surest and soundest basis of character.

What Bulgaria owes to American education was officially acknowledged a few years ago by the Bulgarian government. Two American institutions of learning, one for boys and the other for girls, that have existed in Bulgaria for many years, were officially recognized by the government and granted the privilege of giving diplomas equivalent to those given by the state schools. In making known this decision to the lady principal of the girls' school, the Bulgarian Minister of Public Instruction expressed in an official letter the gratitude of Bulgaria to the United States for all the good these American schools have done to the country by the intellectual moral, and spiritual training they have afforded

the youth of Bulgaria, and the assistance they have
rendered to the country in its efforts for greater progress
and more enlightenment. The letter is of great significance, for it is the first official recognition by a Balkan
state of the educational work done by citizens of the
United States in those parts of the world. It is significant also of the broad tolerant spirit that animates the
Bulgarian people, who are ready to welcome with gratitude what is being done by people alien to them in race,
language, and religion, but akin to them in human sympathy and kindly feelings, for the uplifting progress
and culture of Bulgaria.

VILLAGE LIFE IN BULGARIAN POETRY [1]

The place of village life in Bulgarian poetry is an
especially interesting subject at this particular time, because the village—which has hitherto remained unaffected by the attention or interest of the intellectual
class—is now suddenly increasing in importance and has
already won significance as an element in Bulgarian society. Even now the city feels the invigorating influence
of the great peasant wave; it is permeated and impregnated with new forces. What place does the village
occupy in Bulgaria's poetry? Because it has remained
so isolated, so shut off amid harsh surroundings, the village has attracted the poet soul only by its solitude, by
the blue sky that sweeps above it, or by the free open
spaces that surround it and are alive in summer with
the shrill songs of the women in the harvest fields.

The estrangement between the Bulgarian poet and the
village is chiefly due to his overwhelming interest in foreign culture and to his desire to steep himself in fashionable refinement and in the very essence of modern
civilized life, which carry him even to the imitation of

[1] By N. Dontchev. L'Echo de Bulgarie. 10: 2634-6. August. 19-21,
1922.

French and German verse. Being himself unfamiliar
with the life of the village, the Bulgarian poet naturally
has been able to give us no profound feeling in his
efforts at its interpretations. He has failed to waken
in us thought and feeling about the village; he has failed
to make the village soul live for us—that great and
simple soul, treated with so much power and nobility by
Alexis Koltsov, the Russian poet, in his marvelous songs
of the *muzhik* of Russia.

Koltsov was a great poet of the village, and his
simple verses, free from any trace of artifice, have, even
in our day, the value of inimitable pearls of Russian literature. The Bulgarian poet, on the other hand, still
remains a stranger to the village, and to the calm domes-
ticity of the home, which is stamped with the profound resignation of our peasants. We Bulgarians
have not yet had our Koltsov.

Among the writers whom we do have, the one whose
work approaches closest to that of the Russian is Tsanko Bakalov-Tserkovsky, who, in the delicacy of his
motifs and the pastoral harmony of his rustic poetry,
recalls the Russian verses of Koltsov.

Ivan Vazov, who died in 1922, is another poet who
is sympathetic toward the village. It is with evident joy
that he touches on it in his poems, describing its delights
and its charm, and giving voice to his admiration of the
never-ceasing productive work of those who dwell in it.
His poems, "Fields," "Work," "Read, Shepherd." "To
Nature," and others are characteristic in this respect.
Touched with pantheistic feeling, the poet bows before
the toiling peasant and dreams of finding rest in the
bosom of Mother Nature, in the village calm, where one
hears nothing save the gay murmur of the brook and the
bleating of the herds.

Vazov has given us marvelous pictures of nature and
of the customs of the Bulgarian village, though he has
not sung the joys and sorrows of the peasant, the woes

and losses amid which the peasant soul has grown. In some of his poems—"In the Presence of the Workman," "The Sower," "Let Us Work," and some others—the poet has felt the peasant's suffering; has done honor to this figure, so browned and withered by the sun; and has blessed his horny hands. But these are only scattered examples that complete the feeling and the general tone of the village songs.

Indissolubly linked with the life of the village is Tsanko Bakalov-Tserkovsky, whom we named above. Born a peasant, Tserkovsky remains a peasant still in his poems. The culture of the city has left his peasant nature and his inherent talent unaffected His poetry, simple and without artifice, bears the imprint of no literary school, for in Tserkovsky's eyes one school alone exists—the school of life.

To this is due the personal character of his poetry, in which we find but a trace of popular balladry; yet no warmer words have been spoken of the Bulgarian village than those of Tserkovsky. His songs ring like a revelation, for there is nothing hidden in them and each verse is vivid with the clarity of an emotion that has been lived, an impression that has been experienced. For Tserkovsky the village is not a mere spring or winter landscape; on the contrary, it becomes something alive, something with a soul characteristic of itself.

Whereas Vazov gives us nothing but the external beauties of the village, Tserkovsky depicts for us its inner life. He portrays the scenes in which the peasant soul discloses itself, and he contrives to touch us profoundly by the sight of some joy or some grief in peasant life. His thoughtful, silent glance does not fall merely upon the startling indifferent immensity of the fields, but it pierces also into the houses, and beneath the smoky, tumble-down roof of the poor peasant, to show his suffering, to sing the crushing burden of toil, which, nevertheless, he endures unmurmuring, filled with a

great faith in himself. Even the least significant of
Tserkovsky's works portrays the martyrdom, the weariness of the perpetually burdened peasant; and yet in
this poetry one may also catch a note of the faith that
sustains his soul and gives him joy. This poet, where-
ever he may find himself, never ceases to live with the
thought of his village, of its vast fields and fresh valleys, where the shepherd leads his white flocks and with
his flute accompanies, sometimes the song of a gay and
solitary stream, sometimes the songs of the birds.

Tserkovsky, who lives with the people themselves
and who knows their beliefs, who has listened to their
tales and legends, gives us a cycle of verses wholly
from folk motifs. These are songs in which the poet
can interpret in artistic form the religious and spiritual
aspects of village life; but the content of these songs
has also a ballad character. The imagination of the poet
gives itself free rein in the magic realm of fantastic
creation, and the pictures follow one upon another as if
in a kaleidoscope.

An important part of Tserkovsky's poetry is its social
element. This is the leitmotif of all his work. The poet
never ceases to awaken social feeling in the heart of the
Bulgarian peasant. Even though occupied with his fields,
he follows social problems and solves them in his own
fashion, keeping in mind always the interests and the
good of his village. In the following verses he extols
the ideal of union:

> Under the white spread which covers the earth,
>   One hears in the depths,
> The dull movements of a secret union,
>   Preparing for combat.

Such are the essential characteristics of the Bulgarian village and the life that animates it, in the poetic
work of Tsanko Tserkovsky.

Another poet in whose work the village plays a great
part—almost the only part, in fact—is Nikola Vasilye-

vitch Rakitin. So far his work is represented by some
collections of verse, among which one cycle, "The Native
Village," is characteristic for our purposes. Nikola
Rakitin is perhaps, after Tsanko Tserkovsky, the only
one of our poets who remains wholly original, without
undergoing the influence of any literary modernism. In
his short poems the whole soul of the Bulgarian village
is alive, and yet Rakitin seems to us more a painter of
the village than its poet. He is a naive artist but a
sincere one, who renders the landscapes of life and rustic
nature, full of plastic and picturesque sentiment, and in
his work one feels involuntarily a charm and an individual transparency of color. But the village songs of
Rakitin are stamped with impressionism; they have none
of the mental qualities of Tserkovsky, though they are
distinguished for the sentiment, measured, truthful, calm,
which the poet grasps as if by instinct.

The village lives in silence, in a resigned reverie, in
the calm of the fields that bears with it a charming ex-
pansive realm of feeling. The seasons color it with their
varying nuances, but it retains its fundamental character. "The Native Village" serves the poet as an unfail-
ing spring of inspiration and of poetic musing. The
summer's evening draws his regard with its gently fad-
ing light, with its setting sun that colors the flowery
carpet of the fields, with the merry bells of the herds
coming back from pasture. In the winter the village is
as beautiful as ever, with its white expanses and solemn
silence, which spreads invisible wings above the smoking chimneys.

Rakitin does not remain indifferent to the life of the
village. The stubborn industry of the peasant delights
him, and in some fine songs he expresses that admiration, celebrating the fruits of labor. Among his best
poems I shall mention only "The Storm," "Within,"
"The Plain," "The Return," four faultless poems in
which one feels best of all the pulse of rustic life, and

in which the great, country-loving soul of a sincere poet of the village finds true expression. In his last collection of verse, "Threads of Gold," Rakitin remains faithful to his own nature, for in this book once more he shows himself the same enthusiastic singer of country landscapes and the joy that breathes out from them.

Among other Bulgarian poets, the poetry of Tsanev-Borina possesses a degree of distinction because of some highly characteristic village songs. He depicts for us rather interesting rural landscapes, but these vast canvases are charged with little feeling and are, from a pictorial standpoint, weak. He has neither the profound thought of Tserkovsky nor the contemplative soul of Rakitin—and all poetry is dead if it is not illumined by deep feeling. The great poet of our Bulgarian village, the poet who will seize the peasant soul in all its complexity and will express it in literary works of great compass—that poet has not yet been born. But I believe that he will not long delay his appearance.

BULGARIA'S REVOLUTION OF 1923 [1]

The trials through which Bulgaria has gone in the last decade are not only interesting but highly instructive. Ten years of constant warfare, beginning with the Balkan wars, would have sapped the vitality of a large nation, to say nothing of a small country like Bulgaria. Her catastrophic reverses in the Balkan and the World Wars were enough to drive any state to desperation and civil strife. But, contrary to all expectations, Bulgaria, instead of plunging into revolution and internal disorders, resumed the labors of peace and settled down to cultivate her plains, rendered desolate by prolonged wars.

It was during these initial days of reconstruction that the late Agrarian leader, Stambulisky, made his appear-

[1] By C. Stefanov. Current History. 19: 636-40. January, 1924.

ance; for the next three years he was the central figure not only in his native land but throughout the Balkans. His unique reforms, which attracted so much attention and approval in many foreign countries, justly gained him the reputation of the greatest champion of the peasant class throughout Europe. In consequence, he became the soul of the so-called "Green Internationale," to which Czechoslovakia, Poland, Rumania, Yugoslavia and other states gladly subscribed. For a time, when Stambulisky was supreme in his country and the peasant movement in southeastern Europe was threatening to sweep away all other political groups, the Bulgarian government was cited as an example worthy of imitation by all agricultural states in which the numerically superior peasant class was exploited by the bourgeois aristocracy and bureaucracy. Because he championed the cause of the farm worker, he naturally enough was looked upon with favor by Lenin and Trotsky. On the other hand, Stambulisky himself, though very unfriendly toward the Bulgarian Communist Party, always declared that "the cause of both the communist laborers and the peasant tillers of the soil is one and the same, and the future belongs to these two classes, which constitute the majority in every state." A secret sympathy between the two factions in Bulgaria was in constant evidence, though repeated clashes marred their relations in the struggle against the common enemy.

Shortly after the war, at the close of 1918, the reaction against the old parties was assuming an ugly aspect. It was Stambulisky's turn to loom up at the head of the Agrarian Party, which, under the circumstances, was greeted by all as the savior of the country. The "Narrow Socialists," as the Bulgarian Communists were then called, also gained in prestige. Until then they had never been guilty of any discreditable action, but were known as an orderly faction, albeit of rather extremist views on certain questions. They were not as

yet imbued with the destructive theories of the Third
Internationale, after the rise of which they commenced
to call themselves the Communist Party and became the
pliant creatures of bolshevism. Stambulisky's benevolent
attitude and the unstinted financial and moral support
secretly provided by Soviet Russia so strengthened the
Communists that in the national election of February,
1920, they secured fifty-one seats, as against one hundred
and six captured by the Stambulisky forces, and only
sixty-three won by all the other opposition parties. At
the next general election, in April, 1923, which was a
Stambulisky landslide, the Communists made an impressive demonstration of strength, winning sixteen of the
thirty-two seats which the Agrarians failed to secure.
Moreover, it should be kept in mind that three months
earlier both the Agrarian and the Communists had
united in support of the referendum which approved the
indictment of the bourgeois ministers. After that the
two parties had united against the old parties, but in a
guarded and disguised manner, as Stambulisky feared
that an open coalition with the Communists would injure
his influence and success with the Entente nations, who
considered him, as Poincaré put it, "the greatest Bulgar
friend of the Entente." Stambulisky, it is clear, was
insincere with the Communists and was cleverly using
them as his most effective weapon against the old parties,
who never ceased in their stubborn resistance.

Having convinced themselves of the identity of their
interests, and having pledged their mutual support in the
fight on the "capitalist" parties, the Agrarians and the
Communists felt assured that whatever happened either
one or the other would retain the mastery of the country.
That is why Stambulisky repeatedly taunted the old
parties with having outlived their usefulness, and
prophesied that the future of the country belonged to the
left. This state of things, naturally, rendered both the
Agrarians and the Communists too confident. They were

now cocksure that all danger from below was over, or, if it existed, was insignificant. They also underrated the strength and preparedness of their antagonists. This fact explains why the *coup d'état* of June 9, 1923, engineered by a handful of expert political and military strategists, found the Stambulisky Cabinet asleep and effected its overthrow, meeting practically no resistance on their part.

The disappointment in consequence of the downfall of Stambulisky's government was felt most acutely in Moscow, where it was believed that the Russian propagandists in Bulgaria, masquerading under the title of "Red Cross Mission," had succeeded in organizing the Communists and effecting a strong union of the agrarian and communistic forces. A severe note, therefore, was immediately sent to the Executive Committee of the Bulgarian section of the Internationale, unceremoniously stigmatizing it for its utter incapacity and negligence in being passive on June 9, a day disastrous alike to the agrarian and to the bolshevist cause. One can imagine the fury of the Moscow Bolshevists when early in August the new Bulgarian government peremptorily ordered the so-called Russian Red Cross Mission out of the country within forty-eight hours. A good many Bulgarians were arrested at the same time as accomplices of this secret bolshevist propaganda, which was carried on under the cloak of a humanitarian agency. Some days later the Bulgarian authorities found another secret document, a circular issued by Moscow for the benefit of the Bulgarian peasants and Communists. The following paragraph is typical:

In this hour of severe trial and great provocation on the part of the Government of Tsankov, the Comintern [Communist International] sends its brotherly greeting to the Bulgarian workers and peasants. Let the workers and peasants of Bulgaria tighten up and reinforce their ranks, reorganize all their groups in the country, and never cease in their efforts until they succeed in setting up a Soviet Government. The régime of the White Terror will soon be over, and the triumph of the

peasant and city laborers is soon to be achieved. Long live
the Bulgarian Communist Party! Long live the Bulgarian peasants and working people!

In spite of the repeated warnings of the Bulgarian
government, the Bulgarian Communist Party did not
desist from its wonted methods of inciting the populace
to disloyalty to the government and of preaching obedience to orders from Moscow. The activity of Soviet
propagandists was redoubled in the Balkans, particularly
in Bulgaria. Kolarov, Sapunov and other Bulgarian
communist leaders were repeatedly called to Moscow for
instructions. Already three hundred young Bulgarians
had managed to reach Russia for the purpose of being
schooled in the arts of revolution. These young men had
duly returned home and were getting their districts into
shape for the great day when the flag of the Red Republic was to be hoisted over Bulgaria. Quantities of
arms and ammunition, secretly brought over from
Odessa, had been smuggled into the country by way of
Burgas and Varna. The public demonstrations of the
Communists began to occur more frequently than before.
A preliminary mobilization of all the communistic
brotherhoods in the land under the guise of ordinary
and peaceful evening recreations was fixed for September 15. The general uprising was to take place on
September 21.

The government, however, had not, in the meanwhile,
been asleep. It had managed to get wind of the impend-
ing revolution, which many considered merely a chimera.
On June 12, however, there was no longer room for
doubt. The Sofia police, led by an able detective and
a detachment of troops, arrested the Communist Executive Council at their meeting, in which they had been
taking decisions of a most treasonable nature. The Bulgarian population, so ran proclamations seized by the
police, was "called to arms against the usurpatory government of capitalists, professors and generals." As a

result of the raid by the government, the revolution planned to take place a week later was ordered to commence at once throughout the country. Communist outbreaks occurred in many places, and soon, owing to the scantiness of local police and the absence of government forces, some communes succeeded in proclaiming themselves Soviet republics. It is believed that over a hundred such republics were set up within a fortnight. Some of them lasted but a few hours, the populace being able to drive the republicans out without bloodshed. A number, however, managed to survive longer, among them being the Soviet communes established at Nova-Zagora, Tchirpan, Tchepelary and other places in north Bulgaria. At first both the civilians and the military authorities were lenient toward the rioters. When, however, the communes resorted to the bloody tactics of the Moscow Soviet, ruthlessly butchering a number of innocent people and plundering their homes, their opponents adopted more forceful measures. For over two weeks, until the responsible authorities were able to establish order and security in the affected regions, local civil war raged, causing the death of hundreds, not to say thousands, mostly inoffensive citizens, on both sides.

The most sanguinary struggles occurred at the towns of Berkovitsa and Ferdinand in north Bulgaria. Here, owing to the proximity of the Rumanian and Serbian borders, the strongest contingent of the communist forces had established itself. The most desperate leaders of the Communists commanded the disaffected towns which covered the entire stretch of territory from the Danube to the Serbian frontier. As soon as the revolution was proclaimed in the town of Ferdinand the boys and men between eighteen and fifty years of age were mobilized and formed into bands led by trusted "comrades." Circulars, distributed as the red guards advanced, stated that the "capitalist government" had been overthrown, Soviet rule established in Sofia and all the bigger cities of the country, and that a Russian Bolshevist army had landed at Varna and Burgas to aid their Bulgarian brethren. The Cheka [Summary Court] was set up to try recalcitrants. It is needless to say that the Bulgar communes proved good disciples of their Russian masters, for the terror which they introduced within their temporal jurisdiction will long be remembered by the horror-stricken inhabitants who had the misfortune to feel it. Lawlessness, ruthless killing, debauchery and pillage reigned supreme. The red guards did as they pleased. Unwilling local villagers pressed into service were placed in the front lines, thus exposing them as targets for the advancing royal troops. By the end of September the greatest communist strongholds, Berkovitsa and Ferdinand, were vacated by the reds, who finally crossed the border into Serbia and Rumania, where they found shelter from the Bulgarian militia. The largest number of fleeing rebels found refuge in Serbia, which was nearer. According to the Serbian authorities over seven hundred Communists arrived in the district of Nish, where Kolarov, the General Secretary of the Third Internationale; George Dimitrov, the Commander-in-Chief of the red guards, and Pastermadzhiev, his adjutant, were shown a hospitality which they did not expect.

Thus ended the communist revolution in Bulgaria. Though it was a short-lived one, the sore it created in the nation is a very painful one. It was a great blunder, an aimless and foolhardy undertaking which cost the state very dearly in needless loss of precious lives, for again it was the intellectual class that suffered most, both in life and property, not to speak of the moral torment which harassed the nation during those terrible days of uncertainty and constant fear of foreign invasion. Once, forty years ago, it was Russian Tsarism that considered it its duty and right to meddle in the internal affairs of the then young and inexperienced Principality of Bulgaria. Today it is Bolshevist Russia that regards

Bulgaria as her outpost in the Balkans. Tsarist Russia, it will be remembered, prompted the revolution of 1885 and the expulsion from Bulgaria of Prince Alexander Battenberg. Bolshevist Russia was the prime mover of the September communist revolution. But on neither occasion did Russia succeed in her machinations and intrigues. The Bulgarian people, a race noted for its sobriety, common sense, energy and love of freedom and independence, knew how to free and disentangle itself from those who, masquerading as its liberators, were bent on using it as a tool in a policy of aggrandizement and world dominion. The small peasant state has been able to defend itself and to emerge safe from the Bolshevist danger, as it did from the peasant dictatorship four months previously. So long as Bulgaria occupies a central geographical position in the Balkans, and so long as one-third of her nationals are under the alien yoke of her neighbors, her existence as a state will constitute an object for their fears and apprehensions and her territories a goal for encroachment. Therefore, the Bulgar race has to fight for its existence as few other states are compelled to fight. Perhaps that is the reason why the Bulgarian people have developed such an extraordinary power of endurance, resistance and coolheadedness.

BULGARIA FACES THE FUTURE [1]

Economically Bulgaria has not suffered so greatly as might be expected. Sophia has a prosperous look, but financially things are in bad shape. Danev, the Finance Minister, who represented Bulgaria at the London Conference after the first Balkan war and at Bucharest after the second, estimates the national debt at 12,235,000,000 levas—quite a tidy bit for a country that has only about five million inhabitants. Danev said he hoped to be able

[1] By H. G. Alsberg. Nation. 109: 563. November 1, 1919.

to pull Bulgaria out of financial difficulties if the indemnity to Serbia were not fixed at too high a figure. [The Allies have asked for an indemnity of $500,000,000.] The Bulgarian budget is now about 1,200,000,000 levas in expenditures, and 1,000,000,000 levas in income. New taxes, he hopes, will meet the deficit. The condition of the railways in Bulgaria is rather better than that in any of the neighboring countries, but transportation difficulties are very great.

I think, from what I hear, Bulgaria faces the same difficulties of doing business with the outside world as its neighbors. In the first place, the question of exchange is a huge obstacle to export. Then the government itself is over-controlling both imports and exports, and has fixed artificial rates of exchange so that merchants can work on the basis of the actual rate only at the risk of being punished. There is tobacco and rose oil for exportation and some grain. But I was told the red tape and the conditions on which export permission would be given were so onerous that exports of these much-sought-after articles did not flow as they should. Motor oils from America are competing with those of Rumania and beating them all out. A tax on war profits has already been enacted.

Land legislation of any consequence has not been passed since the armistice. Bulgaria is already a country of small landed proprietors. Kolarov, the communist leader, said his party proposed a law to reduce all holding to ten hectares. I suppose the average Bulgarian holding is not much greater than this. The following laws are to be proposed in Parliament:

1. The public lands to be partitioned among the few landless peasants, with provisions for the working of the land on a cooperative basis.
2. Land credit banks.
3. Agricultural schools (some already exist).
4. Control of rivers.

5. Laws for improvement and government backing of cooperative associations already in existence. The chief strength of the agrarian party, which is the ruling party of Bulgaria, lies in connection with the building up of these cooperatives. More than seven hundred agricultural credit cooperatives already exist; some thirty consumers' cooperatives, and some four producers' cooperatives. Three of these last are dairy associations. The land credit cooperatives have over eighty thousand members which, reckoning five per family, means that four hundred thousand persons are represented in this membership. Dragiev, Minister of Agriculture, tells me that he wants laws passed which will practically make all the cooperatives part of the state, and which will enable him to open branches in every village, to be devoted not only to material ends, but also to cultural and educational purposes.

Bulgaria, among the Balkan states, is perhaps the most literate, showing a percentage of 80. Primary education is compulsory up to fourteen years of age and child labor is forbidden under that age. The proposal in the next session of Parliament will be to make secondary education compulsory; that is to say, the sub-gymnasium, equivalent to lower classes of our high-school, will be both free and compulsory. Then the whole rather old-fashioned system of the gymnasiums is to be overhauled and simplified. Trade schools and schools of commerce and agricultural schools are to be increased in number and improved in quality. Higher technical and professional schools scarcely exist in Bulgaria, and there is no intention to create them.

These are all plans, although laws to carry them out are already on paper. But one good thing that the new government did at once, was to raise the salaries of teachers. As in other countries, teachers were a sadly underpaid lot. In the elementary schools the lowest salary formerly was 120 levas monthly. Now the salaries run from 230 to 500 levas monthly. In the gymnasiums salaries ranged from 250 levas monthly to 350. Now they are 350 to 800 levas. The budget of the Ministry of Education now is 100,000,000 levas, while before the war it was 6,000,000 levas and last year it was only 39,000,000 levas.

I might add a few words as to prices. Sofia stands, in this matter, about on the level of Belgrade. Meals can be had at about sixteen levas and rooms at about twenty-five to thirty levas in the best hotels. In American dollars at present rates of exchange these prices are very low. But for Bulgarians they are inconceivably high, more than ten times what they were before the war. But this is not due to scarcity. There is no real scarcity now, although last winter and spring this scarcity did exist. Meat, vegetables, milk, butter, cream, everything can be had in quantity. But the depreciation of the leva causes a good deal of the trouble. It will be a long time before prices drop. Wages, which run as high as twenty-five levas and more a day, will have to come down too.

In the matter of the reduction of the army, I asked the War Minister, Magarov, whether Bulgaria would disarm in accordance with Allied commands. He said that already it had only forty-five thousand men under arms, the minimum needed to keep order in present troublous times. [The peace terms accepted by Bulgaria allow an army of only 20,000 men.] I do not know how reliable this statement is, but Magarov is one of the most reliable members of the Cabinet. He was always consistently friendly toward the Entente and suffered a great deal for his political convictions.

Finally, I took the trouble to look into the question of Bulgarian treatment of the Jews. Bulgarians have always been liberal in this matter. Recently their liberality has grown enormously, a bit ostentatiously in fact. Every party put a Jewish candidate on each of its election lists during the last elections, rather far down